River, My Mother

I Never Told Anyone...

A Memoir

Kathleen Rossi Marino

ANGELSONG PRESS
PRESCOTT, ARIZONA

ISBN 978-0-578-86330-6

Library of Congress Control Number: 2021904079

Book design by Longworth Creative, LLC
www.LongworthCreative.com

First Edition
Printed in the United States of America
ANGELSONG PRESS

To the children of the world who are victims of secrets
And to all adults who lived with secrets as children:
May you forgive those of us who kept the secrets
And may you become the truth tellers of the world.

First You Must Ride

And you will find yourself on that road again, halfway between the life you left behind and the life you have not yet claimed. And for a moment, breathless, you will forget the destination, forget where you are going because your heart is ablaze, and the wind is in your hair now, and the world cannot keep up with you. You are too fast for this world, too alive to think about consequences.

You have risked everything to ride on this road, risked ridicule and rejection and your precious reputation, but you have chosen life over death, freedom over approval, speed over stagnation.

You have fallen in love with the unknown again.

The destination will show itself, yes, a new life will rise, but first you must ride, guided only by some inner knowing, a little frightened, but in awe of your own courage.

– Jeff Foster

Contents

WORDS OF GRATITUDE

There are no words that can express my gratitude. The abundance of support and love I've received in the past ten years of working on this project is impossible to describe.

Nancy Eichhorn and Irene Tomkinson in New Hampshire allowed me to quietly cry through their writing groups and encouraged me to continue to write despite my depressed state. I appreciate your kindness and gentle mentoring.

When I moved to Prescott, Arizona, by some Divine Grace, I stumbled into a seminar given by Elaine Greensmith Jordan, author of *Mrs. Ogg Played the Harp: Memories of Church and Love in the High Desert*. That was five years ago. Elaine mentored me through the writing of this memoir and invited me to join the memoir writing group she facilitates.

Elaine's guidance, emotional support and dedication to making this book a reality are the reasons you're holding it in your hands today. She is an astute and meticulous editor and has honored the complexity and depth of my story by her willingness to look through my eyes. She is my mentor and my friend. Elaine, I am beyond grateful for your presence in my life and for all you have given me from your generous heart. I cherish our friendship.

The writing group Elaine leads has become a vital part of my creative process. Each member contributes a unique perspective that has shaped my writing in amazing ways. I have grown to love and deeply respect these women: Bobbie Williams, Carol

Rotta, Connie Thacker, Jude Shoemaker, Judy Davis, Margaret Valenta, and, past member, Ella Klein. My deepest gratitude to each of you.

My writing partner, Juanita Hassenstab, has sat with me over tea for years, as we shared our writing. Your soulful presence has enhanced my writing and my life.

Jennifer Longworth is my computer guru and book midwife. She patiently walked me through my tech anxiety, and the fear that I wasn't up to the task of finishing this book. Jennifer, I am grateful for your expertise and for your gentle encouragement. Your Light shines brightly—thank you for bringing it into my home.

And, to my family and my friends who uplift me when I'm feeling down and listen patiently to my stories, I am blessed by your love. I treasure each one of you. If I tried to name all of you, this book would never make it into print.

I do want to acknowledge my long-time friends, Lenore, Lauren, Sandee and Rabbi Jeff, who have helped keep the creative flame alive within me with their insightful wisdom, shared freely with humor and love. To my friend, Elizabeth, I thank you for accompanying me on my spiritual journey, bearing witness from your Vermont home. And, to Kathy, my high school friend who remains in my life to this day, thank you for all you have given. My gratitude to each one of you.

Friend of my heart, Carolynn, has steadfastly supported me since I arrived in Prescott in 2010. She has provided physical, emotional and spiritual sustenance, which has inspired me to value the gifts I bring to the world. Thank you, beloved friend, soul-sister, my spiritual guide.

And, to my dear friend, Khailitha, your love and depth of soul comforts me in the dark places —bless you for all that you give. Jessica, your gentle spirit and your beautiful smile grace my life. Thank you both. To my neighbor and friend, Cheryl, my gratitude for your constant support and endless supply of homemade treats!

And, to the *Prescott Peace Dance(s) and Sufi Circle*, my endless gratitude for the spiritual nectar of the *Dances of Universal Peace*, which have continued to nourish my soul since I moved to this beautiful, high desert town. Chanting and dancing to music from many spiritual traditions is my heart's delight. I am blessed to be part of this Sufi community.

To the members of my Gratitude Circle, thank you for sharing your truth with me and listening to mine over the years. Your wisdom and caring have lighted my way. And, to my Meditation Group, my companions on the spiritual path, thank you for blessing my home and my life with your presence.

My therapist, Dr. Jeff (Dr. J), has accompanied me through the challenges of the past six years and encouraged me to keep writing. He was there each time I wrote about the "hard stuff" and needed a place to process the feelings that arose. I am grateful for your ability to listen with your heart, Dr. Jeff, and for your wise counsel. And to all the healers who have graced my life, I give my heart-felt thanks.

And, my darling children; my daughter-in-law and sons-in-law; and my beautiful grandchildren: to you I have a special message. You are the very breath of my life. Your love sustains me and my love for you is my reason for being. Thank you for accepting me as I am, and for your patience, understanding, and unending love. I am truly blessed to have you in my life! You are the source of my passion to make a difference and leave the world a better place for all of you. My love and gratitude are boundless and eternal, and I will always be with you.

With gratitude and love,

Mom, Nonni, Aunt Kathy, Kathy, Kathleen

PRELUDE

A life guided by the awareness that
all we can see is not all there is.

Dear Ones,

Robert Frost said, "The only way out is through." As we walk through our stories we find our way home. This Memoir is my journey home.

The book is not an easy read. It weaves together strands of my life experiences that many of you may have encountered. The specifics of this story are mine, but the underlying themes have always been with us. It explores the darkness of family secrets, partner and sexual abuse, pedophilia, mental illness and suicide, and religious indoctrination. And, it also describes my spiritual journey, my work as a therapist and chaplain, the fulfillment of lifelong dreams, and the freedom and peace I have found in reclaiming my life. My wish is that this book will bring healing and comfort, and glimpses of the possible to those of you who are living in or have lived through the experiences I describe.

I have written this book to honor all that is good in our family—the love and culture, the courage and strength in face of adversity, and the contributions our family has made to the world. But, as in all things, our family has a shadow side which I've also chosen to illuminate in this book. I do this with the hope that our family's story will help expose the culture of secrets that perpetuates domination and abuse; and, I hope to inspire all of us to find ways to prevent individual and systemic exploitation of other human beings.

This has always been my intent for the book. Yet, I've agonized over the ramifications of revealing the family secrets. After much deliberation, I decided to use a pseudonym and to change the names of all the people of whom I write and some of the names of locations. I know this perpetuates the destructive secrecy that I have silently railed against for years but I feel compelled to protect the innocent and do no harm. This choice to hide my identity rends the fabric of my being. I am a hypocrite immobilized by the fear that I will cause more pain. This is the reality of a secret-keeper.

> *Drowning in secrets,*
> *I risk all*
> *to return to*
> *the essence of*
> *my being,*
> *my truth,*
> *my integrity,*
> *my story,*
> *that I may breathe freely*
> *before I die,*
> *and light the way*
> *for those bound*
> *by secrets*
> *who long to be free.*
>
> *– Kathleen, 2020*

In spite of the changes I have made that conceal the identities of people and locations in this book, everything I have written is the truth as I know it. It is *my* story. The people within my story have their own stories. I speak for no one but myself.

The field of all possibilities blooms just beyond our sight—with love, hope, imagination and passion we can make that field manifest in our world. May all who read this book come away with a sense of the possible, and with a vision of a world transformed by truth and human kindness. May we banish secrets and open hearts.

Blessings and love,
Kathleen Rossi Marino

A NOTE FROM THE AUTHOR

A word about the poem, "Renascence," which appears in the text throughout the book: *Renascence* means the revival of something that lies dormant. This poem by Edna St. Vincent Millay spoke to me at the age of fifteen and speaks to me still, sixty years later. I know the anguish Millay describes, the beauty of nature she extols, and the desire to be raised from the dead into a life of infinite possibilities. If it or any other poetry in the book does not speak to you, please feel free to leave it unread—doing so will not diminish your understanding of the story.

I've taken the liberty of altering time sequences and condensing material. Many conversations recorded here will reverberate within me until the day I die. In others, I've tried to capture the gist of the conversation as I remember it.

I am passionate about making a difference in the lives of those who have suffered or are suffering still from the effects of trauma and neglect in childhood or as adults. At the end of the book I have added a section called **Resources**. There you will find **Crisis-Line numbers** and a recommended reading list. Please reach out and get the help and support you need and deserve.

I never told anyone…
There were no words yet…so how could I tell?
Grey thick fog swirled around me,
as I floated above the earth plane,
ambivalent and afraid,
adrift in possibilities.

It was clear I was being called—
they needed me.
Death was destined to visit
in the years to come,
I was to be an anchor
through their grief.

"Don't ask this of me," I begged.
"It's too soon to go back!"
In truth
I never wanted to go back again.

"Just one more time," a gentle voice implored
and it was the Voice of Love Itself,
so how could I refuse?

But, I dallied.
I could not delay too long—
I knew the discovery of my presence
would cause dismay.
I knew everything that lay ahead.

I dragged my feet,
lingered a little longer
at heaven's door—
wanting only to return
to the cosmic womb,
not the womb of one
who walked upon the earth.

But time was getting short—
I had to establish my presence
so I could be there for them
through the dark days ahead—
fully knowing
I would lose them all to grief.

– Kathleen, 2011

River,
My Mother

My Buddha-self

Oh, I will take you back, Kathleen
To where your heart will feel no pain
And when the fields are fresh and green
I'll take you to your home again

– From *I'll Take you Home Again Kathleen*
by Thomas Paine Westendorf

CHAPTER ONE
Just One More Time

THE POEM, *I never told anyone…* came to me in my late sixties, but its sentiment has been with me since I first became aware of the world around me. When I was three years old, my brother, Joseph, who had a beautiful, resonant singing voice, made a record for me of the song, *I'll Take You Home Again, Kathleen.* I have a memory, which my mother confirmed was accurate, of sitting on the floor listening to the song and crying. I remember a feeling of heaviness in my chest as I sat there and sobbed. When the song ended, I would say, "Play it again!" Somehow, even at that young age, I sensed I was not at home in this family or in this world. I wanted to go *home* wherever that was.

~

My first sense of being at home on planet Earth came one spring when I was about eight years old. The New Hope River ran against the twelve foot foundation of our huge, pre-Revolutionary War home in rural Connecticut. The rushing roar of the snowmelt beneath our cellar windows had mellowed into the river's summer song as May glided into June. As I stood barefoot on the riverbank, the rocks beneath my feet were warm and rough, and there was a new intensity to the sun's rays moderated by a slight breeze ruffling my short brown hair. I knew this was the day.

This was the first time I'd attempt to jump the rocks alone. Usually when I was near the river, one of my big brothers or my sister or cousins or some of the neighborhood children would accompany me. I knew my mother was keeping an eye on me from the upstairs window, but I felt brave and proud that I was venturing out on my own.

A burning determination to get over to the other side of the river fueled my exploration that day. I knew the route by heart, although I had never made it all the way across. I jumped the small rocks to the first boulder, named *Clothes Rock* because that was where we shed our clothes; then I made my way to *Plane Rock* and leapt over to *Flat Rock* with one big jump, landing firmly on my newly tanned legs.

After jumping a few more small rocks onto the biggest boulder in our part of the river, *House Rock*—which was the size of a small car—I stopped to rest, unsure of my next move. There were few rocks between *House Rock* and the other shore—another six feet left to navigate. I decided I would ignore my mother's admonition not to get wet and wade in the still cold water to get to the other side.

Heart pounding, I made it to what seemed like a far distant shore. It was thick with vegetation, and my fear of snakes grew as I tried to find footing in the tangled underbrush. I finally broke through the brush to find light streaming into an inner sanctum. I gasped in awe. The mammoth trees, fresh green and lush with new leaves, formed a canopy high over a circular open space with a floor of stones that turned into a stone pathway trailing in a curve back to the river.

On the left was a huge boulder about five feet tall. On the right, a newly-sprouted bed of lacy green fern lay dappled in sunlight. I scrambled up the boulder and took my place as queen of all I could see. From my perch, the floor of the sanctuary appeared to be a patio of flat rocks, placed neatly together, much like the patio my father had built on our side of the river. It was magical. I was in a Holy Place.

Sitting still, alert to every sound and flutter, I knew I belonged there. A visceral sense of peace and safety I rarely felt within the walls of my house filled me. I was *home*.

I was so excited with my discovery, I slid down the rock, re-crossed the tangled barrier without a thought of snakes, and waded through the water without worrying that I'd get my shorts wet and my mother would know I had disobeyed her. I quickly jumped the rocks back to our side of the river and ran up the stone stairs onto the road, across the porch and into the house— slamming the door, calling, "Mark! Mark!"

I found my big brother, fourteen years my senior, leaning over a drafting board as he created blueprints for a house he was building for a professor—cigarette burning in the ashtray, hair disheveled, wearing an old rumpled tan shirt, his back to me.

"Mark! I found God's patio on the other side of the river. It's so beautiful! There are flat rocks on the floor of it and a path that leads back to the river. It's like a church!"

Mark looked up, took a drag from his cigarette, slowly blew out the smoke and said flatly, "That's just the old river bed." He then launched into a lecture on the destructive hurricane of 1938 which changed the course of the river and made it run against our house.

Deflated by this explanation, I nevertheless held onto the vision of my sanctuary being *God's Patio* and spent many hours, in the years to come, held in its embrace. I now realize this secret haven brought me closer to the Holy than anything I had experienced so far. It was my connection to a deeper, mysterious part of me that seemed to understand things beyond my knowing. It was a call to heart-felt connections with nature and the mysteries of life. And, it informed my life's path, although there were many detours along the way.

Many years later a song came to me:

> *River, my Mother, singing to me*
> *Playing upon the rocks sweet melodies*
> *Words of an ancient song, sung lovingly*
> *River, my Mother, singing to me*

River, my Mother, shining for me
Dancing a dance of love so I might see
Life in its ebb and flow, lived joyfully
River, my Mother, shining for me

River, my Mother, cradling me
Holding me in your arms, I'll always be
Child of your Sacred Soul, held tenderly
River, my Mother, cradling me

River, my Mother, blessing me
Touching my hand and heart on way to the sea
Cool clear waters, Holy, Holy
Cool clear waters, Holy, Holy

– Kathleen, 1996

~

Our home in Wentworth, Connecticut, was two miles from the town of Linden where a painted white fieldstone Catholic Church, St. Anthony's, rested on a gently sloped piece of wooded property. It became the center of my religious life. The Hungarian immigrants, who had put their money, labor and hearts into the construction of the Church some years before, topped it with a traditionally Slavic dome of tarnished green copper as would have appeared on churches in their homeland.

The Church had simple elegant lines, and the inside was bright and airy with sky blue walls and white trim. The stained glass windows were not deeply colored displays of Bible passages, but pale pastel squares that let the sunshine stream through with a diffuse and gentle light. A star-studded azure blue ceiling floated above the sanctuary. A tiny chapel on the right side of the altar, dedicated to the Blessed Mother, was graced by a statue of her floating above a cloud, her blue dress flowing. In a larger gated alcove toward the back of the Church was an exquisitely hand-carved Baptismal Font.

My indoctrination into the Roman Catholic Church of the 1950's had begun when I was seven. To be Catholic in this predominantly Protestant New England culture, was to be *other*.

St. Anthony's

There were some who approached Catholics with curiosity or disdain or out-right discrimination, but because Wentworth was a University town, there was more tolerance for differences than in some of the surrounding areas. In Linden, there had been resistance to the building of St. Anthony's Church and even talk of Klansmen being brought in to deal with what was considered the intrusive presence of Papal Authority in the midst of a purely Protestant population. But, things quieted down once the Church was established and the local community realized it wasn't a threat to their beliefs or way of life.

Although my parents rarely attended Church, I began Catechism every Saturday morning at the start of second grade in preparation for my First Holy Communion in the spring. I began going to Mass on Sundays under my sister Jules's watchful eye. At my Catechism lessons I was mesmerized by the women who were our teachers. They dressed in long black robes with long scarves on their heads framing their faces and hiding their hair.

They were called "Sisters," although none of them were related to me. I later learned they were nuns, women who had dedicated themselves to God and lived together away from their families. Having lived with adult siblings all my life, I knew what they wanted of me and behaved accordingly. I became the Sisters' favorite student because I was so compliant and especially because I began writing poetry to the Blessed Mother by the time I was in third grade:

What Mary Means to Me

When I need her she is always there
Ready to help me with loving with care
When I do something very bad
I know that she is very sad.
And when I fret about the ones I love
She sends me the Heavenly Dove
To tell me I'm a lucky girl
Better off than some in this world

And when it's love I long for
She is the one that opens the door
The Blessed Mother means so much to me

And now I think you can see
The reason why I love her so
And she loves me too, I know.

– Kathleen, age eight

I liked the attention I got from the Sisters, and I loved running around the Church yard at recess. I'd visit a statue on the Church grounds of a friendly looking St. Christopher holding baby Jesus. There was a small stone building adjacent to the basement of the Church that housed the bathrooms and echoed when you spoke within its walls. We played hide and seek near the rectory and sneaked around in the bushes trying to spy on the priest. This all took place under the silent gaze of the Blessed Mother who presided in sculptured white stone on a grass carpeted knoll in the center of the circular driveway at the front of the Church.

I can still see a page of the Catechism titled *The Seven Deadly Sins*. A circle of heads floated on the page—each ugly distorted face representing a sin: *Pride, Avarice, Envy, Wrath, Lust, Gluttony and Sloth.* These words were incomprehensible to me, and the images were frightening. The Sisters said that if you did one of these deadly sins you would go to Hell, which they graphically described.

The cover of the Catechism, a blue and white picture of Christ rising out of the tomb, frightened me, too. My sister had taken me to a movie about the miracle at Fatima where three young children saw a vision of the Blessed Mother and were questioned by the police when they spoke of what they had seen. I feared seeing an apparition of Christ or Mary and suffering the same consequences.

I soon found out that *The Seven Deadly Sins* were not the only sins that could get you in trouble. Lying, stealing, disobeying your parents, being unkind to people, and even thinking bad thoughts (whatever that meant) all warranted going to confession and doing penance. My anxiety grew as we came closer to the time of our first confession.

I envisioned kneeling in something like a dark phone booth, talking to a man I didn't know and couldn't see, telling him how bad I was. This man was called Father, although my father was at home mowing the lawn. Then, after I recited the prayers "father" had given me to say as punishment for my wrong-doing, I would be allowed to go down to the altar, like my sister did during Mass, and eat a little piece of white bread. I had been vigorously trained to be a good girl, so I did my best to follow the rules. I had memorized the prayers, including the *Act of Contrition* which is said during confession, not understanding what the words meant until many years later:

O my God! I am heartily sorry for having offended Thee,
and I detest all my sins, because I dread
the loss of Heaven and the pains of Hell,
but most of all because they offend Thee, my God,
Who art all-good and deserving of all my love.
I firmly resolve, with the help of Thy grace,
to sin no more and to avoid the near occasions of sin.

– Catholic Prayer for Confession

On the day of First Communion, before Mass, I stood in line with my classmates outside the confessional—in a pretty white dress and veil my mother made for me—waiting for my turn to confess my sins. I eventually learned to make up sins when I couldn't think of any, which defeated the purpose of confession since lying was a sin. Having gotten through the ordeal of our first confession, my classmates and I walked down the aisle two by two, in front of the whole congregation during Mass, to receive a communion wafer for the first time.

My anxiety grew with each step. When the priest came near me, I had to remember to open my mouth and stick out my tongue, something that normally got me in trouble. The priest put a white wafer on my tongue that had been turned into Jesus, and I was not supposed to let my teeth touch the wafer because it would hurt Jesus.

I took this responsibility seriously. Once I was back in my pew with Jesus in my mouth, He began to disappear, melting away on my tongue. Then I was able to relax and look around. Everyone's head was bowed so I bowed my head too. After the ordeal was over, my parents and sister took me to lunch at a restaurant in Williamson, a small city nearby, and gave me presents.

I was relieved to have this momentous event behind me, but I soon realized we were expected to go to confession once a week and receive communion, and it was not the end of Catechism. I learned ever more subtle, complicated ways I could sin and began to examine my conscience scrupulously—afraid I might die in the state of mortal sin and go to Hell or get stuck in Purgatory (a temporary hell).

My anxiety mounted as Saturday's confession grew nearer with each passing weekday. Would I remember what to say? What if I forgot some of my sins—would the confession not count? To this day, in my anxious moments, I find myself saying, *"O my God! I am heartily sorry for having offended Thee..."* as if to ward off punishment for my sins. Unless I gather my wits and call on my mature self, I'm constantly in the confessional.

The concept of a devil terrified me. I vividly visualized Hell. The thought of Jesus did not assuage my fear. Other girls in class thought that eating the little piece of bread was great because it was the "Body of Christ." To me, it seemed wrong to EAT someone. In later years, I longingly searched for that connection to Christ through the Holy Eucharist, which Catholics believe is the body and blood of Christ in the form of bread and wine, but that sense of connection continued to elude me except for a momentary sweetness that sometimes accompanied my prayer as I knelt after receiving communion.

I became fanatically Catholic as I grew into adolescence. As things became more chaotic in my home, I appreciated the respite of Saturday morning Catechism with the calming presence of the Sisters and Sunday morning Mass, filled with music and tinkling bells. I wanted nothing more than to please the nuns and thus please God.

When my sister, Jules, took me to Williamsburg on spring break one year, I tearfully refused to go into the historic church on the green because it was Protestant. I'd been told by the nuns that it was a sin to enter any place of worship that wasn't Catholic, and I wanted to obey the rules. My annoyed sister wanted to go in and see the church with her friends who had come with us, but she couldn't leave me outside alone. I felt guilty because I'd displeased her. The memory of being torn between sinning or displeasing my sister is still with me. But, no matter how dogmatic I became and how devoted I tried to be my sense of being worthy did not come from the Church.

As my age allowed for greater freedom, I escaped into nature to find what I was seeking. My spiritual life became deeper and more interior. The sense of direct connection with the Holy in nature was much more comforting than trying to find a connection with God through the prayers and rituals of the Church. In nature, I felt I was part of everything, but in my attempts to connect with God through the Church, I felt I was grasping for something outside myself. Yet, I wanted nothing more than to be a good Catholic girl and to dedicate my life to serving others as the nuns did.

The mystery of Christ's body becoming a small wafer and wine and the stories of Mary appearing in a bush or in the mouth of a cave or her appearance in Lourdes—where she created a spring with healing waters—were mysterious and confounding to my young soul but they laid the foundation, in later years, for my fascination with mystical experiences and the mysticism at the core of all religions.

My mother's heavy black coat that hid her pregnancy,
while she was carrying me, foreshadowed other secrets
held by my Italian Catholic family and the Catholic Church itself.
Beneath the veneer of the moral and ethical ideals professed by both,
secrets festered.

– Kathleen, Journal entry

CHAPTER TWO

Number Nine

MY SISTER, Julia, (whom we called Jules) tells me my parents fought about whose fault it was that my mother was pregnant with their ninth child. My mother, Amelia (Rossi) Marino, was forty and my father, Joseph Marino, was forty-nine, when I arrived. Their oldest child was twenty-one and the youngest was eight. There had been numerous miscarriages and near-death experiences for my mother between the last live birth and this new pregnancy. Her husband and children knew how close they had come to losing her.

The family was recovering from the Great Depression which had destroyed my father's earning ability as an award-winning stonecutter in New York City. They were uprooted from an Italian section of the Bronx with extended family all around them to a place where they were called "fereigners" by their new neighbors. World War II's tentacles had reached the United States with the bombing of Pearl Harbor. This was no time to welcome a new baby.

The first group of eight children spent their early years in a tiny two bedroom house in Iselin, New Jersey. They were a short commute by train into New York City where our Marino and

Rossi relatives lived. Before the economic downturn, my father was making a good income and could provide the little extras for his large brood such as fresh fruit, candy and outings to the City. But as construction in New York came to a halt, my father's income dwindled.

Finally, there was no more work. My father was the last stonecutter to be employed during the Depression. At first, he did not tell anyone, not even his wife, that he had lost his job and couldn't find another. Every morning he continued to get up at 4:00am to get dressed and leave the house in time to catch the 4:53 train into New York City. He searched for work all day and dragged himself home defeated, acting as if nothing had changed.

Eventually the truth became evident. The family had to move back to the city into a series of increasingly shabby apartments in the Bronx. Then, after several years, my uncle bought a farm in rural Connecticut, a few miles from the University of Connecticut, and our family moved into it. There was no running water or electricity, and there was no central heat.

My brothers, Tony, Matt, Jim, Joseph, Tom, and Mark (named after my grandfathers, my father and uncles according to the Italian custom) taught themselves to farm and raise animals for food. Six year old Pete was always by their side, doing his part. Jules, who was ten, helped with the "women's work." The older boys excelled in high school and became an integral part of the community. A few years after the move, one by one, the oldest three went off to war. The fourth son entered the monastery at the age of fourteen. Because my mother had depended on her "boys" to keep the farm running, the family would have to move again shortly before I was born.

My mother hid her swelling belly under her big black coat all winter to keep her children from worrying about her. Little did she know she couldn't protect them from the specter of death that would soon befall the family, a tragedy that would change our lives forever.

The house was freezing so no one questioned her attire, and she made no mention of her pregnancy in letters to her boys in the service. Even my twelve year old sister, Jules, the only girl with seven brothers who had been praying for a baby sister for years, didn't suspect her mother's secret. Jules had been bargaining with God for a younger sister, promising that she would take care of the baby for life. God took her literally.

Jules was ecstatic with my appearance on March 8, 1944. The birth deepened her faith in God and the Catholic Church. My brother, Tom, begged my mother to name me *Kathleen* because his Irish girlfriend had threatened not to date him unless she did. He ended up marrying a French girl and I ended up with an incongruous name: *Kathleen Marino*.

I was the first child Mom had in a hospital. I was delivered by forceps while all the other children had entered the world into the hands of an aunt or uncle. When Mom went into labor with one of the first eight children, Dad would run to fetch the doctor, relieved to have something to do. The doctor always arrived long after the birth. The baby was kept in the bed, next to Mom, and fed on demand.

I was also the first child to be separated from my mother at birth and cared for in the hospital nursery. My mother did not nurse or feed me on demand as she did with my siblings. Instead she gave me a bottle and put me on a strict four-hour feeding schedule which was in vogue at the time.

Since my mother had toxemia during the pregnancy and was ill after I was born, she was unable to attend to my needs. My young, inexperienced sister, Jules, was put in charge of my care. She sterilized the bottles, made the formula and fed me at the ordained time. She says she sat and cried with me as we waited for feeding time. Even though she was overwhelmed by the task of caring for a newborn baby, Jules continued to provide the nurturance and love that sustained me. She is there for me to this day, over seventy years later. Jules was the first mother I knew, and she claims me as her first child.

Seventeen years later, when I went to work on the OB/GYN unit of the local hospital, I met Miss Lowell—the ancient head nurse on the floor—for what I thought was the first time. Miss Lowell, with her cloud of abundant white hair, rather gaunt and austere, greeted me with surprising warmth. She had been the nurse on duty the night I was born.

She embarrassed me in front of other staff members when she said she remembered two of my brothers, dressed in Navy uniforms, tapping on the window of the nursery a few days later, declaring me the most beautiful baby in the nursery. Tony and Jim had hitchhiked half-way across country to get a glimpse of their newest sibling—a girl at that!

Mother was clearly tired and out of patience by the time I arrived. Her strategy was to let me cry myself to sleep. Tom at seventeen was the oldest sibling of the four still at home. When he heard me crying and my mother fuming as she tried to put me to bed, he'd rescue me from my mother's impatience. Mom told me he would come into the bedroom and say, "Let me have her. I'll put her to sleep". He'd close the bedroom door and work his magic. When my cousin, Stella, asked what his secret was, he confessed he walked the floor with me until I dozed off—something of which our mother didn't approve. Tom also repeatedly said, "Kathy was my first child!"

In my mother's letters to her deployed sons during the war years, she often sounded annoyed and exasperated by my presence in her life. In fact, when Thomas or Jules weren't there, which was most of the time, she admitted to putting me on the porch in my carriage and letting me cry until I fell asleep, my breath still catching in soft sobs as I slept. When the insurance man, Mr. Tubbs, came by to collect his fee each week, he would question, "What's wrong with the baby?"

My mother told him, "Oh, she cries herself to sleep." She repeated this story often and with some humor. In later years, I could hear a tinge of guilt in her voice each time she told it. The family stories of my babyhood stop there.

As I look back on it now, I have struggled to contain my tears all my life. Perhaps those unmet needs of the crying baby on the porch created a well-spring of tears which resurface unbidden to this day.

~

Mom regularly had the local baby photographer come to our home to take a formal picture of me at different stages of my babyhood. In a picture of me at about three months old, I see my Buddha-Self: big eyes, long lashes, curly light brown hair, round face with chubby pink cheeks and a shy smile. That picture was sent to the one brother who had not yet seen the new baby. Matthew was serving on a seaplane in the Pacific. He told my mother it was the safest plane in the Navy.

In the exchange of letters between my mother and Matt, during those war years, she often asks his advice and leans on him like a surrogate husband. You can hear Matt's concern for her and the rest of the family in those letters. He maintained correspondence with his brothers, cousins and friends, encouraging each of them to get a good education. My mother called him the shining light of the family. The endearing term she used in the letters to her sons was a word I never heard her say to me: *Darling*. My brother, Mark, has transcribed these letters and in doing so, has captured a picture of the mother I never knew.

When
The violin
Can forgive the past
It starts singing.…
When the violin can forgive
Every wound caused by
Others
The heart starts
Singing

– Excerpted from "Violin" by Hafiz, translated by Daniel Ladinsky
in *The Gift: Poems by Hafiz*

CHAPTER THREE

Music and Tears

MUSIC ALWAYS filled our home. Mom played the piano by ear and sang all the old tunes. She also fostered the love of classical music in her children. My maternal grandfather, Matteo Rossi, who emigrated from Sicily, sang the Italian operas—all the parts—as he cleaned the streets of New York City. My father knew every word of the old songs he had danced to in his youth and sang along when Mom played the piano.

When we went to visit our relatives in the Bronx, mandolins, banjos, guitars, and violins all came out of their cases, and we would have song fests well into the night. Songs from the old country and from the new country received equal billing. The Rossi and Marino families were talented musicians, and their bond grew stronger through their shared love of music.

Music became the healing elixir of my life. I learned all the old songs and listened to the classical music that was the background of our days, including symphonies, operas and musicals. Jules took me to concerts from the time I was nine. I felt excited as we walked down the aisle to take our seats. I'd sit there impatient for the music to start even though I usually fell asleep before it ended.

Those performances of orchestras and instrumentalists gave me an appreciation for the difference between recorded sound and the tonal complexity and vibrational impact of live music, although I would not have described it that way at the time. The music brought me to that place of belonging I felt in God's Patio. I lived within the music not outside of it.

In sixth grade, I started babysitting, and the only thing I wanted to do with the money I earned was to take piano lessons. My mother hadn't been able to afford them, but she made the arrangements with an excellent piano teacher, Mrs. Wilson, and found someone to drive me to and from my lessons.

I became a devoted student of the piano for three years, getting up two hours before I left for school to practice. Mrs. Wilson encouraged and appreciated my ability to interpret classical pieces, although my technical skill was marginal. When I entered high school, I no longer had time to practice because of the academic demands and a long bus commute each day, but I continued to play the pieces I loved.

As I grew older, my brother, Mark, and I would listen to the same symphony performed by two different conductors and compare their interpretations of the work. I learned to differentiate between conductors' styles, recognize the differences in how a phrase was played by one artist or another, and speak to the emotional impact of a piece. One Saturday when I was about fourteen, Mark and I were rearranging the furniture in my bedroom when the radio on my dresser, tuned to a classical station, began to broadcast an orchestral rehearsal of the opera *Tosca* conducted by Charles Munch.

Mark and I simultaneously leaned on my bright blue dresser and stood mesmerized for over an hour listening to Charles Munch, barely audible, sing every part of the opera as he led the orchestra through the score. This is one of my fondest memories of my brother, Mark. He often called our family the "Cultured Poor" because of our passion for music.

~

On September 8, 1944, exactly six months after my birth, my parents received the telegram every family dreads. My brother, Matthew, it said, was missing in action after his plane crashed into the Pacific Ocean. He was the navigator in a sea plane and sat alone in the back. The aircraft was sliced in half by a huge wave on takeoff. All the other crew members, though seriously wounded, survived.

The family was devastated. My father crumbled in despair. My mother, incapacitated with fear and grief, lay on a cot across from my crib for three days, vomiting. Family lore says I didn't cry the whole time. Someone would finally remember to feed me, but I never cried out in hunger. I have a recurring hazy picture of looking out through the slats of my crib and feeling what I now call *profound confusion*. There was a crushing weight all around me. I was pinned to the mattress by their grief. I couldn't make a sound.

Three days after the first telegram arrived, a second one came. It said Matthew's body had been recovered. He didn't return home until three years later on a train in a flag draped coffin. The baby photo of me, which had been sent to him, came back unopened. My smiling Buddha-Self seemed to disappear.

Matthew was a mythic figure to me. Everyone had a story about him—of his generosity, his intelligence, his kindness, his dedication to the family. These heroic portraits of him were like the fairy tales my sister read to me at night. I soon realized I could never be as perfect as Matt, which left me feeling defective from the start. And in the wake of their sorrow, I became invisible. My life's work has entailed bringing my serene child-self back to life over the course of the past seventy-five years.

~

Almost fifty years after Matt died, I was talking to my cousin, Stella, who was close to eighty at the time, and asked her when she and, her husband, Andy, were married. She said, "Right around the time Matt died," and burst into tears. "I've never gotten over his death," she added. A few months later I was talking to my brother, Jim, and told him what had happened with Stella, and *he* burst into tears and said the same thing.

The family was forever changed by this death, and the stories my older siblings tell about my parents in the early days of our family's life describe two very different people than I knew as I grew up after Matt died. My father was never the same and remained bitter towards the Japanese until the day he died twenty years later.

This devastating loss colored everything. When I was ten, my mother and I took our yearly trip into Hartford by train the week before Christmas to see the decorations at G. Fox & Company. We entered the store, extravagantly decorated for Christmas, and spent several hours perusing the treasures within. We left the warmth, shimmering lights and decorations of the store and headed into the cold chill of the descending night to walk to the train station.

As we waited beside the tracks, a train pulled in. It became very quiet. One of the freight doors opened, and six soldiers stood at attention in grey-blue double breasted full dress uniforms with white flat-topped hats. I watched as they gently lowered a flag-draped casket, lining up on either side. In one synchronized movement, they lifted the casket and stood at attention. Then they moved slowly and deliberately through the silent crowd that had opened a pathway for them to pass.

I stole a glance at my mother, who was silently weeping. "That's how my Matt came home," she said. We boarded the train after the hearse drove off, and she never said another word, but I could sense a black coat of sadness draped around her shoulders.

I always knew when Mom was thinking about Matt. She would sit down at the piano and play *Stormy Weather*, Matt's favorite song.

You're the end of the rainbow
My pot of Gold
You're Daddy's little girl
To have and to hold

– *Daddy's Little Girl*, lyrics and music by Robert Burke and Horace Gerlach

CHAPTER FOUR

And Then There Were Ten

JUST A FEW MONTHS before Matt's death, my parents scraped together enough money, with the help of family, to buy their own home for the first time in their married life. It included ten acres of land a mile up the road, which my father planned to divide among his nine children. My parents and the five children remaining at home moved into the huge old house which was a dance hall and tavern in the days of the Revolutionary War. According to local folklore, General Washington had stopped there to eat on his way through town. The room that had served as the dance hall became our living room, which we called The Big Room. Our family filled it with music, lively discussions and laughter and, sometimes, grief and tears.

The New Hope River ran against the five foot thick stone foundation of the house that rose twenty feet above the rushing waters. Sometimes the water was so high during storms my brothers fished through the cellar windows. Only one bare light bulb hung in the middle of the ceiling and dimly illuminated the dark cellar's dank, earthen floor. I rarely ventured down there, imagining it harbored all kinds of crawly things.

Family Home

The first and second floor porches, secured by pillars anchored in an undulating stonewall, ran the length of the house. French doors opened onto the lower porch from the large airy dining room. A round oak, pedestal table stood in the center of the room, surrounded by hulking oak chairs with high backs, elaborately carved with lions and scrolls. From a child's perspective, they looked like monsters in a scary fairytale looming ominously over our gatherings.

The furniture had belonged to my Uncle Jim Rossi, who was an accomplished frame-maker in New York City. He carved and gilded frames for the works of renowned artists that hung in the Metropolitan Museum of Art. He was a cultured, soft-spoken, genteel man who collected antiques. His generosity to our family was boundless because he adored his younger sister, my mother, Amelia, and her children. I remember the same furniture when it was still in his home. The chairs didn't look scary there. I would sit on Uncle Jim's lap in one of those massive chairs, feeling safe and loved. He would give me a hard candy from a pear- shaped pink depression glass container that now sits on a shelf in my living room—one of my most precious possessions—a reminder of his love.

~

Eighteen months after we settled into our new home, another major upheaval occurred in my young life. A tenth child usurped my position as the youngest in the family. Rose appeared two years after I did—another mistake. Rosie was a blue-eyed, blonde Sicilian just like my mother had been as a child. She had huge translucent blue eyes with long lashes and a head full of blonde curls. She was adored by all. I remember my father singing to her: *You're the end of the rainbow, my pot of Gold. You're Daddy's little girl to have and to hold.* There was no doubt Rosie was his favorite. Mom would later say that my father came back to life for the first time since Matt's death when Rosie came into the world.

Rosie and I grew to be inseparable. Responsible for my younger sister by the time I was four, I was supposed to model good behavior for Rosie and keep her in line. My mother used me as an example when she was trying to get Rosie and me to stop sucking our thumbs. Mom put the bad tasting tincture on *my* thumb. Once when my mother punished us by sending us outside to sit on the porch, she overheard Rosie whisper in her adorable lisp, "Suck your sumb, Cassie, suck your sumb!" Her voice was unusually low for a child.

Rosie was high-spirited and precocious. My mother often told the story of putting two-year-old Rosie in her highchair in the morning to await her breakfast until after my father was served. Rosie demanded, "I want my breakfast RIGHT NOW!" banging her spoon on the tray. She was so cute she always got her way!

My older sister, Jules, told me I had a different strategy at that age. I would throw a tantrum standing up in my high chair, crying hysterically, and hold my breath until I almost passed out. I fell out of the highchair several times, scaring the adults in the vicinity—a hard way to get attention.

Every summer evening as we grew older, Rosie and I would trudge up the dirt road to elderly Mrs. Daniels' house to sit on the porch with her in silence and watch the sun set over the river. Each of us sat in one of the appropriately sized green rocking chairs with high slatted backs and wicker seats that stood in a row—large, medium and small. It was the highlight of my day. Invariably, just before it was time to leave, Rosie would say in her husky voice, "I'm hungry."

I'd admonish her in a false whisper, "You're not supposed to say that!" But, secretly I was delighted at her brashness because Mrs. Daniels would disappear into the narrow dark hallway of her house and return with a tin of cookies.

One summer day, I learned it was sometimes dangerous to ask for what you wanted. Rosie was three and I was five when we went on an outing with our mother to downtown Williamson. We were dressed in look-alike ruffled white dresses our mother had just made for us, our hair in banana curls.

Mom offered to buy us ice cream. She said, "I'll get you vanilla cones so you won't stain your dresses." We both protested and insisted on chocolate. She finally relented. "Ok," she said, "but if you get any chocolate ice-cream on your new dresses, I'll give you a spanking!" The inevitable happened. She opened the car door and commanded us to lean over the seat, pulled down our panties and spanked us as people passed by and watched. Rosie seemed unfazed, but I cried all the way home. The memory of that humiliation is sticky and lingers still.

Even at this young age, I was aware of the contrast between Rosie and me. I had dark, unruly hair, hazel eyes, and I cried easily. I couldn't walk across a room without some invisible obstacle tripping me, whereas Rosie seemed to float in her petite body. And, Rosie was tough. She wouldn't give my mother the satisfaction of crying when she was reprimanded while I'd dissolve into tears when spoken to harshly.

Rosie not only resembled our mother physically, she was her mother's daughter: feisty, stubborn, confident and full of life. Mom had no patience with my sensitivity, shyness and lack of mental agility. I was a plodder like my father—a characteristic she couldn't stand in him or me.

Despite my mother's tight rein on the two of us, Rosie and I had fun together. We danced like Shirley Temple whenever Mom played the piano. We played house and had tea parties. Our first nephew appeared when Rosie was three and I was five. The first time we saw him, Rosie bent over his carriage and said, "Look at your little Auntie! Look at your little Auntie."

A month after I turned six years old in April of 1950, Rosie, who would be four in June, woke up from a nap screaming that her throat hurt. The sound tore through me because it was like nothing I'd heard before. Mom tried to console her. She took her temperature and called the doctor who said to bring her in the next morning if she wasn't better. Rosie continued to cry all afternoon.

Mom was scheduled to play the piano for a talent show at the Grange that evening, and she insisted I go with her. I didn't want to leave Rosie—I can still feel the sense of what I now would call *impending doom*. I instinctively knew something was terribly wrong with my little sister. As we were leaving, three of my brothers surrounded Rosie, looking down her throat, and I couldn't get close enough to her to say good-bye. Mom had to drag me out the door. When we got to the Grange, I wouldn't sit down. I remember standing by the piano that evening, fighting back tears, wondering why my mother was there and not home with Rosie.

Usually, Rosie and I slept in the same room in twin beds. That night, when Mom and I returned from the Grange, I was sent to sleep beside Jules in a far corner of the house in a double bed with an arched metal headboard painted an ugly brown. I never liked that bed. When I woke up the next morning my big sister was sitting up beside me, crying. I'd never seen Jules cry before. I was scared and asked her what was wrong. She said, "Rosie's gone." *Gone* was a word that implied she'd be back.

Still in my nightgown, I walked out into the Big Room, which was filling up with neighbors and friends. I climbed onto my brother Jim's lap. He was crying. I didn't understand why everyone was crying, but assumed I should cry, too. That was easy—I wanted to play with Rosie and she wasn't there. I started crying, saying over and over again, "I want my playmate."

Rosie and I shared a favorite song: *Playmate come out and play with me and bring your dollies three, climb up my apple tree. Look down my rain barrel, slide down my cellar door, and we'll be jolly friends forevermore.* (Playmate: Words and music by Saxie Dowell) That song swirled around me for years following Rosie's death.

Later that morning, our distraught New York relatives began to arrive. My favorite cousin, Stella, hugged me and said, "Honey, I'll take you in to see Rosie. There's nothing to be afraid of. She just looks like she's sleeping." My younger sister, who had been playing with me the morning before, was lying in a white box on the dining room table. When I refused to go with her, Stella pulled a fifty cent piece out of her pocket and tried to bribe me to go in. Again, I refused. I didn't want to see Rosie sleeping. I wanted to play with her. Finally, my mother intervened and sent me to stay with a neighbor.

All I remember about the rest of that day is feeling safe and happy at our neighbor Betsy Mason's house. Betsy was a sweet, unassuming, short, round, motherly woman with dark curly hair and kind brown eyes. Although it was clear she, too, was sad, she gave me her full attention. I remember sitting at Betsy's kitchen table in her small cottage-like home that day, having cookies and milk, and feeling like the sun was shining on me. Betsy was a faith-filled Protestant woman who prayed differently than us Catholics. When I was leaving, she put her hands on my head and prayed over me, using my name and talking directly to God in her own words. I felt comforted and calmed by her prayer.

Our copper colored cocker spaniel named Taffy had become Rosie's dog. The night Rosie was sick, Taffy lay on the landing of the stairs and howled in the middle of the night sensing, as I did, that Rosie was in danger. Days after Rosie died and all the relatives and friends had left, a dull emptiness descended on our house. I remember wandering around, not knowing what to do.

One day, I sat on the porch step with Taffy, trying to befriend him. The dog wanted nothing to do with me—he was as lost without Rosie as I was. Within a short time, Taffy, who had always been a well behaved dog, began killing chickens in the neighborhood. I woke up one day and Taffy was nowhere to be found. Mom told me he was sent to a farm in Virginia where he'd be happier. (I now suspect he was put down.) I felt Taffy did not love me as much as Rosie. In my six year old mind, nobody loved me as much as they loved Rosie.

I missed my Rosie terribly. I began playing on the stairs across the hall from the dining room that had been closed up since Rosie's death. An imaginary friend, Olli, joined me on the steps. He was about a foot tall and wore green knickers. The family began to step over Olli as they went up and down the stairs. My sister, Jules, says everyone thought I was adjusting well to the loss with the appearance of Olli. No one knew I was living under the assumption that if someone was *gone* they could come back. Many of my older siblings lived far away. They came and went arbitrarily, so I waited doggedly, achingly for Rosie to return.

~

My brother, Jim, and his wife, Andrea, who had been living with us, left to live in California shortly after Rosie died. I was sure she was with them and would return. I spent most of first grade

Sisters

looking out the window watching the road in front of the school, expecting Rosie to get out of a car at any moment. My teacher, Mrs. Lamson, gently admonished me to pay attention several times a day. Finally, in frustration, she threatened, "If you don't start paying attention, I'm going to tie your head to the chair so you can't look out the window. Now turn around!"

I looked straight ahead at the blackboard and imagined a school bus made into a little house on wheels, curtains in the windows, with someone to drive me around the country to find Rosie. (RVs and converted VW vans were not yet part of the landscape. I would make that journey sixty years later, no longer in search of Rosie, but in search of myself.) Still, I continued to sneak peeks out the window for the rest of the year.

Toward the end of the school year, I brightened one day as a tan car like Jim's pulled up across the street from the school. A man got out and went toward the trunk. I was certain Rosie would jump out and come find me. As he opened the trunk, I held my breath. He retrieved something and closed the trunk. At that moment I knew Rosie was gone forever.

Up until then, I imagined all kinds of ways Rosie and I might be reunited. It's as if the screen went dark and my mind could no longer conjure up a happy ending to the story. I now believe that my family, inundated with their own pain, was unable to acknowledge the depth of my loss. My suffering was more than they could bear to know. I doubt that they understood my confusion either, so they didn't explain the truth to me—that Rosie was never coming back—that she was dead, buried in an unmarked grave beside my brother Matt in the cemetery we visited on *special days*. I later learned these were Matt and Rosie's birthdays and the anniversaries of their deaths.

Our visits to the cemetery in the year following Rosie's death were an outing to me. I ran and played in the grass, stopping at tombstones with carved angels or statues of the Blessed Mother, while my family stood in silence looking down at the ground my mother called "our plot." After my realization that Rosie was dead and buried beneath the dirt, these visits became somber and disturbing events. I stood with the others looking down at the ground.

In pictures taken eight months after Rosie's death, I am a bright, straight backed, smiling little girl full of hope sitting on my daddy's lap. That summer, pictures of me at a picnic reveal a somber, hunched-backed child with dark circles under her eyes. I'd caved in on myself with grief. This was my first depressive episode. I've never been able to stand straight since that spring.

I had no words in my vocabulary to describe my feelings back then. I'm not sure I do even now. Aching with sadness, I wept through that summer, aggravating my mother. She had little tolerance for tears especially when they appeared to have no legitimacy. When I was very young she would say, "If you want to cry, I'll give you something to cry about!" Later, she often swiped my tear-stained cheek with her finger to taste my tears. If she deemed them salty not bitter, which she always did, she called them "crocodile tears," meaning they were fake. I felt humiliated by her dismissal of my feelings and began to question their validity myself.

When I was older, I'd go into the bathroom to cry and then wash my face before I exited into the large upstairs kitchen. I remember sneaking past my mother so she wouldn't detect I'd been crying as she stood at the sink with her back to me, washing dishes. More than once, she said harshly, "You think I don't know what you're doing in there—you think I don't know you're crying!"

My father had a different tactic to stop my tears. He sang an old song to me. The words were: *When you're crying, when you're crying, the whole world cries with you. When you're laughing, when you're laughing, the sun comes shining through. When you're crying you bring on the rain, so stop you're crying, be happy again...* That song only served to make me feel responsible for everyone's happiness. None of the five adults still at home had a clue about what was going on in my head, and I had no way to articulate the depth of my pain. They already had a year of processing the reality of Rosie's death while I was just beginning to grasp the magnitude of the word *gone*.

My inability to fall asleep was the only significant sign of my distress for the year after Rosie died. My sister, Jules, would read to me until I fell asleep. Now, as I contemplated the finality

Filled with Hope

Lost Hope

of Rosie's disappearance after the trunk slammed down on all my hopes, I became terrified to close my eyes even with my big sister sitting beside me with the lights still on.

Jules would say, "Close your eyes. I'm right here." Or, "There's nothing to be afraid of. I won't let anyone hurt you."

But, I was not convinced. From my seven year old perspective, Rosie had gone to sleep and never awakened. I came to the conclusion that something got her *from inside* when she closed her eyes that night. I felt that the danger was within her body, and it could be within mine as well. I didn't understand biology or know about germs or viruses—but I sensed a darkness within that could snuff out the light. More than any outside threat, I feared this "monster" inside me that could attack me in my sleep, and I would never wake up. Even Jules couldn't protect me.

I forced my heavy eyelids to stay open, to the exasperation of my patient and tired sister, until sleep overtook me. Often, in the middle of the night, I'd wake up—heart pounding with terror—and run to my sister's bed. She would always take me in.

She sat by my bed every night until I was twelve years old. She read poetry, stories of elves and fairies, and many treasured children's books until I fell asleep. She seeded my love for literature and poetry. And, at a very young age, poetry began to fall from my pen onto paper. The act of writing was soothing and exhilarating at the same time. When a poem had spun itself out on the page, I was filled with relief and calm. The positive attention I received for my poetry from my family and the nuns encouraged me to continue writing.

At the age of seven I wrote this poem about Jules:

> *Little Lady good as gold,*
> *One that I will always know.*
> *She tells me poems when day is through*
> *And always stops to kiss me, too.*
>
> *– Kathleen, age seven*

~

When I returned to school in the fall, entering second grade, my friends and I formed a small group on the playground at recess. I began telling the story of "the night my little sister died." I developed a following. My friends clamored to hear the story again and again as we walked together around the perimeter of the school yard. My close encounter with the mystery of death gave me status among my peers. I felt important and wise in contrast to the way I felt in a household of adults where I was no longer the big sister to someone less knowing than me.

By that time, my mother had tried to explain what happened the night Rosie died. She said that during the night Rosie was having trouble breathing, so Daddy and she and Jim and Mark took her to the hospital. The doctors put Rosie in a tent with air in it to help her breathe—she was scared so Mom climbed into the tent with her. (I always liked that part of the story.) Then Rosie couldn't breathe anymore. The doctor scooped her up and ran to the operating room, but it was too late. She told me Rosie had strep throat and, if she had lived, she would have been an invalid the rest of her life.

As I grew older, more details (and confusion) were added as I gleaned new information by eavesdropping on the adults as they rehashed the trauma. The conflicting stories only exacerbated my fear for myself and, later, for my children. I assumed that if I knew exactly what had happened to Rosie, I could prevent it from happening again. The different versions offered by family members made the adults in my life seem untrustworthy. Mark said he was holding Rosie at the hospital, and later Jim said he was the one holding her. I didn't know who or what to believe.

I became obsessed with death and this obsession propelled me further into the arms of the Catholic Church as I grew older.

~

Mark began renovating the house after Rosie died. He threw himself into the project which lasted thirty years. Constant chaos ensued as he tore apart one room after another. I hated the mess and the noise and was ashamed to bring my friends home. His excuse for disrupting our home was that he wanted to make it better for our mother. There was often tension between them and they argued about the changes he was making. This situation left me more disoriented and confused.

Even though Rosie was gone, she was present in my life growing up. Each Christmas after she died, I found an abundance of presents under the tree. At some point, when I no longer attributed the bounty to Santa Claus and understood the financial constraints of our family, I asked my mother about it. She said, "Well, I've always figured I would've been doing for two if Rosie were still here."

Mom had sewn adorable look-a-like outfits for Rosie and me. When I was about ten, I finally found the courage to investigate the attic, a place I feared. I used to run past the door, afraid I'd be snatched by the ghosts that lived there. On my first excursion up the creaky staircase, I found a box of clothes from my early years. I ran downstairs excited to show them to my mother. "Mom, I didn't know you saved my clothes!"

Without looking up from what she was doing, she said in a flat voice, "I didn't—those are Rosie's. I gave yours away."

I understand what those clothes meant to her. They were a little piece of Rosie she could hold in her hands, smell and fondle—they were all she had left of Rosie. Still, as I write this now, I feel the sting of her words.

My respect for my mother's strength grew after I had children, and she and I became closer, but it could not make up for the feeling of not being wanted in my early years. I always felt like I was in the way. I had the sense that I should have died, not Rosie.

~

My mother's black winter coat, which she wore everywhere to hide my presence when she was pregnant with me, represents a message that reverberated through my childhood. "Why are you always under my feet," she would say. If I sought the comfort of her lap, her words were "Here comes my two-ton elephant!" or

"Lean on your own appetite!" which I never understood but took as a rejection. "Don't bother me (or your brother, sister, father)." "Make yourself scarce." "Stop being such a *Sarah Heartburn*." "Go find something to do." "What do you want NOW?" I tried to make myself invisible and eventually became invisible to myself.

In retrospect, I see the loneliness of this child and the ramifications of early trauma in her later life. She was forced to learn "to put on a happy face" to hide a layer of her soul, which was probably her first introduction to keeping secrets. It was a family expectation long before she arrived. Yet, the emotions she tried to hold in check often welled up from the depths and betrayed her inner feelings.

(In my sleep I dreamed this poem)

Someone I loved once gave me
A box full of darkness.

It took me years to understand
That this, too, was a gift.

– "The Uses of Sorrow" by Mary Oliver, from *Thirst*

CHAPTER FIVE

The Stonecutter's Stories

IN THE MONTHS following Rosie's death, my six-year-old self trudged a half mile to the end of River Road everyday to meet my father who was dropped off there after work. He wore his white overalls, still clean after spending the day painting buildings at the University. He was meticulous, a perfectionist.

I sensed his weary sadness. I'd take the empty lunch box he carried and hold his hand as we walked back to the house. We never spoke. On Saturdays, he gave me all the change he'd accumulated during the week to put in my piggy bank. One of my earliest memories of my father is the smell of his *Bond Street* pipe tobacco. I found it comforting. It mingled with the smells of baking bread and fresh coffee—the smells of home and family.

My father became despondent after Rosie died. He plunged into months of profound depression, sitting for hours, almost catatonic, in an over-stuffed dark green chair in the upstairs living room, curtains drawn to block out all light. He shuffled when he walked, was hardly able to move, unable to eat. He'd sit at the table crying and repeating stories about the deaths of his children and the death of his mother when he was four. None of the adults in the house seemed to pay attention, but my young heart was breaking for him. When I was eight or nine, I would sit with him at the dimly lit kitchen table and listen to his stories.

He repeatedly told me, "I was four years old when my mother died. My sister, Rose, said it was my fault she died because I was a cry baby." He'd begin to weep. Then he'd break into sobs as he vividly relived losing Matt and Rosie.

His war stories were the worst. He told me countless times the story of being in WWI in France in 1918, where the starving soldiers stood in long lines for their meager rations. "As I stood in line one day," my father said, "one soldier tried to cut the line. The soldier he cut in front of bit him and drew blood—the man died from the bite." Without fail, my father ended the story by saying, "The human mouth is the filthiest thing on earth." My aversion to "filthy" things was already well ingrained, but this graphic image escalated this aversion into a phobia.

My father described an incident in France when he was scouting ahead of his men. "I came upon two German soldiers setting up a machine gun. One fired on me and hit me on my left side, the bullet exited and lodged in the crux of my [left] arm. The impact threw me into a shell hole and then a body came hurtling into the hole after me—it was one of my men who had been wounded too. The Germans kept spraying the field with gunfire. When I saw someone coming toward the hole, I was ready to fire—I thought the enemy was coming to finish us off. Instead it was our own medics coming to help us."

At this point my father broke down in wracking sobs. What he saw as he emerged from the hole was the carnage of bodies strewn across the field—his men. He carried the pain of those losses for the rest of his life.

These stories became embedded in my memory as if I had witnessed them—which I learned, years later, is called "secondary trauma." But, it was the image of my father sobbing as he told them that seared my psyche. I was incapable of offering him comfort. I walked away feeling a physical sensation—like a huge hand was squeezing my heart until I couldn't breathe. Looking back, I realize my family abandoned me to my father's depression, and I attempted to lift the pain from his shoulders by carrying his burden as if it was my own.

~

The river was my refuge. I'd jump the rocks to the middle of the river and stand on Flat Rock, close my eyes and melt into the sound of the water, the touch of the breeze, the sun's light and warmth, the birdsong. The boundary of my skin disappeared—there was no separation between me and the natural world. The house looming behind me vanished, and the pain that permeated our home was washed away by the river's cool waters.

The only other place of respite from the weight of my father's dark and scary world and my family's palpable grief, was the Church—Catechism on Saturday and Mass on Sunday. Our beautiful, airy Church with sunlight streaming through pastel stained-glass windows filled me with a sense of peace. The music, the rituals, the smells of incense and the bells all brought order and grace to my soul. The Church and the Sisters felt more like a safe haven than did my home.

It became the custom to send me to our extended family in New York City for part of the summer from the time I was nine to twelve years old. There my cousins, who were the same age as my older brothers and sister, fussed over me and made me feel special. I played with their children who were my age. We went on excursions to Rye Beach and Coney Island. We went to the movies every Saturday and spent most of the day there.

These visits to the city for a month each summer were to protect me from seeing my father's mental deterioration. Carol, my friend who lived across the street, filled me in on what happened while I was gone. One summer upon my return, she reported that the State Police came and took my father away. Another time, she said my brothers had to tackle my father to take him to the hospital.

My father had a cycle which started with depression around the Christmas holidays. He sat in that living room chair for hours, never moving, staring straight ahead. I felt the darkness exuding from him—as if a menacing presence inhabited his body.

Jumping the Rocks

As summer approached, he slowly emerged from depression into a full blown mania—displaying unpredictable and frightening behavior. He became paranoid, agitated and belligerent, yelling or rambling on with his stories or singing the old songs in a loud voice at inappropriate times and places. The mania escalated until it was necessary for the family to forcibly hospitalize him for his own safety and ours.

In his manic state, he wore khaki nylon swimming trunks, a white sleeveless undershirt and his khaki safari hat, *everyday*. He carried a sturdy stick with a piece of lead pipe on the bottom with which he threatened anybody who didn't jump at his command.

My brother, Mark, a born caretaker who lived at home, would orchestrate our father's hospitalizations and call the other brothers to come help with what was always an excruciating process. My father, with his background as a stonecutter and amateur boxer, was extremely strong, especially when manic. Since he was delusional and paranoid, he believed we were the crazy ones and were all out to get him. He never went to the hospital voluntarily—my brothers needed to use force or call the state police for help.

Years later, my brother, Jim, told me it broke their hearts to have to tackle Dad and hold him down to get him the help he needed. This took the greater toll on Mark as he was the one left behind with Mom and me to visit the hospital and deal with our angry, bitter father. The psychiatrists diagnosed Dad as "manic depressive paranoid schizophrenic." He lived with that label for the last ten years of his life.

I vividly remember one of our visits to see my father in the Norwich State Hospital in Connecticut when I was twelve. Every visit entailed being escorted through several clanging locked metal doors. Inside, the deafening sound of patients' and staff's voices echoed off the drab grey walls. There was always a "Day Room" in these psychiatric hospitals, with men, in various psychological states, talking to each other or to themselves, shouting obscenities, frenetically pacing, getting in fights, smoking incessantly.

My father was furious when we went to see him, demanding we bring him home, outraged that we would leave him there. On one occasion, he said to me, in a low, menacing voice, "I want you to see where they make me sleep." He grabbed my arm and dragged me back through a gloomy hallway to a narrow dark room with twenty beds lined up one after the other with barely room to stand between them. He snarled glaring at me, "See! See! This is where they make me sleep with all those animals."

I silently shook in the back seat of the car the whole way home. That image haunted me for years.

I dreaded each visit, and it was no better when Dad came home heavily tranquilized. His animosity toward us was evident. He would stop me as I walked through a room and aggressively ask, "What day is it? What's the date? What year is it? Who's the President of the United States?"

"I don't know, Dad—it's Thursday, I think it's the 28th…"

"See! See! You're the crazy one! You don't even know the date!"

These are the mental status questions my father was asked when being admitted to the hospital. He went around trying to prove *we* were the *crazy ones* not him. About three months after returning home, Dad would stop taking the tranquilizers, and the cycle started all over again. (Lithium, which is an effective medication for what is now called bi-polar disorder, was available in Europe but had not yet been approved in the United States.)

I resented my father for disrupting our household and preventing me from living a normal adolescence. I withdrew from him, barely acknowledging his existence. One morning, as he was once again escalating into mania, I came to the breakfast table, sat down and reached for the butter. He was sitting across from me. He slammed his fork into the butter, narrowly missing my hand and growled, "Say good morning to your father when you come downstairs!"

On a summer evening in July at dusk, my cousins, Lenny and Bobby, and I were sitting near a window on the upstairs porch. The interior of the house was dark except for the brightly lit kitchen at the back of the house where we could see Mark sweeping the floor. My father came into the room and started instructing him on how to sweep. Mark, who could be as volatile as my father, argued with him, and a shouting match ensued.

My anxiety level started to rise as I watched the scene unfold. I saw my father raise his fist about to strike Mark, who responded in kind. I let out a scream and fled off the porch, down the stairs, running barefoot across the street and up the neighbor's stony driveway with Lenny and Bobby right behind me. I banged on the door crying, "Mark and Dad are fighting!"

I was engulfed in warmth and light as the door opened. Evelyn, my friend Carol's mother, held me in her arms and tried to calm me as Mark and my father came running across the road and up the driveway after me. I'm still shaking inside as I write this.

Mark reassured me in his calm, controlled voice that "everything's alright," and my father tearfully apologized for upsetting me. I was surprised by this because he never seemed to care about me. Evelyn, who was also the neighborhood nurse, tended to my bruised and bleeding feet. We went back home pretending nothing had happened. The incident was never mentioned again.

Another spring, in a manic state, my father trained my dog, Sami, to be an attack dog like the ones he worked with in the army. My gentle companion became aggressive, growling and dangerous. Sami bit my friend, Katie, who lived around the corner from us. Even though it wasn't a bad bite, my mother and brother decided the dog had to be put down. It took me a long time to forgive my father for the loss of my pet.

I wanted a normal life with normal parents and family, to be carefree the way my friends seemed to be. I wanted a father that acted appropriately and didn't scare me. I didn't want to have to tip-toe around him, afraid I'd set him off. By this time I'd become my mother's confidant and a source of support. I felt responsible for her happiness and often took her side against my father and siblings.

~

A social worker began to appear at our home every few weeks. She would remind me not to take anything my father said or did personally because he was "sick." She didn't explain what kind of sickness he had. It was hard for a thirteen-year-old to comprehend this. I felt guilty because I began to hate my father and regularly confessed my sin in the confessional.

The Catholic Church had been my refuge from the time I made my first communion at the age of seven, but the focus on sin and damnation burdened me with guilt and fear. Still, I chose the rigidity of Church doctrine over the chaos of my life at home.

I once asked my mother, as only an audacious thirteen-year-old would do, "Why do you stay with him?"

My mother quietly replied, "It wasn't always like this."

I now know what the social worker was trying to say: "This person you see now is not really who your father is."

In reality, my father, Joseph Marino, was a remarkable man. He came from a family of eight. His father, Antonio Marino, who owned a grocery store in an Italian neighborhood in New York City, worked long hours, although he never made much money. He went bankrupt several times because he allowed his customers to take food on credit during difficult times. He was called "Don," a title of respect in those days because he was an honest, generous man, ready to help anyone in need. Since my father's mother died of tuberculosis when he was four, his sister, Rose, the eldest, took over the mother's responsibilities, but she was young and became bitter and domineering.

The family lived in a dangerous neighborhood, and when my grandfather worked late, he often was unable to open the door when he returned home at night because his children were heaped in a pile sleeping against the door to prevent intruders from getting in. Grandpa Antonio finally decided he needed to break up the family temporarily so the younger children would be safer and get better care and the older ones would be free to go to work.

The younger girls and the baby, Thomas, were sent to aunts, but no one wanted the two boys in the middle. They were sent to an orphanage. Tony, the older of the two, about seven-years-old, became his five-year-old brother Joey's caretaker. My father described how his big brother, Tony, tried to protect him from the raging nuns and the bullying of older children. If little Joey wet the bed at night, which he was prone to do, Tony whipped

Grandpa Marino's Store

off the sheets from his bed and exchanged them for dry ones from another bed so his little brother wouldn't get in trouble.

When my father went to school he faced another hurdle—he was left handed. In those days, left-handedness was considered evil, sinister. He was beaten whenever he went to use his left hand. That alone would make a child averse to learning, but it appears my father also had learning disabilities that weren't recognized in those days. He struggled in the first few grades, never learned to read or write well, a source of great shame for him.

I was captivated by another story Dad repeatedly told me:

"I came down with St. Vitas Dance, [a neurological disorder caused by rheumatic fever]. I couldn't control myself. My arms and body and even my face jerked and moved uncontrollably. I couldn't go to school and was left alone all day for a year. I made friends with a boy in the building across the alley who was paralyzed. We'd sit by our windows and talk to each other. Then he stopped coming to the window. He died."

When he recovered, my father was sent to apprentice in a stone yard. He was strong for his age in spite of all he had been through. Even so, it was a daunting task to handle the huge pieces of stone and learn to cut them precisely with a chisel and a heavy mallet. Dad was a natural at it and loved the work. He became a connoisseur of stone—stroking a piece of stone like a pet, he would reverently say, "Feel the grain. Just, feel that grain!" He finally excelled at something and his left-handedness did not matter. It made him even more valuable in the trade because he could access places that were difficult for right-handed stonecutters to reach.

World War I broke out and my father put down his chisel and mallet and joined the Army. When he returned to the States after the war, seven years later, he fulfilled a promise he'd made to himself when he was twenty-one. The first time he met his new sister-in-law, Marian—his brother, Tony's wife—he could not help but notice her sister, Amelia, who was twelve at the time. She was beautiful, and he promised himself he would wait for her.

Dad, in his youth, was a handsome, dapper man—about 5'8" and muscular, a light-footed graceful dancer. My cousins told me he was in demand as a dance partner. His love of singing stayed with him until the end of his life. My parents were married in 1923 when Mom was nineteen and he was twenty-eight.

My mother, Amelia Rossi, was a beautiful, vivacious woman with a wonderful sense of humor, talented and bright. She was a good student but had to leave school in tenth grade to go to work and help her family. Despite this fact, if she overheard one of her offspring make a grammatical error, this Italian mother yelled, "Speak the King's English!" She was a voracious reader and later in life she did the *New York Times* crossword puzzle every Sunday. In her seventies, she continued to enjoy beating her intellectual adult sons at Scrabble, and often quoted Shakespeare.

Mom frequently sat for an hour or more and played the piano. She went from one song to another, drawing on her stream of consciousness. If she was unhappy, she played songs with a darker tone in a minor key. As she continued playing, her choices of songs became lighter and brighter. She'd say, "This is my therapy."

Her wry sense of humor often caught us off-guard. She was rarely overwhelmed by the multitude of children she birthed, but sometimes, when we were all together, she'd try to get the attention of one of us, calling out a litany of names, "Thomas! Mark! Joseph!" Then, in exasperation, she'd say, "You with the hair on your head!" The object of her attention would coyly answer with a grin, "Yes, Mom," knowing all the while to whom she was speaking.

And, she showed her love through food. When my brother, Jim, was at the table, his portion had no onions. She made special dishes for other family members as well—always remembering our favorite foods. Every Saturday, she took me grocery shopping with her, and she let me pick out a treat, usually ice-cream, even though she was always on a tight budget. And, each Thursday night around 8:00 pm when the Baker-man's truck pulled up in front of our house, she took me outside with her to choose pastries or coffee-cake to be served with the family's evening coffee.

~

The wound in Father's side eventually healed but left a grotesque scar which he bore proudly. During his manic episodes in later years, he often lifted his shirt to display it. The doctors didn't dare remove the bullet lodged in the crook of his left arm so he lost fine motor control in his left hand. He trained himself to use the chisel in his right hand and the mallet in his left.

Meanwhile, he worked to dislodge the bullet from his arm. My brother, Mark, told me, "Cold sweat ran down his face from the pain as he pushed it out little by little—it took months, but he finally succeeded." The bullet remained in a jar on his dresser until he died. He retrained his left hand and became an ambidextrous stonecutter.

As his abilities were recognized, he began to get choice assignments working on buildings all over New York City—the Empire State Building, the Chrysler Building, Rockefeller Center, and The Cloisters. At one of our kitchen table conversations he told me about working on the Cathedral of St. John the Divine.

"You go to work every day knowing you will never see the cathedral completed, but you do your very best because it's a House of God."

I heard echoes of the voices of stonecutters, who worked for centuries on the cathedrals of Europe, saying those same words. In the 1930's, before the crash of the stock market, Dad won a prestigious award for being the best stonecutter in the City. This award hung prominently on the living room wall. Dad always said, "I don't need a monument on my grave—I have monuments all over New York City." His stature as an award winning stonecutter is part of our family identity, and I was proud of my father's skill and dedication to his work.

My brothers and sister remember a father who never hit them no matter how badly they behaved because his hands were so big and strong he was afraid he'd hurt them. As a result, my mother became the disciplinarian. He provided the softness in those early years of the family's life. His eight children thrived, and he was proud of the family he had created and his ability to support them.

When the Great Depression hit, Dad didn't want to be on the dole or accept anything from my Uncle Jim Rossi and Uncle Tony Marino who offered help. My mother resorted to sneaking around to accept their money. Sometimes she sent her young sons on this clandestine errand to get money from our Uncles to pay for the groceries she needed to feed the ten people who sat at her table. A culture of secrets became the family's way.

Eventually, my father had no choice but to accept help. It broke him not to be the family's sole provider. Years later, in his melancholy moods, he sang the depression era song, *Brother Can You Spare a Dime*. He never really recovered and ended up working as a painter at the University of Connecticut for meager pay.

After the deaths of two of his children, my father rarely spoke, and when at home, he would undertake solitary tasks like damming up the river to form a swimming pool for our family and the neighborhood kids. He was still physically powerful, moving huge boulders to create a patio while clearing the area for the pool.

Toward the end of Dad's life he took up stonecutting again for the first time in years. He worked on the back of a scrolled cornice that had belonged to my Uncle Jim Rossi. I heard the clinking of his chisel and went downstairs to the cellar to watch him work. After standing there in silence for a while, I asked, "Dad, what are you making?"

"I'm carving an angel to put on Rosie's grave." His mallet struck the chisel again without losing a beat. The clinking sound reminded me of the bells ringing during Mass when we said, "Mea Culpa, Mea Culpa, Mea Maxima Culpa." I turned and went back upstairs.

~

My father's legacy lives on in his children, grandchildren and generations of offspring who exhibit extraordinary creativity, perseverance, gentleness and innate intelligence. And, some of us have inherited genes that give us a propensity for depression, bipolar disorder, learning disabilities and autism.

I've learned that these seemingly disparate traits often go together. Some family members of the younger generation are on the autism spectrum and/or have learning disabilities. And, I have been distraught when some, including myself, were diagnosed with depression or bi-polar disorder like my Dad.

Then I began to appreciate the gifts that have allowed us to live full and fruitful lives: creativity, an ethic of service and kindness, the ability to be contributing members of society, and the love we share. Now, I practice holding the paradox for myself and my family. We are not defined or diminished by our challenges in life nor are we elevated by our innate gifts and strengths. We are whole, perfectly imperfect human beings.

For each ecstatic instant
We must in anguish pay
In keen and quivering ratio
To the ecstasy

For each beloved hour
Sharp pittances of years—
Bitter contested farthings—
And coffers heaped with Tears

– "Compensation" by Emily Dickinson, from *Final Harvest*

CHAPTER SIX
The Child's Voice

DISORIENTED BY THE GRIEF AND CHAOS of Rosie's death and my father's illness, which consumed our family, I had no sense of myself, what I wanted or where I belonged. The only thing I could cling to was my belief in God, and the Catholic Church was the anchor of that belief. My forays into the mystical center of my being through music and nature still gave me sustenance, but I needed the structure of the Church to ground me.

By the time I was eight or nine, my consciousness was deeply embedded in the family culture and the Catholic ethos of serving others and changing the world. Mom fed anyone who showed up at our door hungry. She baked for fundraisers in the community and offered her time to play the piano for the Grange, the Church and local schools. She was there for her friends with a casserole and words of compassion when they experienced a loss. The New York relatives were generous people, giving tangible help to those in need. And, I watched my siblings model these behaviors in their daily lives. They chose careers in science, teaching, medicine and art. I aspired to emulate them.

I felt proud to be a Marino. I held our family to a higher order of conduct than the average family, not understanding at the time that such elevated expectations would inevitably lead to crushing disillusionment when its secrets were revealed.

~

My position as the youngest living member of the family made it difficult for me to envision how I could live up to the idealized view I had of them. Surrounded by competent adults, I felt there was nothing special about me, and I had nothing to offer. Even my younger sister, Rosie, outshined me in her short life. She was feisty, outgoing, unafraid. I was shy, lacked confidence, and was fearful.

After Rosie died, Mom took a job as a cook at the Buchanan School where I entered first grade that fall. The school's eighth grade class put on a variety show at the end of each year, and Mom accompanied them on the piano. When I was six, she bribed me to sing in the show with the promise of making me a *gown*. Although I didn't want to get up in front of two hundred people and sing, singing was something I *loved* to do, and I really wanted that gown. I became the show's mascot. Every year Mom made me a new gown for the event. I was the envy of all the little girls in my class.

I got up on stage and sang. Standing on a box to reach the microphone, I belted out the old songs I heard sung around the piano at home. I sang with gestures and flair that made the audience laugh. The New York relatives drove five hours to hear me sing. My glamorous cousins did my makeup before the show and applauded loudly when I performed. I felt special and seen. I had something to offer that garnered the attention of *adults*. Standing up in front of these large audiences gave me the confidence I called upon years later as a teacher and speaker.

But, my immediate family offered little praise. One day when we had guests, I overheard my mother say, "Here comes my alabaster beauty." That was the only time I had any indication she thought I was pretty. "You look nice," was usually the extent of the compliments I received. Jules encouraged my efforts to write poetry, paint and explore other creative endeavors, but was sparse in her compliments. The Church prohibited allowing a child to become prideful and arrogant. If I tried to stand up for myself, my mother would say, "Get off your high horse!"

Singing Debut

I was confused by mixed messages. My brothers' discussions around the big oak table went on long into the night and filled my mind with possibilities for myself and the world. No women sat at that table. My mother went back and forth to the kitchen all night serving coffee and homemade baked goods to *her boys*. Women's deference to men was the norm in our family and in the Church. My sisters-in-law fell asleep in various corners of the house waiting for their husbands, while I sat spellbound outside of the circle of men, absorbing every word.

My siblings enriched my childhood immeasurably. They nurtured my curiosity about the workings of the world on every level: history, science, culture, religion, politics and ethics. In my first journal at nineteen I wrote: "Little comparison can be made between my siblings and me. Despite the fact that I was born into a large family, I was brought up as an only child. The brother closest to me is nine years older, and my younger sister died when I was six. My brothers and sister were children growing up together. I was a child growing up among young adults. I found this situation both advantageous and challenging."

Whenever I met a new group of people, I didn't tell them anything about myself. Instead, I told them about my "seven brilliant brothers and sister." I was awestruck by my siblings' accomplishments and envied my mother's sociability, her innate intelligence and many talents. My father held the prestige of being an award winning stonecutter. The more I looked up to the adults in my family, the smaller and more inadequate I felt.

I never felt fully integrated into the lives of the seven male siblings who came before me. And, as close as my sister, Jules, and I are, there is a distance between us that can never be traversed. My siblings had a different history, a different world view, coming through the Great Depression and World War II, and happier parents before their son was lost at sea. The stages of our lives have been out of sync until now when old age has become the common denominator among us.

My seventh grade science teacher, at the Junior High School I attended, Mr. Neilson, took me aside to question how I was doing—he had heard about my father's breakdown. I waxed philosophically about understanding that my father was mentally ill and that I shouldn't take what he did or said personally, freely paraphrasing the social worker's words. Mr. Neilson said, "You have wisdom beyond your years, Kathy." I felt like a fraud.

When Mr. Levine, my junior high social studies teacher, stood before our class one afternoon with an uncharacteristically stern look on his face, I trembled. Everyone quieted down and he said, "There are a few rotten apples in this class that are spoiling the whole bunch." Sitting about four rows back from the front, I turned toward the wall and hid my head in shame, tears silently slipping down my cheeks. In an instant, Mr. Levine squatted beside my desk speaking softly, "Kath, what's wrong?"

"I'm one of the rotten apples!" I said in a whisper.

"You're the last person in the world I'd think of as a rotten apple!" he said. "Where did you get that idea?"

I couldn't stop crying, and tears well up today as I write this. He gently escorted me to the nurse's office and quietly said something to her, shaking his head. He told me he would be back after class to check on me. This short, slightly rotund, balding Jewish man, wearing dark-rimmed glasses, responded to my tears with compassion—not with a reprimand or an attempt to banish them with logic as my mother and brothers did.

Mr. Levine knew my family and took me home that day and a few more times in the following months. Sometimes he engaged Mark in conversation and, one time, he stayed for dinner. I think he was concerned about my home environment. Whatever the reason for those visits, I know I will never forget his kind attention. I was visible to him.

Although I was often the center of attention when my brothers were teasing me or trying to impart their greater wisdom, I felt invisible in their presence. I believed there was something wrong with *me*. I lived in the shadow of guilt and unworthiness.

And, I was trained by the Catholic Church to scrupulously search my soul for sins and to avoid *the near occasion of sin*. The voice of the inner critic became louder and louder until it was all that I heard. Even doing a good deed could be *the occasion of sin* if you did it for the wrong reason—to receive praise or even to feel good about yourself. Suffering, sacrifice and humility led to Heaven. Pride, selfishness, and self-indulgence led to Hell. I walked around feeling intrinsically defective.

~

The Catholic Church strongly impacted another part of my life. When I was about ten years old, rumors circulated on the playground at school that "older girls bleed from their private parts every month." This was a frightening prospect. My sister finally took me aside and quickly and sketchily explained menstruation to me. She was as embarrassed as I was. She handed me a small pink book with diagrams in it and said, "If you have any questions, just ask me." That was unlikely, considering her demeanor.

It was about the same time that the Sisters began instructing the boys and the girls separately. They repeatedly warned us that it was a sin to touch yourself *down there* or to let anyone else touch you *down there*. This was a puzzlement to me because, being germ phobic and trained to wash my hands thoroughly after using the bathroom, I had no inclination to do either. According to the nuns, even *thinking* about doing these things was a sin.

My strategy to keep myself *pure*, which seemed to be an important word to the nuns, was to never think about *down there* and avoid any information on that forbidden part of my body. When I turned twelve, there was no escaping the need to deal with my private parts. I woke up one morning feeling sick, and I found blood on my pajamas. I was mortified, confused and scared. I stuffed some toilet paper in my underwear when I got dressed and went to lean against the warm chimney in the upstairs dining room for comfort.

My sister came into the room and, crying, I told her what had happened. She was angry and curt. "I told you all about that! Just go get a pad from under the bathroom sink and get ready for school." In those days, pads were big bulky things, and I remember finding some kind of belt that was supposed to keep it in place. I lived in fear that the pad would show or blood would seep through my clothes and give away my secret. My friends at school helped me adjust to this new reality in my life.

These same friends also began talking about boys: "Chuck is *so* cute." or "I hope Rick asks me out." I was uncomfortable with this kind of talk. It was difficult for me to understand why this had become the topic of conversation. I became more of a loner and escaped into reading stories about the female Saints who were chaste and pure along with *Cherry Ames* and *Nancy Drew* who were equally so. Immersed in classical music and opera, I thought popular music was immoral and beneath me. I felt rather superior to my peers and, of course, that was a sin.

I graduated from eighth grade with honors and won several awards. I was also crowned queen of the eighth grade dance. I had gained some confidence by then, but didn't feel worthy of these accolades. My mother made me a beautiful white graduation dress, and my still unruly hair looked perfect that day. I presided over the dance in a blue, silvery, full-skirted dress she also made— with three crinoline petticoats under it—costing my mother more than she could afford.

Everything was perfect, but the teachers who cared about me, and the Principal and the Superintendent of Schools, who were family friends, knew about my situation at home. Had they orchestrated this triumph for me? Fifty-eight years later, I still question whether I earned those awards or if they were given to me out of concern or worse, out of pity, for my life circumstances.

~

My sister, Jules, was an integral part of my life until I was twelve. We did everything together. I felt secure and cared for in her presence even though she would correct me on my manners, and sometimes showed displeasure with my behavior. She was, and still is, a quiet, introverted homebody. My mother was convinced her oldest daughter would end up an *old maid* if she didn't get out of our small town. She pressured Jules to apply for a job teaching overseas. I was crushed when my sister left for Japan. It was the summer I realized Dad was being hospitalized for a mental disorder not a physical one. I had no idea what this meant for my life, especially without Jules.

Two years after she left, Jules announced she was getting married to a British-Japanese man. The wedding would take place in Japan. I was angry and hurt. Our family could not afford to attend. I felt betrayed, cheated out of fulfilling my dream of someday being Jules's bridesmaid. I stopped corresponding with her. She reached out to me many times with presents and notes, but I was unmoved. It wasn't until she came home for a visit with her one-year-old son that I cracked the door open again.

The spring I turned thirteen the nuns at Catechism chose me to lead the May procession in the yearly celebration of Our Lady, Mother of God. The children of the parish processed around the statue of the Blessed Mother that stood in the center of the circular driveway. When the circle was complete they stopped, prayed and sang while I solemnly climbed a ladder to crown the statue with a wreath of flowers. I was chosen again the next year. No one had ever been given this honor twice. Once again, I felt honored to be chosen *and* unworthy of the honor. I was so fearful of doing something wrong or committing the sin of pride that the beauty of the moment eluded me.

So much of my life entailed this struggle with sin. Every year that I sang in the eighth grade show, I resisted taking in the hearty applause. I was supposed to be humble but, secretly, I relished the applause and praise. Instead of making me feel better about myself, these achievements made me more aware of my sinful tendency to credit myself and not God for whatever good I did. The massive cross above the altar, on which the almost naked, wounded, bleeding Jesus hung, served to make me feel an abyss of guilt for my sins.

The Rite of Benediction of the Blessed Sacrament, observed at an evening service once a month, was the most holy ritual to me. We sang my favorite hymns: solemn, deeply resonant and, what I now know, in a minor key. Waves of incense were sent wafting through the dimly lit Church. The Presence of God was palpable. Awestruck, I'd remain silent for the rest of the night. With the familiarity and richness of the rituals, and the attention I received from the nuns, the Church was the only place I felt I belonged.

It doesn't have to be
the blue iris, it could be
weeds in a vacant lot, or a few
small stones; just
pay attention, then patch
a few words together and don't try
to make them elaborate, this isn't
a contest but the doorway
into thanks, and a silence in which
another voice may speak.

– "Praying" by Mary Oliver, from *Thirst*

CHAPTER SEVEN
A River of Faith

SITTING ALONE in the backseat of the car as a child, I enjoyed a myriad of wonders as we drove the back roads of Connecticut on tree canopied winding roads. The northeast corner of Connecticut is verdant: rolling hills, huge old oak trees, magnificent maples which turn a stunning red in autumn, slender swaying birches. The fast running rock-strewn streams are flanked by an array of flowers and blossoming bushes in the spring and inhabited by a diversity of wildlife and birds in every season. The area used to be called *The Quiet Corner*. Today it is called *The Last Green Valley* because the astronauts on the Space Station noticed it is the only place on the Eastern Seaboard that is completely dark at night.

Humans have complemented the landscape. Farms, stonewalls, open fields, elegant old houses and barns, and simple white clapboard churches appear along the country roads. In spring, newborn colts, calves, and lambs appear in the fields. The green of the trees deepens as spring gives way to summer. Hillsides become lush and inviting; the woods cool and dark; the rush of the river's waters offer mercy from the heat.

The sound of the river was a constant in my life as it ran against our home and murmured quietly in the background day and night. The rough waters that raged in spring hurled kayaks downstream. The January thaw sent blocks of ice crashing against the foundation of our house shaking the timbers.

As I grew into adolescence and my teenage years, the river continued to be my refuge. I sat beside the water in solitude, drinking in the sound of birdcalls and of water splashing against rocks. Here I watched chipmunks scurry in pursuit of food for their winter larder. The dragonflies flashed shimmering turquoise; the gold finches, the lone scarlet tanager, the red-winged blackbirds offered their distinct songs. It was here, on this sacred river, that I directly experienced what I now call *Holy Oneness*. I melded into the Life around me.

One spring vacation, when I was in my early teens, my mother, father and I took a road trip to Florida with another family. Dad was between his depressive and manic episodes for a brief period at that time of year. My brother, Mark, who was working at a photography store, gave me a camera with seventeen rolls of film. He developed the film when I returned home.

"Seventeen rolls of trees. I just developed seventeen rolls of TREES!" he said in mock outrage when I walked into the store to pick up the prints. Not one human inhabited my film. There were flowers, ponds, birds, beaches and predominately TREES!

My connection to *The Holy* expanded over the years. One day when I was walking the beach picking stones a song came to me. First the melody fell out of the sky, then the words. I had to sing it all the way home to remember it.

All of these joys
Lay at my feet
Silvery white pebbles
Strewn on the beach

Birds in the sky
Flowers and trees
Children's bright faces
My joys are these

Moments alone
People filled days
Love that's expressed
In a thousand ways

Visions of Life
Beauty I find
In the creations
Of human minds

And to my God
I sing this praise
Source of the joys
That fill all my days

– Kathleen, 1978

~

I loved the beauty of winter with its silent white presence bearing witness to the crisp blue sky. Each year, before ice skating season began, I envisioned myself floating gracefully over the ice. That image never turned out to be the reality. Staying upright on skates was a challenge for me. The winter I was fourteen, I fell on the ice and hurt my back. My mother took me to the doctor, and he told her I needed surgery on the tail end of my spine—I was mortified by the prospect. And, I was even more distressed because it was called "jeep sickness," and occurs in servicemen who bump around in jeeps.

The doctor chose to leave the surgical site open to let it heal from within because the incision was so deep. My mother had to clean and dress it regularly, which I found embarrassing. I finally convinced her to let me do it myself. The surgery and healing period were extremely painful. My body was *other* to me—anything having to do with it made me uncomfortable. The nuns told us the *flesh* was the source of sin. They also imprinted on our young minds that our lack of modesty could lead others to sin, which would then be our fault and sinful. My body was the enemy and this surgery was forcing me to deal with it.

I was operated on that summer which gave me time to heal before I entered high school the following fall. Ours was the first

freshmen class to attend the new Nathan Hale High School,
affiliated with both the University of Connecticut and the town
of Wentworth. After coming from a relatively small Junior High,
the new school appeared enormous and daunting. I felt reassured
when I walked into my homeroom class the first day and heard
a familiar aria coming from a record my teacher, Mr. Moran,
was playing. I quietly said, under my breath, "Ah, *Tosca*" as I slid
into my seat.

Mr. Moran had heard the remark, "You know this opera?"

"Yes, my brother and I listen to it all the time. We both
love opera."

Mr. Moran's approving smile bolstered my confidence. "I've
never had a student who knew anything about opera!" He was
clearly pleased and impressed.

I soon found my place in the flow of classes, made new friends
and reconnected with old ones. I met Cindy Allen that year. We
shared many interests that were foreign to our classmates: classical
music, a love of nature, and deep discussions about life. I was
often invited to Cindy's house for sleepovers and would join her
family in taffy pulling, popcorn making and playing games. These
were things my family never did. Hers was a household geared to
young people; mine was a household focused on adult activities.

As in any rural community in Connecticut, our bus route
was long and winding, and teenagers from various villages in
the town often came together for the first time on the ride to
and from school. That's how I met my friend, Mandy, the oldest
of eight children. Soon we were back and forth to each other's
homes, often celebrating our differing holidays. She would come
to our Christmas and Easter celebrations and I would go to her
Passover Seders, Bar and Bat Mitzvahs and Chanukah parties,
despite my previous misgivings about going into non-Catholic
houses of worship. Our families also bonded. We learned that
Jewish and Italian mothers speak the same language.

One evening when Mandy and I were quietly talking on my
front porch, something came out of my mouth that shocked us
both. I firmly said, "If I was ever anything other than Catholic,
I'd be Jewish." We both laughed at something as absurd as my

NOT being Catholic, but I felt no desire to take back my words. And, it was true. I had come to love the Jewish traditions almost as much as the Catholic ones.

I enjoyed the warm, lighthearted atmosphere in the homes of my Jewish friends. Their lives were not weighted down by the concept of sin. One day a year they fasted and atoned for their sins on Yom Kippur, and they were assured of forgiveness. Then their sins were wiped from the Book of Life. They began the Jewish New Year with a clean slate.

The Catholic Church, on the other hand, impressed upon its believers at a very young age that we were sinful creatures. We came into the world with sin on our souls and needed to be baptized to clear it. And, to be accepted into Kingdom of God, we had to suffer, fast and do penance to gain merits in Heaven. The concepts of Hell, Purgatory and even Limbo, for un-baptized babies, were ever-present in my consciousness. But I trudged on holding fast to my faith despite the glimpses of different paradigms in the glen by the river and in the Jewish traditions.

~

I met someone else on the school bus that freshmen year. Our bus stop was at the beginning of the route, so I was one of the first students to board. I sat alone, reading the *New York Times.* It was my daily assignment for a Social Studies class. As we climbed Laurel Hill Road, the bus stopped at a huge red house on the left. A long, lanky teenage boy with laughing eyes folded himself into the seat beside me.

The first words out of his mouth were, "I bet you don't understand a word you're reading!"

I was indignant and shot back, "Of course, I understand what I'm reading!"

That was it. Brian Andersen, the son of a university professor, and I, the daughter of a stonecutter who struggled to read and write, began an on-going dialogue for the rest of the year. Brian started by quizzing me on current events. When he found that I was well versed on that subject, our discussions expanded.

Soon we were discussing my favorite topic—religion. Brian was fascinated by my belief in God and the Catholic Church. He challenged me and made compelling arguments against religion, yet he also shared his own struggle with me of "wanting to believe in something." I clearly understood how he believed in nothing, for my faith had faltered from time to time, but he couldn't understand how I believed in something.

It turned out those discussions later affected my decisions about my children's spiritual education. I determined I'd give my children a religious foundation and then allow them to choose to not believe rather than give them nothing to believe in at all.

Brian was a senior, four years older, and he had quite a reputation as a Casanova. He soon got the message that I wasn't to be a romantic conquest, that I was saving myself to either be a nun or an untouched bride. He only tried to kiss me once when I was leaning against a wall at a party in my favorite high-waisted brown and gold paisley dress, feeling pretty (which was a highly unusual state for me). He hovered over me with his hands on either side of my head, and as he went for my lips, I laughed and slid down the wall, escaping under his arm.

He became protective and brotherly toward me after that. Sometimes he walked down the hill, across the bridge and up River Road to my house, playing his guitar and singing, on his way to see me. He found my brother, Mark, fascinating and loved my Mom *and* her cooking.

One day he and Mandy came over to visit. Brian was sitting between Mandy and me with his arms around each of us as we listened to popular music, foreign to my ears. I only remember the words *to know, know, know him is to love, love, love him*. I felt that way about Brian—he was funny and smart, and he had a sweetness few people saw because he was constantly joking. That day I was so happy to be with my two friends in this shared moment. I began to feel warm and almost drowsy. When they left, I panicked. I called Mandy as soon as I thought she was home.

Me: "Can we get pregnant from what we did with Brian this afternoon?"

Mandy: "You don't know ANYTHING, do you?"

Me: "No, I don't, but I want to stay that way so I can't think bad thoughts."

Mandy: "I'm giving you a book tomorrow and *I want you to read it!*"

The next day she put the book in my hands, and I immediately knew I would not open it. It was a book about SEX—the word I was not supposed to think about. I accepted it graciously and kept it for a while and returned it unopened. From that point on my friends created a circle of protection around me. If I went to a party with Brian and it began to get rowdy, he'd take me home and return to the party. But, Brian was not the only one who tried to protect me.

At pajama parties with my girlfriends, they would keep their talk clean. On one occasion they even skipped playing a song from Camelot so I wouldn't hear the words "bonnie breast." (I didn't hear that song until years later.) I was grateful to them *and* embarrassed that I was so different from a normal teenager, but I was firm in my conviction that God wanted me to remain pure.

My obsession with staying pure was abnormal and dangerous. It gave me some status among my peers, but at great cost. I felt like an alien in the culture of the late fifties and early sixties when old paradigms were beginning to crumble. I was isolated and alone in the midst of these changing social attitudes which my peers embraced. One day, my mother said in a disgusted voice, "Margery, [another Catholic girl in our neighborhood] was seen necking with a boy in the back seat of a car on Saturday night." I didn't know what the word "necking" meant, but I thought it was my mother's way of saying that being seen in the back seat of a car with a boy was disgraceful and a sin. Lesson learned.

~

As I look back, I can see I missed a normal developmental stage by not allowing myself to learn about relationships, experience different social settings, and acknowledge and explore my natural sexual stirrings. The subject of sex was as taboo in our household as it was in the Church. There was no adult with whom I could discuss the subject and had no inclination to seek more information. And, I also learned years later, that not all Catholic girls internalized the Church's precepts to the degree I had. I still speculate as to why I was so susceptible to an extreme interpretation of religious doctrine.

~

When Brian graduated, he gave me a picture of himself with the inscription: "To my funny Catholic sister, if she is as nice about trying to convert people as she has been to me, it will be a Catholic world again! Love, Brian."

Brian and I lost contact when he went away to college. Years later, I walked through our family room and glanced at a musical sit-com my children were watching and said to myself, "That looks like Brian Andersen!" This happened two or three times. I finally called my high school friend, Mandy, and asked her if it was possible Brian was on TV.

"Oh, yeah," she replied. "He's on a comedy show playing his guitar and singing. The kids love it." After I told my kids Brian was an old friend of mine, my esteem in their eyes went up a notch, and they begged me for stories about him.

Memories of sitting by the river with Brian brought a smile to my face. Our friendship flowed by quickly that year, and ran deep. It was formative. I came to believe that men could be trusted and would respect my boundaries. That was the gift and the curse of my relationship with him.

I wept and raged and cursed the corpse that still remained
A vase now void, which once my hope contained.

– Kathleen, 1965

CHAPTER EIGHT
The Enigma

IN MY JOURNAL, the first entry reads: "The phrase I remember hearing most frequently throughout my nineteen years of life is "Oh, so you're one of the Marinos!" Invariably, this comment was followed by the observation that I looked exactly like my mother or sister or one of my six living brothers. I would then hear lengthy praises of the individual I resembled."

My handsome brother, Mark, often was the one on whom these praises were heaped. He was loved by everyone in our family, especially the children. He was jokingly called the Pied Piper by the adults because a trail of children followed him around when family or friends were visiting.

Mark was constantly teaching and explaining the world to his awestruck devotees. The nieces and nephews and, of course, Rosie and I, adored him. He'd squat to our eye level and speak in a soft, mesmerizing voice or pick us up to give us a view of the world from a different perspective. Rosie had total trust in him and allowed him to lift her straight little body high into the air as he held onto her ankles.

Mark left for Korea shortly after Rosie died, disappearing from our household as others had before him. The house was bigger and scarier without them.

I had not seen Mark for almost a year when he appeared at the hospital in his uniform to take me home after my tonsillectomy. He brought me a twirly yellow dress with a white peter-pan collar and red cherries all over it. He let me wear it home. I loved that dress!

I held his hand as we walked out of the hospital. He looked down at me and said, "Let's get something to eat! I'll get you anything you want."

When I emphatically said, "Potato chips!" he winced, thinking of my still raw throat.

"OK," he said, "if you promise to chew each one twenty-one times!" So, for years after, I tried to chew each bite of my food twenty-one times.

Mark made magic. Our house was in total chaos every Christmas Eve. Mom baked and cooked and Jules attempted to clean and finish the never ending laundry as other siblings and nieces and nephews came and went. Mark was in charge of cutting down a tree. He brooded, paced and procrastinated all afternoon. I was frantic—usually in tears—sure that Christmas would be a disaster and there would be no tree! At dusk, he finally went out to find the perfect tree. He never failed to bring back a spectacular one.

One Christmas morning I woke to find the Big Room transformed—a barn-like structure, divided in three sections, spanned the huge room. In the middle section, the decorated Christmas tree stood on a raised platform. Train tracks ran beneath it with the trains my brothers played with as children circling around and around. The three walls of that section were covered in aluminum foil that reflected the Christmas lights. A painted cardboard fireplace with a fire of yellow and red cellophane, and an ethereal nativity scene, filled the other two sections. Magic! Of course, I attributed this amazing overnight miracle to Santa Claus.

Until I was twelve, I woke to another mysterious transformation of our Big Room each Christmas morning. I thought Mark was a scrooge because after he took pictures of us opening our gifts, he'd go to bed for the day. I'll never know how he accomplished these feats of fantasy from the time I went to bed on Christmas Eve to early Christmas morning. I didn't hear hammering or other indications of the construction that was going on one floor below me.

My fascination with the unseen, magical and spiritual world was fueled by the inexplicable appearance of these elaborate structures on Christmas day—they made plausible the miracles I learned about in the Bible and in books about the Saints of the Catholic Church.

After Mark returned from Korea, he took the role of the good Italian son who stays home after all the other siblings leave. In my family, this included being the protector, mentor, and caretaker of his younger sister as well as caring for his aging parents. Our home had become a scary place for me after the morning I woke up to find Rosie gone. There seemed to be danger everywhere. I believed Mark would shield me from all harm.

My anxiety grew beyond generalized fear to include the fear of being snatched when I ran past the attic door to my mother's room in the middle of the night, nightgown flapping around my legs; or the terror of a witch coming out of the wall in the dark hallway and pushing me down the stairs (which was a frequent nightmare). I feared a man with a fedora like my father's, lurked on the upstairs porch outside my bedroom window, ready to grab me and take me away forever.

In those moments, Mark again worked his magic. His soft, soothing words were a calming salve to my terrified little soul: "There is nothing to be afraid of. I'm here to protect you. If you need me, just call…I'll come to you."

Mark became the emotional rock on which I stood when the world began to quake beneath my feet as eruptions of rage roared from my father. Or, my mother's angry outbursts screamed from the depths of her frustration and unspent grief after Rosie's death. I remember one time when I heard my father and mother arguing in their bedroom as I lay in the next room, my heart gripped in fear. My father sounded so angry I was afraid he would hurt my mother.

Shivering, I ran down the stairs and across the expansive cold floor of the Big Room to where Mark was sitting on the edge of the couch leaning forward, elbows on knees, listening. He was wearing a worn, faded, maroon plaid, flannel shirt that somehow gave me immense comfort. He opened his arms to let me into the circle of his care and said, "Do you think I would let anything happen to you or Mom? That's why I'm here…"

Mark was always there—in place of my father at parent-teacher conferences; when the bus driver scolded me and made me cry; when my two best friends dumped me in fourth grade; when my Physical Education teacher pushed me too far and I got hurt, or when, as a teenager, I needed a ride to work at 6:30 in the morning.

In time I learned that Mark was an avowed atheist, unlike some of my other brothers, who called themselves agnostics, and three who remained Catholic. He inspired others with his impassioned rhetoric about a world transformed by kindness, compassion, elegant design, and enlightened capitalism. His message was that one person could change the world or, in the words of the *Christopher Brothers*, a Catholic TV program we watched as a family every week, "If you light one little candle, you can light the world."

This brother, who had stayed behind to help his parents and younger sister, was especially loved and respected throughout our community. Mark was invariably polite and kind, willing to help anyone in need. He was a problem solver and became a resource to family and friends. His brothers, who had far more formal education than he did, went to him for advice on their scientific endeavors.

When someone in the family died, it was Mark who was there to give hands-on help. He was the one to make the arrangements, help direct traffic at the funeral, and comfort others with his quiet cadenced words of compassion. Mark went to identify the body of our friends' thirteen-year-old son, who was killed in a horrible accident, to spare them the agony of seeing their son's mangled body.

When a doe, having been chased onto the ice by dogs, was wounded on the partially frozen river, Mark was the one who took his gun and waded into the frigid waters to put it out of its misery with one shot. My mother had the animal dressed by a local butcher because food was scarce. She served it for Sunday dinner. Mark turned white at the sight of the roast and left the table saying he wasn't hungry. He said, "All I can see are those big brown eyes looking at me."

~

My memories of Mark include a side of him I didn't understand until later in life. I was about thirteen when a nine-year-old boy, Danny, became a frequent visitor to our home as Mark's guest. Mark said his parents both worked, so the boy was lonely. Danny followed Mark around like a puppy. Mark doted on this boy and talked to him in a sugary sweet voice.

My brother's attention for me diminished, and I was jealous of the time he gave to this intruder. Both my parents became annoyed with the boy's constant presence. My father was especially upset when Danny followed Mark into the bathroom. On several occasions, I heard my parents arguing about this situation. I remember my father's face darkening during one of these arguments. He said in a seething voice, "He had a boy in Korea, too!"

In the spring of 1959 when I was fifteen, our family life continued to be complicated by the presence of Mark's shadow friend, young Danny. Mark was a gifted photographer and often used family members and neighbors as models, so I wasn't surprised when Danny became one of his subjects.

Soon a huge photographic portrait of Danny looking over his left shoulder—in a suede honey-colored jacket with fringe—hung over our piano in the Big Room. Danny had grown into a handsome boy, but the image of him gazing out from that picture made me uncomfortable. The portrait of Danny had a quality I could not then explain. I now would call it seductive. My brother had carefully posed the boy. I had no idea at the time how this portrait would haunt me.

One Saturday early that spring, my mother and I were waiting in the car for my father to return from getting a haircut. It was a dreary day, and Mom was unusually quiet in the front seat. She took out a folded piece of paper from her purse and quietly said, "I found this" as she unfolded it.

She began reading a love letter from Mark to Danny. The gist of it was: I don't understand why you are treating me this way. I've been good to you (listing numerous gifts he had given Danny and activities they'd done together). Then she read the only sentence I remember verbatim, "I even let you piss on me." There was more, but I didn't hear anything after that. My mother cried as she read this letter. She rarely cried. I sat in stunned silence. She folded the letter and put it back into her purse and never mentioned it again.

I was shaken by this revelation. I had no idea what it meant, but it made me nauseated. I shook as I am shaking now as I write about this incident sixty years later. Somehow I knew my world would never be the same. I didn't speak a word of this to anyone until I was in my forties. I cannot imagine why my mother read that letter to me and why she never spoke of it again. I feel now that she transferred her torment onto me, and I was to carry it for her for the rest of my days. It was one of the cruelest things she ever did.

It's about coming alive. It's about waking up to grace. It's about unconditional friendliness and infinite kindness to yourself. It's about making it safe, finally safe for all of those unloved, un-met, unseen [parts]…of yourself to crawl out of the depths, out of the darkness, out of the corners and holes and crevices of experience and come into the light, blinking and full of wonder.

It's about giving birth to yourself…

– Excerpt from *The Extraordinary Painting of You* by Jeff Foster

CHAPTER NINE
I'll Be Seeing You

MY BROTHERS, Tom and Pete, frequently rescued me from the chaos of my home life in early summer, to spare me the sight of my father slipping into another manic psychotic episode. Both brothers lived in New York State. Tom lived only a few hours from western Massachusetts where my father was hospitalized. He expected me to accompany him when he visited our father in the psychiatric hospital. I hated going to see my father, but I loved having time alone with my big brother.

On those trips, he taught me how to fill his pipe with tobacco and tap it down just enough. We talked about geology as we drove through the varied landscape on our way and sometimes stopped to hunt for interesting rocks. He told me stories about the days before I was born. We'd meet Mark, Pete, and my mother at the hospital and then we would go out to lunch together. All three of my brothers were handsome and soft-spoken. I was proud of them and relished the time sitting around the table with them over lunch even though I was not part of the conversation.

In March of 1959, I turned fifteen and started to plan my summer escape months before my father's yearly descent into madness. By June, I saved all my babysitting money, $100, to take a bus trip to San Diego to visit my brother, Tony, twenty one years older than me. Although I was terrified at the thought of traveling alone, I was determined to get far enough away that I wouldn't have to visit my father in the hospital. And, I longed to be free of the pall that hung over our home during the summer when his absence left the lingering scent of insanity throughout the house.

Tony was career Navy. He designed pilot simulators and ended up teaching electrical engineering at college level without ever going to college. I had seen him about four or five times in my life, always briefly. I informed my mother that I had enough money to get myself out there, but if she wanted me back she'd have to pay my way. My mother had no qualms about putting me on a Greyhound bus alone at age fifteen and sending me off to a brother I hardly knew. Tony and, his wife, Liz, welcomed my visit.

On the first day of my trip, I sat next to a middle-aged professor of anthropology, and by the time he disembarked, I was convinced I wanted to be an anthropologist. Sometime in the afternoon of the second day, a young college student boarded the bus and sat next to me. He was pleasant and nice looking. We chatted for a while and then turned our attention elsewhere. I was determined to read several books as I traveled across the country.

That night, sometime after our supper stop, I woke up in the darkened bus with my head on this sleeping man's shoulder. I jumped up from my seat in terror and flopped down next to an elderly woman closer to the front. She had a soft halo of white hair and a finely wrinkled face. She looked at me with a grandmotherly smile and said, "Dear, don't you know we won't let anything happen to you on this bus? Just relax and go to sleep." She asked the impossible. She did not understand—something had already happened. I'd slept with a man.

The only thing I had gleaned from overhearing a few adult women's conversations was that a woman got pregnant by "sleeping with a man." And, she knew she was pregnant if she didn't get her period. It would be a while before my period was due and I'd know if this fate had befallen me. This kind of ignorance would later have horrific consequences.

I was exhausted when we reached San Diego, still harboring the nagging worry that I might be pregnant. As I was standing waiting to disembark, I looked out the window and saw the smiling face, inviting eyes and dark curly hair of my oldest brother. I knew everything was going to be all right.

Tony was a stunning human being: warm, funny, soft-spoken, affectionate, loving, and forever intellectually curious. As we got reacquainted, he treated me as a peer, not the younger sister of the family. He even asked my advice and listened respectfully to what I had to say. An extraordinary father and husband, he left tender, sometimes funny notes for Liz to find throughout the day. Every morning, in full uniform before he went to work, he stopped to gently comb his young daughter's curly, tangled, strawberry blond hair.

I kept my concerns about being pregnant to myself. When my period started three weeks later, I said a prayer of gratitude for having been spared. I can only imagine if I had confided my fear to Tony or Liz—their laughter would have shattered every glass in the house!

On Sundays, Tony and I took the four children to Balboa Park to give Liz a break. During one visit, we came upon a replica of an international village with tiny houses, each representing a different country. Tony and I both instantly gravitated to a house from which came the sound of someone playing *Autumn Leaves* on the piano. We shared a love for that song because it was one of Mom's favorites and she played it often. And, we heard another song that day we both loved: *I'll be Seeing You.* I remember Tony quietly singing along as we listened.

In true military tradition, Tony was harder on his three boys than he was on his daughter. One day Tony and I stood at the screen door watching his youngest son, Tim, about three, strut down the sidewalk away from us. Tony said, "Look at that little back—so straight, shoulders back—too bad I have to break his spirit." My heart sank. I couldn't believe those words had come out of my gentle brother's mouth. Our discussions about child-rearing years later had their origins in this remark.

Tony joined the Navy at the age of seventeen, immediately after Pearl Harbor. It became his way of life. Liz had to keep the house "shipshape." As soon as you could smell the coffee brewing, you had to take it off the stove or it would "lose all its flavor" according to Tony. The towels were neatly folded lengthwise in three equal parts and then rolled up. I still fold my towels that way. Tony may have applied Navy disciplinary tactics on his three boys to make them into men before their time, but there was never a doubt about how much he loved his sons and his beautiful daughter.

Every evening, Tony and I would read to the children before bed. He loved to read anything humorous, and he introduced me to Ogden Nash and poems like *The Cremation of Sam McGee*. When the kids fell asleep, Tony and I sat on the floor reading to each other and laughing quietly. We also shared a love for the kind of music Liz didn't appreciate, so we'd go to the car to listen to it on the radio.

I felt at home with Tony and his family. I had chores like everyone else and knew my help made a difference. I was an integral part of the household. I had a curfew, too, which I'd never had at home—it made me feel cared for, valued. I felt extraneous in my mother's house, either unseen or in the way. Here, even though the quarters were small, and I shared a bedroom with my niece, Sharon, I felt more comfortable than in my own home. I could be myself. I didn't have to make myself disappear or be someone I wasn't. Tony was both brotherly and fatherly, and seemed to like having me around.

Tony gave me my first driving lesson on a narrow road leading to the military cemetery on Point Loma overlooking the Pacific Ocean. We were stopped by a MP who said I couldn't drive there and the lesson ended. But, some of Tony's instructions live in my head to this day, almost sixty years later. "When the light changes don't hesitate! Go! Or the guy behind you will get annoyed." That one always makes me chuckle. I knew he was "the guy behind" me. I still try not to hesitate when the light changes.

One afternoon when Tony arrived home, I was sitting on the meager grass of the front lawn, reading some uninspiring book. He tossed a book at me and said, "Read this!" It was a book of poems by Edna St. Vincent Millay, and the poem he had bookmarked was *Renascence*, written when Millay was nineteen:

All I could see from where I stood
Was three long mountains and a wood;
I turned and looked another way,
And saw three islands in a bay.
So with my eyes I traced the line
Of the horizon, thin and fine,
Straight around till I was come
Back to where I'd started from;
And all I saw from where I stood
Was three long mountains and a wood.

The poem was long and beyond my comprehension, but Tony gave me the book as a gift. I secretly thought I'd never look at it again. I couldn't have been more wrong. The poem came to echo my own voice, describe my experience, and hold out hope for my own renascence.

I began walking a mile to church every day to attend Mass. Tony was an agnostic and we began discussing religion. Like my friend, Brian, Tony wanted to find a way to believe, but more than anything he wanted his children baptized in the Church. The specter of his un-baptized children spending eternity in Limbo still haunted this non-believer. He had approached a priest about baptizing the children and was denied this request because he was not a practicing Catholic himself. He implored me to talk to the local priest to see if he'd do the baptisms.

I had come to like this priest because when I confessed to *hating* my father he said, "Love is the icing on the cake. Do you honor and obey him?"

I said, "Yes, I do" without mentioning that I did so because I feared him.

The priest assured me, "That's all the commandment asks— to *honor* our Mother and Father—nothing is said about love." I was relieved.

But when it came to my request to baptize my three nephews and niece, the priest refused. He wouldn't even consider it unless both Tony and Liz were practicing Catholics. Liz, who wasn't Catholic, was a good woman and mother, and a devoted wife. The decision seemed unfair, and I questioned the wisdom of Church doctrine for the first time.

How could the Church be so rigid when Christ was so open and accepting? He embraced everyone, sinners and saints alike. Where was the justice for these children who, through no fault of their own, would be relegated to eternity in Limbo or worse? This seed of doubt tentatively rooted in my soul, although I did not see the first hesitant shoot break through my consciousness for another year.

A teenage girl, Christy, a few years older than I, also lived in Navy housing near us. She took me to the USO to meet the young sailors. I'd never dated, I didn't dance, and I was painfully shy around boys, so her attempt to socialize me failed. None of the young men approached me to ask for a dance. I assumed it was because I wasn't pretty or thin enough. Meanwhile, Christy never stopped dancing, going from one boy to another, until she went off with one of them.

A handsome, quiet young man always offered to walk me home. He never touched me, just kept up a quiet conversation until we got to my door. I developed a crush on him. If Tony was home, he invited my escort in for some lemonade and they talked at length about a wide range of subjects. I sat on the periphery.

One day, Christy told me that none of the boys were ever going to ask me to dance because Tony was their Chief Petty Officer—they didn't dare come near me. And, the young man, who walked me home in such a gentlemanly fashion, thought the world of the Chief and wanted to "pick his brain" and learn from him. My heartthrob finally told me that Tony was "the smartest, most well-read man I've ever met." It was clear he was in awe of my unassuming brother. That's why he wanted to walk me home— to have a chance to talk with him. I stopped going to the USO.

As the summer wore on, it was clear that things back home weren't getting better. My father was still hospitalized, and my brother, Mark, tore the house apart doing renovations. My mother reluctantly agreed to let me start school in San Diego. Tony and I had talked about my staying with him for the year. I felt freer and happier with him and his family than I ever had in my fifteen years. Maybe the constant sunshine had something to do with it. Or, maybe it was because being near Tony was like sitting by a soothing river in the warm sunlight.

~

About a month into the school year in San Diego, my mother called and wanted me home. She gave me no real explanation. I told her I wanted to stay with Tony. I reminded her she would have to pay my way back, thinking that would deter her, but she and Mark insisted I return. I dreaded returning home—I felt angry that I was given no say in the decision. Shortly after that call, I boarded a plane and cried my way across the country.

When I arrived home I wouldn't speak to anyone. After a week of my stony silence, my mother barged into my room, glaring, and said in a cold voice, "Enough of this! You're just like your father!" That was all I needed to hear. I started talking again and was polite and helpful. Trapped in the maelstrom of my domineering mother, my crazy father, and a brother who had turned into someone I didn't know, I now feared I was like my father—a horrifying thought. I plunged into depression as profound as when I was seven and realized Rosie wasn't coming back.

The intuition I had as a child, about a darkness within me that would extinguish all light, seemed prophetic. The blackness of depression saturated my cells and banished the light from my world. I could no longer feel my connection with God and nature. I lost all pleasure in the things I usually enjoyed, even food. Although exhausted, I couldn't sleep. Usually I was driven to succeed academically; now I was lethargic and unmotivated. Nathan Hale High School was an accelerated learning environment. The San Diego school system had been behind ours and it took me months to catch up in my classes.

I withdrew from my friends—unable to describe what was going on inside of me and ashamed of my feelings. I lost all hope in the future—something I now know is called *anhedonia*, a symptom of clinical depression. It was the first time the thought of killing myself felt compelling. All of a sudden the poem "Renascence" made perfect sense to me. I read it to my English class and later memorized it. Mr. Taylor, my English teacher, was so impressed with my understanding of the poem he gave me a valuable first edition of the book, *Renascence.* The poem continues…

Over these things I could not see;
These were the things that bounded me;
And I could touch them with my hand,
Almost, I thought, from where I stand.
And all at once things seemed so small
My breath came short and scarce at all.

But, sure, the sky is big, I said;
Miles and miles above my head;
So here upon my back I'll lie
And look my fill into the sky.
And so I looked, and, after all,
The sky was not so very tall.
The sky, I said, must somewhere stop,
And — sure enough! — I see the top!
The sky, I thought, is not so grand;
I 'most could touch it with my hand!
And reaching up my hand to try,
I screamed to feel it touch the sky.

With the help of some empathetic teachers and friends, including Cindy Allen who had become a steadfast friend, I weathered the throes of depression through the winter of my sophomore year. Music, as always, lifted me out of myself and provided relief from the dark imaginings which haunted me. And, perhaps because they sensed my struggle, Mom and Mark bought me an Acrosonic Baldwin piano, one of the best pianos on the market at the time, which they could not afford.

I began to play again—Mozart, Bach, Beethoven, Schumann—all the classical composers who had been with me since childhood. By spring, I started to slowly emerge from my depressive state. I read, jumped the rocks on the river, or just sat on the bank, watching nature unfold around me. Eventually, I became more social again and participated in school events I had shunned in the previous months.

~

Years later, I came to understand the complexity and tenacity of the unrelenting clinical depression that stalked me—that engulfed me in a numbing fog, tethered me to a leaden despair, and immobilized my instincts for self-preservation. I denigrated myself for not being able to fight it. Friends and family subtly inferred that I should snap out of it, that I was just sulking, looking for attention or I was overly sensitive and should toughen up. I believed them, which only led to more torment. Understanding mental illness and helping those who suffer from it eventually became my life's work.

Dear God, please reveal to us
your sublime beauty
that is everywhere, everywhere, everywhere,
so that we will never again
feel frightened…

– Excerpted from "Dear God" by St. Francis of Assisi,
translated by Daniel Ladinsky in *Love Poems from God*

Chapter Ten
A Calling

I was attending CCD classes for teenagers. The acronym stands for Continued Catholic Development. I'd been confirmed in the faith and still adhered to its precepts, but I began to silently question some of the basic teachings. Still, I was drawn to the contemplative life while the social life of my peers felt increasingly alien to me. I didn't party, smoke, drink, or even think about sex. These were all taboo activities according to my strict interpretation of the Catholic faith.

The nuns' indoctrination on sexual abstinence, even in thought, became my obsession. It was the sin I most feared. I aspired to be holy and pure like the saints who dedicated their lives to Christ and died for their faith. I was continually disappointed in myself for my lack of devotion during prayer, for my failures in patience, humility and compassion. Purity was the only virtue I felt I could attain. It was concrete, controllable—you were pure or you were not—there was no ambiguity.

And, I believed it was in my hands to preserve my "virginity"—a word I didn't really comprehend. To me it meant untouched by a man. In those days, no one talked about rape and, if they did, it was whispered behind closed doors. I didn't even know the word at the age of sixteen. I should have known.

Looking back, I now question why I developed this obsession with being pure when other Catholic girls did not. It came to define who I was in my teens and early twenties. Somehow, I felt it redeemed me from all my perceived failings. At least I was pure. (Ironically, in my forties, I learned the name *Kathleen* means "Pure.")

~

Sometime in the early spring of my sophomore year of high school in 1960, I overheard my father, who was now retired, say to my mother, "If it wasn't for her [meaning me], we'd be free now."

I took that personally, and when the nuns invited me to a "Vocation Week" at the convent that summer, I chose to escape into prayer and meditation in what I assumed was a quiet, peaceful setting. That decision had ramifications that reverberate to this day.

It was then that I learned the actual name of the order from which my Catechism teachers came. It was *The Sisters of Charity of Our Lady, Mother of Love*. The order originated in France and was founded in the 1800's. The nuns devoted themselves to charity work, teaching and providing medical care for the poor.

The American Motherhouse was in Westfield, Connecticut, about forty-five minutes from our home, where the Sisters ran *The Academy of the Holy Trinity*, a girl's high school for boarders and local day students. A Greek-revival brick building, that had been a hotel built in 1914, was converted to serve the Sister' needs. It was a stately structure with white trim, a block long and five stories high.

The left side of the building had been converted into dormitories for the boarders, girls from wealthy families, some of whom were there against their will. Many of these boarders remained at the school even during vacations and holidays, including Christmas. The middle section was converted into classrooms, offices and an auditorium. The right side of the building became the *Cloister*, the nuns' private quarters, a secluded area where only the Sisters and novices could enter.

Several rooms outside the Cloister were set aside for the aspirants, taking their first step toward joining the Order: a dining room, sitting room, and a small kitchen. Vocation Week activities were centered in this area. A large Chapel was in one half of the basement, and a huge laundry was in the other—the sacred and profane side by side.

As my mother and I walked up to the building, I was intimidated by the size and formality of the structure. A wide brick stairway led to an elegant white portico with fluted columns capped with scrolls and ivy carvings. As we stood under the portico waiting for someone to answer the door, I felt the excitement of my new adventure. I anticipated being surrounded by elegance and classical beauty inside. I'd become enthralled with the architecture of the Greek and Roman revival era when my freshman Latin teacher required us to locate examples of both in our community.

The huge door opened, and a diminutive nun in a pristine white habit greeted us with a smile. "Please, come in," she said in a high young voice. As I stepped into the foyer, I was taken aback by the contrast between the white portico ablaze with sunlight outside and the darkness of the narrow high ceilinged foyer within. The walls were covered in dark mahogany paneling, and long high-backed deacon's benches of the same wood lined the walls. In front of me, a steep narrow stairwell curved to the left and disappeared into the darkening shadows.

I had a moment of misgiving about my mother leaving me in this foreboding place. Years later, I would reflect on the difference between the elegant outside appearance of the building and the dark and gloomy interior—a metaphor for the Catholic Church itself.

Sister said, "Mother Provincial would like to speak to you for a moment, Mrs. Marino. She needs information in case of an emergency." She escorted my mother to a room adjacent to the foyer. "She'll only be a few minutes," Sister reassured me when she returned.

The serene nun stood at the foot of the stairs in silence. Her hands, locked together, disappeared into the wide sleeves of her habit, her eyes cast down. She looked like an alabaster statue. When my mother finally stepped through the parlor door, we hugged in a short good-bye and she disappeared out the massive front door. Anxiety rose out of the void I felt as I stood in the dimly lit foyer.

The Sister instructed me to leave my suitcase by the stairwell, and we proceeded through a series of narrow drab hallways, leading to a bright, open sitting room with a large window where other participants of the Vocation Week chatted quietly. Cookies and lemonade awaited us, and my anxiety began to lessen as I talked with some of the girls I knew from school or CCD classes.

When all the girls arrived, Mother Provincial, who was head of the American branch of the Order, welcomed us and spoke briefly. She introduced Sr. Elizabeth, the Mistress of the retreat, and Sr. Ruth who had greeted us at the door. Sr. Elizabeth told us to bring our suitcases upstairs to get settled in our sleeping quarters.

Single file, we traipsed up one flight, two flights, three flights to the attic following Sr. Ruth into the increasing darkness of the poorly lit stairwell, with Sr. Elizabeth bringing up the rear. The attic was a huge open space with the rough hewn beams of the peaked roof-line floating high above our heads. Bare light bulbs hung from the cross beams on long electrical cords.

The space was partitioned off into "cells," each surrounded by three six-foot high walls and a curtain. Each cell was as wide as a single bed and a small dresser. The attic probably had formerly held thirty or forty aspirants and postulants in the years when a religious vocation was held in high esteem. In those days, every family wanted to have a son who was a priest or a daughter who entered the convent and became a nun.

The nine of us got lost in the vacant, semi-darkness of this immense space as we put our things away. Sr. Elizabeth was clearly in charge, and she made sure we were scattered throughout the room, not side by side. She admonished us to always keep silence in our sleeping quarters. I was terrified to sleep in this gloomy, creaking—probably rat and bat infested—place, but I spoke not a word of this to anyone. I vowed to conquer my fears.

The outward appearance of the building belied the drab, run-down interior reeking of stale air and mold. I imagined ghosts of Sisters past roaming through the dark corridors at night. The only comfort was the other girls sleeping in the attic with me. I think everyone of them felt the same way. We became a close group. We did everything together: eat, sleep, pray, attend lessons, clean, do laundry, and start all over again the next day.

I was assigned to help Sr. Veronica in the sewing room one day and surprised to find a short, slightly overweight nun, who reminded me of the Fairy Godmother in *Cinderella*— with one arm. I watched her quickly cut out a pattern and sew a bright blue jumper for one of the new Aspirants. She was friendly and cheerful and matter-of-fact. I was amazed at her skill and dexterity working with only one hand. She had an aura of peace and serenity about her and a lively sense of humor. I wanted to be like that—able to overcome any obstacle and remain content.

I loved the bells that rang to call us to the *Liturgy of the Hours* (sometimes called the *Divine Office*) six times a day. Along with the nuns, we retreatants stopped whatever we were doing and went to the chapel to pray the prescribed prayers, sing hymns, and listen to readings of psalms. The Major Hours included *Lauds* at sunrise, *Vespers* in the evening and *Compline* at nightfall.

We were allowed to pray the Minor Hours alone in the chapel or in the terraced garden on the steep hill behind the convent, and we kept the Grand Silence from after *Compline* until after breakfast in the morning. This period of silence is kept by Catholic monastics all over the world. In contrast to my chaotic home life, the order and rhythm of the days calmed and comforted me.

During the week, we were introduced to many of the nuns, and three of them immediately won my heart: Sr. Valaria, Sr. Elody and Sr. Dennis. The Mother Provincial, Mother Helen Marie, who had greeted us in a talk the first day, was a mountain of a woman with a military posture, an aquiline nose and piercing eyes. She spoke in an authoritarian manner, but with enough warmth and humor to make her likable, while at the same time—intimidating. At the end of the week, she took each of us separately into her office and asked questions about our experience that week.

To me she said, "My dear," in her aristocratic voice, "The Sisters and I think you have a vocation. We would love to have you join us. Is that something you'd like to do?"

I stuttered, "W...w...well, Mother, I've enjoyed this week very much, b...b...but I would have to think about it and consult with my family." I was completely taken back. I thought a "vocation" was something you did after you finished high school and maybe even after college. I was entering my junior year and didn't want to change schools. Later I learned this order of nuns attempted to enlist girls at a young age so they could more easily mold them into good, obedient, unquestioning nuns.

Mother Provincial continued, "If at any time you decide you want to join us, the door will be open for you. It's clear you have great devotion, and I think this is where you belong." She smiled for the first time since I'd met her. She added, "You can continue your studies here. Your family would pay a small tuition, and the Sisters will pay for everything else. Tell your mother we can work out tuition payments. We would even send you to college."

"Thank you, Mother," I said in a state of shock. "I promise I'll think about it." I slipped out the parlor door in a daze.

~

Back home I found myself missing the routine and quiet of the convent. I was lonely in our big empty house. I had enjoyed the company of the Sisters and the other girls at the retreat. The words I overheard my father say in the spring, "We'd be free if it wasn't for her" continued to haunt me. I was in the way.

One day, as I sat at the kitchen table while my mother cooked dinner, I said, "Mom, Mother Provincial asked me to join the Order. I'm thinking of entering this fall. She said she'd even send me to college."

My mother continued stirring the spaghetti sauce on the stove, her back to me. "Oh, is that something you really want to do?" she queried without turning around.

"Well, I liked the quiet and the time for prayer and being with the nuns. I want to see what it's like to live there. The Sisters would pay for everything except tuition. Mother said she'd work something out with you."

She took a breath and said, "Well, your brother was only fourteen when he entered the monastery, so I guess if it's what you want, we can make it happen." Mom didn't question my decision any further and made arrangements with Mother Provincial for tuition payments. She seemed relieved to have me out of the way.

I'd eventually be wearing a black habit not unlike the heavy black coat my mother wore to hide my presence within her womb. I now wonder if my desire to wear the black habit and veil of a nun was an attempt to hide myself—perhaps to disappear. The increasingly frightening social, sexual, and intellectual expectations of living in the world of my peers and my family overwhelmed me. Did I mistakenly think I could elude the complexities of life by becoming a nun? This may have been my unconscious motivation more than my aspiration to be pure and pious.

My mother and I made a visit to the convent the next week so Sr. Veronica could take my measurements and sew two bright blue loose fitting jumpers and three white shirts to wear underneath. At home I had a huge wardrobe my mother had sewed for me with accessories to match. Now, every day I'd put on the same outfit, and it felt like a relief.

We also made a trip to the shoe store to buy the clunky-heeled, old-lady black-tie shoes and thick black cotton stockings that Mom said my grandmother had worn. I'd also be issued a long red grosgrain ribbon that would circle my neck under my shirt collar and be tied in a bow at my throat.

And, as an aspirant to the Order, I'd ceremoniously be given long black rosary beads to loop under my blue belt. The most important item of all was the gauzy black veil we were to wear on our heads at all times except when we were sleeping or bathing. The boarders and day students had uniforms, but our attire, especially the veil, identified us as future nuns, the *Brides of Christ*. This status gave us prestige and accorded us privileges the other students did not enjoy.

I hoped that in this new environment, free of family turmoil, I could maintain my equilibrium and never again slip into the quagmire of desolation as I had when I returned home from California. Those months of living without hope frightened me worse than any nightmare or fear I had endured as a child.

It was easy to love God in all that
was beautiful.

The lessons of deeper knowledge, though, instructed me
to embrace God in all
things.

– Excerpted from "In All Things" by St. Francis of Assisi,
translated by Daniel Ladinsky in *Love Poems from God*

CHAPTER ELEVEN
Behind the Cloister Doors

THE DAY FINALLY ARRIVED for my departure on the last
Sunday in August of 1960. My father, who was home from the
hospital subdued on heavy tranquilizers, came with Mom, Mark
and me on the ride to my new home. When we all got out of
the car in the parking lot, I said a brief good-bye to my brother
and father. Dad started to weep. I was surprised by his tears—I
thought he'd be happy to see me go. My mother explained later
that Dad felt it was his fault I was leaving home.

My mother and I climbed the stairs with my half empty
suitcase. The nuns had instructed us not to bring any of our
worldly belongings so we could begin the "practice of non-
attachment and devotion to God alone." The only thing I snuck
in and planned to hide was my copy of Millay's book of poems,
Renascence, my English teacher had given me.

Mom and I entered the paneled vestibule and Sr. Ruth asked
us to wait on one of the high-backed deacon's benches. My mother
was called in to have a few private words with Mother Provincial,
and when she came out, we said our good-byes. I stood in that
dismal space and felt my heart sink as I watched her go out
the door and down the stairs. I found myself enshrouded in the
darkness of the foyer once again. Had I made a terrible mistake?

Then, Sister brightly announced she was going to find the clothes Sr. Veronica had made for me. I exchanged my misgivings for the excitement of wearing *the habit.* When she came back with a neatly folded bundle of clothes, Sister accompanied me upstairs to the attic to put my things away and change. Besides the two jumpers and shirts, I was also issued sleeveless undershirts, plain white cotton underwear, and two long, roomy nightgowns. All the items were marked with my name. Somehow that was significant—I belonged.

I liked the feel of the jumper. It was soft, almost satiny, but the white shirt was scratchy, and the black stockings made my legs itch. The big clunky black shoes were probably the most comfortable shoes I'd ever worn and added at least an inch to my height, which had the surprising effect of helping me stand straighter and feel more confident. But, it was the veil that made me feel special. Unlike the Sisters' veils, under which they wore skull caps to hide their hair, ours were a headband covered with a flowing gauzy black cloth. It sat on the top of the head and had strings that tied at the nape of the neck. It covered my ears, but the front of my hair was visible. It proved to be hot in warm weather and often would slip down the back of my head—adjusting it became automatic.

As the new aspirants gathered in the sitting room, I was grateful that I knew what to expect, although I dreaded sleeping in the attic again. I soon found that life as an aspirant was quite different from being a guest of the Sisters for a week. After praying *The Hours* in the afternoon, Sr. Elizabeth gave us a long list of rules to follow and assigned chores for the week.

Our chores ranged from helping in the kitchen, scrubbing floors and washing windows, to cleaning bathrooms. We spent Saturday afternoons working together in the garden and on the grounds. One aspirant, named Jackie volunteered to make cleaning the bathrooms her regular job, sparing the rest of us from what we deemed a disgusting task. Her explanation for doing so was, "I want the chance to gain more merits in heaven." We all blessed her for that.

"Merits" were earned by suffering and sacrifice, toward the goal of entering higher levels of heaven when you died. There were ample opportunities to gain merits in the days ahead.

The main rules for aspirants included obeying any request from a Sister, immediately and without question; being respectful at all times; not having special friendships with the other aspirants or any Sister. (The real meaning of the word *special* would only become clear to me years later.) We were not allowed to talk to the boarders or day students even though we'd be attending classes with them. Confession weekly, Mass daily, and keeping the daily silences were required.

Sr. Elizabeth instructed us to dress and undress under our nightgowns to protect our modesty. We should wear our undershirts in the shower so as not to see our own bodies. There were no mirrors—an attempt to deter us from committing the sin of vanity. Detachment from the body was the goal. Already in denial of my physicality, this strategy led to greater self-alienation as I became estranged from my body's needs, wants, and emotional desires. My body became suspect as the *occasion of sin.*

Sister instructed us to sleep in our tiny cells at night lying on our backs as if we were in our coffins—hands, with rosary beads entwined, folded over our hearts while we meditated on death as we fell asleep. Of all the rules we were given, the mandate to pretend I was in my coffin while going to sleep was my greatest challenge. It was too close to the nightmares that had haunted me after Rosie's death.

The eerie creaking of the floorboards every time someone went to the bathroom during the night, and scratching sounds of rodents in the walls, made it impossible to get a good night's sleep. Each week we spent two or three days in a row in silence, again meditating on death. Silence became the default setting of our days.

We were fortunate to have Sr. Elody for our Aspirancy Mistress. She was a short, round, elf-like, sweet-natured woman with a lovely unlined face, a quiet sense of humor and a loving soul. She tried to soften the hard edges of convent life for us. Her assistant, Sr. Frances, was Sr. Elody's opposite: tall, painfully skinny, wrinkled face, nervous laugh and prone to back-biting and gossip.

The Academy was scheduled to begin classes in two weeks, so we had a long list of things to accomplish before the students arrived. One of our first projects as a group was to strip the yellowed coating of wax off the long hallway floors in the classroom area. These floors had received many coats of wax over the previous year. It was our job to remove all the wax so the process could start all over again with the new school year.

In silence on our hands and knees, we scraped the dark maroon tiles with razor blades. The Sister in charge told us to offer up our suffering while we worked by saying "All for you, my Jesus" over and over again. The bells that rang for the *Divine Office* released us from this drudgery for as long as it took to say our prayers, and then we went back to the task.

My body, unused to manual labor, began to scream at me. My back, neck, arms and hands seized up. I wanted to cry, but I continued to scrape little curls of wax from the floor and brush them into small piles to be picked up by the Aspirant with the dust pan and brush. We stopped for lunch and a quiet time— which was normally used for prayer, reading, or a walk, but we all fell into a deep sleep until Sister came up the attic stairs ringing a hand bell to wake us so we could begin again. We labored at this chore for three more days.

Mealtime was a form of slow torture. I suspect the Sisters had a low food budget and limited culinary experience. The nuns found countless creative ways to make bland, mushy, foul-smelling meals which they served with pride. One of the cooking Sisters always served us so we had no control over portion size, and we had to finish everything on our plate or we'd be sinning against the vow of poverty. Nothing could be wasted. Professed nuns took three vows: Poverty, Chastity and Obedience. As aspirants we were called upon to practice these vows.

On Thursdays, all the leftovers from the week before were placed in one large pot and stewed all day—the smell was indescribable and permeated the whole building. We dreaded that meal each week and sat at the table for an hour trying to clean our plates, sometimes crying. Here was another occasion to gain merits in heaven as we forced the food down our throats saying, "All for you, my Jesus."

After dinner and clean up, and before *Compline* and the Grand Silence, we would have an hour of recreation in the sitting room.

We did jigsaw puzzles and played games. Sometimes there were instructions on how to mend our clothes, or time to write notes home. On birthdays and holidays there might be something special awaiting us at recreation hour: cookies from the nun's kitchen or candy sent from home to be shared, but these treats were rare.

I especially savored those sweets. My mother was an excellent baker—there were often homemade goodies awaiting me after school and on weekends. I missed her baked goods, but even more I missed her delicious Italian meals. Despite this, I began to gain weight on all the starchy food we were served. I was grateful there was room in my jumper for this expansion.

~

The morning bell rang at 4:30 a.m., and we aspirants filed through long dark corridors in prayerful silence making our way to the Chapel in the basement. The Chapel was the width of the building and half the building's length. Small, high windows lined the two long walls, and the Stations of the Cross hung in the spaces between the windows. Jesus hung on the cross over the altar, his tortured body before us.

The antiquated heating system in the building didn't keep us sufficiently warm but made loud clanking and hissing noises reminiscent of the stories we heard about Hell. The lighting was dim, and an eerie silence hung in the air. There were twenty rows of dark wood pews. The boarders, day students and any guests filled the first five rows; we aspirants sat in the row behind them; the postulants were behind us; the novices behind them.

Then the Sisters who had made temporary vows were followed by the Sisters who had made final vows in the order of their seniority. Then came the nuns called *Mother* or *Mother Superior*—Sisters who were part of the administration and held positions of esteem. Mother Provincial sat alone in the last pew to catch the smallest infraction of the rules and maintain total control over those in her charge.

We genuflected and made the sign of the cross as we took our places in the pews and knelt to say our individual morning prayers. We then joined the others praying in unison, reading the psalms and singing the hymns of *Lauds* as the sun rose. We recited the rosary together. When we were finished, the boarders and day students filed in to take their places in the front pews. They were exquisitely silent knowing the consequences of making any sound that might disrupt the Sisters' prayerful concentration.

One morning, a day student, sitting toward the front in the middle of the row, in full view of the aspirants, rose up from the pew gesticulating madly, making weird groaning sounds, her body contorting. The students surrounding her started to scream and emptied the pews. Sisters ran toward the girl as she collapsed. We aspirants never moved or made a sound. We were frozen on our knees with fear.

A few of us gathered after breakfast to whisper about the incident. The consensus was that this girl was possessed by the devil and would need to have an exorcism. The devil was ever present in our minds, luring us into temptation to sin. Later that day, Sr. Elody praised us for remaining calm and not joining in the hysteria of the students. She said the girl had had an epileptic seizure.

In truth, I couldn't reconcile the concept of a devil with some of the other Catholic teachings. I questioned that if God was All Good, as the Sisters told us, and All Loving and Creator of All Things, how could there be something Evil from that Loving Source? It was one of the many questions that kept floating through my consciousness. I finally asked the teacher of our religion class another question that had been bothering me: "If faith is a gift from God, how can it be a sin not to have faith?" The Sister snapped at me that it was an inappropriate question. I never again openly questioned anything while within the convent walls.

There were many elderly Sisters in the order, and when one died there was a huge celebration because, as a professed nun, she was the Bride of Christ and now reunited with Him in Heaven. One day two of these Sisters died within hours of each other. As was the custom, the next day they were *waked* in the main aisle of the Chapel. They were laid out in their coffins in their best habits, with their hands crossed over their hearts holding their rosary beads, just as we practiced each night in bed.

Because there were two coffins, one was placed alongside the aspirants' pew. The proximity of a body so close to us heightened the eeriness of the Chapel before dawn. Suddenly, I heard the aspirant next to me gasp and whisper, "Her rosary is moving..."

I looked over, and it looked like Sister was saying her beads, moving from one bead to the next. Then I watched as a fly flew off her hand. I breathed a sigh of relief. I did not want to witness any miracles!

Convent life was rigorous, demanding and emotionally draining at times. But there were moments of friendship and joy, and there was always music. My richest, deepest experience in the convent came from a frail, bent lay-woman in her nineties who came to teach us Gregorian chant in the choir loft of the Immaculate Conception Church next door. She was one of the oldest living teachers of this ancient form of chanting, and she relished sharing her knowledge of the music she loved.

Miss Dunn tottered as she moved her baton through the air to keep us singing at the pace she decreed. Her eyes, set deep in her tired wrinkled face, sparkled in spite of their pale color. Her hair was a yellowish grey pulled back into a bun at the nape of her neck, and she always wore a tailored white blouse and a straight brown skirt.

In spite of her brokenness, there was an elegance about her that spoke of old world decorum and genteel upbringing. She provided small books covered in faux-leather which contained about a dozen of the most common chants used during Mass. The notes were different from the ones I had learned for the piano, and there were decorative illuminations around the first letter of the chants—all of which were in Latin. Everything was right with the world when I was singing Gregorian chant.

~

Some of the aspirants formed quiet friendships, careful not to break the prohibition against having "special" friends, although none of us knew what that meant. Angela, Helen and I had an immediate connection which deepened as the months went by. All of the aspirants were friendly accept one aspirant who stood apart from the group. She was ostensibly devout and ingratiated herself to the nuns in charge. She stood ramrod straight and ignored us. Her name was Lucia.

Not talking to my classmates from the other side—the boarders and the day students—became more of a challenge as the school year unfolded. We could converse with them only in the classroom or when we did projects together, which made it hard to keep the boundaries between us clean at other times. Many of the boarders were lonely, unhappy girls. They felt neglected and abandoned by their parents and hated being at the school.

The aspirants and students joined together for a school project that year, under the direction of Sr. Valaria. We were rehearsing an abbreviated version of the popular musical, *West Side Story*, to perform for our parents, classmates and the Sisters at the end of the year. Sr. Valeria led us in prayer before every rehearsal. One day, three cousins, from a wealthy family in Puerto Rico, who struggled with English and homesickness, stood behind me while we prayed. As we started to say the *Hail Mary* which begins with the words *Hail Mary, full of Grace*, I distinctly heard all three of them say, *"Hail Mary, full of Grease!"*

I suppressed the urge to giggle! Later, I discretely told them the word was *Grace* and we had a good laugh together. They were friendly and high-spirited. It was the beginning of our forbidden friendship, my small rebellion against the rules that kept the boarders and the aspirants separated. Some of the Sisters and aspirants believed that the aspirants were superior to the boarders and that they would be contaminated by mingling with them. I didn't concur with that theory.

On several occasions, when I passed Mother Magdalena's office, I heard her screaming at some poor boarder for a minor infraction. Mother Magdalena was the Principal of the Academy. She was perpetually on a rampage. Short, rotund, and quick on her feet, she'd attack the subject of her ire verbally and, sometimes, physically. Her flushed round red face reminded me of the floating heads in our Catechism book that depicted the seven deadly sins. I couldn't decide if it was lust, anger or gluttony.

If I saw one of the boarders upset or crying, I'd break the rules and quietly carry on a conversation with her, trying to offer comfort. Some nuns pretended not to notice when we transgressed this rule. Two in particular were Sr. Valaria and Sr. Dennis. They were young—not yet fully professed—and kindly, gentle souls who were also full of fun. They took special interest in the boarders who were struggling. Their example inspired me to strive to be kinder and more devout.

Mother Magdalena was not the only nun who lashed out at the students. Many of the nuns believed it was their responsibility to mold these "errant" young souls with harsh and unyielding discipline. Everything I'd learned about love and compassion from these Sisters, who taught Catechism on Saturday mornings, seemed like a flimsy veneer over a philosophy that assumed guilt before innocence. And with that assumption of guilt, some nuns felt free to mete out discipline, deliberately causing humiliation and suffering. The boarders in their charge were young girls struggling to find their way through adolescence in this harsh environment. What they needed, I believed, was compassion and empathy, not punishment.

Even some of the Sisters who were kind to the aspirants treated the borders and day students cruelly. I became acutely aware of the disparity between the Catholicism I had been taught and the Catholicism I saw being lived behind the cloister walls. I was also disturbed by the Sisters' treatment of each other. The word "sister" had a strong connotation for me based on the caring and love I had received from my own sister, Jules.

Sr. Frances was not the only nun who was capable of back-biting and gossip. I witnessed competition, divisiveness, and often a coldness and lack of empathy among the nuns. Even some of the Mother Superiors, who supervised other nuns, were guilty of favoritism. Others disengaged from the nuns under their direction and barely interacted with them. I began to wonder if the convent was truly where I belonged.

~

About mid-year, the Sister who served as the school nurse checked my back, concerned that I might have scoliosis because I was so severely hunched over. She did not accept my explanation that my back fell when I was seven after I discovered my younger sister was never coming home because she had died the year before. No matter how hard I tried—walking with books on my head, doing stretches and other exercises—I could not stand up straight. I felt deformed, ugly, and self-conscious. Mortified that Sister was making a big deal of it, I wanted to disappear through the cracks of the attic floorboards where she was examining me.

In the course of checking my back, she noticed a hole at the end of my spine. She was upset and concerned. I explained that I'd had an operation two years before, and the doctor had left it open to heal. "Not for TWO YEARS!" she exclaimed and was quickly on the phone with my mother to arrange a doctor's appointment.

When Dr. Yates, my surgeon, saw the hole, he was angry with me and questioned why I hadn't told anyone that the incision had never closed. I was afraid to say, "I didn't want to go through this whole embarrassing ordeal again." Before I could think of a reason, he said, "I'll fix you! This time I'm sewing you up!" And he did—which made for a long and painful recovery. (My mother likened it to how she closed the flap on a turkey at Thanksgiving, crisscrossing the string and pulling it tight.)

The surgery took place over the Christmas break. Mom was busy with company. She decided that since I had been through the surgery before, she didn't need to be there when I woke up after the operation. I didn't protest her decision, but I was frightened to be left alone, feeling vulnerable and at the mercy of people I didn't know.

When I opened my eyes after the surgery, my gentle brother, Jim, who had just arrived from California for a visit, was sitting at my bedside. At first I was embarrassed. I hadn't seen him for several years, and I knew I looked terrible and was about to vomit. But, he just beamed at me and said, "Just relax—I'll be right here to keep you company." He apparently told my mother he wouldn't

think of letting me wake up alone after the surgery. I was grateful
he was there and will never forget his caring and love.

~

My ruminations about possibly leaving the convent continued
while I recovered at school, keeping a modified schedule with time
to rest. There were so many aspects of convent life I loved—the
deep meditative practices, saying the *Divine Office* in the garden on
the hill, singing the hymns and Gregorian chant, the camaraderie
of the aspirants, the sense of having a greater purpose in life—to
live close to God and serve humanity. And yet, I couldn't reconcile
the discrepancies between the Catholic doctrine I was taught and
how the Sisters acted behind closed doors.

I decided to discuss my concerns with the only civilian teacher
who lived on the premises. Miss Champlain was our Physical
Education teacher. She was straight-forward and painfully
truthful. I felt I could trust her to speak to me honestly.

I went to her office, a small dingy cube of a room with a
high ceiling and one small window halfway up the wall. "Miss
Champlain, may I talk to you about something?"

"Sure, sit down. What's on your mind?"

Taking a deep breath, I said, "I'm beginning to think I don't
belong here."

"Have you talked to Sr. Elody about this?"

"No, she'll just tell me I have a vocation and should stay."

"Why do you think you don't belong here?"

"Well, I thought it would be different. The nuns always taught
us about being kind and patient, not gossiping. They said Christ's
message was about love, taking care of the poor, and accepting
everyone." The room was turning dark as the sun went down. I
fidgeted in my chair, uncomfortable talking about my superiors.
"Yet, it's hard for me to watch how they treat the boarders
sometimes and even each other."

"Oh, so you thought everybody behind the cloistered doors
was going to be perfect? There is no such thing as perfection

here on earth, but I feel the same way about the boarders—the Sisters are very hard on them. You need to think deeply about why you're here. When you've given it some thought, come see me again."

I was disappointed with her response. Miss Champlain was usually decisive and direct. I wanted her to tell me what to do. I went outside to the grotto and prayed for guidance. None came.

One afternoon in late spring, I came down the foyer staircase and froze a few steps from the bottom. I witnessed Mother Magdalena pacing in front of a boarder who was lying on a deacon's bench. Mother was screaming, "How could you do this to us? How could you ruin the reputation of this school? You are a disgrace!" She went on and on.

I felt sick. I heard footsteps behind me. I looked up and saw an ashen Sr. Dennis coming down the stairs. My eyes questioned hers. With tears, she whispered to me, "She made a suicide attempt—they're waiting for the ambulance." An ambulance arrived a few minutes later, and Sr. Dennis disappeared up the stairs.

I was shaken and crying. Although I didn't know the girl well, my heart broke for her. I knew the last thing she needed in her moment of desperation was to be accosted by an angry nun. I didn't need to talk to Miss Champlain again. I knew I had to leave.

A few days later, I made an appointment with Mother Provincial and told her I wanted to leave the order after the school year ended. She was adamantly against my decision and tried to convince me I had a vocation. She even promised she'd send me to medical school if I stayed. I have no idea how she knew my dream was to be a missionary doctor in Africa where the order had a hospital, but her offer did not dissuade me. My faith was shattered.

I felt ashamed for having put so much faith in the Church. And, I felt bereft and anxious at the prospect of leaving my friends and going home to the on-going chaos. I was seventeen years old. The weight of all the pain I had experienced and witnessed descended upon me and crushed my spirit. The tentacles of depression began to squeeze the life out of me once again. At the age of seventeen, I wrote:

I am weary of this world
of this life
of this being that I am

The day my mother came to pick me up was wrenching. I had grown to love many people within the convent walls: my sister aspirants, boarders with whom I had made friendships in spite of the constraints, Sr. Elody, Sr. Valeria, Sr. Dennis—still my favorite nuns. (Sr. Dennis left the order a year after I did.) I'd even miss Mother Provincial, who followed my mother and me out the back door. As she stood on the cement steps, she called out to me, "You'll be back! You *will* be back! You have a vocation!"

~

Readjusting to home life and battling what I now know was clinical depression, proved to be a challenge. My mother's words echoed in my head, "You're just like your father!" With the freedom and lack of structure in secular life, I wandered around not knowing what to do next.

In the convent, I felt safe and contained by our schedule and the predictability of our days. So much had changed in and about me during the nine months I'd been away. Besides the weight gain that became obvious when I tried to fit into my old clothes, I walked with a "convent stride," which had become my natural gait, in my clunky, comfortable old lady shoes—traversing the endless corridors, always late for something.

I found it hard to enter a conversation or initiate one. I fell into long silences that had been part of daily life within the convent walls. Although I loved praying the Divine Office, I lacked the motivation to continue saying it. Still, I longed for those blessed interruptions in an ordinary day. And, I was lonely without other young people around me. I lived in a household of adults, and school was out for the summer. I was estranged from friends who didn't understand my choice. Now I didn't understand it either.

I particularly missed my aspirant friend, Angela, who was a lovely, devoted French Canadian teenager with whom I felt a deep connection. She seemed fragile and even a little despondent when we began the year together, so I had reached out to her with encouragement, and she had done the same for me when I was feeling down.

About two weeks after I returned home, the phone rang and my mother answered. She held out the phone, "It's for you."

I heard a man's voice yelling, "This is Angela's Father! How could you let this happen to Angela? She was your friend! Why didn't you tell me that nun was a lesbian? Why didn't you tell me she was seducing Angela?"

I could not respond. Crying, I gently placed the phone back in its cradle and turned to my mother in dismay, asking through my tears, "Mom, what's a lesbian?"

Not until recently, when I read *An Unquenchable Thirst*, a memoir by Mary Thomasson, who was a nun in Mother Teresa's order for many years, did I understand that lesbian relationships in the convent are not uncommon, nor is sexual exploitation. I couldn't imagine exactly what had taken place, but I knew Angela was hurt. Nor did I comprehend how a nun could prey upon my vulnerable, innocent friend. I was broken-hearted for her, but made no attempt to contact her. Disillusioned and emotionally drained, I wrote these words.

> *Sometimes I am so weary*
> *it is a great effort*
> *to put one foot*
> *in front of the other.*
> *Only rarely*
> *do I find joy in living.*

~

Clinical depression's hallmark is exhaustion, a sense of being drained of one's life-force. Everything becomes hard. Morning brings dread for the day ahead and night brings tortured sleep, if any at all. Life becomes meaningless. This is why many people with depression become suicidal. Taking one's own life, at that time, was deemed a mortal sin by the Catholic Church, and those who committed suicide couldn't be buried in a Catholic cemetery.

~

I chose life over death each time I came to the precipice of ultimate despair because I feared dying in the state of mortal sin. And, every time I held on long enough to ride out that impulse, there was a glimmer of hope that this would be my last depressive episode. Hope was the thread I followed back into the light. I emerged from each depression as if reborn. My arms wrapped around the world more tightly than ever before. My energy, creativity and ecstasy soared again. This pattern is now called a bi-polar disorder. My mother was right—I was just like my father. Millay's "Renascence" echoed in my ears.

> *I screamed, and — lo! — Infinity*
> *Came down and settled over me;*
> *Forced back my scream into my chest,*
> *Bent back my arm upon my breast,*
> *And, pressing of the Undefined*
> *The definition on my mind,*
> *Held up before my eyes a glass*
> *Through which my shrinking sight did pass*
> *Until it seemed I must behold*
> *Immensity made manifold;*
> *Whispered to me a word whose sound*
> *Deafened the air for worlds around,*
> *And brought unmuffled to my ears*
> *The gossiping of friendly spheres,*
> *The creaking of the tented sky,*
> *The ticking of Eternity.*

The place in which you find yourself
isn't nearly as important
as where you place your attention
while you are there.

– Stephen C. Paul from *Inneractions*

CHAPTER TWELVE

Where is Home?

AFTER LEAVING THE CONVENT, the long summer loomed before me. I walked around as though I was blind, feeling my way with each step. The Church had been my spiritual home, and now I was homeless, banished by my own inability to accept the hypocrisy, the cruelty, the pettiness I'd seen behind the cloister walls. Bereft from the loss of my North Star, I floundered not knowing what to believe or trust. I questioned the existence of God. Hope fell away like the wings of a fallen angel.

The environment of my earthly home was no less confusing and unsafe. There was tension in the house even when Dad was hospitalized. Mark was as moody and volatile as my father. He and my mother constantly fought about the progress of the renovations Mark was making on the house. Mom was impatient with his slow, methodical pace and long periods of inactivity when Mark was "thinking things through." He was often unemployed. This aggravated my mother since his income was needed. She went to work every day to cook for a nursing home with over thirty patients.

Mom was also annoyed with my lack of direction that summer as I continued to struggle with depression. I was exhausted from my ordeal in the convent and pictured myself reading and spending time by the river. My mother suggested I take driving lessons at the high school. I hadn't pursued a job because we lived ten miles from the nearest city, and I didn't drive, so getting my license made sense. When I signed up for driving lessons, there was another signup sheet for career counseling. I signed my name to it without much thought since I now had no idea what I was going to do with my life.

My first session was with the Counseling Department supervisor in charge of training counseling interns at the University of Connecticut. He was probably in his early forties, balding, and a little overweight. He wore a wrinkled beige suit and looked hot. During the interview, he was soft spoken, gently attentive, although somewhat aloof at first. He explained he was doing the initial interviews so he could assign each client to one of the student counselors. He began by asking me questions about my family life and my interests. "Tell me why you signed up for career counseling."

"Well, I just spent a year in the convent with the Sisters of Charity. I left because I saw how the nuns didn't live up to what they taught us in Catechism. It was very upsetting to see how they treated each other and the students who live at the school. Now, I'm not sure what to do with my life. I don't even know what I believe anymore." Tears welled up and overflowed onto my cheeks. He moved a box of tissues close to me.

The room felt barren. It was sparsely furnished and painted a muddy tan. Shadows slipped into the room as the sun made its descent. There was no air conditioning, just a standing fan swinging from side to side. "How are things at home?" he asked.

I tried to compose myself. "My father is in and out of the hospital—he alternates between depression and mania. He gets very agitated and belligerent in the spring, and then he keeps getting worse until my family has to put him in the hospital."

"What happens when he's released from the hospital?"

"He returns home in the fall on tranquillizers and just sits in a chair—he hardly moves. Then he stops taking the medication and he gets extremely sad—talking about all the bad things that have happened in his life. Then, the mania comes back."

"And, how do you feel about all this?" he asked.

"Oh, I'm use to it, but it's still pretty upsetting. Sometimes my father is really scary. When I was younger, my mother used to send me to my cousins or brothers when Dad was getting manic. Now I just try to make plans not to be around."

As my story unfolded, he became quiet and finally said, "I don't think you need *career* counseling right now, but I do think it would be helpful if you talked to someone, so you'll be seeing me."

What a gift this man was, although I don't remember his name. We spoke for an hour twice a week for six weeks. He sat in disbelief at the complexity of my young life and helped me unravel the tangle of emotions about my family and my experience in the convent. He listened with compassion. I felt valued and respected in his presence. I was more centered and positive by the time the sessions ended. The darkness began to lift. I also successfully completed driver's education. My confidence returned to the point where I felt ready to get a job.

Since I was still enamored with the idea of becoming a doctor, I walked into the local hospital in Williamson, the small city ten miles from home where we shopped and received our medical care. I applied for the position of nurse's aide. Miss Cane, the Director of Nursing, reminded me of Mother Provincial, straight-backed, self-assured and well-spoken. She looked over my application and hired me.

The job entailed being fitted for a light green uniform which obviously had been worn by many before me. It was faded and soft, almost silky from wear. As I tried it on, a sense of familiarity and relief filled my cells. I'd missed the feeling of slipping on my bright blue convent jumper everyday—and the simplicity it brought to my life. I took to the job. The discipline and schedule gave me a feeling of being in safe waters again.

My shift started at 7:00 am, but there wasn't a car available for me to drive to work. Mark, who was a night owl and probably went to bed at 2:00 or 3:00 am, was up without complaint to take me to work. As my confusion about him and the young boys who followed him around our home increased, I'd begun to distance myself from him. He didn't seem to notice. He took me wherever I needed to go, and willingly renovated my bedroom to my specifications.

My convent stride was appropriate in the hospital where I needed to get from one end of a long hallway to the other in seconds. I learned quickly and was given increasing responsibility because there was a nursing shortage. I was needed to fill in the gaps in patient care. I started on the OB/GYN floor. My first assignment was to sit with an unwed mother who was in labor. She was relegated to a room at the far end of the hall by herself. I entered her room and found a pretty young woman about my age with pale skin, long dark hair, long limbs and a huge belly. She was crying. I asked her what was wrong.

"I don't know what's going to happen."

I replied, "I don't know either, but I'll sit with you if you like." She gratefully accepted and reached for my hand. We eventually were crying together as I witnessed her pain with each contraction. Being of service became my life-line that brought me back into the world.

The end of summer came quickly, and Miss Cane said she didn't want to lose me. She asked if I'd work weekends during the school year. I agreed to the weekend shift—anything to escape the ceaseless turmoil in our house. My father came home from the hospital in September, heavily tranquilized, and our world revolved around him again.

I re-entered Nathan Hale high school as a senior. I'd lost ground academically during the year I spent in the convent. My Parisian French teacher was appalled at the accent I picked up from the French Canadian nun who taught me the previous year. She'd call on me every day to read in front of the class, then ridicule me for my horrible pronunciation. I was behind in every subject. And I was even more alienated from my peers than I was before my year away.

It was clear my fellow-students were curious about where I had been, but no one inquired or made an effort to welcome me back. (It never occurred to me that they probably thought I went away to have a baby!) And, with those friends who knew where I had been, I felt embarrassed by my decision to enter the convent and humiliated by my failure to stay. I was more reserved than ever.

Desolation began to color my days, once again. My good friend, Cindy Allen, and I reconnected and picked up where we left off, which was a great comfort. My work at the hospital continued to be my refuge—I felt needed and confident in that role.

Participating in the Catholic rituals and prayers at our Church became meaningless as I grappled with the contradictions I discovered in the convent. I was in an emotional and spiritual freefall. I put on a cheerful face and pretended everything was fine. Only a few friends knew the dark state I was in and were willing to sit with me while I wept.

Some of my journal entries that fall of 1961 included:

This life is alien to me.
Why am I all thumbs at living?
Do I belong on another planet?
In another Universe?

***

There is disbelief
in all my faith
and hate
in all my love.
There is emptiness
in all I am.

***

What is it with my life
That it possesses
The light of time
Yet passes by
Unlived?

~

In the spring of 1962 a few months before high school graduation, I received acceptance letters from Duquesne University and the Catholic University of America. I wanted to go to a Catholic college in hopes it would rekindle the flame of faith. My mother and I took the bus to Washington, DC to visit Catholic U. I fell in love with the city and the university. The university offered me financial aid, dependent on my maintaining a 3.5 grade point average. I usually maintained closer to a 4.0 average, so that seemed doable.

I spent the summer before college working at the hospital. I befriended another nurse's aide who had been a year ahead of me in high school. We rode the same school bus for years but never connected. She was painfully shy. Her name was Susan Black. She'd been accepted into a prestigious college on scholarship and was entering her sophomore year in the fall.

We began to share our stories during breaks at work and soon realized we had much in common. We both struggled with depression but held onto our high ideals and aspirations for making a difference in the world. Her childhood was much like mine, a household where life revolved around her sister, Mary, who was disabled with cerebral palsy. We were both introverts and relished our time alone. Our friendship was tentative that summer because we were assigned to different floors. My work at the hospital gave my life meaning, and I looked forward to getting away from home in the fall. My mood brightened.

I was sent to the fourth floor with critically ill and terminally ill patients. My nursing supervisor trusted me to count the number of drops in atropine drips, which is crucial to the patient's stability. This usually required a Registered Nurse and now is done by computer. I was assigned to patients who had complicated medical needs and/or required emotional support. I helped orient a degree nurse on her first assignment as charge nurse of the floor. I felt respected, seen and trusted by my superiors and colleagues. My sense of myself as a competent, caring nurse's aide heightened my desire to become a doctor.

Miss Cane tried to convince me to go to nursing school instead of pre-med. She said, "You have a wonderful way with patients, and you won't be able to work with people in the same way if you become a physician." Only now can I admit that I wanted the prestige of being a doctor, and I saw nursing as women's work. I wanted to be like my brothers, not like my mother and sister.

~

In late August of 1962, my mother put me on another Greyhound bus with everything I needed for the semester. I was nervous. Ten hours later I arrived in Washington DC. A Catholic University shuttle picked me up at the bus station and drove past the gleaming white buildings of the Capital which stood against the deeply azure sky. Many of these buildings had pillars and porticos and other features of the Greek and Roman architecture I loved.

The shuttle brought me to the entrance of my college dorm. A residential advisor showed me to my room and introduced me to my roommate, Michelle. I watched as Michelle and her parents hung her stylish clothes in the closet and made her side of the room into a cozy little haven. Her family lived in an affluent suburb of New York City. A small wave of envy swelled in my heart, not for the material things she possessed, but for the attention she received from her two doting parents. Rejecting that feeling, I increased my resolve to be independent and responsible for myself.

School officially began the day after I arrived. The first morning was filled with General Orientation in a huge auditorium. Then, in the afternoon, we were divided according to our majors. Mine, of course, was pre-med. I was amazed to see the smaller auditorium filled with over two-hundred pre-med students, mostly male.

The Dean of the program wasted no time in warning us that he intended to weed out anyone who didn't belong in the program. The curriculum for the first semester included: Biology, Chemistry, Math, English, and a foreign language. In high school, I'd struggled with all these subjects except English, but somehow maintained a good grade-point average. I assumed, if I worked hard, I could do that again. Before I left home, my brother, Pete, pulled me aside and pointed out that my strengths were in the Liberal Arts and suggested I change my major. I wasn't about to do that, but a low level anxiety nagged at the edges of my consciousness. I knew he was right.

~

We had a few days before classes started, so I began to investigate the surrounding area. Not far from the school, a massive Cathedral was under construction. It would become known as the *Basilica of the National Shrine of the Immaculate Conception.* It was breathtaking even in its unfinished state. I discovered that the underground level was finished and included a Crypt Church where Mass was held daily. It was dark and cave-like and had an Eastern Orthodox look—bejeweled statues and rich colors, deeply silent and beautiful.

I stood in the doorway awe-struck. I fell in love with this chapel, and it became my soul's home. I attended daily Mass more for the beauty of the place than for the ritual. I started my own personal discourse with the Holy while listening to Gregorian chant in this low-ceilinged chamber. At the same time, I was growing more removed from the Catholic dictates and doctrines.

There were many concepts I rejected in the Church's teachings. One was eternal damnation—how could an All-Loving God banish a soul to hell for eternity? I could not accept the concept of Original Sin on which the whole premise of redemption rests. I believed the innocent babies I'd held over the years, as an auntie and as a nurse's aide, could not possibly be blemished by sin. Yet, I felt *I* came into the world with some moral defect just for being alive. It was like the dye from my mother's black coat had seeped into the womb and stained me. I came from the womb drenched in darkness.

One day I wandered into the unfinished sanctuary on the main floor of the Cathedral. Pews were in place, but no glass filled the mammoth arched windows floating high about the huge open space. Swallows flew in and out of the windows and across the sanctuary as if at home in this divine milieu! I sat there after the workmen left for the day while the low rays of the sun streamed through the windows and the birds sang evening vespers. My spirit started to soar again as it did when I was a child sitting on the huge rock in my natural cathedral across the river that I called God's Patio.

Here, I was untethered from the dogma and rituals that had kept me bound to an imperfect human institution that had betrayed my faith. I was as free as the birds flying above me. Although my heart was free to soar, the indoctrination of the Church, imprinted on my cells, would echo within me for years to come.

~

I dutifully went to classes and labs and tried to keep up with my assignments. My Parisian French teacher also disparaged my pronunciation and became exasperated with my slow progress. I had never taken advanced Math courses in high school, a serious disadvantage. Biology was challenging, but fascinating, and chemistry was beyond my comprehension. As always, I was entranced by my English course.

But, in truth, my heart was elsewhere. Every Saturday morning I visited the *National Museum of Art*, ate lunch at the museum cafeteria and stayed on to attend the free concert that was held there each Saturday afternoon. I sometimes walked to the *Cultural Center at Georgetown University* on weekends to attend programs there. I learned my way around the city at a time when it was safe to walk the streets even at night.

There were countless little parks around civic statues with small gardens and benches, often enclosed in high hedges to create an oasis of calm in the middle of the hectic city. I would take my books to study in one of these quiet corners, away from the noise and distractions of the dorm where I felt like an outsider.

I'd imagined attending a Catholic college with like-minded people who shared my values. My high school was on the UConn campus where I was shocked by the behavior of the college students. It was no different here. Many of my fellow students had gone through twelve years of Catholic school before they entered college. They went wild and ignored curfews and snuck in and out of the dorm at will. I judged them harshly.

Nevertheless, I had a small group of friends who did share my values. I even went on one date—my first. Paul was in my

Math class, and he invited me to a movie. We were both a bit awkward, but we had a pleasant time together. Then, as we were walking home, he reached for my hand. Although this seems absurd to me now, I actually said to him, "Oh Paul, it's been such a nice evening, let's not spoil it." He never asked me out again. I didn't question my extreme aversion to physical touch by a male or to anything remotely sexual. Now I wonder if there was some early sexual abuse in my past.

Meanwhile, as I settled into college life, my cultural interests and my spiritual life cut into my studies. The goal of keeping my grade point average at 3.5 began to slip away. The sense of freedom and my immersion into the world of culture were intoxicating. I lost perspective on why I was living in this beautiful, exciting city. I was feeding my thirsty soul away from the stresses of my home life, and I wanted to savor the experience. I didn't consider the consequences.

I went home for Christmas and returned to school to take finals. It wasn't long before I received the notice that my grade point average was not high enough to keep my funding. I had to withdraw and return home.

As the depression, that manifested with each loss or failure, descended, my salvation was to go back to work at the hospital. My friend, Susan Black, was there, too, having dropped out of school because it was too stressful. She was in the same depressive state as I was.

We asked ourselves: *Were we trying to escape from life? Were we taking the easy way out, feeling sorry for ourselves?* We both felt shame for our weakness and for succumbing to depression over and over again.

I knew Susan wasn't a weak person—she had lived through so much and remained thoughtful and kind. I didn't judge her for being depressed, but I judged myself and I felt the judgment of others. *Just pull yourself up by your bootstraps. Think happy thoughts. Get busy. You're too serious—lighten up.* I tried to follow the instructions, but my efforts never resulted in the desired outcome. I felt Millay's words were written for me:

I saw and heard, and knew at last
The How and Why of all things, past,
And present, and forevermore.
The Universe, cleft to the core,
Lay open to my probing sense
That, sick'ning, I would fain pluck thence
But could not, — nay! But needs must suck
At the great wound, and could not pluck
My lips away till I had drawn
All venom out. — Ah, fearful pawn!
For my omniscience paid I toll
In infinite remorse of soul.

~

At the time, neither Susan nor I knew how pervasive mood disorders are or the destruction they wreak on individuals, families and society. Historically, these disorders had been judged as character flaws. It took another twenty years before mental illness was viewed more objectively and compared to other diseases like diabetes. Yet, the stigma of mental illness is tenacious to this day. And, so is the shame.

~

Back at the hospital, working the three-to-eleven shift, I was once again assigned to the OB/GYN floor. This time I was put in charge of the Newborn and Preemie Nurseries. I was nineteen years old. Miss Lowell, whom I had worked with before, was a demanding supervisor. She was used to having complete control of the floor even when she wasn't there. Our paths now crossed only when we were doing report at the start of my shift and the end of hers. She would admonish me, "Now don't you go spoiling those babies by picking them up every time they cry!" Of course, the first thing I did after changing all the diapers in my charge was to pick up the babies. No baby was going to be left crying on my watch. I loved this work.

When a mother was in labor, I'd be called to the delivery room just as the baby was crowning. Watching through the window in the door, I'd witness the birth and be handed this wet, sticky howling newborn to take down to the nursery to clean up, weigh, measure and dress. Then the nurse came to check the vitals, put ointment in the baby's eyes, and recheck the Apgar score, an assessment of the infant's skin color, pulse, grimace, activity and respiration.

One infant entrusted to me looked pale with bluish lips and seemed to be struggling to breathe. I picked up the baby and ran down the hall calling for help. A nurse grabbed the baby out of my arms. I was shaking on my way back to the nursery. The nurse came to me a little while later and gently told me the baby had died. "The baby had a birth defect, Kath. Nothing you or I could have done would have saved him. You need to let this one go." I sobbed in her arms.

I became more vigilant for signs of trouble with *my* babies. The preemies were even scarier to handle. I grew attached to these tiny ones who sometimes ended up in our nursery for weeks or months. I was the only person who consistently cared for them, and many of them were children of poor parents who couldn't visit often.

How many of these babies would end up in foster care because the conditions at home were unacceptable? Some babies were abandoned. I wanted to take them home with me. I was cautioned to keep a professional distance from my little patients and their families, but it was too late. I had fallen in love with all of them, and I couldn't undo what my heart had already embraced. And, I bore witness and grieved for all those who suffered and sometimes died.

These words from Millay's Renascence expressed my feelings:

All sin was of my sinning, all
Atoning mine, and mine the gall
Of all regret. Mine was the weight
Of every brooded wrong, the hate
That stood behind each envious thrust,
Mine every greed, mine every lust.

And all the while for every grief,
Each suffering, I craved relief
With individual desire, —
Craved all in vain! And felt fierce fire
About a thousand people crawl;
Perished with each, — then mourned for all!

To go into the dark with a light is to know the light.
To know the dark, go dark. Go without sight,
and find that the dark, too, blooms and sings,
and is traveled by dark feet and dark wings.

– "To Know the Dark" by Wendell Berry from *Collected Poems 1957-1982*

CHAPTER THIRTEEN
Comforting Arms

ALTHOUGH MY WORK was deeply fulfilling, the impact of the suffering and loss I witnessed began to take its toll. The acutely and terminally ill patients I worked with on the fourth floor haunted me. I grew attached to some who lingered in the hospital until they died.

One terminally ill patient with bone cancer, pale, emaciated and in excruciating pain, was demanding and caustic. No one wanted to care for her—we all dreaded going into her room. As soon we crossed her threshold, she'd start yelling commands at us.

Every pillow had to be exactly where she dictated. She gave detailed instructions for everything she wanted done and loudly reprimanded us if we didn't follow them to her liking. It would be two to three hours before you would be released from her grip if you had her that day. We closed the door behind us with a sigh of relief.

She intrigued me—refined and elegant, even in her wrinkled nightgown and disheveled long grey wispy hair. I learned she had grown up in the family that owned the mammoth brick mill that loomed over the town, yet she never had visitors. She was very proud that her ancestors were among the first settlers in the new world.

I did not wither under her patronizing treatment and stayed present—looking her straight in the eyes with all the kindness and respect I could muster. She calmed down and began to soften her tone with me. I became "her" nurse's aide and was assigned to her every shift I worked to the relief of the other aides working on the floor. From the stories she told me, she had been a proud independent woman. Now she couldn't even brush her hair or care for herself in any way. It was humiliating and she was angry. I saw who she was and she was grateful.

A few doors down, a man with an Irish brogue was dying of the same disease. When I walked into his room he'd say, "Top o' the mornin to you, darlin! How are you today?" He, too, was in horrendous pain yet he never failed to greet anyone who entered his room with warmth and humor. I mourned them both when they died.

I also felt the weight of responsibility for the little ones I loved in the nurseries. I was afraid I would make a lethal mistake. I was exhausted from the intensity of the job. If I couldn't do this work, what could I do?

In time, the miracles of everyday life no longer touched me. Even my connection with nature was frayed. My mood was flat, detached, unmoved. And, I was even more estranged from the religion of my youth. I doubted God's existence.

I could no longer tolerate the constant upheaval in our home. All my nerve endings were on fire—I needed space and time to listen to my own voice. It was impossible to do that under my mother's roof. Nothing had changed at home, except my father was hospitalized for longer periods and was becoming increasingly ill and physically weak. He was diagnosed with a heart condition in his fifties. Now, in his late sixties, he had chronic pancreatitis which became pancreatic cancer. And he continued to suffer from untreatable mental illness.

Mark's young companions followed him around the house while he worked on the never-ending renovations. He seemed obsessed with these adolescent boys and talked to them in that syrupy sweet voice, laughed at their unfunny jokes, and made sure they weren't hungry or thirsty. And, Mark became more like our father, with periods of frenetic energy and volatility, followed by long despondent periods. I felt he had vacated his body and some stranger had stepped in.

Mark was working at the local newspaper as a photographer. He started bringing a young woman home from time to time. Her name was Judy Feingold, and we all loved her. She was bright, funny, and warm. Both Mom and I became close to her. Mark perked up, and the young boys disappeared. It was quite obvious that Judy was in love with him, and Mark liked her. He was his articulate and caring self in her presence

We all hoped that "this was the one," but Mark abruptly broke off the relationship with Judy after about six months when a young boy, Billy, began to show up at our house. She was inconsolable. Mom and I tried to comfort her. I'd meet her in Williamson for lunch, and we would talk for hours. Her theme song became: *If it takes forever, I will wait for you* from the movie, *Umbrellas of Cherbourg*. My sister Jules was still in Japan, so Judy took over the role of my big sister. She was Jewish, and we often talked about religion.

Mark slipped back into the old patterns after Judy was gone. The young boys began to reappear around our house again, and Mark was abrupt, angry and cynical with everyone except these boys. His grandiosity and self-righteous attitude escalated. It was as if he had died—I grieved the loss. A poem about him spilled out of me.

My brother died a slow and painless death
and when he spoke, I sensed his soul depart.
His words had grown meaningless and weak.
He lived no longer mindful of his art—
creating hope in all who heard him speak.

He lingered long and softly did he leave
and only empty flesh remained...
and, yet, I was deceived
and missed him not nor grieved.

Some thoughtless god
aroused him from his grave
and with his life brought knowledge of his death.
He was more precious now that he'd been saved.

When he abruptly died again
I wept and raged
and cursed the corpse that still remained
a vase now void which once my hope contained.

– Kathleen, age nineteen

~

I knew I had to escape this toxic environment, but how was I going to save enough on the meager salary I made at the hospital? I approached my Godparents, Carmine and Marie, to see if I could stay with them in the Bronx while I looked for better paying work in New York City and could afford my own apartment. They opened their home to me.

I grew to love the City as much as I did Washington D.C. Even though everything about it was antithetical to my usual sensibilities—the noise, the density of people and cars, the hectic and pressured pace—my soul was stirred. I was fascinated by the people—diverse in every way—their faces, ethnicities, the way they dressed, the various dialects and how they freely expressed themselves. I was enamored with the architecture—as diverse as the people. I stood in awe in front of the buildings where my father's mallet and chisel had made their mark. There was beauty everywhere I looked.

I found my way down to the tip of Manhattan and mustered the courage to walk into the Personnel Department at the Chase Manhattan Bank—a sixty floor skyscraper. I was hired as a secretary in the Personnel Department based on my typing skills. The subways were crowded when I got off from work, and I had a few unpleasant experiences with men pushing against me while I was standing holding on to a strap or pole. To avoid this, I walked around Battery Park near my office to calm my nerves after work and to delay getting on the crowded subway.

I'd end up at the Staten Island Ferry, to ride back and forth several times for a nickel, and then meander up Wall Street, silent except for the echoing of my footsteps. Sometimes I'd wander into Harlem and eventually get on an almost empty subway car, reaching home well after dark.

This routine caused Marie and Carmine to worry about my safety. They urged me to come directly home. But no one had ever bothered me, except in the crowded subway, so I continued my routine. One morning I came down to breakfast, and there was a newspaper clipping beside my place setting. A young woman had been killed on Wall Street around the same time of the evening that I usually walked through there. That was it. I got on the subway with everyone else as Manhattan emptied into the boroughs and suburbs of the sprawling city, praying I'd get a seat.

Another morning, I found a letter from my mother on the breakfast table. A newspaper clipping fell out with the obituary of my friend, Susan Black. She had committed suicide. Shocked and grief stricken, I sobbed uncontrollably. I anguished over my decision to leave. I had deserted her. Perhaps I might have been able to save her if I'd been there as she plummeted into the abyss. I was overwhelmed with guilt. My godparents tried to comfort me, saying there was nothing I could have done to stop her. But I was not convinced.

Suicide had haunted me during my periods of depression. As a teenager living in Connecticut, I had driven fast and recklessly, swerving in near-miss swipes at the walls of rock lining the curved entrance to the highway. I wanted to demolish my life, but still leave it in fate's hands so my death wouldn't be a suicide, which was a sin.

Susan had been much more deliberate—she hanged herself. I could not get that image out of my mind. I was desolate that my friend was in so much pain she saw no alternative to ending her life. And, I was afraid that one day I, too, might not be able to control my self-destructive impulses. I vowed that I'd help people like Susan who do battle with suicidal ideation. Again, Millay's "Renascence" spoke to and for me.

A man was starving in Capri;
He moved his eyes and looked at me;
I felt his gaze, I heard his moan,
And knew his hunger as my own.

I saw at sea a great fog bank
Between two ships that struck and sank;
A thousand screams the heavens smote;
And every scream tore through my throat.

No hurt I did not feel, no death
That was not mine; mine each last breath
That, crying, met an answering cry
From the compassion that was I.
All suffering mine, and mine its rod;
Mine, pity like the pity of God.

~

It would be many years before I understood and accepted that suicidal
thoughts and impulses are part of the mood disorder that hijacks the
brain chemistry and neural pathways of people like Susan and me.
In the 1960's, science and medicine were only beginning to touch
upon the genetic, neurological, biochemical, and external factors that
are involved in mental illness, including clinical depression and
bi-polar disorders.

I watched a friend who had juvenile onset diabetes act erratically
and hallucinate when his blood chemistry was out of balance—I never
judged him for his thoughts and behavior because I knew there was
an organic reason for it. I wish I had known that was true for my
friend and me as well.

~

One bleak day in November of 1963, I tumbled out of the Chase
Manhattan Bank with the crowd onto the darkening streets,
heading for the subway at the day's end. There was a great deal of
commotion but I was so tired I didn't pay attention to it at first.
Soon, the sidewalk was blocked with people gathered around
a store window where a TV showed Walter Cronkite looking

straight at the camera, clearly upset. We couldn't hear the sound, but someone whispered to me, "The President's been shot."

I gasped and burst into tears. A woman put her arm around my shoulder and handed me a tissue. I thanked her and broke away from the crowd, stumbling toward Fifth Avenue. I reached the steps of St. Patrick's Cathedral, my sanctuary in the City.

Hundreds of people were flocking to the same destination in a state of confusion and grief. Inside, it was quiet except for the muffled sobs that could be heard throughout the huge edifice. A group of nuns started to pray the rosary. I joined in. I needed the comfort of those familiar words.

After several hours, I found my way to the subway and arrived at Marie and Carmine's house where they were waiting to comfort me. Marie's arms encircled me with warmth and love as Carmine held us both.

Many years later, when my precious comforter and God-mother, Marie, lay dying at the age of 93, memories of her came flooding back to me in the form of a poem.

My dear, sweet Marie,

You have lighted my life
since the day I was born.
I love the picture of you
holding me at my baptism,
your wide brimmed hat
and beautiful smile,
with Carmine by your side.

I could always feel
your and his love for me.
You have been with me
in good times and bad,
coming to see me sing
in the school show each year,
taking me to Coney Island
when I visited New York.

You were there when I needed
someplace to live,
when my friend
committed suicide,
when J.F.K.
was assassinated
and I lost
all hope for the world.

You were there
each time a death
shattered my heart.

You exude love, wisdom and light
You have mothered my heart and soul,
as well as my body.

You are embedded in my heart
and I will cherish your memory
forever.

My love...always...Kathy

After about six months with Marie and Carmine, I finally found a small studio apartment I could afford. I looked forward to having time and space to write, which had been my goal since I was introduced to great literature in eighth grade. I'd just bought a used typewriter and settled in when my mother proposed she join me and look for work.

My father was now hospitalized indefinitely. Mom was fifty-nine and had looked for a job back home with no success. I opened my apartment to her, but resented the intrusion on my solitude. She still couldn't get a job so money was tight. We rarely went to the movies, which was one activity we enjoyed doing together, and we shopped only for necessities.

Every Sunday we went to see our Bronx relatives for a traditional Italian meal that lasted for hours. It always lifted my spirits. Once a week, we went out at 10:00 pm and stood at the bagel factory door until it opened. Someone would hand us a bag of steaming hot bagels in exchange for a pittance of money.

There is nothing like a hot, fresh, New York bagel! That was the highlight of our week.

The silence and solitude I sought when I moved to my own place were nonexistent. Finding my voice would have to wait. I turned twenty that March, disappointed that I was not yet a published author. Edna St. Vincent Millay had written "Renascence" and won international acclaim at the age of nineteen.

Mom and I moved back to Connecticut shortly thereafter because it was clear my father was coming to the end of his life. It all seemed too much—Susan's suicide, the President's assassination, my father's illness and impending death. Millay's words described the suffocating pressure I felt:

> *Ah, awful weight! Infinity*
> *Pressed down upon the finite Me!*
> *My anguished spirit, like a bird,*
> *Beating against my lips I heard;*
> *Yet lay the weight so close about*
> *There was no room for it without.*
> *And so beneath the weight lay I*
> *And suffered death, but could not die.*
>
> *Long had I lain thus, craving death,*
> *When quietly the earth beneath*
> *Gave way, and inch by inch, so great*
> *At last had grown the crushing weight,*
> *Into the earth I sank till I*
> *Full six feet underground did lie,*
> *And sank no more, — there is no weight*
> *Can follow here, however great.*
> *From off my breast I felt it roll,*
> *And as it went my tortured soul*
> *Burst forth and fled in such a gust*
> *That all about me swirled the dust.*

Longing is the nature of the soul
the seed sown by the Eternal
to call us back to Love.

– Kathleen, Journal entry from July 2015

CHAPTER FOURTEEN
"—the eyes of love—"

MY FATHER was failing fast. We brought him home to celebrate what was to be his last birthday. He was tranquilized and frail, withdrawn and apathetic. My niece, Jen, who was five years old, sat beside him all day holding his hand as if she knew this would be the last time she'd see him. We went through the traditional ritual of lighting the candles on the birthday cake and singing 'Happy Birthday' with little response from my father. That evening we took him back to the hospital.

We continued visiting regularly in spite of the fact that he was consistently angry and belligerent with us for not taking him home. One night, after the three-hour drive from the Veterans hospital in Western, Massachusetts, the phone was ringing when we walked through the door. Mark sprinted up the stairs to the second floor hallway to answer it. My father had stockpiled his medication and taken an overdose. Although it wasn't a lethal dose, he was in such a compromised condition it killed him.

I was numb—relieved, actually. My brother Tony flew in from California. My sister couldn't get back from Japan, but relatives from New York descended upon our home and friends gathered round us bringing food and their comforting presence.

I had returned to work at the hospital with the babies once again. It was the only place I felt any peace. Still, my mood was darkening with each passing spring day and through the summer. I felt numb to the beauty of the world.

A new general practitioner came to town, Dr. Bret Weston. He was often on the OB/GYN floor where I worked. He was kind, soft spoken and his patients loved him. I decided to see him to find out if there was something physically wrong with me because I was exhausted and in pain all the time.

After taking a short history and doing a brief exam, he assured me there was nothing physically wrong, but he thought I was depressed. He had done a residency in Psychiatry and felt qualified to counsel me to resolve the issues underlying my depression. I'd had a positive experience with my first counselor, so I thought it might help.

Dr. Weston offered consolation. I felt seen and understood in his presence, even when our paths crossed in the hospital. I began to check for his car at the window overlooking the doctor's parking lot. It calmed me to know he was in the building. I looked forward to seeing him alone at his office each week. He sometimes held my hand if I was crying or he gently pushed a strand of hair out of my face.

I was falling in love with this man who was at least fifteen years older than I and married. Knowing what I know now, I can see his culpability in crossing the ethical boundaries between doctor and patient, but back then his actions just proved to me how much he cared. His kindness undid me, and his gentleness and humility endeared him to me. I also think he was shy. When he discovered how ignorant I was about sexual matters, he became flustered, almost blushing. "Just don't let anyone touch you below the waist," he said. I was equally embarrassed about the subject so didn't ask him to explain. In retrospect, I feel he failed me by not being more explicit.

Working together also complicated things. It blurred the boundaries between us. I knew him as a person not just my doctor or therapist. Standing at the Delivery Room door, I'd watch him bring a baby into the world. His blue eyes would

brighten as the baby slipped into his hands. I'd take the baby to
the nursery, feeling proud to be working with him. I respected
him as a physician and heard nothing but praise for him from
his patients. I felt privileged to know him. I sent him this poem:

> *My love for you is a quiet thing*
> *which overtook my soul in little ways.*
> *Unnoticed, it began to shape my life,*
> *and unadorned it showed itself to you.*
>
> *My love for you is an awakening.*
> *With new awareness I embrace each new day*
> *With greater joy I say my morning prayers*
> *No longer sadness rules and tortures me.*
>
> *My love for you is a gentle thing*
> *from which there flows a stream of tenderness.*
> *Although it's meant for you, it overflows,*
> *and touches all who wander near its path.*
>
> *My love for you enriches me*
> *it gives my life a reason to be lived,*
> *perfected, cherished, not to be forgot.*
> *And, through the eyes of love I see my God*
>
> *– Kathleen, 1964*

Dr. Weston never addressed this poem with me except to say
these kinds of feelings are common in therapy, and I'd work
through them in time. He may have been embarrassed by my
declaration of love, but for whatever reason he never mentioned
it again. Meanwhile, that March I turned twenty-one, still naïve
and vulnerable. As spring spread across the hills of Connecticut,
I began to face the reality of my relationship with Dr. Weston.
I knew therapy was coming to an end because I was emerging
from the depression that brought me to his door. It would be
less painful if I was the one to make the break.

Terminating therapy made perfect sense to Dr. Weston
because he felt his work with me was successful. So we stopped
our sessions, but all summer I continued to see him at the
hospital. It was painful not to have private time with him. My
mood shifted into the shadows and began a downward spiral.

One night after work at 11:00 pm, I got in my car and impulsively started driving toward New York City. I arrived at the Staten Island Ferry about 3:30 am. I took the ferry back and forth several times, watching the black water rush against the hull, contemplating how it would feel to drown. Slowly the sun began to rise and the sky was transformed into hues of pink.

My heart lifted with the rising sun. I was suddenly hungry. I drove to my favorite deli to get some breakfast and then to an upscale thrift shop on Madison Avenue that I'd frequented when I was living in New York. There I found a stunning red wool suit with the jewel neckline Jackie Kennedy had made fashionable. I tried it on and looked in the mirror—I liked myself in it, a rare phenomenon. As I drove from New York back to work that day, never having slept or called my mother to let her know where I was, I plotted my escape from the torture of working with Dr. Weston. I sent him one more poem:

There is no need in me, nor need for me.
Untouched by life I am unhurt by it
and touching not another cause no pain.

And so I live as planets long exist
in orbits far removed and lacking aim…
perpetuated by a nothingness.

– Kathleen, 1965

He tracked me down at the hospital, and said he wanted to talk to me. We went to a quiet corner of the floor. I leaned against the brick wall, and he hovered over me, his face close to mine, one arm blocking my escape. He said he was concerned by the tenor of the poem, and he wanted to know if I was in danger of hurting myself. I stayed aloof and cold and said, "No, I'm fine!"

He again voiced his concern and told me I could come back into therapy with him if I needed to. I declined his offer and told him I was moving to Boston at the end of the month, which is exactly what I did. I could not bear being in such close proximity to him, knowing he did not return my love. My heart was aching, but I did not want him to see how much I cared for him. He was my first love, and he remains in my heart to this day.

Oh, my God, I am heartily sorry for having offended thee...

– Excerpt from Catholic Prayer for Confession

CHAPTER FIFTEEN
The Unfathomable

ONE THURSDAY MORNING in August, I borrowed my brother's car and drove to Boston for the day. I found my way to *Boston Children's Hospital* and applied for a job as a nurse's aide. I was hired. I had already enrolled in Bay State College to take a few classes. My last goal was to find a place to live. I wandered around for a while and then turned onto a street lined with trees and small gardens that graced the narrow spaces in front of the brownstone row houses. The late blooming flowers splashed color against the dark bricks.

Several of the brownstones had "Room for Rent" signs in their windows. One had an orange door—my favorite color at the time. I chose it for that reason. I rented a room on the third floor and would be sharing a bathroom with two other people. The building had been a single family home which was converted into a boarding house.

I was charmed by the signs of old-world elegance, which had been spared in the renovation. The raised entrance had a short brick stairway with black wrought-iron filigreed railings. The banister on the staircase inside gracefully curved at each landing. There were delicately carved moldings in the large sitting room.

I wanted to start fresh, away from my mother and Mark. I longed for a minimalist life like the one I lived in the convent. Before I left home, I gave away most of my clothes and belongings, including all of my precious dolls and the red suit I'd bought on Madison Avenue. Without Dr. Weston nothing seemed to matter.

I returned home that day and told my mother what I had done and that I would be leaving on Sunday. She seemed unfazed. Friends drove me to my new home on Sunday, although they questioned my sanity for making such an impulsive decision.

"Are you going to be ok?" one queried.

"I'll be fine," I answered, "Remember I lived in Washington DC and New York City." They were still dubious, but wished me well and went on their way.

I settled into my tiny room, which was not much bigger than the cell I slept in as an aspiring nun.

The next morning I stepped into the brilliant sunlight. The sky was a crisp end-of-summer blue. The flowers greeted me with their sunny disposition, waving in the breeze. I was falling in love with Boston. I started up Brookline Avenue on a mission to get to know the city. As I passed *Beth Israel Hospital*, a red sports car drove up to the curb and stopped. A man with dark hair, wearing a green madras plaid shirt and sports jacket jumped out and approached me.

"I'm looking for the entrance of Beth Israel—can you tell me where it is?" he asked. I couldn't have known then he lived in Boston all his life and knew the answer to that question.

I said, "I have no idea. I just moved here." I kept walking. I was taught never to talk to strangers. He kept following me.

"Where did you come from? What are you doing here? Where are you living?" His staccato questions hung in the air as I walked faster.

I shot back, "I do NOT talk to strangers."

He was not deterred. "I just want to get to know you. Let's go have a bite to eat."

"Absolutely not!"

"Look, I come from a good family. My father is big-time tort lawyer in Boston. Every two years he buys a new Thunderbird with cash," he offered like a fisherman trying another lure when the first one doesn't work. Probably realizing I was unimpressed with this information, he switched tactics. He said, "I share an apartment in Brighton with my cousin, Jason, and I have two brothers and a sister and four nieces and nephews."

I continued to ignore him and kept walking, determined to lose this intrusive man.

He tried one more time. "I'm a graduate student at BU doing research in Sociology, and I've proven blacks are mentally inferior to whites."

I stopped and spun around to face him. In a surprisingly loud voice, I said, "What? Are you crazy? That's impossible!" I turned and started walking away, even faster than before. He kept up with me.

"Well," he said, "it's only a preliminary study, I might be wrong. Why don't we have a cup of coffee to discuss it?"

I was passionate about Civil Rights and thought I might enlighten this man on the subject (the sin of pride!), so I finally relented. "Fine," I said coldly, "but I'm not getting in your car! It will have to be someplace around here."

There was a coffee shop up the street. We made formal introductions as we settled into a booth across from each other. His name was Stanley Cohen—he was called Stan.

Ready for a heated discussion, I sat up straight, prepared for his first volley of words. Instead, Stan's demeanor became softer and his voice quieter. We ordered our coffee. Stan began asking me personal questions again. My answers were curt. I did not want to reveal anything to this stranger. He changed the subject—began telling me more about himself, never mentioning the topic we had come there to discuss.

"I'm Jewish," he said, "and extremely pro-Israel. Kids threw rocks at me and my brother every day as we walked to and from grade school."

"That's horrible!" I said, shocked by this revelation.

"Yeah, my philosophy is: *You step on my foot, I step on your HEAD!* That's how Israel operates," he said proudly.

I was taken aback by the vehemence of his words. He went on. "I had polio when I was ten and was in an iron lung for months, and then I had acute nephritis when I was twelve and spent another few months in the hospital and a year in bed. The nephritis left me with kidney damage—I'll be on blood-pressure medication for the rest of my life. And, I'll never be able to lose this weight." I felt compassion eroding my anger.

Then his tone became wistful. "My dream is to buy a place in the country where I can have animals, including horses, and grow my own food. I want to have a bunch of kids—I love hanging out with my nieces and nephews." I was beginning to see him as a person and not a stranger. I really looked at him for the first time. He was handsome, a little on the heavy side, with dark wavy hair like my brothers.

A man who loved children and animals couldn't be all bad. And, his dream of a country life with a family was one I held but was too afraid to hope for. I felt ugly and deformed with my hunched back and considered myself overweight. Not a likely candidate for marriage.

I began giving Stan a little more information about myself in answer to his questions. When he found out I was staying in a brownstone, sharing a bathroom with two other people, had only $100 to my name, and I didn't know anyone in the city, he became solicitous and protective.

He advised me to open a checking account and put most of my cash in it. He took me to a bank in the vicinity and waited while I opened an account. In case I had a medical emergency, he gave me the name and phone number of his uncle who was a doctor. Then he insisted he needed to see where I was living to make sure it was safe.

Touched by his concern, I finally consented to get in his car and let him drive me to the orange-door brownstone. Still nervous about being in a car with a man I didn't know, I was ready to jump out if I felt he wasn't taking me to our destination. Then I recognized Beacon Street and saw the orange door.

We entered the building and climbed the two flights of stairs in silence. He checked out the bathroom while I unlocked the door to my room. He wanted to know if there were any men on the floor. I said I knew there was one but wasn't sure who was in the other room. We both stepped into my bedroom which held a single bed, a stuffed chair and a small dresser. I thought he would just peek in and go on his way. Instead, he walked straight to the chair and sat down.

Trying not to be impolite, I left the door open a crack and sat cross legged on the bed, my back against the wall. As always, I was wearing a calf-length dress with a full skirt, so my legs were modestly covered. After a little more conversation, it dawned on me that I was alone in my bedroom with a strange man. With a shudder of fear, I started to cry.

Stan showed concern. He asked, "What's wrong?"

"Here I am alone with a strange man in my room, and I've never even been kissed."

I heard a quiet gasp, and he said, "I promise you I'll never do anything to hurt you." I took him at his word because other men, Brian from high school, the young sailor in San Diego, and Paul from my Math class in college, had respected my boundaries without question. So, when Stan asked me to go to dinner with him that night, I accepted his invitation.

He got up to leave. I walked him to the top of the stairwell. He turned and took my face in his hands and gently kissed me on the lips. He said, "Consider yourself kissed." He pulled the hair pins out of my upswept long hair and handed them to me. "Wear your hair down tonight."

I was excited—a real date. The only pretty dress I'd kept when purging my wardrobe was one my mother made. It was a soft silky fabric, red with a subtle yellow, blue and green plaid pattern barely visible. The white peter-pan collar was starched and ironed. It had a long fitted bodice which stopped at the hip and dipped at the center into a V and flowed into a gathered, calf-length skirt. I loved that dress.

I ran across the street to a store and found an inexpensive plastic molded horse to give to Stan. When I returned to my room, I began to get ready. I gingerly took a shower in the shared bathroom, afraid of the germs that might be lurking there, and started to get dressed for the evening. Standing in front of the mirror, I tried to stand up as straight as my hunched back allowed. Although always embarrassed by my stooping posture, I felt pretty when I finished dressing, brushing my hair 100 times and putting lipstick on my lips and cheeks. I wrapped the horse in the tissue paper I had bought and put it back into the brown bag.

Stan arrived on time, came around the car and opened the door for me. I thought that was a good sign—he was a gentleman. As he settled behind the steering wheel, I handed him the bag.

He said, "What's this?"

"Just a small gift to thank you for helping me this afternoon."

He un-wrapped the gift and looked stunned. He said, "I can't believe you did this for me!" His eyes were glistening.

"Oh, it's nothing," I said, feeling uncomfortable. "I'm sorry it's plastic but it's all I could afford. There were some beautiful wooden horses there."

"It's perfect!" he said, giving me a quick hug.

Stan explained, as we drove to the restaurant, that although his father had money and had given him the Alpha Romero we were riding in, he was on his own to pay for his education. He claimed he was just a poor student and could not afford to take me to a fancy restaurant. I said, "That's fine. I'm not a fancy person."

We ate at a bar and grill in Kenmore Square. After we finished, we took a walk around the square. Stan said, "I wish I could take you to the movies but I don't have any money. Why don't you come to my apartment and we'll watch TV and then I'll take you home." I didn't want to embarrass him by ending the evening early, so I agreed.

The apartment was not far from Kenmore Square. Stan drove through a maze of crisscrossing back streets with dim street lights to his apartment on Liberty Ave. It occurred to me that I would never be able to find my way back to Beacon Street on my own.

The apartment was almost completely below ground. We descended a half flight of stairs, and he unlocked the door. We entered a dingy, sparsely furnished living room and dining area with a small dark kitchen behind it.

Stan's roommate, Jason, was not at home. I hadn't noticed there was no television in the living room, when Stan opened the door to his bedroom. He explained that Jason and he each had a TV in their bedrooms because they rarely wanted to watch the same thing.

As I walked through the door of his bedroom I realized there was only a bed in the right far corner, with the headboard under the basement window and no chairs. The TV was at the foot of the bed. I was uncomfortable with this arrangement but didn't say anything, again not wanting to hurt his feelings. Stan took some pillows from the living room and offered me a place on the bed near the wall in a nest of pillows. He turned on the TV and asked what I liked to watch.

"Nothing scary," I replied. Those words later rang in my ears.

He turned the TV on to a sit-com I enjoyed and came to sit by me on the bed. He put his left arm around my shoulder. I remembered his promise and tried to relax. He started to rub my arm and then gently kissed me on the cheek. I was getting very warm and feeling pleasantly strange. I did not ask him to stop—my skin felt thirsty for this kind of touch. His right hand began to roam lightly around my waist—it felt intoxicating. When he put his hand on my breast, I froze in fear.

I said, "I want to go home."

"We just got here. Relax!"

Before I could protest any further, he yanked me down on the bed and was under my skirt, roughly pulling down my panties and entering me. He made strange movements; his face contorted; he breathed hard and made groaning sounds. He looked crazed. I was terrified. I was sure he was going to kill me. I'd never seen anyone look or sound or move like this. Suddenly, I felt something wet, and he seemed to relax, dropping his full weight on my body. I didn't move. I didn't know what he was going to do next. Would he kill me? He began to gently kiss my face again.

Numb with shock, my voice barely audible, I said, "I want to go home now."

He said, "OK," and stood up.

"You promised not to hurt me," I said, as I started to shake.

"I didn't hurt you," he said gruffly. "I didn't penetrate all the way. You're still a virgin."

Shivering—as I am now as I write this—I went to the bathroom to pull myself together. There was a sticky, white substance between my legs. I was trembling. Feeling disgusting and filthy, I cleaned up as best I could. He was waiting at the front door when I came out, casually talking about showing me around Boston and finding me another place to live. We got in the car, and he continued to talk as we drove back to my place. I sat in silence still shaking. He came around and opened the car door for me and walked me up the steps to the entrance. He gently kissed me on the lips and said he'd see me in the morning for breakfast at nine.

I unlocked the front door as quickly as I could, slammed it behind me and ran up the stairs. My hands shaking uncontrollably, I unlocked the door to my room and started to sob as I closed it behind me. I made a dash for the shower. I quickly undressed in the bathroom, I knew I never wanted to see these clothes again and threw them in the trash, including my much loved red dress. It was August 31, 1965.

Holding back the flood of pain and fear roaring through my body, I cried quietly through the shower, so as not to disturb my housemates. I collapsed on the bed and sobbed into my pillow until, exhausted, I fell asleep. Early the next morning I woke up feeling like my body was bruised from the inside out. My head felt huge and heavy, and my eyes were swollen from crying. I felt sick to my stomach. The feeling of disgust sent me directly to the shower again.

Even after scrubbing my body for twenty minutes, I felt defiled, dirty. No one would ever want me, not even God. I had sinned. I felt abhorrent and ashamed. I determined that the only way I could rectify this sinful state was to marry this man and learn to love him. How did he know exactly what to say to make me turn around and talk to him? I wondered if the V in my long torso dress had been seductive and led this man to believe I was a loose woman. I berated myself for being so stupid as to go to his apartment.

I knew I had to meet Stan for breakfast and pretend nothing had happened. My face was a mess. I put an icy cold wash cloth on my eyes to get the swelling down. This was my third day in Boston.

Much later, I discovered this was a textbook description of a woman's reaction to that for which I had no name, other than "my sin."

And, it wasn't until fifty years later that I learned I was not the first woman Stan had assaulted this way. Ten months earlier, he'd done the same thing to another young woman—but, unencumbered by Catholic doctrine, she realized she was a victim of rape and pressed charges.

She filled out a police report after the assault and described exactly what I had experienced—in fact Stan even used the same line about being a poor graduate student and suggested they listen to music at his apartment because he had no money. I have tremendous admiration for her courage, but Stan's father pulled strings and got the charges dismissed.

~

I dreaded seeing Stan again but by then I was beyond fear—the worst had happened already—I now knew to be on guard. I wouldn't allow myself to be put in a vulnerable position. I was numb, almost in a trance, when Stan arrived at 9:00 am. I was waiting at the door. He opened the car door for me and placed a quick kiss on my lips. Neither of us mentioned the night before.

He proudly took me to a famous deli in Brookline called *Jack and Marion's*. He said his father was paying for breakfast and to order anything I wanted. I had no appetite. After we ordered, while we waited for our meal to arrive, Stan said he wanted to marry me. Shocked, I remained silent. My head was spinning—how could this be? He then told me we were going to the business district in downtown Boston that afternoon so his father could meet me.

Stan kept hounding me on the subject of marriage all morning, talking about the life we could have together. He was gentle and affectionate, unlike the night before when he handled me so roughly. My instinct was to run as far as I could from this man, but the Church's indoctrination was so deeply etched in my psyche that it didn't occur to me until years later that this assault wasn't my sin.

The Church taught that God has a plan for each of us and although we might not understand it, we are called upon to accept what happens. *God's Will Be Done!* I thought marriage to Stan was part of God's plan for me so I could be forgiven for the mortal sin I had committed. With silent desolation, I said, "Yes," to Stan's proposal of marriage. He immediately went to a phone booth and called his father to give him the news.

On the way to his father's law office, Stan took me to the Boston Public Gardens, a large open green space in the middle of Boston, with gardens, a pond with lily pads, swan boats, and walking paths with small foot bridges over waterways. I was enchanted.

Then we went to meet his father. I was nervous, and I sensed Stan was, too. The receptionist showed us into his father's large, barren, high-ceilinged office with long fluorescent lights. David Cohen was a big man, over six feet tall and well-over three hundred pounds. He had wavy gray hair and a warm smile. He got up from behind his huge mahogany desk, piled with stacks of files, and came around it to shake my hand. He indicated for us to sit down on the hard straight-backed chairs across the room from him with a huge expanse of an empty worn wooden floor between us. He took his place behind the desk and began to grill me with questions as if I was on the witness stand.

"Where did your family come from? What did your father do for work? Are you going to college? Why did you come to Boston?" The questions continued for a half an hour, and then he stood up. Stan and I jumped to our feet—this man's stature and status commanded respect. He came around the desk with a big smile on his face, his eyes sparkling and his arms opened wide. He enveloped me in a hug and said, "Welcome to the family! You can call me Papa, like my grandchildren do."

Stan looked relieved to have his father's blessing on the marriage. I was taken with this smiling, charismatic man and began to feel a little better about saying *yes* to Stan. Papa, as I now called him, was warm and fatherly. He seemed to like me, so I felt certain he would make sure Stan treated me well.

Later I learned that Papa did not treat his own wife well. He could be demanding and controlling, though generous. Stan's mother and father often argued in front of the family. They raised their children in a huge old mansion on Sherwood Lane in Lansing, an affluent Boston suburb, with all the advantages money can buy.

That night, Stan took me out to dinner again and told me my conversion to Judaism was not a prerequisite to marriage, but it would make his parents happy. I said, "I'll think about it." I loved the Jewish traditions and was searching for a spiritual home, so I considered conversion a real possibility. Although my Catholic conscience clung to me like seaweed, I felt a sense of hope that Judaism would alter my perspective. I wanted to embody the joy and aliveness I saw in my Jewish friends and their families.

~

Later, Stan also made it clear that now we were engaged he had sexual privileges with me, although he didn't want anyone to know we were having sex. I protested that sex came after marriage, not before. Stan ignored this, and my resolve did not hold for long as my body responded to his every touch. I had never felt these sensations before and found them baffling. I had always imagined that love was a prerequisite to sexual feelings— now it seemed my body was alien to my heart.

That night, Stan forced me to perform oral sex, holding my head down until he came in my mouth. I was mortified and disgusted, appalled someone would do this to me. It was as traumatizing as the first night with him. This was beyond my comprehension. I walked around bewildered, ashamed, terrified. Stan demanded oral sex frequently no matter how much I objected. In my naiveté, I thought it meant he was gay. Some months later, I finally got up the nerve to tell a friend about it and asked her if this was a sign he was gay.

She laughed and said, "No! My husband wants it that way all the time, too." I was stunned to hear this, but it did allay my fears about Stan being homosexual.

After the second night of trauma, Stan insisted I call my mother and tell her about our engagement. I was reluctant to do so because I expected an angry response. I called her as he hovered over me.

I said, "Mom, I've met a nice Jewish man and he wants to marry me." This was my fourth day in Boston.

She said, "Good, Jewish men make good husbands. When's the wedding?"

I was shocked. I wanted her to say, "What are you thinking? Come home right now." I couldn't tell her why I had made this reckless decision. I was supposed to be her pure, untouched alabaster beauty. She seemed relieved that a man actually wanted to marry me and would take care of me. She wouldn't have to worry about me anymore. I felt utterly alone standing next to the man I was going to marry.

~

Thirty years later, an osteopath I'd seen regularly for years and trusted implicitly, put his finger in my mouth to check my jaw alignment during a treatment. I froze and he quickly pulled his finger out of my mouth and asked, "What's wrong?"

I couldn't speak. Finally, I said, "I don't know" and ran out of the room. My heart was pounding on the drive back to my apartment and I huddled under the blankets in bed until I could manage to call my therapist and make an appointment to see her. She couldn't see me for three days.

Still not knowing what was going on, I stayed sheltered in my apartment not even taking phone calls until the day of my appointment. I curled up in a chair across from my therapist, Loretta, and wrapped myself head to toe in an afghan she always had handy, feeling totally ashamed and humiliated.

I finally explained to her what happened with my doctor and together we began to unravel the memory this innocuous event had triggered—the second traumatic night with Stan. We worked on this trauma for weeks, with talk therapy and a method called Eye Movement Desensitization and Reprocessing (EMDR) which uses eye movements to rewire the brain. It was an experimental form of therapy then, but now is used routinely with Veterans and other trauma victims. This therapeutic work helped lesson my reactivity to triggers around the trauma.

I went back to my osteopath who had called me after the incident in his office, upset about my reaction and fearing he had done something wrong. I explained what had happened and assured him it was not his fault. He understood, but after that he was afraid to touch me. We had a strong connection, and yet I couldn't continue to see him. I didn't want to put him through another episode of what was now being labeled PTSD (Post Traumatic Stress Disorder).

~

On Friday, five days after I met him, Stan took me to Shabbat dinner to meet his family at their huge brick mansion on Sherwood Lane. Their home was magnificent with mahogany paneling, a long sloping staircase, high ceilings, elegant décor and a multitude of rooms.

Stan introduced me as his fiancée. There was no exclamation of surprise. There were a few mumbled prayers, but the evening wasn't a religious ritual, it was about the food and being together as a family. Stan's brothers and sister and their spouses warmly accepted me. No one in this Jewish family questioned our hasty decision to get married or seemed concerned that I wasn't Jewish. It never occurred to me to wonder why.

~

When I learned about the previous rape fifty years after it happened, I realized Stan must have immediately told his father he had done it again—that he had raped another woman. Knowing Papa, I could picture his red-faced response and booming voice, "How could you be so stupid! This time I'm not going to bail you out! Either you marry her and make it right or you're on your own!" Thus, the urgent proposal the very next day. Papa probably assumed I'd press charges or demand financial reparations, not knowing I blamed myself for losing my virginity. I suspect the rest of his family knew Stan had assaulted me and were relieved I had agreed to marry him. My heart freezes at the thought.

The first rose on my rose-tree
Budded, Bloomed, and shattered,
During sad days when to me
Nothing mattered.

Grief of grief has drained me clean;
Still it seems a pity
No one saw,—it must have been
Very pretty.

– Excerpted from "Three Songs of Shattering" in *Renascence*
by Edna St. Vincent Millay

CHAPTER SIXTEEN
The Shattering

MARRIAGE would be my redemption. I was determined to kill myself if Stan did not marry me. Not a rational response to my dilemma since suicide was considered the ultimate sin against God, but I could not bear the thought of living in this defiled state. And I was sure no one else would ever want me. The only way I could reconcile what had happened was to believe God had given me a mission to love Stan so he'd be transformed into a good, caring person. Why else would he have known exactly what to say to make me turn around and talk to him?

Although this all sounds farfetched in a world where pre-marital sex is the norm, the sexual revolution had just begun and was still under the radar for those of us born in the 1940's. The Church dictated abstinence before marriage, but even those who were not religious were expected to wait to have sex until the wedding day or at least to *appear* to have waited. I didn't understand until many years later that the Catholic Church's teachings left me vulnerable to a predator like Stan.

I was shattered by the sexual trauma. The stain of sin was imprinted on my body and soul. And, I was pummeled daily by

Stan's constant rage in those first few weeks of our relationship. He had been so insistent that I marry him, I assumed he loved me. Now he seemed to hate me. With each passing day it became harder for me to envision loving this man. Stan's rage now makes sense if his father forced him to marry me to "make things right."

I soon learned that he didn't need a reason to be angry. He was angry all the time. If I contradicted him in any way or didn't respond to his commands fast enough, he called me vile names. I had never heard anyone speak to another person like that even in my emotionally volatile home. He passed judgment on what I wore and how I looked. He demanded I buy more stylish, revealing clothes and insisted I wear make-up, "So you won't look half-dead." Everything I did and said was under scrutiny. What little confidence I had diminished.

He told me where to live and work—he ordered me to get a secretarial job downtown because it would pay more than the hospital. And, he insisted I forget my plans for college. There was no discussion.

A few days after we met, Stan found a place for me to live in the home of an elderly Irish Catholic woman, Mrs. Clark. My room was on the third floor, in a dark attic space, again reminiscent of the sleeping quarters of my convent days. It had its own bathroom which was important to Stan because he didn't want me to have contact with other men. I was relieved that it was clean. Mrs. Clark was lonely and demanded my attention whenever I was around. She had a grand piano in her living room, which I played quietly when alone. It was a source of comfort in those early days with Stan.

I dutifully found work downtown as a research secretary at Loomis, Sayles & Company, a highly regarded financial investment firm. It did pay more, but I longed to be caring for the tiny patients at Children's Hospital. I felt competent as a nurse's aide. I never felt competent as a secretary. Although I had a kind British boss, the job left me frazzled and drained at the end of the day. I was out of my element working with numbers and charts.

But, the Office Manager, Olive, and another secretary, Cassie, quickly became my friends, supporting me through the next three years. Finding sources of support became crucial to my ability to survive in the midst of the emotional battering I experienced at home.

Stan started to give me pieces of the truth as things slipped from his friends' and relatives' lips: he was not a graduate student at Boston University. He had never graduated college, although he spent over five years going to classes when he wanted to, flunking out or dropping out of various academic institutions. His father paid for everything and would've continued paying for him to go to school indefinitely. He begged Stan to go back to college. His son refused.

When I met Stan, his father still supported him, paid for his apartment, food, gas and insurance for his car. Stan's line about being a poor student was a lie. He had never had a job by the time I met him—he was 25 years old. He was in no hurry to find work but made sure I went to work on time every morning. Always an early riser, Stan would come by Mrs. Clark's to walk me to my trolley stop and send me off each day with $1.00 in my purse, which was barely enough to pay for the trolley and a cup of coffee. I would have to account for every cent I spent when he picked me up to take me back to his apartment for the evening. He also took control of my paycheck.

Often I would round a corner on my lunch hour and find Stan standing there checking up on me. One time he caught me eating an ice-cream cone. He got angry because he wanted me to lose weight, although he had a greater weight problem than I did. If I mentioned a male co-worker, he flew into a rage. I learned to say as little as possible, and if he found out something I hadn't mentioned, he called me sneaky and said he couldn't trust me.

Stan verbally harassed me in loud tirades calling me a fucking idiot, stupid asshole, God damn bitch, and countless demeaning names. I was used to my parents arguing. They yelled at each other, but they didn't call each other names and never used obscene language. Stan was louder and more frightening than any of my sometimes scary family members, especially when he was drinking. I would take it at first, determined not to give this man an excuse to call off the wedding. We were told by the nuns that women must be subservient to men. It was a woman's job to take care of her husband and follow his commands. I complied.

These same women, who had never been married, told us that we were to give into our husband's sexual demands or it was our fault if he strayed. I carried these messages into the marriage. The lack of sex education in the schools, and the inability of my family to discuss sexual matters, added to my ignorance. But, ultimately, it was my obsession with remaining pure that was my undoing.

When I met Stan's roommate, his cousin Jason, I thought he was more sophisticated and cultured than Stan. Jason and I talked about classical music and art. I began to think I had met the wrong man. Then Jason brought a young woman home. Her name was Sherry—very pretty, an only child of wealthy parents. She and Jason began going steady, and I saw another side of him emerge. He was as abusive to Sherry as Stan was to me. He also could be loud and crude and domineering.

Stan and I often socialized with Sherry and Jason—we'd have supper together in the apartment or watch a TV show on the newly acquired living room TV set. Everyone drank copious amounts of liquor, except me. I didn't like the way liquor tasted or how even a sip of it made me feel. The drunker Stan and Jason got the more competitive they became.

One night, in front of Sherry and me, they started comparing their conquests with woman before they met us. They talked about *cruising* the streets for a *matinee* each day, which was what Stan was doing when he picked me up. Then, they started arguing about who had gotten the most Catholic virgins in bed. It was like they had notches on their belts to represent each woman they had defiled. I felt sick. Sherry seemed to think it was a big joke—she'd had many sexual experiences before she met Jason. It was not a joke to me. This man who wanted an untouched bride had violated countless women, including me, but to my mind it was still the women's fault because they and I had allowed ourselves to be duped.

Stan and Jason's lives mirrored each other. They had been close since childhood. Whether it was the result of competition between them or their affinity for each other, they always seemed to be doing the same thing at the same time. Thus, Jason proposed to Sherry, and they were married shortly before our wedding.

~

Several weeks after we were engaged, we went to see the Rabbi to discuss the possibility of my converting to Judaism. Stan's parents belonged to Temple Israel in Brookline, one of the most esteemed Reform Jewish synagogues in the country. Rabbi Roland Gittleson presided over the congregation with his Assistant Rabbi, Harvey Fields. Rabbi Gittleson was the first member of the clergy to speak out against the Vietnam War from the Bema (Pulpit).

His liberal political stance was refreshing to me after the conservatism of the nuns with whom I had lived. I attended Saturday Services at *Temple Israel* several times and was inspired by Rabbi Gittleson. According to his book, *Man's Best Hope*, God, the Source and Creator of all, had brought Creation into existence and is One with that Creation, experiencing its unfolding, not controlling it. This paradigm meant I could not credit or blame God for what was happening in my life. I was to accept my fate as the unfolding of the Universe.

My dilemma was that I was comforted by the assumption, fostered by the Catholic Church, that it was God's will at play in the story of my encounter with Stan. I couldn't imagine how a loving God would let this happen to me unless there was an underlying plan that led to good. However, I was also intrigued by Gittleson's idea that God sets everything in motion and then cannot intervene in Creation. There was no comfort in this concept of God—and I needed the solace of God's Presence and Love at this time. Still, reading Rabbi Gittleson's books set forth a shift in my consciousness to a more cosmic, integral concept of God that would grow roots and spring to life in the future.

By the time we arrived at Rabbi Fields' book-lined office, decorated in warm honey tones, I was certain I wanted to convert to Judaism. I loved the Jewish traditions and the depth and beauty of the teachings. Catholicism had been all about sacrifice and dying. Judaism was life-affirming and joyous. Rabbi Fields questioned both Stan and me about our beliefs.

When we were finished, he looked at me and said, "You're already Jewish!" Then, he looked at Stan and said, "You need to come to conversion classes with her. Your beliefs come from another era!" So, for six weeks Stan and I showed up each week for a two-hour class. Rabbi Fields chose the Hebrew name *Barucha* for me, which means *blessing*. I was touched by his choice. We set the day for my conversion and our wedding to be January 9, 1966.

In the interim, Stan's father brought me to a jewelry store to pick out my wedding band for which he was paying. We had a lovely afternoon together. He took me to lunch and began to confide some of his disappointments in life. The greatest was that none of his children wanted to finish their education and take over his law practice.

Then he explained why he hadn't bought me an engagement ring. He told me Stan had been engaged to an opera singer in New York City the year before. Papa had bought them a house in Natick, an expensive suburb of Boston, and the red Alpha Romero Stan was driving. He paid for the engagement ring and wedding bands and a huge expensive wedding because the bride's parents couldn't afford it.

Stan broke off the engagement and called off the wedding days before the event. Papa was left with a financial mess. He was not going to make the same mistake twice. He bought me a beautiful wedding band that day. I cherished it more for the memory of spending time with him than for the meaning it had as a marriage bond between Stan and me. I feared marriage to Stan would be more bondage than a bond.

Some weeks later, I finally got up the nerve to tell Stan what his father had told me about his previous engagement. I asked him why he had called it off. He said, nonchalantly, "I found out a few days before the wedding that she wasn't a virgin when I met her." He told me he wanted to marry someone who was completely untouched, who had never even been kissed. He'd given up hope of finding a woman who met that criterion until he met me. Now I wonder about the timing of this decision and speculate that it may have had more to do with the fact that he raped another woman while still engaged to the opera singer. I will never know.

Stan's sexual/emotional degradation continued unabated even as we neared the Big Day. I kept telling myself he would change once we were married. He was just nervous, like all bridegrooms, and besides he was going to start his first job the day after our wedding. Things would settle down after we got into a routine.

I wept the night before the wedding. Something deep in my heart whispered a warning I would not heed. The next morning, Mrs. Clark informed me that she would not be attending our wedding. She said she wanted to, but a mixed marriage was against her Catholic faith. My brother, Joseph, a fanatic Catholic, called at the last minute and said the same thing. Many years later he apologized for not being there.

My Jewish conversion ceremony was held the morning of our wedding in Rabbi Fields' office with only Stan and his parents present to witness the event. It was simple, yet profound. Rabbi Fields gave me my Hebrew name. I felt welcomed and respected by him as I dedicated myself to Judaism.

In the late afternoon, both our families gathered at the Cohen mansion to witness our wedding. My in-laws arranged a buffet supper after the ceremony, knowing my mother could not afford the expense. I hadn't tried on or even seen the dress my mother made for me. She chose a beautiful white satin brocade fabric. The dress fit perfectly, the bodice flowing into an A-line skirt which fell below the knee, in spite of Stan's and his mother's displeasure at my longer than *mini-skirt* hemlines. Mom sent me some of the dress fabric at the last minute, and I made a headpiece for myself the night before the wedding.

I felt beautiful as I solemnly walked down the lovely old staircase into a living room full of people. Papa beamed at me. Rabbi Fields presided over the traditional Jewish ceremony which included Stan stomping on and crushing a wineglass under his foot. I identified with the broken glass. After the ceremony, Papa gave me a diamond engagement ring as my wedding present.

My mother-in-law was less than enthusiastic about her son marrying a "goy" (a derogatory word for a gentile) even one who had converted to Judaism. I was allowed to call her "Mother," although I did not find her to be a motherly woman. She dressed with an aristocratic elegance, and she was determined to make me over into a worthy daughter-in-law.

She started with criticizing my clothes as outdated and "goyisha" colors. My skirts needed to be shorter, above the knee, because that was the latest style. It did not matter that I was uncomfortable in skirts that short or that I loved color. She also wanted me to stop writing poetry. I made the mistake of sharing some of my poems with her, and she found them too depressing. She was an artist, so I showed her my art work which she deemed amateurish. It was, but I had enjoyed painting until that point. I was to drop these creative endeavors and concentrate on being a good wife to her son. I never felt good enough around her although in later years she softened towards me and respected me as the mother of her grandchildren whom she adored.

Recently, one of my mother-in-law's grandchildren wrote a beautiful tribute to her on what would have been her hundredth birthday. I realized how harshly I had judged this woman because of my experience with her in those early years. Now I feel compassion for her. No doubt she was appalled by her son's actions and a daughter-in-law who was not Jewish and did not conform to her standards. She did her best to make a place for me in her family—for that I am grateful.

~

The secret the Cohen family held for fifty years, that Stan raped another woman ten months before he raped me, had devastating consequences. Stan's parents were aware that he tormented his siblings and that his anger was out of control. They withheld those vital facts and let me walk into the lion's den.

Secret keeping is a form of betrayal. I understand this now: I kept our family's secrets and was the victim of the Cohen family's secrets. Still, I hold the responsibility for not speaking the truth or even acknowledging the truth of what Stan did to me; instead I viewed everything through the lens of the Catholic doctrine of sin and the need for redemption.

~

My love for Judaism deepened even though I was living among a secular Jewish family. They celebrated the major holidays and adhered to some of the Jewish rituals, but they were assimilated Jews and blended in with the affluent society around them. One of the first of many songs that fell from the sky and sang through me was a Jewish sounding melody that started with the words, "I am...I am...I am a Jew and I'm proud." When I excitedly sang it for my mother-in-law, she informed me that Jewish people do not call themselves Jews. I felt ashamed that I didn't know that. (And, later found out it isn't true.)

Before the wedding, Stan and I had rented and set up an apartment on the second floor of a brand new concrete building on Brighton Avenue in a working class neighborhood. Stan had insisted on keeping up the charade that we weren't having sex and always took me back to Mrs. Clark's no matter what the hour. We returned to our apartment after the ceremony for our first full night together. Stan made no pretense at playing the thoughtful husband. We had unromantic, perfunctory sex, and he watched TV as I discreetly cried into my pillow.

We both got up the next morning and went to work. People asked if I was upset that I didn't have a honeymoon. I said, "Absolutely not! He's going to work for the first time in his life! I'm so relieved!" I thought I might be the sole bread-winner forever. With his father's help, Stan was hired as a salesman in the textile industry. He complained endlessly about having to work, but he stuck with it and developed a good work ethic. He became an excellent salesman—it was a job that suited his personality.

Perhaps most tragically,
when we work so hard to be special
there is no time to be alive.

– Excerpt from "Celebration of Being Ordinary" by Jennifer Louden

CHAPTER SEVENTEEN
Stolen Tears

EACH EVENING, I climbed the stairs to our apartment wrung out from the day at work and the long crowded trolley ride. Stan, who was already home and relaxing, would demand I start cooking immediately, usually for both himself and a friend. I was determined to be a good wife. However, my own mother had never allowed me in the kitchen to learn to cook. Mom had run out of patience with children under her feet in her kitchen by the time I came along. I didn't know anything about cooking or baking.

Stan and his family assumed that since I was Italian I must be a good cook. The second time I went to dinner at the family home, his mother asked me to make the salad. I had no idea what to do but tried to remember how my mother's salads looked and made something that resembled hers.

My Jewish father-in-law, not my Italian mother, taught me how to make pizza and how to cook lobster. He also taught me how to broil kippers since Mother would not allow him to make them at home because she couldn't stand the smell. (Neither could I, but I would do anything for Papa.) I even tried to make him homemade bagels and a beautifully braided, golden crusted challah bread. *Tried* is the operative word here: the bagels turned into rocks in thirty seconds, and I left the salt out of the Challah. As Papa bit into the first piece of bread, I could see from his expression that something was wrong, and he was trying to decide if he should tell me. He said, "Bread tastes flat without the salt." I never forgot the salt again.

My first efforts at cooking for Stan were failures, which would set him off, especially if one of his male friends was with us for dinner. I got better with time, but if the meat was too well done or something did not come out just right, he would rage at the dinner table. I began to dread each meal.

Meanwhile, Stan wanted a Siamese cat and brought home *Chocolate*. He would cook steak for the cat, affectionately stroke her and hold her, give her the kind of attention he never gave me. I became jealous of this beautiful animal.

Perhaps if we had a baby, I thought, this nurturing side of Stan would come out, and we'd be a happy family. Besides, I wanted someone to love and love me. As much as I tried to love Stan, I felt wounded and afraid most of the time. Although he would rarely say he loved me, I think he did in his own way, but I couldn't feel his love through the barrage of criticism and bullying.

Every once in a while Stan would do something kind and thoughtful, and I'd try to convince myself that was the *real* Stan. If he hadn't been drinking, which was rare, he could be a gentle lover. Those momentary lapses in his usual indifference or outright cruelty made me long for more kindness and tenderness.

Meanwhile, I was losing pieces of myself by the day. I had no time alone, didn't write in my journal for fear Stan would find it, and was too self-conscious to sing through the day as I used to do. I didn't play the music I loved on the radio because Stan hated classical music. Time with my family diminished as did time with friends. My world became circumscribed by Stan's needs.

~

In time, I began to feel more at ease and less self-conscious when I was with Stan's family on Friday nights. I bonded with Stan's nieces and nephews. Before dinner, the children, my sisters-in-law and I went to the front of the house to stand on the massive stone steps and wait for Papa to arrive home from work. He brightened when he saw us, and as he stepped out of his Thunderbird, we surrounded him with hugs and chatter. I think it was the highlight of his long week.

There was a great deal of laughing and good-natured kidding at the dinner table. I'd seen this joy for life in the homes of my Jewish friends. It was something I loved about the Jewish traditions. After dinner, Papa would sometimes ask me to play the piano even though I was out of practice. He loved hearing the classical music I played, knowing it was just for him.

On Sunday nights, the Cohen family gathered again—this time at Papa's favorite Chinese restaurant—and consumed ten or twelve huge trays of food with an array of appetizers and entrees. My own scattered family only gathered once or twice a year. The Cohens ate together twice weekly. I began to have a sense of belonging I'd never felt in my own home. Stan was on his best behavior in front of his father, so I was guaranteed a peaceful evening when we were all together. Although I was still nervous in the presence of my mother-in-law, Papa beamed at me from across the room.

~

Judy Feinberg, my brother Mark's, ex-girlfriend, moved to Boston shortly after I did. She started to come over to visit or have dinner with us. Stan liked her—she was Jewish and had a great sense of humor. But, Judy didn't like Stan. She finally said, "I can't see you anymore, Kath. I can't stand the way Stan treats you." She was a feisty woman, and she didn't understand why I didn't fight back. I could never tell her why I had married him, and why I felt I had to stay. The shame and guilt I felt about losing my virginity outside of marriage haunted me.

In time, I lost other friends for the same reason. Stan had no compunction about yelling at me or belittling me in front of others. One day, after we moved to a garden apartment in Watertown, my mother came to visit. I found her looking out the screen door quietly crying—the mother who rarely cried. I asked her what was wrong. She said, "I want to go home. I can't watch Stan mistreat you like this." She never mentioned it again in the fourteen years she lived, although she continued to witness Stan's persecution not only of me, but of our children as well. Of course, in all those years, I never told her what happened the day I met Stan that made me feel compelled to marry him and remain married.

My discontent and loneliness in those early days of the marriage became a shroud around my personality. I was repressed, less articulate—like I had been after leaving the convent. I was constantly monitoring myself so as not to upset Stan. I felt like a commodity, a possession. The symbol of his sexual prowess now became how many orgasms I had when we had sex. My body, without my consent, was very responsive. He counted my orgasms like he had counted his conquests when comparing notes with Jason. I wrote:

> *Making love*
> *with a knot in my throat*
> *unseen tears in my eyes*
> *having orgasm after orgasm*
> *and wishing only*
> *that I could die*

~

While attending a conference on domestic violence thirty years later, an expert on sexual assault explained that, "The unbidden response of one's body when being sexually abused is the most confusing and disturbing aspect of the violation for many victims. The victim often interprets this response as meaning "she wanted it." This leads to tremendous self-loathing and a sense that her own body has betrayed her." I wept with recognition and relief.

~

During those years, I went underground, numb, holding my breath; I tried to erase myself—it was the only way I felt safe. As Edna St. Vincent Millay wrote:

Deep in the earth I rested now;
Cool is its hand upon the brow
And soft its breast beneath the head
Of one who is so gladly dead.
And all at once, and over all
The pitying rain began to fall;
I lay and heard each pattering hoof
Upon my lowly, thatchéd roof,
And seemed to love the sound far more
Than ever I had done before.
For rain it hath a friendly sound
To one who's six feet underground;
And scarce the friendly voice or face:
A grave is such a quiet place.

~

Six months after Stan and I were married, my mother called and said my brother, Tony, was sick. She and Mark were going out to San Diego to check on him. I questioned what was wrong. Mom said, "He had minor surgery and there were some complications."

"Mom, I want to go with you!"

"Oh, there's no need for that, besides you shouldn't take time off from work. I'll call you when I get there and know more."

Tony and I had continued corresponding ever since I'd been with him on my second visit when I was eighteen. We were having a slight disagreement via the mail about how to raise children. He was military, a strict disciplinarian, and I was reading a book by A.S. Neil called *Summerhill* about a liberal form of child-rearing. I hadn't received an answer to my last letter.

Three days after my mother and Mark reached his bedside, Tony was dead at the age of forty-three. It was June 7, 1966.

Information was again withheld from me for my *protection*, even as an adult. My mother and brother had decided not to tell me how serious Tony's situation was. They didn't tell me what they knew as they flew to his bedside. Tony was in a Navy hospital. He had started to bleed internally after the surgery, and he was given the wrong type of blood, a sure death sentence. He was dying for three days, and he knew it and so did everyone else, except me.

Once again, the *baby* was not told. My family continued to see me as a child, when I was already a woman honed by adversity. I was "protected" by secrets, kept in the dark, forbidden access to the truth, which denied me the right to make informed choices in my life.

Shattered by the news of Tony's death, I wanted to fly out to be there for the funeral. My mother firmly said my presence would just add to the confusion, and Stan said we didn't have the money. I knew Papa would give it to me if I asked, but my mother was adamant.

I was inundated with grief. I felt my heart falling out of my chest—hardly able to catch my breath. Tony was more than a brother to me: he was a friend, a father, a mentor. He was rooted in my soul. Just knowing he was in the world grounded me and gave me hope. Now he was gone. I was in shock. Pinned down by sorrow—I could not move, sleep or eat—unable to control the tears that flowed unabated from my unseeing eyes.

Then, on the third day after Tony's death, the day the funeral was being held in San Diego, Stan insisted I go back to work—that it would be a good distraction for me. I pulled myself together and put on makeup in an attempt to hide my swollen eyes.

Everyone at work was astonished to see me walk in the door. My boss and friends were kind and tried to comfort me as I struggled to contain my tears and be productive. By late morning I felt sadness overwhelming my defenses. I called Papa and asked him to meet me for lunch, something I had never done before. I hoped I could just let go and cry on his massive shoulder. When we met and he saw tears in my eyes, Papa said, "You've cried enough." I was stunned, but assumed he knew what was best. From then on, I internalized my grief, leaving me numb and lifeless.

Tony and I had not spoken on the phone for some time, so I began to question if my last letter had caused a rift between us. I felt so guilty for having questioned his parenting. I knew what a wonderful parent he was even if he was strict. This concern became an obsession. The pall of my grief hung over my days. I entered therapy after several years and was encouraged to openly grieve. The log-jam in my heart began to break up.

Then, I had an amazing dream. I saw a one-story California redwood house with a huge tree hanging over the left side of it. My brother, Tony, came out and walked across the lawn to about three feet in front of me—he was smiling, tanned and relaxed—vividly alive. I recognized his voice when he said, "Don't worry about me. I'm fine. I'm happy here." And, I awoke.

Twenty years after this dream I asked a friend, who was going to San Diego, to find my brother's grave in the military cemetery on Point Loma and say a prayer at his gravesite. She sent me a picture of his resting place. There, hanging over the left side of Tony's grave, was the tree I had seen in my dream. I later learned the tree wasn't there when he was buried—it had grown out of his grave.

I saw his grave for the first time thirty years after he died. He rested high on a hill covered with perfectly aligned rows of white gravestones overlooking the Pacific Ocean. A deciduous tree, like the one I saw in my dream, grew to the left of his grave and hung over it. I remembered standing with Tony on a similar spot in the cemetery when I was fifteen. He was thirty-six. And, I remembered his words: *This is where I want to be someday.* He got his wish seven years later.

When I returned to Point Loma, fourteen years after that, the tree was gone. It had to be removed because it had knocked over Tony's headstone and disturbed some other graves around it. I believe he was so full of life when he died, his energy could not be contained in one small plot of earth. I was saddened by the loss of his tree.

I told Tony's three oldest children about the dream, but his youngest son, Tim, continued to struggle with the loss of his father, so I chose not to tell him until I visited San Diego in 2010, forty-four years after his father's death. I now regret keeping my dream a secret from him as others had kept secrets from me. When I told him, he asked, "Aunt Kathy, do you know where we were living when my father died?"

I said, "I thought you were living in Navy housing."

"Let me take you there," he said.

We drove through a quiet neighborhood with modest houses and lawns, a rare sight in San Diego. Deciduous trees lined the street. We stopped at a one story redwood house, with a thriving lawn and trees surrounding it. Tim said, "We moved here six months before Dad died." He burst into tears.

~

On Christmas Eve, ten years after Tony's death, I received a letter from my brother, Jim, who had been with Tony when he was given the wrong blood. Since Jim had been a medic in the Navy during the war and now was a Ph.D. researcher and practitioner in nuclear medicine, he immediately knew the consequences of receiving the wrong blood type. Years before this letter arrived, Jim had described to me how he frantically ran all over the hospital looking for someone to intervene, knowing there was nothing anyone could do. He remained at Tony's beside for three days, along with other family members, and watched his oldest brother die.

In this letter, Jim said, "I do not know if I did the right thing, but I took the letter Tony was writing to you while he was dying and put it away. I thought it would be too upsetting for you at such a young age. [I was twenty-two at the time of Tony's death.] I'm sending it to you now. I hope you will understand and forgive me for holding onto it for the last ten years."

As I opened the unfinished letter my brother Tony had been writing to me, I felt some trepidation that it would be a rebuke. Tony's words proved me wrong. It was a heart-felt letter saying how much he loved me and how proud he was of me. He told me what had happened—that he had been given the wrong blood, and he was dying. It ended mid-sentence. As I read it, I could feel him with me like I did at fifteen when we were outside in the dark gazing at the stars together. I couldn't see him, but I could feel him. Every time I think of Tony, I still hear him singing the song *I'll Be Seeing You.*

I'll be seeing you
In all the old familiar places
That this heart of mine embraces
All day through

*****

I'll find you in the morning sun
And when the night is new
I'll be looking at the moon
But I'll be seeing you

— Excerpt from *I'll Be Seeing You* by songwriters: Irving Kahal, Sammy Fain

I wasn't angry with Jim—I knew his intentions were to spare me more pain. But I felt the weight of family secrets, like my mother's Black Coat hiding her belly when she was pregnant with me: the secret of my father's illness; the mystery of Mark and young boys; and the truth of Tony's condition. Now, a letter hidden from me for ten years. Did I have some complicity in these secrets? Was there something I was doing to elicit my family's protective instincts?

I was extremely sensitive and cried easily. My family was uncomfortable with my emotions. But, many of the secrets preceded my birth and had nothing to do with my sensitivity like my father pretending to go to work when he didn't have a job and my mother sending her sons on clandestine errands to accept money from our relatives against my father's wishes. All I know is that secrets, kept with good intentions, troubled my spirit and eroded the fabric of our family life.

About six months after Tony died, Liz, his wife, and their four children, went to live with my mother and Mark in the big house on the river. We all spent Christmas at my mother's that year and enjoyed the holiday with Liz, the three boys and their sister. The children seemed to be doing well considering they had lost their father so recently.

My brother, Thomas, and his family, lived about two miles up the road with children approximately the same ages as Tony's. I felt it was a good arrangement for Tony's wife and children to be with our extended family. At one point a few months later, I heard that Mark and Liz were getting married. I was stunned by this news but since it's common in Italian families for a brother to marry his deceased brother's wife, I thought maybe Mark was trying to fulfill this traditional obligation.

Then I heard that Liz and the children abruptly left and returned to California. I was unable to bring myself to question my mother about all this. She never said a word, so I would not breech her silence to learn the truth. Instead, I lived with another secret.

What is life?
It is the flash of a firefly in the night.
It is the breath of a buffalo in the wintertime.
It is the little shadow which runs across
the grass and loses itself in the sunset.

– Crowfoot, Blackfoot warrior and orator 1830 - 1890

CHAPTER EIGHTEEN
And, On This Day...

AFTER TONY'S DEATH, I began to beg Stan for a baby. He finally said, half joking, "If you save a hundred dollars in pennies by Christmas, you can get pregnant." I wasn't going to miss this opportunity, as bizarre as it sounded. I sent out the word: Start saving pennies for a baby. Pennies began to pour in. My mother filled my stocking with pennies at Christmas. Though Papa gave me an expensive diamond watch for our first anniversary—which he said was a reward for sticking with his son for a year—those lowly pennies meant more to me than the shiny watch. By Father's Day 1967, I was able to write Papa a note saying:

We have on order for you
One small grandchild
Due on January 21, 1968

On Father's Day, Papa sat quietly alone in his big overstuffed red leather chair in the den. I sat on the arm of the chair and put my arm around his shoulder. I handed him a card with the note. He seemed quietly pleased, but not his usual exuberant self. He said he was very tired. I think he knew he would never see this new grandchild.

A month later, he had a massive heart attack. Stan and I went to the hospital to join the family and wait for news of his condition. When the doctor came out to talk to us, he did not need to say a word—his face said it all. Papa was dead. This vibrant, hearty, bigger-than-life man would never fill the room with his beaming smile again. My mother-in-law collapsed in a chair and wept, quietly saying, "Did he know that I loved him. Did he know that I loved him?" The waiting room where we all gathered was a sea of tears.

I was once again overwhelmed with grief. How could God take this father, more real than my own, away from me after only two years with him? Stan was stoic. He and I went to stay at the family home that night. Seeing that I was still coping with nausea and almost fainting, Papa's sister, Betty, tried to dissuade me from attending the burial the next day. She repeated an old superstition that the baby would be marked, if I went to the gravesite. I would not be swayed. I was going to stay with Papa as long as I could.

I wrote a poem and read it at the gravesite:

> *Papa, you permeate this house.*
> *You're everywhere—*
> *And yet you are not here.*
>
> *Your voice which now is silent*
> *Resounds through empty rooms*
> *And broken hearts and gloom.*
>
> *Your love is felt forevermore*
> *It filled your heart*
> *And spills into our own in part.*
>
> *Thus, each of us holds much of you*
> *As you were and are*
> *And will always be to us.*
>
> *– Kathleen, 1967*

In the Jewish tradition, burial must take place within twenty-four hours of the death. Countless family, friends and colleagues went to the service and cemetery. The immediate family returned home after the burial and sat Shiva for seven days while friends and family came laden with food to pay their respects.

Shiva is a wise custom. The first few days are heavy with sadness, second-guessing what could have been done differently to have prevented this death. Then things begin to lighten, and sentimental stories are told about the deceased. By the end of the seven days, everyone has a funny story to share about the one who has died, replacing tears with laughter. I was denied that healthy process when my brother Tony died.

But, seven days could not take away the ache from my heart after losing Papa. I felt a tremendous void every time we met as a family. I'd been seen by Papa, valued and appreciated. He had bought me a sewing machine when I voiced an interest in sewing. I was not very proficient, but I made him a dark blue velour pullover shirt with a collar and open neckline. When it was finished I realized the nap of the velour was running in the wrong direction. That did not bother Papa. When he tried it on, it would not fit over his three-hundred-pound, six-foot-four inch frame.

I would not be defeated. I put gussets on each side, which allowed the shirt to snuggly fit over his belly. Papa loved that shirt. The man who wore expensive suits and shoes went to his club every Saturday to play cards in the shirt I made for him. Mother Labb, who adhered to the latest fashions, was mortified her husband was wearing this lowly homemade garment to their fancy club. She and Papa argued about it every week as he went out the door. I'm not sure if he wore it because he loved me or to spite her, but at the time, I chose to believe he loved the shirt because I had made it for him. And, I believe Papa loved me, and I know I loved him.

~

I started to have problems with the pregnancy, including bleeding and anemia which caused debilitating exhaustion and fainting spells. Even so, Stan expected me to meet all his needs. Then he badly sprained his knee playing basketball and was in a cast for weeks. He was immobilized and more demanding than ever. His verbal harangues against me escalated. I attributed it to the loss of his father and the pain in his knee.

I tried not to cause him further stress. He berated me, called me vile names, and disparaged me and my family. His roaring rage had a visceral affect—my solar plexus froze and I couldn't breathe. A prickly numbing sensation spread through my body. I wondered if my unborn child could feel the same sickening waves of emotion I felt. I know now that he did.

I also remembered Aunt Betty's superstitious warning that my baby would be marked if I went to Papa's gravesite. I brushed the thought away.

~

One Friday night, when I was twenty-six weeks pregnant, I couldn't sleep. The practice contractions, called Braxton Hicks, were persistent and strong. I walked the floor all night in my light blue, chiffon nightgown given to me by my friends at work, trying not to wake Stan. This went on throughout the next day until late afternoon. My friend from work, Cassie, called to check on me, and when she heard what was going on she said, "Call your doctor right now and get to the hospital!"

Cassie had given me wise counsel on many occasions, so I dutifully called the doctor, Stan's Uncle Mike. In a gruff, irritated voice, he demanded Stan immediately rush me to the hospital. Uncle Mike had just scolded me for gaining nine pounds at my last check up. He was a no-nonsense, old-timer and wouldn't hear of my taking Lamaze birthing classes as I'd planned. He had delivered Stan and his siblings and countless other babies—he was calling the shots.

I was settled into a hospital bed when Stan, his mother, Uncle Mike and his wife, Aunt Helene, who were there ostensibly to offer support, proceeded to go out to dinner, leaving me alone. The room was dark except for one small light on the wall behind me.

I was instructed not to get up, so I sat in the dimly lit room and cried. I felt deserted. Although I'd witnessed many women in labor as a nurse's aide, I did not feel prepared for what might lie ahead. All of a sudden I felt a gush of something warm and wet. I buzzed for the nurse.

She sauntered in. I said, "I think I'm bleeding again," which I had done on and off during the pregnancy.

She checked and said, "No, dear, your water just broke. You're going to have a baby tonight."

"That's impossible!" I protested. "I have ten weeks more to go!" She called Uncle Mike to come back. I was so frightened and embarrassed by my body's failure, I couldn't speak.

Stan offered no comfort, nor did Uncle Mike who couldn't tolerate my tears any more than Stan could. He finally said gruffly, "Forget about this baby! We just have to get you through this so you can have other babies!"

"But I want THIS baby!"

"Pam and Daniel went through this with their first one and look what a nice family they have now," he said in reference to his son and daughter-in-law.

I began to pray fervently for this little baby within me. I reverted to the Catholic prayers of my childhood. The pain increased and became unbearable. After a couple of hours I was rushed to the delivery room, and with three pushes my newborn son was launched into Uncle Mike's hands. As if to say, "You said to forget about me, take this!" the baby urinated all over the good doctor.

The infant was three pounds—thanks to the nine pounds I had gained in the last month. He would quickly go down to two and a half pounds, and by morning we knew he had a serious problem. He stopped breathing every few minutes and needed to be coaxed to start up again. By some Divine grace, an elderly nurse named Francis Nichols noticed he had stopped breathing shortly after he got to the nursery. She stood guard over him all night, flicking his feet to make him take a breath.

I had not been allowed to see my newborn son. The next morning I stood at the window of my second floor room and watched a nurse carry a black box the size of a shoebox, with wires and tubes protruding from all sides of it, to a waiting police car. She climbed in the back seat with the box, which was a portable incubator with my baby inside hooked up to life support. The police car took off and my tiny son was on his way to Boston Children's Hospital.

At my insistence, I was released, and Stan took me directly to see our baby. I stood outside the window of the NICU (Neonatal Intensive Care Unit) and was shocked by what I saw. In the middle of the huge nursery in a large incubator under bright lights, my skinny, fragile son lay listless. He was hooked up to IV's and machines, breathing tubes and an Apnea Monitor with a blue flashing light which had recently been developed at Stanford University. It was the only one in use other than the prototype at Stanford.

Every time he stopped breathing a harsh sounding alarm rang out through the nursery and a red light started flashing on the monitor. Doctors and nurses ran toward my baby from all sides of the NICU. They would flick his feet to try to arouse him and escalate their interventions until he took a breath. Every time the monitor went off, my heart stopped until his tiny form started breathing again.

We decided we wouldn't name the baby until we knew he was going to live—which was very much in doubt. In 1967 babies that small rarely made it, especially boys. We wanted to name our first son after Papa and, according to Jewish tradition, if we gave the baby that name and he died, we could not use the name again. We waited. The nurses loved this scrawny little baby with the long dark eye-lashes—like I had come to love the preemies I cared for when I was working as a nurse's aide. These nurses started calling him "Charlie Brown."

A week later, my mother came to see her new grandson. She overheard the nurses calling him by that name and turned around to question us about it. I said, "Mom, we decided not to name him yet because we are afraid he won't make it."

She said, almost yelling, "You name that child! He's going to LIVE!" We promptly named our son, David Aaron Cohen, after his paternal grandfather and great-grandfather, a formidable name for such a little one.

For a month, I went every day and stood at the NICU window. I could not touch my baby. The hospital rules prevented me from expressing my breast-milk to feed him. Across the street, the Boston Lying-in Hospital was encouraging mothers to do just that, and researchers were proving how beneficial breast-milk is to preemies.

Instead, I could only watch in horror each time the alarm sounded and little Davey was poked, pinched, slapped and needled into breathing. I made the decision to go back to work and visit the NICU less frequently. I was emotionally exhausted.

Years later, as an adult, David told me his infant-self sensed my energy leave that hospital, and he felt abandoned by me. I've always regretted not standing by him. The first time I was allowed to hold him, he was two months old. When the nurse put him in my arms, he turned his whole body away from me as if in rebuke, almost falling out of my grasp. Now seven pounds, he came home two weeks later on his due date, January 21, 1968, and we were no closer to being comfortable with each other.

When Davey was released from the hospital, we were given a hand-held resuscitator in case he stopped breathing again. Stan and I took turns watching over him day and night for a week until we both got sick. He didn't sleep more than an hour at a time, and he took an hour to drink his bottle and then he'd projectile vomit across the room. And, he still was hard to hold. This was not what I had expected when I begged for a baby. And, the doctors told us we wouldn't know if our son was brain damaged from the prematurity until he was two years old.

Stan resented all the time and attention I gave the baby, although he liked the idea that he had fathered a son. He proudly showed Davey off at family gatherings and to friends but had nothing to do with his care. I hoped he'd understand if dinner wasn't on the table on time or the house wasn't kept in perfect condition, or I was behind in the laundry, but that was not the case. The flow of verbal and emotional harassment never stopped. His drinking escalated. Two months later I found I was pregnant again. I was shocked. We were using precautions which had obviously failed.

When I announced this to Stan's family a month later, my mother-in-law said, "Horrors!"

My sister-in-law, Linda Cohen, forever endeared herself to me by chiming in, "Well, I think it's wonderful!"

~

Little David survived and grew, although he made slow progress, always below average in weight and height until he was a teenager. At first, he was fussy, startled easily and barely slept at night. His nervous system began to settle down when he was about six months old, although he continued to wake up three or four times a night until he was three. At the same time, he was developing into a curious, bright, happy baby. He learned quickly and laughed at my silly antics when I tried to entertain him. Our bond grew stronger over that first year.

My mother gave Stan and me the last five acres of our family's land about a mile up the road from my childhood home, adjacent to the land on which my brother Tom, and his wife, Lily, had built a house twenty years before. We would be neighbors.

We started to build a house on our little piece of Connecticut while still living in Massachusetts. We went back and forth from Boston to Wentworth on weekends to oversee construction. It was then I found out my brother, our neighbor, Tom, was no longer talking to anyone in our family.

Apparently he had cut off all connections with the family after Liz and the children went back to California. No one told me that Tom had stopped communicating with all of us. His children were forbidden to have contact with the family, but his daughter, Renee, refused to accept her father's order. About a year after this break, Renee walked down the road to tell her grandmother that her father, Mom's fifth son, had had a heart attack. *No one told me.* And, no one could or would give me an explanation for his disappearance from our lives. Tom and I had drifted apart since my marriage, so I wasn't surprised that he hadn't been in contact with me, but I couldn't imagine why he had cut-off the whole family.

When I was about eight months pregnant, and Davey was eleven months old, I moved in with my mother and my brother,

Mark, who had never left home. Our apartment lease was up, and our house wasn't finished. My mother had taken a job as a house mother at the University of Connecticut. She lived in a dorm on campus and came home once a week. Mark was still renovating the house, and it was in chaos, not ideal for a toddler. He did help me with Davey, but our relationship was strained.

On one of her days off, Mom came home and found Mark had made some changes in the dining room that she didn't like. I was standing close to the two of them, with my huge belly and Davey on my left hip, when they began to argue.

Mark went into a rage and yelled, "I'm going to kill her!" and lunged for my mother's throat. I screamed and pushed the right side of my body between them. Mark turned in his fury and picked up Davey's metal high chair, swung it over his head and crashed it to the floor. It was in pieces.

This kind of trauma lives in your cells, so as I write this I can feel the adrenalin rush. And, it also impacts the baby in utero with long term effects. The incident was never mentioned again by Mark or Mom, and I certainly wasn't going to say a word—fearing the wrath of both. In disbelief at what I had witnessed, I immediately moved out of the house to stay with a friend up the street. I knew Mark could be volatile like my father, but I had never seen him this out of control. How could I ever trust him again? Other suspicions about him were gnawing at my consciousness as well.

As I was exposed to more information on sexual matters, I was stunned to learn that some adults had sex with children. I wondered if Mark was one of those adults. There was a name for people who did this: *pedophiles*. I didn't want to believe it. I kept turning away from the possibility. If I knew this was the reality of what was going on in our family home, what would I do? Who should I tell? Who would believe me? What if Mark committed suicide if his secret was revealed?

I had no proof so I put on my mother's black coat and hid my concerns from others and myself. Although I never left my children alone with Mark, I did nothing to protect all the other children who crossed his path. I told myself he would never touch one of our own. But, I was aware that, if what I suspected was true, I left a vast number of children at his mercy. I pulled the black coat tighter around my shoulders and kept silent.

While we were still working on our house, I was so certain of Tom's love for me I walked up the hill and knocked on his door. Although there were cars in the driveway, no one answered. I thought maybe they were sleeping or in the back room. As a child, I had sat at their table eating elbows and butter, watching the sun go down through the picture window. I always felt safe and at home in their house.

I tried to make contact numerous times, bringing them a fruit basket on Thanksgiving, pleading with them in a note to join the family for dinner. At Christmas, I left a tin of home-made baked goods with a note begging their forgiveness for whatever I did to cause them to be upset with all of us. I assumed they were angry that my mother had given Stan and me more land than they had been given. I was tortured by this rift in what I had always believed was a close family.

It was difficult for me to believe that Tom and his family weren't anxious to meet my son. I was heartsick and confused by how the short distance between our two houses could feel like hundreds of miles. I loved Tom and Lily's children. I had lived with them in upstate New York for a month in the summer when I was thirteen, and visited them often at other times. I looked forward to watching these spirited children grow into adulthood. I was denied that joy, and the children were denied a relationship with people they loved. Still, there wasn't an explanation from my family or Tom for his relentless silence. It never occurred to me the rejection might have something to do with Mark.

~

In the spring of 1968, still in our apartment in Watertown, I sat in disbelief as first Rev. Martin Luther King, Jr. and then Robert Kennedy were assassinated. I sat with tears running down my cheeks in front of the TV for days, watching each event unfold as my toddler played at my feet and my belly grew with my unborn baby. I feared for my children's future and questioned how I could justify bringing them into this world.

But it was in the midst of a world gone mad, the loss of connection with Tom, the recent deaths of my brother, Tony, and Papa, and Stan's incessant degradation that I brought into the world, my beautiful daughter, Rachel Beth Cohen, on November 29, 1968. She was the perfect baby. She arrived on her due date, nursed well, slept through the night at two weeks, rarely cried and quietly watched the world go by in her baby swing. I later heard the adage, "some babies are born too scared to cry" and wondered if my brother's violent outburst had traumatized my baby daughter in my womb.

~

The heartache from my recent losses didn't touch the love and joy I felt for my beautiful babies or the house we built and the land on which it stood. Our brother-in-law, who was an architect, designed the house for us. From the road it looked like a small brown New England Cape-style house with a red door in a circular clearing surrounded by woods. I had walked these woods to the river many times when I was young. The house was built into the hill that sloped down to the rock-filled rushing waters of the New Hope River, the same river that ran against our family home downstream.

The front door opened into a foyer with tall windows that filled it with light during the day and stars at night. A curved stairwell led to the downstairs bedrooms and laundry. The main floor included the kitchen with deep red counters I loved and a dining area that opened into a huge living room with a cathedral ceiling. On the far wall, covered in diagonal pine boards, was a wide fireplace with a raised stone hearth and a brick herringbone chimney that rose to the ceiling and dominated the room. I finally was able to reclaim my precious piano that Mom and Mark had given me. The honey-colored spinet was dwarfed by the huge room, but filled my heart as I played it in stolen moments.

The back wall of windows and sliding glass doors opened to a deck off the main floor. There was a patio underneath. One of the oldest oak trees in the State stood fifty feet from the wall of windows. At night we illuminated the magnificent tree with spotlights. Living on this piece of land made me happy.

My little piece of Heaven

Beloved Oak Tree

Stan had begun working as a salesman for a staid old Yankee company in Williamson, which was only ten miles from our home, although he travelled all over New England on his route. He often left me alone to go socialize in Boston, leaving me with two babies, a puppy— which he insisted we get against my protestations—and our Siamese cat, Chocolate. He went into the city to hang out with the guys or go to a game. He often returned in the middle of the night, inebriated and belligerent, waking me from much needed sleep, roughly forcing himself on me, ignoring my protests.

~

There was no name for marital rape in those days and I certainly wouldn't have known to define my experience as that. The nuns had taught us that a husband had the right to demand sex from his wife. Even today, marital rape is not considered rape in some states. The Ohio State Legislature refused to outlaw marital rape when a recent bill to do so came to the floor in 2017.

~

Meanwhile, when Stan was gone at night, if I heard anything outside or Chocolate started pacing the floor, I called Mark. I could count on Mark, although I tip-toed around him after the violent incident with my mother. No matter what time it was, Mark would come up and check things out. If both the babies were crying, and I was overwhelmed, I called Mark. He came and played with them and helped me soothe them to sleep. He'd also come to fix anything that needed fixing whatever the hour.

I couldn't count on my husband for anything, except paying the mortgage and providing food on the table. Emotionally he was not there for me, and the degradation of my personhood continued. I began reading books on relationships and tried to get Stan to read sections I had underlined. He ignored me. When he was home, he spent hours in front of the TV watching sports. We barely talked unless it was about what was on the calendar for the next week. Any important conversation often led to an argument. We were on opposite sides of most subjects. And, there was no affection, no foreplay, no romance, only sex at his demand. I felt cheated, angry and alone.

One day, with the baby on my hip and Davey wrapped around my left leg, I picked up the phone and called a lawyer. I explained my situation. The lawyer said, "With two small children there is no way you can make it on your own. You just have to stay and make it work." I felt hopeless and trapped.

~

Stan hated living in rural Connecticut in the woods. After less than a year he wanted to return to Boston. We argued about it. My tone sounded angrier then I intended. (He yelled all the time, but if I raised my voice I was a "fish-wife.") "After all we put into this house, you want to SELL it?" I said.

"There's nothing HERE! There's nothing to do—it's in the middle of nowhere! Besides we could make a quick $20,000 and buy something bigger, in a nice area outside Boston."

"I do *not* want to move! I love it here! This land has been in my family for years. It's like you're throwing Mom's gift in her face!"

"It's always all about YOU, isn't it? What about me? I'm the one who has to go out to work every day. You're a selfish bitch! You don't care about anyone but yourself! You don't give a damn about me or my happiness. How stupid can you be not to understand the economics?"

After several more rounds of this, I said, "Fine, sell it."

It sold quickly, and we did make $20,000 on it—a huge sum of money in 1969. I grieved another loss, the home and land I loved. We packed up our life in my treasured piece of Connecticut and moved back to Massachusetts to a new development in the small town of Stanford. I was reminded of a quote by Kahlil Gibran in *The Prophet: The deeper that sorrow carves into your being, the more joy you can contain.* I prayed this was true.

Whoever you are, no matter how lonely,
the world offers itself to your imagination,
calls to you like the wild geese—harsh and exciting—
over and over announcing your place
in the family of things.

– "Wild Geese" from *Dream Works* by Mary Oliver

CHAPTER NINETEEN
New Beginnings

AS WE SEARCHED for a house in Massachusetts we found many towns still restricted: No Jews allowed. I was shocked. We finally found a house an hour from Boston and the major medical centers. I moved in with a heavy heart. The new house was a two story brown colonial that stood on a small lot. There was only room for a sandbox and a small-swing set in the back yard and a few lawn chairs. The house was still in the process of being finished, so I was able to get red counters in the kitchen again. That was some small consolation for what I had lost. And, my piano found a home in a living room that was more proportionate to its size. Each time I entered the room, it felt like a puzzle piece had fallen into place. Something in me loosened with a sigh. Music was still the corner stone of my life.

There were neighbors all around us, and I made myself reach out and meet people. In a short time, I had many friends in Stanford. I met a new friend at a Hadassah meeting (a Jewish women's organization) held at the only synagogue in town. It was Conservative and the men and women were separated during services—men on the main floor and women in the balcony.

The day Sarah and I discovered we were both from Connecticut our friendship was sealed. By coincidence, our husbands met a few days later when Stan was walking around the neighborhood. Sarah's husband, Jim, was sitting on his front lawn in the sun. Stan introduced himself and sat on the grass beside him.

Sarah later told me that Stan listened with compassion as Jim told him about their infant son who was in precarious condition and still in the hospital. They didn't know if he would make it. Stan's response to Jim kindled a spark of hope in me that my husband was a caring person in spite of his abusive behavior. The two men bonded over that conversation and remained friends for many years.

When I was young, my father used to sing a song to me if I was sad or crying: "Look for the Silver Lining." At the time, it annoyed me, but I have come to appreciate its wisdom. My new friends eased my sense of loss and helped sustain me. *They* were the silver lining of our move to Stanford. They offered me on-going support as the abusive dynamics in my marriage became more obvious.

~

My children, David and Rachel, kept me connected to life. We took daily walks, and their delight in the world was contagious. Davey spent hours in the sandbox with his Tonka toys, totally absorbed. Inside he played endlessly with his plain wood blocks—creating intricate structures. He was an intense, sensitive child with snapping brown eyes and shiny straight black hair. The doctors said we wouldn't know until he was two years old, if he had cognitive damage from his prematurity. At nine months, he pulled himself up on the window sill, pointed outside, and said, "Truck!" I breathed a sigh, knowing that his brain was working just fine. And so was his heart. He was a sweet little boy and grew to be a kind, gentle man.

Rachel looked like a china doll, with curly honey colored hair and big brown eyes. She sat wherever I put her and observed the world. She delighted in anything furry or crawly—worms, caterpillars, dogs, cats, squirrels, chipmunks. She loved books even before she could talk. Sometimes she would sit in the middle of the floor and just giggle.

When she woke from her nap, Rachel would pull the string on the music box hanging above her crib and greet me with a smile when I walked into her room. But she didn't talk, barely crawled, and had no inclination to stand up and walk—I held my breath. Then shortly before she turned two she started talking in full sentences. She knew that Nana was Daddy's mommy and Grandma was Mommy's mommy, and she took off running. She hasn't stopped since!

I remember finding the two children standing at the dining room window at dusk, in silence—barely able to see over the window sill—watching the first snowfall of the season. I groaned thinking of boots, mittens, scarves and skidding cars—until I looked at their faces. They were enthralled. I saw the snow through their eyes as if I was seeing it for the first time. It was beautiful and magical as it fell against the darkening sky. I had no idea I was capable of feeling as much love as I felt for these two little beings.

The children also helped widen my social circle. The neighborhood mothers gathered for coffee and let the children play together, usually at my house. Sarah and I started a poetry group and were surprised when many women in our small community joined us. Few of them had shown any interest in the arts.

Each week we brought in poems to read and, eventually, we began writing our own poetry to share. We encouraged and supported each other and remained together for two years, until I moved. The group brought light into the emotional void of my home life and mediated my increasing depression.

~

Late one cold rainy night in March I went into the family room before bed, bare feet on cold tiles, to lock the back door. Stan was watching TV and started yelling, "This place is a pig sty! What do you DO all day?"

Tired as I was after a long day with two small children, I yelled back at him, something I rarely did. "What do you THINK I do?"

He was on his feet, looming over me in a split second, screaming in my face. "You fucking bitch!" He opened the door and shoved me out into the cold rain, then locked the door behind me. He wouldn't let me back in.

Barefoot, I ran down the slippery driveway, up the street to the home of a friend. Her sleepy, pajama-clad husband answered my frantic knock on the door. He let me in as I hysterically relayed what had happened. My friend joined us, getting me a towel, dry clothes and shoes, trying to comfort me. Her husband got dressed, put on his raincoat and went to talk to Stan. He came back and said it was safe for me to go home.

Stan opened the door, snarling, "You had to go to the neighbors, didn't you?" He was furious, but he did not touch me. Shivering with cold and fear, I went to bed.

This episode led me deeper into the darkness. I contacted a doctor friend and told him how depressed I was. He came to the house with his wife and took me aside, away from Stan and the kids, and said, "You're strong, you can pull yourself out of this." He validated what I feared to be true—I was weak to succumb to depression. (Many years later he apologized for giving me this advice after he experienced clinical depression himself.)

Continuing to sink, I locked the children and myself in the family room for most of the day with PBS children's shows playing in the background. I'd give them a box of band-aids to play doctor and let them use me as the patient as I lay on the couch. I could not move. At two and three years old, these children would cover me with band-aids before I'd put them down for naps and crawl into bed. Rousing myself a couple of hours before Stan came home, I'd clean the house and make dinner, feeding and bathing the children and putting them in their pajamas so they wouldn't disturb their father at dinner time. One day, a snippet of a poem I had written during my first year of marriage echoed in my mind.

This life
Which haunts my tortured being
Continues to live no less
This death
Which woos and tempts my spirit
Will not give me rest

– Kathleen, 1966

On a windy grey afternoon after putting the children down for naps in their cribs, I took a bath, put on the red kimono my sister had sent me when she was in Japan, and took a bottle of painkillers from the medicine cabinet.

I brought the bottle of pills and a glass of water to bed with me and started to take the pills one at a time. Little Rachel uncharacteristically cried out. The spell was broken.

~

Dr. Nathan E. Bennett, OB/GYN, was a tall, elegant man in his fifties, with glints of silvery grey in his dark hair. His office was decorated in muted shades of blue. Pictures of the New England countryside hung on his walls. He instantly made me feel comfortable.

"Please, sit down and let's chat for a few minutes," he said. The tone of his voice was reassuring.

"Thank you," I replied as he held the chair for me.

As he walked around his desk to take his seat, he said, "Tell me, what brings you here today?"

I was nervous seeing this new doctor for the first time. I stammered, "Well—I—I'm due for a checkup and my husband wants another baby—and—and—I have an I.U.D."

"Ok," he said. "Let's start by getting a little history."

He proceeded to ask me questions about my health and my previous pregnancies. Dr. Bennett listened intently to my answers. His respectful tone contradicted what I lived with daily.

Then he asked, "What about your marriage—how is your relationship with your husband?"

I started to weep.

"What are those tears about?"

"Nothing, really…"

"I think they're about something, Kathy—you can tell me."

"I can't seem to do anything right. Stan is always yelling at me, and then I get impatient with the kids. I want so much to be a good mother, and I feel like a failure. And I'm exhausted all the time."

Dr. Bennett handed me tissues and said, "It sounds like you're being much too hard on yourself. And, you sound very unhappy. Have you ever thought about hurting yourself?"

I nodded.

"I think you're depressed, Kathy," he said gently. "It's time you got some help with this depression. I know an excellent psychiatrist, and I can set you up with him."

"Stan would never agree to it!"

"I'll call Stan and take care of that, and I'll also tell him you are in no condition to have a baby at this time," he said firmly. Tears of relief flooded my eyes.

I will never know what Dr. Bennett said, but Stan accepted my seeing a psychiatrist and stopped pressuring me about another baby.

~

I arrived at the psychiatrist's office a few days later. He had a list of questions he seemed to be checking off. How was my appetite? Energy level? Mood? Sleep? He then questioned if I had ever been suicidal. I suspected Dr. Bennett had told him I'd come close to taking a bottle of pain killers, so I couldn't lie.

He was adamant I needed to be on an antidepressant. I held out against the medicine for three weeks until he said he couldn't continue seeing me if I didn't comply. I relented, and after a few weeks on medication, I began to come back to life.

Sitting with this kind doctor week after week, I soaked up the rays of attention and caring I felt in his presence. It became painful in contrast to what I experienced at home. I gave the doctor this poem:

> *Your compassion is showing.*
> *Please, put it away.*
> *I cannot bear to see it*
> *knowing it is not mine to keep*
> *or share with you*
> *for I cannot stay.*

Where my life is going
I'll find none there
to listen to my words,
see beauty through or in my eyes
or hear with me
the songs I hear.

Your kindness is undoing
years of cold denial
of my need to ask another
to look at me and see me as I am
and to hear the silent cry
of my outstretched hand.

– Kathleen, 1972

I'd entered the psychiatrist's office without hope. I looked forward to nothing in my life. The future felt dark and empty, but with the medication and his expertise, I began to hope again, to believe in the possibility for change. I started to attend a yoga class in the basement of a local church. There was child-care that gave me two hours of freedom and peace.

I grew to love the yoga asanas which were followed by meditation. I drifted into a liminal space floating in complete relaxation. After one of these meditations, the instructor told me she had looked up and seen an apparition of a little girl with blonde hair standing beside me while I meditated. I never went back. I swore off yoga and meditation because I feared that in an altered state I might encounter presences from the other side—including Rosie's. Rosie's death still twisted my thinking and haunted my heart.

I continued to see the psychiatrist for a year. His validation and encouragement gave me a different perspective—I started to see and hear *myself*. The creative well that had gone dry with the depression, began to bubble up with poetry again.

I began to reclaim myself—the young woman who crossed the country by herself at fifteen; went away to college; went to live and work in New York City, and picked up and moved to Boston alone. I had been cowering under Stan's constant tirades of criticism and rage, but now I was beginning to stand up to him in small meaningful ways.

I asked permission less and took care of myself more—seeing friends more frequently despite Stan's displeasure. Occasionally I'd fight back when he attacked. I even called another lawyer about getting a divorce. When I explained my situation to him, he said, "Don't aggravate him—just get dinner on the table on time and be a good wife." I practically slammed the phone down in his ear.

Meanwhile, my psychiatrist and I agreed it was time to terminate therapy, but he wanted me to continue on the medication I was taking. I protested: I wanted to claim this victory over depression as my own. He reluctantly agreed to help me get off the medication safely before our last session. I held on for a while, but I could feel a foreboding undertow of melancholy as spring gave way to summer, always my worst time of year. I felt weak, ashamed, alone, helpless, as hope faded once again.

The stigma of mental illness hung like a pall over my life, even when I was not depressed. I feared being dragged under without warning by the monster at the depth of my soul. I felt defective and tried to hide my defective self from the world.

~

Many who suffer from mood disorders echo these words. The origins of these feelings and thought patterns are complex. Neurological and biochemical factors may be hereditary, and in utero influences may also play a part in these disorders. We now know that Adverse Childhood Experiences (ACE) contribute to the development of mood disorders as do traumatic experiences in childhood and adulthood. Medication, various therapeutic modalities, and life style changes can help alleviate the symptoms of these disorders and even reroute the neural pathways that have been affected. If I had known this when I was younger, my sense of self worth may not have been diminished with each depressive episode.

~

In the months sitting with this insightful doctor, I glimpsed a reflection of myself I had not seen in the six years I had known Stan. In that time, I had died to myself—sepulchered away from the beauty of life and my own intrinsic worth. During therapy, I heard, for the first time, *"the pitying rain"* falling with mercy upon the *"lowly thatched roof"* of my grave. It was a sound I would not forget. It gave me hope. Millay continues:

> *The rain, I said, is kind to come*
> *And speak to me in my new home...*
> *I would I were alive again*
> *To kiss the fingers of the rain,*
> *To drink into my eyes the shine*
> *Of every slanting silver line,*
> *To catch the freshened, fragrant breeze*
> *From drenched and dripping apple-trees.*
> *For soon the shower will be done*
> *And then the broad face of the sun*
> *Will laugh above the rain-soaked earth*
> *Until the earth with answering mirth*
> *Shakes joyously, and each round drop*
> *Rolls twinkling from its grass-blade top.*
>
> *How can I bear it; buried here,*
> *While overhead the sky grows clear*
> *And blue again after the storm?*
> *O, multi-colored, multiform,*
> *Beloved beauty over me,*
> *That I shall never, never see*
> *Again! Spring-silver, autumn-gold,*
> *That I shall never more behold!*
> *Sleeping your myriad magics through,*
> *Close-sepulchered away from you!*

Your friend is your needs answered.
[S]he is your field which you sow with love
And reap with thanksgiving.

– "On Friendship" by Kahlil Gibran in *The Prophet*

CHAPTER TWENTY
Leticia

SOMEHOW I got through the summer without medication. Stan was working at American Thread Company. His supervisor became a family friend. He told Stan in front of me, "Get out of this company! You were hired as the token Jew. You don't have a future here." I was shocked. I thought Stan's paranoia about anti-Semitism was all in his head. I had grown up in a University town where professors and their families of all races, religions and ethnicity were accepted. This revelation threw Stan into turmoil. He had minimal work experience.

Money was always tight but we managed to save a considerable amount in case of an emergency. Stan's two brothers had started a successful tire business a couple of years before, and Stan decided to use these emergency funds to buy into it. He worked with his brothers for a while, but they insisted he open his own branch because his angry outbursts and controlling behavior made it impossible to work with him.

I was unhappy with our non-descript house in this new, barren development. Both Stan and I had envisioned living in a rural area with land. In early fall of 1971, we found the house that fulfilled our dreams. It was in Sheridan, Massachusetts, just a few miles away from Stanford. It was a big old house on a winding back road with seven acres of land and a barn. The house was the Ebenezer Hill House built in 1690 with a huge addition added on in 1720. We were told it originally had been a parsonage. Red, sitting sideways on the lot to get the morning sun, it was a typical two-story New England colonial. There was a fireplace in every room downstairs, except the kitchen.

After signing the papers that made the house ours, we went to walk through it alone for the first time. The dining room was not electrified. The previous owners wanted to faithfully preserve the antiquity of this one room. When we stepped over the threshold it felt like we had stepped into another era. We decided to leave it as it was.

The living room was dark with rough hewn boards and exposed beams. There was a square covered well in a closet at the end of the room, which would have been a luxury in 1690. It made me uneasy. I filled it with boxes of old books and never opened the door again. I would hurry through the room at night, but Rachel, who was three at the time, would lie on the couch in the dark. One day I asked what she was doing. "I'm talking to the people, Mom." I questioned no further.

And there was a large sunny room in the front of the house I envisioned as my study, but it was destined to become our bedroom. The kitchen had been a shed attached to the house for the animals in the winter and was in deplorable shape.

I missed the ancient family home of my childhood, and this house felt familiar and welcoming. Its rich history and rustic interior filled the crevices of my longing, even though I knew it might take years to authentically restore it.

Stan and I climbed the stairs to the children's bedrooms where the previous owners had left twin beds. Stan insisted we "make love" for good luck in our new home. I protested and said I didn't have my diaphragm, which I was now using for birth control. In truth, I had no desire to be intimate with this man, and had determined in therapy I didn't want any more children. He persisted and said he would be careful and pushed me not so gently onto one of the beds. There was nothing loving about it.

Dream House

We moved into the house about six weeks later, and I knew I was pregnant. I will never know if Stan had calculated a way to get me pregnant, perhaps in response to my standing up to him. I was furious. I would not pay heed to Dr. Bennett's warning to take it easy for the first few months. We had begun renovations to make the house livable, and I intended to make that happen as quickly as possible.

Contractors did the major work, but I scrubbed the walls and floors, painted kitchen cabinets a buttery yellow, ran up and down the stairs working on the upstairs bedrooms and cleaning out the attic. On a Thursday night, when I was about three months pregnant, I noticed I was spotting.

I called Dr. Bennett early the next morning, and he saw me immediately. I stopped at Stan's workplace on my way home and told him that the doctor thought I'd lose the baby over the weekend. It was 10:00am. Stan opened the bottom drawer of his desk and took a swig of whisky. I was crying at the thought of losing a baby, even though I hadn't wanted it. This life would go unlived. Stan didn't try to comfort me.

I called my friend, Sarah, from Stanford, and asked her if she could pick up the kids and keep them for a couple of nights. I didn't mention the reason for my unusual request—in those days a miscarriage wasn't discussed. Without hesitation, Sarah said, "I'll be there in a half hour." I was grateful but embarrassed that I had to ask this favor. Years later Sarah said, "I knew something had to be terribly wrong because you never ask for anything."

By Saturday night, I was hemorrhaging, and Stan was driving madly through the rainy streets to the hospital, forty minutes away. Losing blood fast and getting weak, I thought I was going to die. I was whisked into surgery for a D&C and given plasma. Dr. Bennett was not on duty so I was treated brusquely and spent a lonely night crying and shivering from loss of blood, overcome by sadness and shame at the loss of my child.

Dr. Bennett visited the next morning and tried to console me. "Kath, if this had been a viable pregnancy it would have withstood the activity. Miscarriages are common—you're not to blame." Despite his comforting words, I grieved my baby's death and felt guilty for my part in it. I imagined the baby was a girl and silently named her Leticia, the name my mother had wanted to give me.

~

We continued to work on restoring the house, a constant disruption of our daily routine, but the results were gratifying. Was I replicating the chaos of Mark's renovations to our family home? I didn't want my children to experience the upheaval I had as a child. They seemed to be oblivious to the commotion and played outdoors most of the time. The family room was the first room to be restored. It was open and light with windows on three walls.

My piano sat between two windows on the far wall. As I played it in the spring, I could glimpse the lilac bush outside the window to my right. This room became the children's sanctuary and the TV room. I painted the trim and wainscoting a quiet blue with white walls. The room had a serene feel in spite of the mayhem that ensued within its walls.

We slowly acquired animals and ended up with dogs, cats, a pig, a heifer, a horse, two geese, chickens and several ducks. Stan and the children were in heaven. I was allergic to all of them and trekked to Boston every week for allergy shots. My allergy doctor questioned why I didn't just get rid of the animals. I said, "My husband and kids would get rid of *me*."

Although I had to account for every cent I spent, Stan had no restraint when it came to spending money on what I called "his toys." He smoked four packs of cigarettes a day. He preferred expensive liquor, which he drank daily. The horse was an extravagance. Stan insisted he needed a high-end tractor and all the accouterments of a gentleman farmer. Later, he bought a fancy boat.

Yet, I couldn't spend money on a pair of shoes or a new outfit without scrutiny, no matter how inexpensive. My clothes budget for the children was meager—sometimes my mother, who was on Social Security, helped me buy their school clothes. I felt humiliated to have to ask my mother for help and angry at Stan for putting me in that position.

I eventually opened a small gift shop in the room attached to the barn, hoping I'd be able to make a little money I could call my own. It enlivened my creativity as I worked on crafts and arranged displays. Local artists and craftspeople sold their work in the shop on consignment. And, I did some buying.

Repeat customers found their way to this rural location and the business started to take hold. However, my expenses outweighed my income so I was still at Stan's mercy financially. Yet, the experience of creating and running *The Bittersweet Barn Shop* gave me a sense of myself as capable and creative. Besides hanging sprigs of bittersweet around the shop, I hung a plaque on the wall that said:

> *Bittersweet is chocolate*
> *Bittersweet's a berry*
> *Bittersweet's the life you lead*
> *No matter whom you marry.*

> – Anon.

~

After the miscarriage, I became obsessed with having another child to somehow make up for the one I'd lost. Dr. Bennett said, "I'd like you to wait awhile, Kath, to give your body a chance to heal." We became close during that time. Each visit began and ended with a warm hug. I wouldn't be deterred. I had sinned once again by causing my baby's demise, and I had to make up for it.

He finally gave me permission to get pregnant about nine months after the miscarriage. Months went by and nothing happened. I thought I was being punished by God for blatantly disregarding the doctor's instructions to take it easy. The Catholic mentality about sin still controlled my thinking even though I did not consciously believe in it.

It took almost a year before I joyfully experienced morning sickness. I felt somehow exonerated by the pregnancy and was careful to obey the doctor's orders to the letter though Stan's verbal and emotional abuse continued unabated. I was afraid the stress of living under his constant onslaught of negativity was going to compromise my ability to carry this baby to term.

When I was six months pregnant, I met a new friend, Karen, who was also pregnant. Her son and my daughter were in nursery school together, and they had fallen in love at the age of five. Karen spoke the language of feelings and allowed me to do the same. After hearing stories about my marriage and realizing how unhappy I was, she encouraged me to see her therapist. A week later I met with Arthur Randall, and we made a good connection. We set up my next appointment, but before I could see him again, I started to bleed.

I was rushed to the hospital and stayed for a few days until the doctors determined I had a condition called *placenta previa* where the blood rich placenta lies over the birth canal. I was at high risk for losing the baby, and possibly my life. Sent home on complete bed rest, I wasn't allowed even to get up to go to the bathroom. My mother came to take care of me and the whole family. Fear of losing my baby and concern for my family engulfed me.

I couldn't bear the thought of losing another child, and I felt terrible for my mother, now in her late sixties. She and Stan didn't get along, so there was constant tension in the house. The two small children were still a handful. Sarah came every weekday morning to pick them up and take them to school, going miles out of her way. Karen came to visit and brought me a bouquet of spring flowers I will never forget—purple irises, pink tulips, and daffodils. A few weeks later, her baby died in utero. I was heart-broken for her and her family. Our bond of friendship strengthened as we supported each other through our difficult pregnancies.

After a month in bed, I began to hemorrhage. Again, Stan was speeding all the way to the hospital as I sat beside him sure I was going to die from the loss of blood or a deadly accident. When I arrived at the Emergency Room, I was prepped for a Caesarian section. Dr. Bennett was not there.

No one talked to me as I lay stripped on the gurney, shivering, blood being drawn from one arm, an IV inserted in the other and someone shaving me. Monitors were attached as tears streamed down my cheeks. All of a sudden I was looking down on the scene from the ceiling. I felt detached from my body and calm. The bleeding abruptly stopped. The presiding doctor put me on complete bed rest in the hospital to try to hold the pregnancy long enough for the baby to have a chance.

Dr. Bennett was at my side the next morning and every day on his daily rounds. On Sundays, he'd stop to see me after church, sitting on my bed to chat. We talked about his garden and strawberry patch. I described my children to him. Just small talk, but those brief times we spent together took the rough edges off the hours I spent alone confined to my bed in the hospital room.

Six weeks after entering the hospital, I went into labor and started to hemorrhage. I was rushed into surgery and ended up with a difficult C-section. Dr. Bennett had promised he'd let me stay awake so I could see my baby. He held my newborn son up for a second for me to see and all I could say was "My beautiful biblical boy!" before he quickly put me out as my blood pressure plummeted.

Although I was in excruciating pain after the section, I insisted on holding my baby as soon as I was fully awake about an hour after his birth. Jacob Ely Cohen arrived on April 19, 1973 to bells ringing throughout Newton, Mass., for the two hundred year centennial of the City. He was healthy and round, and turned out to be as easy-going as his sister, Rachel.

Jake's presence seemed to ease some of the tension in the family. Rachel and Davey thought he was funny and cute. They fought less because of this new distraction. Stan was pleased with his second son, a robust, out-going and happy baby, who turned into an adventurous, mischievous, charming little boy.

I was still recovering from the C-section when I began seeing Art, Karen's therapist. After a few sessions with him, I started to regain my equilibrium. Art caught onto my issues quickly, including my marital life with Stan. He noted my propensity to push myself and encouraged me to take time to heal. He said, "You need to put yourself in the equation. You tend to put everyone else's needs before yours." Wise advice, but impossible to follow with three children and a demanding husband.

My trust in Art grew. Our pediatrician recommended we have our oldest son, Davey, tested for cognitive issues because of his premature birth. I asked Art, who also worked with children, to do the tests. Davey was entering first grade in the fall, so Art tested him that summer.

I was over protective to the extreme, constantly admonishing my children to "Be careful!" "Don't touch that dirty thing!" "Wash your hands!" "Don't go near the road!" "Someone is going to get hurt!" I gave each child an elaborate party on his or her fourth birthday because I considered it a miracle they had lived that long—Rosie had died two months before she turned four.

With the vivid memory of my younger sister, Rosie, screaming with a sore throat thirteen hours before she died, I panicked every time the children complained about their throat hurting. Our pediatrician took note after several frantic office visits. He'd take a throat culture and assure me we would have the results in a couple of days. I'd protest that we couldn't wait that long. Finally, he asked what was going on.

When I told him Rosie's story, he said, "Your sister didn't have strep. Strep develops slowly, it's not acute. She more than likely had acute epiglottitis." I had mentioned her husky voice. He said, "Her deep voice was a clue that she had a small airway which was closed off by the infection." This possibility did nothing to assuage my fear, but I was grateful to have any reasonable explanation for what happened to my sister.

By now, Davey was six and Rachel, five, and I still did not let them leave my sight or ride bikes. I never questioned what effect all this had on my children. I was trying to keep them alive.

Art came out of the office after the test and shook his head. He looked at me and said, "Mother, stop! You wonder why Davey is anxious? Let me tell you why. Each time I showed him an object, he attached some dire consequence to it: a bat—you could swing it and knock someone out; a ball—you could hit someone in the eye with it; water—you could drown in it."

Art proceeded to lecture me about my constant warnings and being overprotective. He advocated for the children to get dirty, ride bikes, and to be allowed to explore. He said I was thwarting their natural development. He advocated what he called "benign neglect." I began the slow process of letting go of my need to control the children's every move to keep them safe and allow them to *live*.

In the darkness of night's falling
In the depths of my despair
I can hear your
sweet voice calling
And I know that You are there.

– Excerpt of a song by Kathleen

CHAPTER TWENTY-ONE
Peace Amidst Chaos

AS WE SETTLED into some semblance of a routine, I became more active in the children's schools. Davey was in first grade. His class was singing Christmas Carols when a little boy named Adam stood up and said, "I don't have Christmas in my house. I have Chanukah."

Davey jumped out of his seat and waved his hand saying "I'm Chanukah, too! I'm Chanukah, too!" When the teacher told me this, I was stunned. I never realized my son needed to have contact with children who shared his traditions. Adam and Davey became friends.

I went to Davey's class at the invitation of the teacher and taught the children some Chanukah songs and games, and told the Chanukah story. When the students heard Jewish children receive presents for eight days, Adam and Davey's status rose with their classmates. Everyone wanted to celebrate Chanukah. I went to Rachel's classroom and did the same thing. This became a tradition each year while we lived in Sheridan.

Davey and Rachel were in third grade when they got off the bus one day and asked, "Mom, what's a dirty kike?" My heart sank. The epithet was hurled at them by two older children who lived in the house down the road. Stan went into a rage when he heard what had happened. He immediately went to confront the children's father who he knew was the source of the slur. The man would not open the door, but Stan got his point across raging on the doorstep. The children never heard those words again, but the discussion about prejudice and the persecution of Jews had been opened.

Stan insisted, from the beginning, that we wouldn't raise our children in what he called "a Jewish ghetto." He said he wanted his children to have a realistic idea of where they stood in the world as a small minority. He felt that would strengthen them so they'd be able to stand up for themselves as Jews. Stan told the story many times about being pelted with stones by his non-Jewish classmates when he was a child on the way home from grammar school. Later, his family moved to where they were no longer in the minority, but Stan felt the lessons he learned in those early days were invaluable.

It turned out we were one of only three Jewish families in town. There wasn't a reform synagogue close enough for the two oldest to receive religious instructions, so I taught them what I could at home. I started to make Shabbat dinner and, of course, we celebrated Chanukah. We also celebrated the High Holy Days and Passover with Stan's family as well as Christmas and Easter with my mother. Still, our children were living as "other" in a Christian community.

More troubling was the atmosphere the children had to endure in our home. As hard as I tried to create a safe, love-filled and secure home for our three children, Stan's daily drinking and angry outbursts shattered my hope for a peaceful home. Perhaps my expectations were part of the problem. I was trying to create what I had so sorely needed as a child—a calm, child-centered home. As I continued to read books on parenting and child development, I became more critical of Stan's harsh parenting style and my own failures as a mother.

In the summer of 1973, my niece, Joann, came to stay with us to help with the children. She was wonderful with them, and I enjoyed her company. I felt less lonely with her around, but

Stan's eruptions continued. One day, I went grocery shopping and came back with bags of fresh produce and canned goods. Joann and I worked quickly trying to get everything put away before Stan came home from work so as not to upset him with the mess. We filled a counter with canned goods in preparation for putting them in the pantry.

Stan walked in the door and inquired if I'd gotten an item he'd asked for. I apologized for forgetting it. He began yelling, swearing, calling me an idiot. Then he swiped his arm across the counter and sent all the cans flying onto the floor. He growled, "Pick them up!" and stormed off. By now both Joann and I were in tears as we knelt on the floor and picked up the cans. I was appalled that my niece had witnessed this scene and that my children had witnessed so many like it.

I could not know then that the hopelessness I felt in that moment would be transmuted, many years later, into a motivating anger to change my life and the lives of other women.

~

The kitchen in our Sheridan house and the downstairs bath next to it were destined to be demolished and replaced. A contractor came in October and tore off what had been a shed made into a kitchen at the turn of the century. I was left with a hot plate and refrigerator in the dining room, plugged into a long extension cord since we were determined to keep that room authentic, without electricity. The only source of water was up a steep flight of stairs to the antiquated upstairs bathroom. Jake was only six-months-old, and I was still nursing him. The contractor promised the renovation would be done by Christmas.

About six weeks into the work of building a new wing on the house, I found out I was pregnant again. I cried when Dr. Bennett told me. He calmed me down, and said he had to remove the I.U.D. I was using for birth control or I could get septic poisoning. He assured me the pregnancy would terminate with the procedure. I breathed a sigh of relief.

I adored Jake and had enjoyed the first six months with him before the chaos ensued with the renovations. Now I felt I was being cheated out of my time with him with so many distractions and constant exhaustion. I worried I couldn't give him enough of me. The two older children were attentive to him, but I couldn't imagine how another baby was going to fit into our family.

Dr. Bennett was wrong—the life within me held fast after the removal of the I.U.D. When I returned for my next appointment, he offered me an abortion because he knew I wasn't in an emotional state or a marital situation to handle another pregnancy. I refused. The thought of losing a baby by my own volition, even an unplanned one, was impossible to bear.

That day as we parted, Dr. Bennett held me in his arms as I wept into his chest. He said, "I'll always be there for you, Kath. You won't go through this alone." I never forgot his words.

~

The remodeling was going more slowly than anticipated, but the contractor demanded the first installment on the bill in early December. He proceeded to take off to Florida and did not return. We had to hire another contractor who would not be available for two months. I was dealing with morning sickness, an increasingly mobile eight-month-old baby, and two young children over-stimulated by the coming of Chanukah and Christmas.

Art, my therapist, supported me with his patient, low-key counseling. Dr. Bennett would take time to talk with me at each of my frequent visits. He was watching closely for any sign of trouble since I had already had problems with three of my four previous pregnancies. My friends were steadfast, especially Sarah and my new friend, Karen, with whom I had become very close.

And, yet, I was sinking into the black quicksand of depression, once again. I had stopped taking medication for depression years before, and would not consider taking it while I was pregnant.

The kitchen and downstairs bath, and a master bedroom and upstairs bath, were finished by my mother's seventieth birthday,

March 11, 1974. I had turned thirty, three days before. The renovations were everything I had hoped for: a huge country kitchen with a large fireplace and a trestle table for at least ten people. The kitchen had my signature red counters, and my mother had made red-checked curtains for it.

The master bedroom was painted candlelight yellow which I loved. Moving our bedroom upstairs freed up the light-filled room we had been using as our bedroom. As promised, Stan had bookshelves built and made it into a study. It was all just as I'd envisioned it. But, a heavy darkness continued to swirl around me and my child within—sucking me into its vortex. I knew this little one could feel everything I felt. Guilt and fear festered under my invisible black coat.

~

Stan loved to entertain. I felt indebted to him for my beautiful new kitchen. I had to pay my dues. In spite of my advancing pregnancy and the daily exhaustion from tending to three children and a big house, I often cooked for ten to twenty guests. Stan was in his element on these occasions. He never noticed the toll it took on me to prepare, serve and clean up the multi course meals he expected me to make. I was invisible to him— just a functioning part in the machinery of his life. If I couldn't function, he would take note without empathy or concern for my well-being—other than to do what was necessary to make me functional again.

Stan and his cousin, Jason, remained close. When Jason divorced Sherry, he was given full custody of their only child, Leah. He frequently came to spend the weekend with us. He walked in the door, opened the refrigerator and made himself at home. He assumed I'd take responsibility for his daughter so he'd be free to hang out, drink and watch ball games with Stan. I loved Leah, and knew she rarely saw her mother. I felt she needed my attention.

One evening Jason called and said he was getting married again and wanted us and our children and Leah to be the only witnesses. A couple of weeks later, our family piled into the car and made the trip to Burlington, Massachusetts where Jason lived. I met his wife-to-be for the first time. Ann was a small, soft-spoken woman with long brown hair and a beautiful smile. I liked her immediately.

I would come to find out she was a true Yankee—reserved, practical, stoic and frugal. We tentatively began our friendship. She was a very private person, and I was trying to hide my depression. We spoke superficially about life events at first, but it didn't take long for our friendship to deepen and grow into a strong bond.

Ann, Karen and Sarah were the three friends in whom I confided about my depression and marital situation. It became evident that others were aware of my struggle, too. My next door neighbor, Louise, urged me to take a Transcendental Meditation course with her—I knew it was her way of reaching out to me.

I was reluctant at first because of my previous experience many years before when my yoga instructor had seen an apparition of a little blonde girl standing beside me while I meditated. I was terrified because I thought it was my younger sister Rosie's ghost. But I was desperate to fill the longing for spiritual connection. Judaism had filled that void when we lived in Boston. I could go to services at Temple Israel or walk down Harvard Avenue in Brookline to buy the Jewish foods I had grown to love, peruse Jewish bookstores and shops, and feel connected with the Jewish community. Now, I seemed to be in limbo.

The tension in our home made it impossible to have an inner life. And, I needed to find something to alleviate the recurring depression. Also, I was four months pregnant and anxious about delivering a healthy baby. The cost of the TM class was $126, a fortune at the time, and Stan refused my request to go with Louise. I mentioned it to my therapist, Art, in a session, and he was sure TM would help me. He convinced Stan to let me take the course.

I went off to class with my friend, enjoying a night out away from Stan and the kids once a week for three weeks. TM is not a religious practice (or so we were told) and there was nothing contrary to my religious background in its teachings.

I loved this meditation program. Although my teacher denied it was a spiritual practice, it connected me to the esoteric teachings and mystical experiences I loved in Catholicism and Judaism. It validated my own spiritual life—spending time in nature, listening to music that sent my heart soaring, and finding moments of silence in a busy day. And, I was intrigued by the concept that Hindu meditation leads to a state of enlightenment, *Oneness with All That Is*.

When the day of my TM initiation came, I was nervous. I gathered the fruit and flowers I'd been instructed to bring for the ceremony and dressed in my best maternity outfit. An alcove off the main room of the Meditation Center was draped in bright blue satin cloth with gold trim, creating a sacred space. Against the far wall of this space stood an elaborate altar filled with Hindu artifacts and flowers. Two chairs faced the altar.

I sat in one of the chairs and the teacher stood and performed a Hindu ceremony in Sanskrit using the fruit and flowers I had brought. He sat beside me and quietly gave me some final instructions. Then he whispered the mantra in my ear.

I proceeded to meditate as I had been taught, repeating the mantra, noticing other thoughts and bringing my attention back to the mantra. I quickly realized I had just paid $126 for something I'd been doing since childhood, sitting by the river. I went home from this peaceful encounter with *The Sacred* to preside over a ruckus birthday party for my one-year-old son. A strange sensation came over me: I was happy.

Stan was determined to get his money's worth from my $126 venture into meditation, so he insisted I meditate twenty minutes twice a day as I had been instructed to do. He'd even watch the children, although that didn't disrupt his napping or watching sports on TV. It was a godsend to have these moments of respite. The meditation renewed me and made me more resilient. My days were filled with a lightness I hadn't felt in years. The boundaries of my body melted and a profound peace settled over me. My mood stabilized and my anxiety decreased.

~

I was doing so well that I convinced Dr. Bennett to let me try to deliver the baby naturally, although Jake had been delivered by C-section. Allowing natural childbirth after a C-section wasn't an accepted practice back then. Dr. Bennett was hesitant, but he promised he'd let me try. He said, "At the first sign of trouble I will not hesitate to take you into surgery and do a C-section."

On August 21, 1974, I went into labor. I meditated between contractions. I was on multiple monitors because of the problems I'd had before. It became clear that the meditation was effective in lowering my blood pressure, heart rate and skin resistance. TM was relatively new then, and doctors and nurses from all over the hospital came to check out this phenomenon. Seeing those machines document what happened in my body when I meditated helped me continue practicing TM faithfully for twenty years.

I was in labor for eight hours when I started to hemorrhage. I had placenta previa again. The condition had escaped the ultrasound, and the placenta remained intact until the baby started pushing through the canal. True to his word, Dr. Bennett rushed me into surgery. This time he couldn't let me stay awake to see the baby because my blood pressure spiked dangerously high. The nurses later told me they'd never seen this calm, professional doctor, so upset. I woke up fourteen hours later not having yet seen my baby girl. I've always felt that first abrupt separation from me disrupted little Debbie's whole system.

Deborah Jean Cohen was petite and beautiful. My sister had returned from Japan five years earlier, and she was there to help me when I came home with little Debbie, along with her five youngest children. Although the baby was peaceful while we shared a room in the hospital, she cried incessantly when I brought her home. Nothing would comfort her. She never slept through the night until she was three years old, and when she did sleep she sounded like she was gasping for breath. I would stand by her crib at night to make sure she was breathing, so even when she slept, I often did not.

Stan was impatient with her and with me. He was definitely getting less and less of my attention with each additional child, and he resented it. He was as demanding as ever and was getting even more vicious. He would rip me apart with his words, and his verbal and emotional bullying of the children escalated. By now we were seeing Art together, but even *he* did not get the full picture of our abusive household. He thought it was a triumph when Stan started to put his socks in the hamper.

I now understand the physical consequences of the verbal, emotional, physical, and sexual abuse I endured on me and the babies within my womb. I often wondered what impact the daily stress of Stan's constant negative tirades and assaults had on my pregnancies. Years later, when I researched studies on domestic violence, I learned it was often linked to complications during pregnancy such as miscarriage, low birthrate, premature birth, and even placenta-previa which had put both my life and my last two babies lives in peril.

~

During my first check-up with Dr. Bennett after the birth, he quietly told me, "I was afraid I was going to lose you on the table, Kath." He was close to tears as he spoke. He wanted to keep track of my progress, so we met frequently over the next few months and each parting after our time together became harder. One day, as we hugged good-bye, he bent down and kissed me gently on the lips. I nearly fell apart as I hurried out of his office before the dam broke and tears came gushing. The pain of leaving him, knowing how much he cared for me and how much I loved him, was unbearable.

I knew I couldn't go home feeling this way, so I ended up on my friend Karen's couch. She understood everything. She covered me with a blanket and let me cry. When the tears began to subside, she made me a cup of tea and we talked. I will always be grateful for her healing presence on that day.

My next appointment with Dr. Bennett was six months away, so I had time to reflect on our relationship. A poem sprung out of that reflection:

From that pain
you wrought inside of me
I grew.
Pushed through the dark
and moistened dirt,
unfolding one hesitant
green leaf
and grasped the sun.
Built a bud—
force fed it into blossom
on the ambrosia
of your love
and gave it voice—
my own—
strong
clear
longing
whole

— Kathleen, 1975

I tucked it in an envelope and sent it to him. I never received a response.

And the world cannot be discovered
by a journey of miles
no matter how long
but only by a spiritual journey,
a journey of one inch,
very arduous and humbling and joyful,
by which we arrive at the ground at our feet,
and learn to be at home.

– Excerpt from "Spiritual Journey" by Wendell Berry
from *Collected Poems 1957-1982*

CHAPTER TWENTY-TWO
For the Love of Houses

I WAS NOT ALONE in my desire for a peaceful home. As Ann, Jason's new wife, and I got to know each other better, our conversations deepened. It was obvious that Jason treated her as abusively as Stan treated me. She, too, had bouts of depression. On one of their visits, when I was struggling with depression once again, I had made brunch for the nine of us. The long trestle table in the kitchen was strewn with dirty dishes, napkins and food.

Ann must have heard my sigh when I went to clean the table. She quietly said, "Don't look at the whole table, just take a small section at a time. I'll help you." And she did, not only that day but for years to come. Our despondent moods seemed to be on reverse cycles: when she was down, I was up and vice versa.

We were both unhappy in our marriages. We started talking about our options for extricating ourselves from these destructive relationships. Nothing seemed feasible. Both Jason and Stan were powerful men. Jason was a lawyer, and Stan had family friends who were lawyers. We, half jokingly came to the conclusion that our only options were homicide, suicide or stay—two intelligent women who could not imagine how to break free from angry, controlling husbands. I didn't know then that our conversation would be prophetic.

A short time later, a friend and I started a consciousness raising group with women in the neighborhood. I brought this dilemma to the group. It became evident from our conversations that although Stan's behavior was extreme, the subservient role of women in our society was universal. I began to get angry, which gave me the strength to occasionally stand up for myself.

I took a daring step. Stan insisted I wear my long thick hair halfway down my back. It gave me headaches when I tied it back, and when loose it fell in my face while I tended to the children, cooked, or did other daily tasks. And, I hated that it made me look dowdy and unkempt. One day I left the children with a babysitter and went to a hairdresser. I had my hair cut to shoulder length. I liked what I saw in the mirror.

As I walked up the back steps to the screen door of the kitchen, Stan started screaming, "What did you do to your HAIR? I can't believe you cut it! That's proof you don't love me! I'm going to DIVORCE you—you don't care anything about me" As I stepped into the kitchen I noticed our friend, Don, standing by the sink with a drink in his hand. He was watching the scene with amusement.

He said to Stan with good humor, "Are you crazy? It's her hair! She can wear it any way she wants!" Stan shut up. I was stunned that a man had stood up for me. Something shifted. I began to challenge my assumption that somehow Stan was always right, and I had to acquiesce to his demands.

There were moments when I could see a spark of good in Stan's soul. Those moments kept me hopeful. One spring he planted rose bushes against the split-wood fence at the front of the house. Their blossoms splashed red against the grey weathered wood all summer long. Every year, they appeared again as if to remind me of what I infrequently glimpsed in Stan. I wanted to love this man, to make sense out of my world and fulfill what I still thought was God's mandate for me to love and transform him. I wrote:

To Stanley

You know you gave me pleasure
the day you brought me those rose bushes—
bare branches, roots wrapped in burlap.

I was pleased with your perception
of what would make me happy
and appreciative of the time and energy
their planting incurred.

But do you know what an on-going joy
those growing, blossoming bushes
have been to me each late spring
and long into summer?

Did you suspect
when you gave them to me
that the sight of them in bloom
would cause me to love you more?

If you had,
there probably would be roses
growing from every inch of earth
we own.

– Kathleen, 1976

He never acknowledged the poem.

One of my favorite stories is Antoine de Saint-Exupéry's *The Little Prince*. In it the Little Prince, who lives on a tiny planet, patiently tends to an ornery Rose. She is boastful and is never satisfied with his care. Yet he is invariable kind to her. When he goes exploring other planets, he finds he has learned to love the Rose by caring for her so long. He misses her while he's away. The Little Prince's friend, the fox, says, "It's the time you have wasted for your rose that has made your rose so important."

I tried to apply the lessons of *The Little Prince* to our marriage. I hoped I would come to love Stan if I patiently cared for him. Instead, I grew to hate him more. With each cruel word he uttered; each time he denigrated one of our children or disregarded their needs or forced himself on me for sex, enmity grew in my heart.

I later wrote: "The most painful result of the constant abuse was I realized I was a person who could hate."

~

Tension always increased as the supper hour drew near in our home—in part because my anxiety about getting everything right grew exponentially the closer we got to sitting down for the meal. The list would tick off in my head—make sure his salad is ready when he walks in the door, get Davey or Rachel to set the table, check to make certain they fill his water glass to the top and, for God's sake, don't burn the meat. Get everything to the table on time and HOT! We held our breath when he came to the table—what would he find to yell about? There was always something.

One Friday evening I prepared a beautiful Shabbat meal. I liked to eat by candlelight in our elegant, blue, unelectrified dining room on the Sabbath and holidays. As I surveyed the table set with good china, food hot and steaming, I was pleased with my efforts. I called Stan and the kids to the dinner table. They settled in their seats, and before I could light the Shabbat candles and say the blessing, he spotted the baked potatoes on the table. He went into a rage. As the food got cold, he ranted.

"POTATOES! You made POTATOES? They're a useless food! How could you be so stupid to serve them? What kind of idiot are you?" I was crushed. My heart froze. I felt nauseous. The children sat in stony silence—no one could eat, which made him even angrier. In tears, I removed the potatoes from the table. It was the last Shabbat meal I ever cooked.

~

Looking back, I wonder why I did not object to this pattern of subjugation. It was so pervasive and familiar; I was like a fish that doesn't see the water in which it swims. I was consumed with anxiety—trying to do everything *right*. I thought I was a terrible wife. One day in the middle of one of his rages, Stan turned to the children and said, "Your mother is crazy and her family is crazy, and she has passed the genes onto you." I stood there astounded that Stan could be so cruel as to sow doubt in our children about about me, my family and their own mental well-being.

His vicious diatribes against me messed with my sense of reality. I could no longer trust myself because I'd internalized what Stan said—"You're making a big deal out of nothing." "You're an idiot!" "You're a crazy, selfish bitch!" "How stupid can you be?"

Again, I contacted a lawyer. He basically said, "You made your bed, now you have to lie in it." Divorce seemed out of the question.

Above all, I wanted stability for my children and myself. Our home life was chaotic and unpredictable. Yet, we had established a stable sense of *place*. I loved the town we lived in, our land and the house we'd just finished restoring after six years of work. I told Stan I wanted to be buried in the field behind the house.

Both Stan's tire business and *The Bittersweet Barn Shop* were doing well. The children were in a good school system. I had a community of friends, neighbors, and health care professionals on whom I depended. The TM community was a life-line to me—as was the consciousness raising group.

Without any discussion, Stan announced he wanted to move again in spite of the fact that we had just finished restoring the house and his mother had recently been diagnosed with terminal lung cancer. Since his brothers couldn't work with him, they were glad to buy out his share of the tire business. He wanted to invest in a convenience store in Vermont, Maine or New Hampshire. I protested vehemently! David and Rachel were going into fourth grade, a difficult time to make a transition. Jake was in an excellent nursery school and Debbie was not yet two. I would be moving farther from my mother who was now having health problems.

My nearby friend, Karen, and I continued to support each other. We spent many hours together with all seven of our children, and occasionally would get some time alone. Our bond continued to grow over the years as we shared good times and celebrations, and leaned on each other through crises. Moving away from her was the greatest loss of all. Stan was jealous of anyone who took my attention away from him—even our children.

At one point, he said, "It's Karen or me!"

In a flash of defiance I said, "Then it's Karen!"

Maybe this move was a ploy to break our bond, but it didn't work—Stan would move me away from Karen, but he couldn't move her out of my heart. We remain friends to this day.

Stan was unmoved by my arguments. Many years later, a leading expert in domestic violence said, "…frequent moves are a common strategy of men who abuse their partners. It keeps their victims off balance and disconnected from a support system." That was exactly what Stan accomplished. I left my rose bushes behind and the hope that anything would ever change.

~

The quote was by Lundy Bancroft, an author, workshop leader, and consultant on domestic violence, in his book "Why Does He Do That." It went on to say, "Abusers thrive on creating confusion including confusion about the abuse itself." That summed up my experience—I was confused and unbalanced by arbitrary and cruel decisions. "If you try to leave," Stan said, "I will demolish you; I WILL destroy you; I will get custody of the kids because you're crazy!" I believed him.

~

Stan began to look for a business to buy. By this time, I felt empowered to make some stipulations about the move. I wanted to live less than an hour from a major medical center, less than two hours from my mother and in proximity to a reform Jewish Community. The search went on for months. Stan finally found a convenience store in Sheffield, New Hampshire, in July of 1976.

The day he signed the papers, his mother died. Stan and his mother had a contentious relationship when he was young, but on her last visit to our home in Sheridan, she said to me, "The one I can always count on is Stan." I hoped he would take comfort in her words which I repeated to him. Instead of openly grieving in the months following her death, his drinking increased, his anger escalated.

This small New Hampshire town was over three hours from my mother. We were one of only six Jewish families and the closest synagogue was conservative. But, the world famous medical centers of Boston were only an hour away, which gave me some peace of mind.

Stan bought the large building that housed the store and several apartments. One apartment became our temporary home while we waited for our house in Sheridan to sell. The new property was in the Town Center which included the Town Hall, a post office, a bank, the volunteer fire department, the library and several beautiful old homes. It was ten miles from the city of Danforth and three miles from Windsor, the home of the Windsor Academy.

Stan hung a red stained-glass Jewish Star of David in the store window the first day he owned it. As the town's people began to stream in, he claimed that they were coming to see if we had horns and tails. Such images are found in materials by anti-Semites, including a small book with graphic illustrations of Jews as devils. It was initially published in the middle-ages and is in circulation to this day.

Once, shortly after we moved to Sheffield, I was standing in the store parking lot talking with Stan, Debbie on my hip. He said, "When they come for us, you'll go to your mother's with the kids and change your name back to Marino, and I'll head for the hills and fight!" Even after the incident in Sheridan with my children being called an anti-Semitic slur, and with Stan's company hiring him as a token Jew, I could not fathom this kind of thinking.

Stan joined the Sheffield Volunteer Fire Department which entailed our attending social affairs at the firehouse. Socializing in large groups of strangers was difficult for me. The first night we attended one of these gatherings I made an effort to mingle and make small talk while waiting for the program to start. The program consisted of several speakers talking about the work of the volunteers and plans for the expansion of the firehouse.

Then the entertainment portion of the program began. A small nervous man got up and began telling anti-Semitic jokes. Stan laughed. Appalled, I stood up and walked out. I was aghast to find blatant anti-Semitism in this town. The realization that my children would have to deal with this kind of prejudice for the rest of their lives brought me to tears. The words, "Never Again," the cry of Jews everywhere in remembrance of the Holocaust, reverberated through my soul in a way they never had before.

When Stan returned home, I angrily asked, "Why did you stay and listen to that garbage?"

He said, "Oh, you get used to it!"

I swore I would not get used to it and would confront anti-Semitism wherever I encountered it. The next day I went to the firehouse to find Phil, the short thin man with greasy dirty blond hair, who had told the jokes.

"Phil, I was very upset by the jokes you told last night—do you realize they're anti-Semitic—against Jews?"

"I didn't mean anything by it," he said his faded blue eyes cast down, avoiding my gaze.

"Those jokes are offensive and reinforce Jewish stereotypes. I found them extremely hurtful."

Phil looked like a little kid called into the principal's office. Without looking up, he said, "I promise I'll never tell those jokes again, Mrs. Cohen."

I realized he was saying he would not tell them *in front of me again.*

~

One day, a man posted a "for sale" sign on the lawn of the house across the street from Stan's store. The house looked like something out of a horror movie. Old and dilapidated, it stood on a small hill, with tattered curtains and torn green shades in the windows, the exterior paint peeling. Stan grabbed his checkbook and started out the door.

"Don't you *dare!*" I yelled. I wasn't going to do another six years of renovations—living in the same chaos of my childhood through the years Mark was *working on the house.* And, we still hadn't sold our house in Sheridan. Stan took his checkbook out of his pocket and bought the house on the spot without consulting me. I was so furious I refused to see it for three weeks. When I finally walked through the double-doors of the front entrance, I fell in love.

Although it was in deplorable condition, the large foyer was elegant: high ceilings, a long wide sloping staircase with wainscoting leading to a landing where a six-foot, small-paned window looked out on the backyard and the woods beyond. Three high-rise steps called "Good Morning Stairs" descended onto the landing from each of the two small bedrooms on either side. A short continuation of the main staircase led back to a wide sitting area between two large bedrooms in the front of the house.

Carved moldings graced every room. Six fireplaces were closed and filled with dirt and sand. The seventh, a large open fireplace in the dining room, had a beehive oven. There were gun-stock posts in the oldest section of the house, a more rustic look than in the front, which had been added on in 1720. The house had been the first parsonage in the area, similar to our Sheridan home. It sat on five acres of land with an ancient locust tree dominating the woods at the back of the property.

The wallpaper dated back to the thirties and was faded and peeling off the walls. There was a layer of soot over everything. The owner, Mrs. Cole, was a widow in her eighties who had lived there alone for the past forty years after her husband died. She proudly told us she was an aide at a nursing home and took care of "the old people." Her frail frame and gnarled hands belied her strength and energy. She chattered non-stop, determined to impart her deep love for her home.

The back part of the house, in which Mrs. Cole lived, was the original house built in 1690. She used the back staircase to get to her bedroom. It was sharply curved with narrow high-rise steps and was enclosed in what looked like a closet by the dining room fireplace. It was called an *Indian Staircase*, built to protect the occupants during an Indian raid.

While waiting for the papers to be signed, Mrs. Cole gave us permission to enter the house while she was still living there to take measurements and make preparations for the needed repairs. We would enter the premises with bated breath, afraid we would find Mrs. Cole dead at the bottom of those stairs.

My Soul's Home

Good Morning Stairs

When we passed papers on the house six weeks later, mine was the only name on the deed. The business was in Stan's name, and he couldn't risk losing everything in a lawsuit against the store. I felt I now had some leverage—he couldn't sell this house without my signature. His mother had left us a small inheritance which we poured into restoring the house.

Contractors overran the property, first raising the house off its foundation to replace the rotted sill beams on which it stood. They re-wired the electrical system, replaced all the plumbing, painted the outside and tore off the lath and plaster—used to cover the walls in Victorian times—and thus uncovered beautiful wood panels.

I told Stan we didn't need to open all the fireplaces after he'd opened the first one making a mess with sand and dirt scattered everywhere. Still, every Saturday when I went to the Laundromat to do twenty-five loads of wash, I came home to find he'd opened another fireplace, until he had opened them all. The mess was left for me to clean up.

In order to save money, I stripped wallpaper and removed layers of milk-based paint from hundreds of feet of wainscoting, the panels over the fireplaces, and all the trim. Then I applied an undercoat of paint to the bare wood. I cleaned up after the workers at the end of each day. This went on for months.

We moved in amidst the bedlam. My piano didn't come with us—I can't remember why—but I soon regretted that decision. Although the living room was in terrible condition, its high ceiling, finely finished panels above the fireplace, carved moldings and hardwood floor assured me it could be restored to its previous elegance. It was a room for a Baby Grand and old world furnishings. It remained empty for as long as we lived there, except for a decrepit old upright piano that Stan dragged home.

Meanwhile, when the weather got cold in the first few months after the move, before the kitchen was renovated, we came downstairs in the morning and found the water pipes had frozen overnight. I called Mrs. Cole. "Mrs. Cole, how did you keep the pipes from freezing in the kitchen at night?"

Quiet Elegance

"Oh, dear, I should have told you. You have to keep the water running a trickle and you need to open the cabinet door beneath the sink and the one to the left of it." We never had a problem again as long as I remembered her instructions before going to bed.

One day, Stan came out of the downstairs shower shaking his head. "I think Debbie is confused about using the potty—there's *shit* in the shower." I questioned little Debbie to see if perhaps she had misunderstood my potty training instructions, but she was insistent that she was going in the right place. I called Mrs. Cole again and asked what she knew about the septic system.

"Dear, I can tell you what you need to know," she said. "The tank number is 58723554, and I just had it pumped out in 1943!" This was 1976. A septic crew came in and opened up the spot Mrs. Cole had indicated and found the tank had totally disintegrated. We needed a new septic system.

As we began the finish work, the house spoke to me room by room as I chose the wallpaper and paints for the interior. Working with a gifted painter and wallpaper hanger, each room took on new life—all in six months! I felt more at home in this house than I had in my childhood home or in any other house in which I'd lived. There was an intimacy in my relationship with it as if I'd walked through these rooms in other lifetimes.

I once again declared I wanted to be buried in the field behind the house at the edge of the woods. The children quickly acclimated to their new surroundings, building forts in the woods and making new friends. One early spring morning, I found myself on the landing of the stairs looking out the large small-paned window onto the back yard.

"What have those kids done now?" I thought in exasperation. The back yard was strewn with what looked like brightly colored toys. I marched outside and gasped at the sight. Before me lay a huge perennial garden—crocus, tulips, daffodils, hyacinths, day lilies and pink poppies—in a marvelous disarray like the English gardens I had admired in *House Beautiful* magazines.

I excitedly called Mrs. Cole and exclaimed, "Mrs. Cole! You didn't tell me about the garden!"

"Oh, yes, dear, I planted some of those bulbs thirty years ago. You have to weed the garden EVERY DAY. It will get ahead of you real fast! There's also a strawberry patch in the back field."

Millay's cry for new birth rose in my own throat.

Oh God, I cried, give me new birth
And put me back upon the earth!
Upset each cloud's gigantic gourd
And let the heavy rain, down-poured
In one big torrent, set me free,
Washing my grave away from me!

I ceased; and through the breathless hush
That answered me, the far-off rush
Of herald wings came whispering
Like music down the vibrant string
Of my ascending prayer, and—crash!
Before the wild wind's whistling lash
The startled storm-clouds reared on high
And plunged in terror down the sky!
And the big rain in one black wave
Fell from the sky and struck my grave.

*When despair for the world grows in me
and I wake in the night at the least sound
in fear for what my life and my children's lives may be,
I go and lie down where the wood drake
rests in beauty on the water, and the great heron feeds.
I come into the peace of wild things....*

– Excerpt from "The Peace of Wild Things" by Wendell Berry
from *Collected Poems 1957-1982*

CHAPTER TWENTY-THREE
Finding Strength

STAN'S EXPERIENCE owning and running a tire business in Sheridan did not prepare him for the rigors of owning a convenience store. The store was open from 6:00 AM to 11:00 PM. Stan and his employees worked nonstop to keep up with the gas pump sales, the meat counter customers, and filling the beer coolers and shelves. Stan enlisted me to work several night shifts a week to save money. He agreed to "watch" the kids, although he was only vaguely aware of them as he sprawled on the couch watching TV. He did not oversee their homework or bedtime routine. Chaos ensued the next morning as I tried to get them off to school.

In the first few months that we owned the store, the hectic pace at home kept me numb to the losses incurred by the move. I slowly began to thaw and missed the friends I had left behind. One evening, alone in the cavernous, creaky old building which housed the store, with its well-worn paths in the wooden floor and dark unlit corners, a young woman came in. She said, "I'm escaping my crazy household for a few minutes. I have a three-year-old and I'm nursing my two month old twins. I haven't been out of the house in weeks!"

I was sitting at the cash register on a break and welcomed the company. She introduced herself as Dee and sat on the counter to chat. We talked for over an hour. She was funny and smart. Our friendship began that night.

Dee invited me to join a group she was starting. It was based on a form of peer counseling called Peer Counselors United or PCU. I missed my therapist, Art Randall, and the consciousness raising group I had co-founded in Sheridan. I gratefully accepted Dee's offer.

Thus began my seventeen year involvement with this peer-counseling community. The theory behind the practice is that humans have natural healing abilities which are suppressed in our society. These abilities can be reactivated with good attention from another person or a group of people. With all the issues that were surfacing in my life, the timing of Dee's offer was fortuitous.

I attended weekly classes at her house with a group of seven people I did not know. She taught us how to give our undivided attention to the person we were counseling [the client] and to not give advice, interrupt or redirect. She instructed us keep our eyes on the client and to listen with interest and caring attention. Then we would reverse roles and the counselor became the client.

In one of our first classes, Dee read a quote from the PCU manual: "Studies show a connection between emotional expression and physical, mental and emotional health. According to these studies, crying, laughing, shaking, raging, yawning, talking animatedly or reluctantly all have healing effects and should be encouraged, not suppressed." I had known this intuitively, but hadn't trusted my instincts.

As peer counselors we were to watch for these emotional signals when counseling someone and gently encourage the person to feel the emotion. With the counselor's quiet attention, the client was often moved to express what he or she was feeling. It took me a while to trust the process and my fellow peer-counselors. For someone who had been taught not to cry and yet was always fighting back tears, this form of counseling brought relief. Dee and the members of the group proved to be trustworthy and supportive.

I slowly started to disclose what was going on inside our home. The group listened with compassion and identified my husband's rage-filled outbursts as domestic violence. One counselor said, "Nothing you could possibly do could warrant Stan's cruel and abusive treatment." That sentence reverberated in my head and carried me through many of Stan's verbal assaults. The group's view of me and my situation contradicted Stan's distorted perception of reality and my own low self-evaluation.

Peer Counselors United also promoted a form of parenting that was aligned with my parenting philosophy: respect for children, allowing emotional expression, encouraging the child's interests, and re-directing rather than punishing unacceptable behavior. I attempted a balance between parenting more liberally *and* ensuring the children didn't incite Stan's ire, so they would not be subjected to his wrath.

One day, when I returned from my PCU class, Stan confronted me. He said, "It's this counseling group or me!" I calmly said, "If you put it that way, it's the counseling group!" He backed down and never questioned my involvement with the organization again. I hoped Peer-counseling was my path to freedom.

~

When my children walked in the door each day after school, they would greet me, and then ask, "Is Dad home?"

If I said "Yes," their next question was "Has he had a drink yet?"

If the answer to that question was "Yes," they scattered. They would also inquire if I had meditated, knowing I was in a much better mood if I had.

Stan's withholding of affection, validation, simple kindness and expressions of love had an insidious effect. My heart would sink when I watched as one of the children approached him with a work of art or a good grade on a school paper. He would barely acknowledge their presence, his eyes riveted on the TV. It was obvious that the children felt diminished and disappointed when this happened. I wanted nothing more than to free my children from their father's angry glare, from his iron-fisted control, from his alcohol induced diatribes, from his indifference.

In one journal entry I wrote: "He [Stan] makes our lives miserable and then he wonders why Davey shakes and Debbie gets so anxious. ... He can come storming in here and start yelling if supper is a few minutes late. He can crush a child verbally for the least little thing. I know I give him power to do this to us, and I must find the strength to stop him from destroying us."

Another journal entry illustrates my own desire to be free: "I am frightened. I am trapped. I want to be beautiful to someone. I want someone to make love to me like I was there. Talk to me, touch me, listen to me, *see* me. I feel like I ache to ends of my soul. I've always labeled it selfishness, self-pity, being spoiled. Now I want to call it human."

Our dinner times were still fraught with tension. I decided to introduce a diversionary tactic, applying a practice we used in peer-counseling. In class, we would go around the circle and appreciate something about each person. I transferred this practice to my family. Everyone had a "Love Day" one day a week, including Stan and me. On the person's Love Day, he or she could choose a favorite food for supper, and we would go around the table and offer the Love Day recipient a sincere compliment or appreciation.

I encouraged everyone to give examples and look at the person to whom they were speaking. Stan sputtered over this for a while but he gradually seemed to enjoy the process. The Love Day recipient also got to have tea time with me after supper and could choose an activity for us to do together.

David and Rachel were in early adolescence by then, so spending time with Mom wasn't high on their list of fun things to do. David occasionally shared his music with me or brought me to the cellar to view his latest diorama of a well researched battle which took him weeks to set up. And, Rachel sometimes shared her poetry or we'd watch a TV show together.

Jake, who had taught himself to read at the age of four, was into science projects by third grade. He set up his "laboratory" in a closet under the stairs. Our time was spent huddled in the closet where we worked on experiments together. Debbie loved to dance so we watched a TV show, *Solid Gold Dancers*. She was a natural and learned all the moves on the show. These Love Days went on for almost two years.

However, even this attempt to distract Stan at the dinner table did nothing to dampen his explosive behavior. I finally sought out another lawyer, this time a woman, in my fourth attempt to extricate myself from the marriage. My expectation was that a woman lawyer would be more understanding than the male attorneys I had previously consulted. Instead, this woman was cold and patronizing. She said, "I will need an advance payment of $3,000 to start any kind of legal proceedings." I thanked her for her time and left.

Stan still had complete control of our finances, doling out money to me as if I were a child. I brought my discouragement to the counseling group. They coached me to think about my options. One option was to get a job and save the money I'd make. I hadn't been employed outside the home in twelve years, and I knew Stan would object. But, inspired by my peer-counselors' support, without saying a word to Stan, I prepared a resume, put on my only suit—a bright yellow linen—and went in search of a job to earn my own money to finance a divorce.

My first and only stop was the University of New Hampshire Personnel Department. I was immediately hired as an assistant secretary in the Plant Science Department. I was thrilled and terrified. Telling Stan was my biggest hurdle. Then I had to face my fear of failure.

Stan predictably blew up when I gave him the news. He forbade me to go to work. I stood firm. I assured him it was only twenty hours a week and I had made arrangements for childcare. This did not dissuade him. I would not give in—my counseling group cheered me on. That Monday I went to work. My anxiety must have been evident because my co-workers in the Department took pains to reassure me I would do fine.

The first task I was given was to make coffee in a large drip coffeemaker. Having never encountered one before, I stood in the break room blankly looking at the machine. Dr. Stuart Clemens, Chair of the Department, came in and introduced himself. He quickly assessed my dilemma and chuckled, putting me at ease. He kindly showed me how to make the coffee.

The next gadget I had to tackle was the copier which also confounded me. The secretary in charge, Carolyn, patiently helped me unravel its mysteries. She and I soon became good friends. The Office Manager, Stella, who was a grandmotherly woman with a cloud of dandelion fuzz-like white hair, took me in hand and bolstered my confidence with her praise. I couldn't have landed in a softer nest to hone my secretarial skills and reintegrate myself into the outside world.

I became a productive and valued member of the Department. Work was a respite from Stan's constant criticism at home. The professors and my co-workers treated me with respect and appreciation. However, my plan to save money to pay for a divorce was thwarted because Stan insisted I turn over my check to him. He gave me a pittance to get to and from work.

When Stan found out one of my benefits was a free course at the University, he insisted I enroll in a class so we would "get our money's worth" out of my working. I was more nervous about going back to school than I'd been about going back to work. The last time I was in school was at the age of twenty-one—I was now thirty-six. I didn't know how I would juggle the kids, the house, my job *and* school, but I signed up for *The Psychology of Women* taught by a graduate student, Susan Goldstein.

When I went to my first class, I was the only "non-traditional student," as we older students were called in those days. I looked at the sea of fresh young faces and wanted to run. Susan, the instructor, only a few years older than my classmates, was a bright young woman and an excellent teacher. She, too, recognized how nervous I was and encouraged me to relax and enjoy the class.

As I read the assignments, a new consciousness dawned. My plight in a dictatorial marriage was a fate I shared with many women—it was the result of male dominance in our society. Words like *feminism, patriarchy, misogyny, sexism, oppression,* and *empowerment* became part of my vocabulary.

My entrance into college life gave me a legitimate excuse to write, something I had always loved to do. A *Reaction Paper* was due at the end of each week. As shock waves overwhelmed me from our class discussions and the reading material, I revealed my truth to Susan and myself in those papers. She praised my courage and my writing. This was not a mere intellectual exercise. I was putting my life on the page.

Until I delved into the writings of the prominent feminists of the time, I had not grasped how embedded the denigration of women was in all aspects of society. A weight lifted off my shoulders as I realized that my marital situation, in part, grew out of societal inequities not personal failure.

I began to take up the cause—standing up to Stan, my brothers, and even a family friend, who was a judge—about the equality of women. I now understood the reality of oppression at a visceral level. I became articulate again, as I had been before my convent days. I felt myself coming alive after suppressing my opinions for so long, ardently trying to be a "good girl" all my life.

Still, when I faced my first final exam, I froze. I could not put my pencil onto the paper. I closed my eyes and tried to calm myself. I looked up to find Susan squatting next to me. "Having a little test anxiety, Kath?" I nodded and tears began to roll down my face. She said, "Take your time." The tears cleared my head, and I went on to ace the test. The taste of academic success was exhilarating. I was coming alive as Millay so beautifully describes:

> *I know not how such things can be;*
> *I only know there came to me*
> *A fragrance such as never clings*
> *To aught save happy living things;*
>
> *A sound as of some joyous elf*
> *Singing sweet songs to please himself,*
> *And, through and over everything,*
> *A sense of glad awakening.*

CHAPTER TWENTY-FOUR
Moonrise

IN THE SPRING OF 1980, with my first academic achievement, I felt a small sliver of hope. Education could be my path to freedom from my marriage, but I was still dubious that I could succeed. I made a deal with myself: if I could get a decent grade in *Statistics* (a requirement for a degree in Psychology), I would go back to school. If not, I would give up the dream and reconcile to what one lawyer had said to me, "You made your bed, now lie in it."

Statistics was a summer class starting in June and ending in mid-July. When I picked up my text book at the university bookstore, my small quotient of hope diminished. It looked like it was written in a foreign language. By some Divine Grace, my statistics instructor, Tim Ober, was a gifted, perceptive and kind teacher.

Once again, I was the oldest student in the class. When I walked into the large, echoing classroom, Tim immediately acknowledged my presence and suggested I sit close to the front. I took a seat in the first row on the right side of the room, close to the door. The walls were painted a dull shade of green and the blackboard covered the whole front wall. My classmates were newly minted mathematicians—well versed in advanced algebra and calculus.

After I went to Tim several times for help, he got a feel for the way I learned and how I thought. He would lecture the class for ten or fifteen minutes and then look over at me to see if I was getting the lesson. If he saw a blank or scared look on my face, he'd slide over to my side of the room and raise his arms as if conducting a symphony and say, "Intuitively speaking…" He would then launch into the same subject from a different perspective—one that I could understand. I will be forever grateful to this man for his patience. He taught me that there was more than one way of learning and teaching, knowledge I would draw upon several years later.

~

Meanwhile, my mother had just been diagnosed with uterine cancer and was scheduled for a hysterectomy. The weekend before her surgery, I piled the kids into the car and made the trek to Connecticut to see her. When we arrived, I walked in and found my brother, Thomas, who'd been estranged from the family for twelve years, sitting across the table from my mother playing Scrabble. The children clamored all around me to get to Gram as I stood, frozen in shock.

Tom looked up and said in his nonchalant low-key voice, "Hi! Who are all these people?" I introduced him to my four children.

My mother looked immensely happy in spite of her impending surgery. Mark disappeared into his workshop downstairs, which surprised me since he usually participated fully in our family gatherings. Tom began talking to my children, trying to get to know them.

I asked about his children and his wife, Lily. He told me he and Lily were divorced. I tried not to register my surprise. I found out that Tom, who had been a highly respected chemist and had worked on the first U.S. satellite, had left his career in scientific research and now owned a used bookstore.

Not a word was said about why he'd abruptly stopped talking to the family, or why he was back again. I left, still in the dark about the hiatus in our relationship. I did not know, nor dare to ask, if it was because Mom had given me a bigger, better piece of land than his. I felt confused and unsettled.

A few days later I arrived at the Massachusetts General Hospital in Boston to be with my siblings as we waited for Mom to come out of surgery. My final exam in *Statistics* was scheduled that week. I brought about a hundred 3X5 cards with me with questions and answers that might be on the test. I studied for hours while my siblings talked and paced. Finally, the surgeon came to talk to us.

"There was nothing I could do," he said in a defeated tone. "I opened her up and closed her up. She has an advanced form of sarcoma, and I couldn't remove the tumor because it just crumbled in my hands. She won't make it through the summer." He recommended chemotherapy to which my mother consented.

After one round, she said, "Enough of that!" It made her ill—she vomited for days. She was not willing to sacrifice quality of life for a few extra weeks on the planet. She wanted to enjoy the things she loved: playing the piano, listening to music and spending time with family and friends. By then she and Mark had sold the big house and bought a smaller one. It was her sanctuary. A small pond graced the property—she spent hours looking out the window watching the wildlife that was drawn to its waters.

I reminded Mom that my son David's Bar Mitzvah was in November and that he was counting on his grandmother being there. There were still many devout Catholics in the family, and the prayer chains and novenas began. I recited the Jewish prayers for healing, but in my anguished moments the Catholic prayers of my childhood formed on my lips.

My final grade in *Statistics* was B+, good enough for me to continue pursuing a degree. I dove back into my studies after things settled down to the usual level of pandemonium.

As I was beginning my new classes, I started to prepare for our son's Bar Mitzvah. Since we had no affiliation with a local Jewish community, David—as he now preferred to be called—had been studying his Torah portion with a tutor for almost a year. I wrote the service following some of the traditions and creating some of our own, and David illustrated the cover on the order of service. We decided to hold the celebration in the newly finished firehouse hall on the second floor. Mom was holding on.

We invited sixty townspeople who had become our customers and friends, in part to help demystify Jewish traditions and dispel any myths they might hold about Jews. Our family and friends from around the country accounted for another seventy guests. A friend, who was a Cantor, came to lead the ceremony. I cooked and baked for months, making huge pans of lasagna, kugel and chopped liver—this was an Italian Jewish Bar Mitzvah! Mark made a multi-layered rich yellow cake and decorated it with his usual flair. It was stunning.

On the day of the Bar Mitzvah, November 4, 1980, my mother had to be carried up the stairs to the hall on a chair. She was thin, frail, and her wig kept slipping to one side of her bald head, but she was there. David was poised and confident. He read his Torah portion with ease and gave a short speech he'd written.

The celebration was a huge success. It was hard to believe that thirteen years earlier we almost gave up hope that our son would survive, and now he was flourishing. Only his maternal grandmother believed this day would come when he was lying in an incubator thirteen years before. Now she was there to witness his coming of age in the Jewish tradition. I was immensely grateful for the gift of her presence.

Mom made progress after the uterine surgery. Her hair grew back in soft white curls. She gained some weight and started cooking and baking again. She had lost her leg four years earlier at the age of seventy-two, but she got up on a prosthetic leg and did everything she used to do. Now, she fought her way back again.

I cherished every moment with her. The children and I went down to see her as often as possible. We spent all the holidays together and enjoyed her lively presence. Every time she sat down at the piano and played the old songs, I stored away the memories. It was a miraculous reprieve from the diagnosis she had been given after the surgery. Still, knowing it would not last forever, I could feel the impending grief gathering within me and often took it into a peer-counseling session to give it voice.

~

I decided to do an internship as an independent study during the spring semester and made an agreement with a local shelter for battered women to work fifteen hours a week. I thought I could help these battered women and their children with my newly acquired peer-counseling skills. No classroom could have given me the education I received at that shelter.

I was assigned to individual women to help them cope with their emotions as they sifted through painful memories and reclaim the parts of themselves lost through years of domination by their abusers. As a court advocate, I supported the women during legal proceedings and provided a buffer from unwanted contact with their perpetrators. There were some frightening moments—as one woman and I pulled out of the court parking lot to return to the shelter, her abuser began following my car. Making some quick turns, I finally lost him. We were both shaken.

I facilitated groups, made safety plans with women who weren't ready to leave their perpetrators, and supported women planning to live on their own. My favorite assignment was working with the children. We went on outings and I kept them occupied with art projects, story time and music. I will never forget one nine-year-old boy, Kenny, traumatized by the violence in his home, reticent and untrusting. He barely talked.

I took him to the beach one day—we walked the whole length of the beach. When we got to farthest point, standing on a rocky breakwater jutting into the sea, I asked if there was something he'd like to bring back to the shelter with him. Without saying a word, he pointed to a large white rock. I picked it up with some difficulty and carried it all the way back to the car. That was it—he started pouring out his story—I had earned his trust.

One woman in her sixties had been battered for forty years by her husband who was a professor at UNH. She reluctantly came to the shelter after an especially egregious attack. As she sat around the kitchen table with other residents of the shelter and talked with the counselors, she came to realize what she was experiencing at the hands of her husband was unacceptable and she did not deserve this vile treatment. She made the decision to leave.

Her mood immediately lightened, relief was evident on her face. She asked me to drive her to the Catholic Church she attended so she could talk to her priest. We chatted on the way over—she was almost giddy with the prospect of living a life without the violence she had endured for so many years.

I sat in the car while she went to talk to the priest. As soon as she emerged from the rectory door, my heart sank. She was bent, walking slowly and pale. I knew what had taken place. Her priest told her she had to honor her marriage vows and stay with her husband no matter what he did. We returned to the shelter in silence.

These "battered" women gave me so much in return for the time and attention I gave them. Their authenticity, sense of humor, resiliency and compassion reminded me they were not "battered women." They were women—wise, caring and strong—who had experienced domestic violence. They shared their stories with me to use in my final paper, and in describing their lives they helped me see that I was one of them. One woman who had lost her eye when her husband punched her in the face said, "The verbal abuse is what haunts me since leaving him. His words ring in my ears every day."

Many others said the same thing—physical wounds heal; verbal and emotional abuse leave lasting scars. Many years later I wrote, "Sometimes I feel like I ran into a glass door and I'll be picking slivers of glass out from under my skin for the rest of my life. His [Stan's] words are like shards of glass, imbedded deep within me, painfully and unexpectedly, coming to the surface from time to time." It became clear to me that what I had endured for the past fifteen years was a form of battering. My peer-counselors held me with their gentle attention while I faced this reality on a daily basis. I spent the next eight years studying and working in the field of domestic violence.

~

When Mom ended up in the hospital again the following November, right before Thanksgiving, we all knew the miracle had run its course. She no longer could eat without vomiting. The doctor said, "The cancer has metastasized to her stomach, and she won't make it until Christmas." She was adamant that she wanted no heroic efforts, and she wanted to go home to die.

After the doctor left, and minutes after receiving this heartbreaking news, my mother proudly turned to her roommate and said, "This is Kathy, my daughter. She's working as a counselor in a shelter for battered women."

The woman in the next bed teared up. "I wish there had been something like that when I was young and being beaten up by my husband," she said through her tears. I spent the next halfhour talking with this patient. Mom was beaming at me like Papa used to do. I finally felt visible to her.

My mother once again defied the doctor's prognosis. The doctor underestimated her. Since two of my brothers couldn't get home until Christmas, my mother said, "I'll wait!" She could not eat and lived at home on sips of Michelob beer which was the only thing she could keep down.

Mom celebrated her last Christmas with her family all around her. Then, on New Year's Day, when my brother, Pete, walked into her room to wish her a Happy New Year, she admonished him to go to the hospital. She said, "I don't like the way you look!"

He protested, "I just ate too much last night and didn't get to bed until 2:00 a.m. I'm fine, Mom."

She was not convinced. "Humor your dying mother!" was her response. He didn't want to upset her so he complied. As he walked through the Emergency Room doors, Pete had a massive heart attack. She tenaciously held on until she knew he was out of danger.

Each weekend, Jules and I came from opposite directions to give Mark respite, but Mom wouldn't let him leave her side. She insisted that only Mark could care for her—no one else would do. So, Jules and I helped with the cooking and cleaning. My brother, Joseph, who was a nurse, had come to help as well, taking meticulous notes about her condition and medication.

It was a Friday night in early February. Usually I left for Connecticut after making dinner, but I was exhausted and decided to go the next morning. As the sun went down, something tugged at my consciousness. I changed my mind and left earlier than usual.

Traveling over three hours on a deserted highway in a blinding snow storm, I arrived just as Mom's doctor was leaving. He said she was in a coma and it was only a matter of hours before she died. I had not seen her for a week. I was shocked to see her beautiful hand curled unnaturally against her chest, her breath raspy and labored. I had stood beside many dying patients in my days as a nurse's aide, but this was different. This was my mother.

In the early hours of February 6, 1982, Joseph, Thomas, Mark, Jules, my niece, Lynn and I gathered around my mother's bed. I felt calm and aware. My children had made a tape for their Gram which I played softly next to her ear. Her eyes were open, unseeing and glazed. All of a sudden I saw consciousness in her left eye.

I said, "Mom, if you can hear me, blink your eye." She blinked.

"Do you know we all love you?" She blinked her eye. "And the kids love you, Mom." Again she blinked her eye. Then I looked in her eye and could see she was trying to communicate something. I said, "Mom, do you want to tell us that you love us, too?" And, she blinked her eye slowly with what seemed like relief that I understood.

A few moments later she took her last breath and her hand uncurled and she lifted it as if in a blessing. I said, "She's saying good-bye."

Joseph said, "Maybe she's also saying hello."

Mom was buried two days later on my father's birthday, February 8, 1982. Stan drove the kids down for the service and burial. Driving back, I took Debbie and Jake, and he took the older two. I had held it together fairly well during the funeral and the gathering of friends and family at the church hall. But now, as I was driving home, with the skies darkening and my two youngest children asleep in the back seat, the weariness and sadness began to break through.

It was dark and frigid. I began to cry. "Mom's alone in the dark and cold," I cried. At that moment, a huge orange full moon crested on the horizon. I felt certain God was saying, "Oh you silly girl, do you think I'd leave her alone in the dark and cold?" I woke the children to see this spectacular moonrise. They fell back to sleep, and I wept all the way home.

Two years later, my suppressed feelings about my mother surfaced and this poem fell onto the page.

Woman in Black,
you come unbidden
stone-carved face
stoic, beyond grief

forever unreachable
your presence
permeates.

Woman in Black,
there is nothing more to say,
my words have gone dry
as have my tears.

You, who have no arms
to hold me
then or now,

I cry no more for you
for what
should have been.

Did you not know
every day
I followed
that white coffin
to the grave?

– Kathleen, 1984

~

I jumped right back into the madness of my busy life. I had decided to matriculate as a full-time student with a Pell Grant and loans. I carried five courses and studied late into the night. The children saw less and less of me for which I felt mounting guilt that almost undermined my resolve. Stan somehow managed to start a fight when I was studying for a test or working on a paper. His sabotage was anything but subtle.

I knew Stan was too harsh with discipline, but I never thought he would physically abuse one of the children. I came home one evening and found Debbie in tears. Rachel told me, "Dad hit her hard with his belt." I looked at her back. There was a huge red swath over her kidneys. I put cream on her back and tried to comfort her. Then, I drove her over to my friend Dee's house so she could witness and document the evidence of his violence.

When I returned home with Debbie, I fixed steely eyes on Stan and said, "If you ever touch one of the kids again, I will immediately leave with them and start divorce proceedings. I have a witness to the welt you left on her back!" I spent the rest of the evening with Debbie. She was eight years old.

Forty years later, I learned this was not an isolated incident. Behind my back, Stan had tortured our children for years. Fear of Stan had kept them silent—as did, what one son called, my "emotional detachment" from them.

This incident only increased my determination to get my degree. All my professors encouraged me, but two in particular were especially supportive. Dr. Ernest Fredrick, my Experimental Psychology teacher, sensed my trepidation at taking his course—I was not good at hiding my anxiety. He guided me through the semester, making the material assessable to me as Tim Ober had in Statistics. I ended up with an A in his class, and he told me he was impressed with how I had conquered my fears.

Another psychology professor, Dr. Robert Cantor, said, "Kathy, I'm worried about you—you haven't taken time to grieve your mother's death."

I assured him, "I'm fine. I worked on anticipatory grief in my peer-counseling sessions before my mother died. She lived a lot longer than anyone expected. I'm grateful for that."

But on Mother's Day morning that May, with my children making me breakfast and giving me homemade cards and gifts, my heart broke open: I couldn't call my mother to wish her a Happy Mother's Day. Unable to stem the tears that fell onto everything, I tried to explain. "I'm just missing Gram." In that moment I realized my children must be missing her, too. My life had been so pressured in pursuit of my goal that I hadn't acknowledged their loss of the grandmother who had given so much of herself to them. We ended up crying together.

By not dealing with my own grief, I had inhibited the acknowledgement and expression of theirs. I hadn't stopped to look in their eyes with the attention and love they needed to allow their feelings to flow. I will always regret abandoning them during that time.

Beyond words
secrets lay
darkening the soul
of those who say
"All is well!"
when it's not
siphoning joy
from the heart.

– Kathleen, 2012

CHAPTER TWENTY-FIVE
Truth Denied

DURING THE YEAR AND A HALF between Mom's diagnosis and her death, the children and I visited her at least once a month. Tom was often there when we arrived. He and I began to rebuild our relationship. His bookstore became a neutral setting for us to get reacquainted. We talked about books and our differing philosophies while the kids played in the yard behind the store. I started lobbying him to carry books on feminism. He resisted at first, but after some months, he added a section on Women's Studies. Next, I cajoled him into creating a section of books on holistic health and spirituality. His customers began to take an interest in both sections.

It was wonderful to be in dialogue with this handsome dark-haired brother again.

A memory of him patiently teaching me to tell time one Sunday afternoon when I was five bubbled to the surface. He had the ability to explain abstract concepts in a way I could grasp, and I had learned to read the hands on the clock by suppertime. I remembered many occasions when he had taken me rock hunting. He taught me, in painstaking detail, about their origins and composition. I never remembered the lessons, but my love for rocks grew with each excursion.

Classical music constantly wafted through the store as it did in his home when I, at the age of thirteen, spent the summer with him and his family. He often hummed and waved his hands in the air as if conducting the symphony that was blasting from the radio in his store as his bemused customers continued to browse. This was the Tom I knew and loved.

Slowly, over several visits, he told me why he stopped communicating with the family. He assured me it had nothing to do with me or the land. He had never been angry with me. He had been broken-hearted by our brother, Tony's, untimely and tragic death, and was relieved when Liz decided to bring the children east to be near the family. Tony and Tom's children began to hang out together.

One of Tom's children casually mentioned that Tony's son said, "Uncle Mark taught us everything we need to know about sex." Tom was alarmed and questioned the boys. He found out that Mark had molested all three of them. Horrified, he went to our mother and told her what had happened. He wanted to confront Mark, report him to the authorities and/or get him help. He never told me exactly what Mom said, but it was clear my mother forbid him to bring up the subject ever again.

Tom wrote a letter to all the siblings but me, describing what had happened and enlisting their support in addressing this issue with Mark. He said to me, "I didn't send you the letter because I thought it would be too upsetting for you."

His intent was to protect me. He had no idea I had been grappling with confusion about Mark's relationships with young boys since I was fifteen when our mother read me the love letter from Mark to his young companion, Danny. Tom's letter was ignored by our siblings, because no one wanted to cross my mother. He felt he had no recourse but to cut ties with the whole family.

I was sickened by this news which made real my suspicions about Mark. It was crushing to hear the truth. At the same time, I was relieved to know Tom's long absence was not my fault. More questions than ever flooded my mind. I could not fathom why Mom blocked Tom's attempt to confront the situation or how my siblings could turn their backs on Tom and the boys Mark had sexually exploited.

How could my righteous brother Mark live with himself? My mind was spinning with thoughts of all the boys that were probably my brother's victims. And I still could not reconcile why I had lost all those years with my brother Tom. Why didn't he just tell me what was going on? In my family's eyes I'd always be the "baby"—innocent and vulnerable. I had grown stronger and less naïve during my years with Stan, but either I didn't project this or my family refused to see it.

It never occurred to Tom that I might have felt something was terribly wrong about Mark's attachment to young boys. It never occurred to Tom that I carried a sense of loss and guilt for his disappearance. It never occurred to him that I was an adult woman with children of my own and deserved to know the truth. I did not dare to broach these subjects for fear of losing him again.

I wanted to be angry with him, but I couldn't. He had obviously struggled with his decision about the family and regretted the time we had lost. And, I could not escape the reality that I had *not* acted on my intuition or questioned what was going on in our home. How could I hold Tom culpable for not telling me what he knew when I hadn't spoken of my fears to anyone? He had the courage to speak the truth. I had remained silent.

~

Two years later, my sister, Jules, and her children, traveled to New Hampshire to join us for Easter. Jules had three boys and six girls. The youngest boy, Stevie, two years younger than my son, David, was a wiry, high-strung and mischievous little boy who was turning into a defiant, angry adolescent. He was the main target of his father's emotional and physical abuse.

On the drive from Delaware to our home in New Hampshire, Stevie attacked his siblings and threatened to jump out of the car. Jules detoured to "Mom's house" where Mark now lived alone since Mom's death. Jules and Mark had always been close and had become even closer since her divorce the year before. She called me and told me she would be late. She was dropping Stevie off with Mark for the weekend because she couldn't control him. My breath caught in my throat.

I asked to speak to Mark. He got on the phone and said gruffly, "What this kid needs is a good kick in the ass!" I was relieved—it wasn't that surgery, sweet voice he used when he talked to *the* boys when I was growing up. But, I held my breath all weekend. I thought my sister had received the letter that I did *not* receive about Mark's molesting our nephews, so I assumed she trusted Mark would never touch one of her children, if she believed the letter at all.

We had an enjoyable Easter together, and after Jules left, I called Mark to tell him she was on her way. I asked him how it had gone with Stevie. His voice changed to the timbre I dreaded to hear. In a soft, melodic voice, he said, "Oh, he was fine. He just needs to be loved and guided."

My heart sank—I feared that Stevie had become one of Mark's victims. Shortly thereafter, Jules made the decision to move in with Mark with her five youngest children. I protested that decision without saying anything about Mark. I couldn't risk making my sister choose between us.

Stevie's rebellious behavior escalated. He and a friend stole a gun from a neighbor. There was a high-speed police chase, and when cornered, Stevie put the gun to his head. His friend stopped him. They both were sentenced to Juvenile Detention for a year. Stevie was fragile, depressed and suicidal. Mark and Jules began pouring money into rescuing him. Love? Concern? Guilt? Buying his silence? I will never know.

As months turned into years with Mark and Jules and her family living under the same roof, I naively assumed Mark would not act out with Stevie while living with Jules. And, I imagined he was a surrogate father to Jules' children—doing for them what he had done for me: chauffeuring them to different activities, helping with homework, talking to them about life, instilling in them the need for education. I was afraid that someday their idol would crash from his pedestal, and they would be as crushed as I was when it happened to me. I never thought to check out these assumptions, to my great regret.

Only recently I learned that my imaginings were not the reality. In fact, Stevie was the center of Mark's attention, and Mark gave him power over the other children who were neglected. Every night, Mark and Stevie slept together in the larger of the two bedrooms on a water bed. My sister slept in the other bedroom. The other children had to scrounge for space to sleep in the tiny house, and sometimes resorted to sleeping in the cellar.

My silence made me an accomplice to Mark's actions. Although I only had suspicions about him until Tom revealed what he knew, I still did nothing to expose Mark as a predator. I was fully conscious of the consequences of my silence and was overcome with guilt and shame for doing nothing to prevent Mark from continuing to perpetrate these crimes against children.

I feared Mark would commit suicide if the truth of his pedophilia became known. I feared my mother's wrath and my sister's condemnation. I feared I would do more harm to the victims and their families by revealing Mark's secret.

I did not want to believe that my "high-minded" family was so horribly flawed, that everything I believed about our ethical mandate to help others and change the world was a fraud. I was no longer the innocent younger sister who knew nothing about these worldly things. I was compelled to face the truth. As Edna St. Vincent Millay wrote in Renascence:

All sins was of my sinning, all
Atoning mine, and mine the gall
Of all regret.

[The Warrior] is not intimidated by silence, indifference or rejection.
(S)he knows that behind the mask of ice that people wear,
There beats a heart of fire.

– Excerpt from *Warrior of the Light: A Manual* by Paulo Coelho

CHAPTER TWENTY-SIX
Light Illuminates Darkness

LIGHT ILLUMINATES the Darkness. It does not turn it into Light. It reveals what's hidden. We are left with the revelations. Only we can transform them into Light.

My nephew, Stevie, was in crisis and suicidal at the age of twenty-three in 1992. I rushed to his side. He and I sat in my car talking outside the apartment his mother shared with Mark. Stevie told me that Mark had sexually abused him over the course of several years. I forced myself not to overreact, but my heart broke open.

I chose my words carefully. "Stevie, I am so, so sorry! What happened is in no way your fault. Mark is responsible for doing this to you! There is nothing wrong with you that caused this to happen—you're the victim! I will *do anything* you want me to do—go to the police, confront Mark, find a counselor to help you cope with this trauma, *anything!*"

"No, no, Aunt Kathy! Don't do anything! And, don't tell anyone what I told you!"

"I promise I won't do anything without your permission, Stevie. And I won't tell anyone. But, I want you to know I am here for you whenever you need me. Have you told your Mom?"

He looked down and quietly said, "Yeah." I knew from his tone that his disclosure had been ignored.

To give him complete control, I decided not to broach the subject with him again unless he brought it up. He never did, although he or his mother would reach out to me when he was suicidal. I would drop everything and go to him no matter where he was living. We would talk about what was going on in his present situation, but never about the past. I pleaded with him to get help, but he'd assure me he was okay. Stevie committed suicide when he was thirty-nine, leaving four children and a broken-hearted family.

~

At the age of seventy-four I was still grappling with how we break the silence around issues of domestic violence, sexual violation, incest, and systemic abuse in institutions. In part, I began writing about my life to understand these crimes, and why people collude with the perpetrator(s) by remaining silent. We had yet to uncloak the dark secret of our family: Mark's pedophilia.

Those of us who knew about his transgressions against these boys were his accomplices. Every moment of our silence put a child at risk. There was no escaping our culpability. I will be haunted by that fact with every breath I take for the rest of my life.

Research on the effects of Childhood Sexual Abuse is plentiful. My training in psychology provided some insights about the effects of this kind of violation including mental illness, suicidality, PTSD, guilt, shame and self-loathing, and the inability to form lasting relationships. In the course of my training, I learned to identify some patterns of behavior in childhood sexual assault victims.

Among Mark's victims that I knew, most were prone to exceptionally risky behavior during their teenage years after the abuse. One was severely injured in a motorcycle accident and lost his arm. Another was killed in a car accident. One was hit by a car and died. Two committed suicide (that I know of). Two others died of lung cancer at an early age. Many became addicted to drugs and alcohol. Were all these events related to the sexual exploitation Mark perpetrated against these boys? We will never know.

But, we do know that Adverse Childhood Experiences (ACE) have life-long impact on many victims' physiology, including a higher incidence of cancer, heart disease and other medical conditions; emotional and mental instability; inability to function according societal expectations; unable to hold a job; difficulty maintaining relationships; and they often suffer from shame, guilt, poor self-esteem and self-loathing. There are now treatment modalities to help mediate these effects, but these programs are not widely available. There are some victims who appear to be unscathed by the abuse, although the repressed memories and emotions may at some point overwhelm them.

My brother, Tom, told me that one night when he was staying with Mark someone pounded on the door. When Mark opened it, a neighbor shouted at him, "You are a monster! You have ruined my son's life! I should kill you!" Mark slammed the door and never said a word about the incident; neither did Tom, who had given up the fight.

At a family reunion a few years ago, two of my nieces asked me to tell them about a rumor they heard regarding Mark. I hesitated and questioned if they really wanted to know the truth. They firmly asserted they did, so I told them the truth as I know it.

I thought they would register shock. Instead, I saw a click of recognition as they turned to look at each other. Their brother, the second oldest in a family of six, had been a mystery to them. The laughing, bright-eyed, good natured ten-year-old boy turned dark and sullen after being sent alone to visit Mark and Gram. He turned into an angry adult. Was he one of Mark's victims? He died in 2007 of lung cancer at the age of fifty-four.

About five years ago, I felt compelled to look up Judy, the woman whom Mark had dated briefly when I was nineteen. After six months, Mark dropped her when another young boy named Billy came into his life. Now fifty years later, some intuition made me want to contact her, although I had no idea where she was. I feared she blamed herself for the split. I found her on the internet and sent her an email.

I wrote, "Judy, I want you to know how much you meant to me during the years of our friendship. You taught me so much and were so supportive. I will always be grateful. And, I want to make sure you understand that the breakup with Mark had nothing to do with you."

She wrote back: "It's wonderful to hear from you, Kath." She told me she was terminally ill with cancer. Then she said, "I actually knew the break-up was not about me. Billy's parents and I sat at their kitchen table one night and talked about the possibility that Mark was a pedophile. But, I still loved him."

I was shocked that Judy suspected Mark was a pedophile and still loved him! She died not long after this exchange.

Mark had great charm. He groomed his young victims with attention and gifts. I realized the tentacles of his abhorrent behavior ran through every part of the family; he had groomed us all to keep the secret and everyone colluded, except Tom, who was silenced.

In the wake of the Pennsylvania priest scandal in 2018, I watched a program on the subject. A sixty-year-old man, a victim of childhood sexual abuse by a priest, wept as he said, "He [the priest] groomed me, he groomed my parents, and the priests in that diocese groomed the whole community."

Although I adored my sister, Jules, it was hard to visit her because she lived with Mark almost to the end of her life. When I visited, Mark dominated the conversation. He made it difficult for Jules and me to have time alone. Sometimes we'd say we were going to take a nap in the room we shared, so we could talk.

Worse yet, Mark would follow me around espousing the Man/Boy love thesis to which he ascribed as a defense of his pedophilia, although he never admitted to being a pedophile. I would shut him down and walk away, but my sister did not flinch when he referred to this topic. She was in a trance around him, not unlike the women with whom I worked at the battered women's shelter.

In September 2018, I went to visit Jules to help care for her. She was in the end stages of her twenty year battle with cancer. At that point, she was still sweet-natured, grateful and compliant in her lucid moments, but Mark's antagonistic and controlling behavior had increased with age. He was decrepit, could not stand for more than a few seconds and had difficulty breathing.

Jules was hospitalized while I was there. I spent three days by her side—leaving briefly to shower and change clothes once. On the fourth day her daughter came to stand watch. I went back to the house to shower, eat something and get some much needed sleep.

Alone with Mark for the first time in years, I sat down at the kitchen table to eat my lunch and Mark, who was now eighty-eight, pulled his wheelchair up to the table across from me. He launched into his usual diatribe about the lack of compassion in the world and the ignorance and violence in our society today. He spoke with the self-righteous implication that he was better than everyone else.

Then, out of nowhere, he began an attack on our niece, Abby, one of Jules's daughters. He claimed she was "fat and lazy" and continued with a barrage of denigrating remarks. Abby had been devoted to Jules and Mark. In spite of a demanding job, she traveled five hours each way every few weeks to help them maintain their independence. She cooked and cleaned and made sure they had everything they needed.

I was appalled. I pointed out our niece's contributions to our family, her creativity, her work ethic, her kindness and compassion. He continued to spew hateful epithets about her—demanding I listen to him. His face was contorted, his voice growing louder. Fear was rising in my belly. I said, "STOP! I'm not going to listen to this!" He was relentless and enraged. I stood up and yelled "Good-bye, Mark!" and stormed out of the room. I was shaking in disbelief. It was the last time I spoke to him.

My head was spinning. "How could this man who had destroyed so many lives berate a woman who gives so much to our family and the world? Why didn't I confront him on the sexual violations he perpetrated on so many boys? Though he is decrepit, unable to stand, why do I still fear him?" I quickly made arrangements for a hotel and fled what felt like a house of horrors.

All through the years, two questions haunted me: How do we break the codes of silence that perpetuate patterns of personal and systemic abuse? And, how can I live with myself if I continue to keep the secret of Mark's pedophilia that has festered in our family and damaged so many lives?

The guilt and pain of keeping the secret eroded my sense of self. I felt unworthy and hypocritical. I berated myself for my cowardice. Then I'd imagine the impact the truth would have on the people I love. I was immobilized by the fear of causing more harm. But in describing this encounter to Jules's other daughters, I assumed they knew that Mark had sexually molested their brother. I said, "I'm outraged that Mark would vilify your beautiful sister after all the damage he's done to the young boys he defiled, and to their families and our family."

One niece was shocked and angry. "Why are you telling us this now when our mother is dying? Why hasn't anyone spoken of this before?" She went on to question how the elders of the family allowed this to happen, including her mother and grandmother. It was painful and messy. I immediately regretted breaking my silence. I also felt relieved.

Since that disclosure, reverberations of my truth-telling have continued to ripple through our family. I have asked for forgiveness for my part in this travesty. More evidence of the extent of Mark's vile behavior has come to light. Denial is no longer an option.

My nieces and nephews have stepped in to deal with the ramifications of these discoveries. I am grateful to them. Their goal is to insure the pattern of victimization and silence stops here. I will continue to tell my truth. That's all I have to offer at this stage of my life.

Those in the next generation are the *Warriors of Light* valiantly illuminating the Darkness and bringing Light to the web of secrets woven through our family's history. Let the healing begin.

Energy moves in waves
Waves move in patterns
Patterns move in rhythms.
A human being is just that
Energy, Waves, Patterns, Rhythms…

– Excerpt from *5RHYTHMS* by Gabrielle Roth

Chapter Twenty-Seven
Beloved Friend

AFTER MY MOTHER'S DEATH IN 1982, my own chaotic life overwhelmed me. The constant tension from Stan's vicious attacks on my children and me made it easy to detach from the complex issues with my siblings and their children. We lived only seven miles from the beautiful shoreline of New Hampshire, my refuge. The children and I would escape to the beach. While they built sand castles and romped in the water, I kept one eye on them as I walked along the cool hard sand collecting beach stones, the spent waves lapping at my feet.

I especially loved finding heart-shaped rocks. They called to me—like magnets drawing me into their energetic field. I imagined they were love notes from God deposited by the Angels. My heart lifted at the sight of one. Soon I had my children and nieces looking for what we called "heart rocks." Finding them has become a family tradition. For me, it's a spiritual practice. My connection to Spirit was rekindled on those beaches.

I started a non-religious Sunday school with Dee's children and mine. Every Sunday morning the children and I would go on an excursion into nature. We would look for repeating patterns in the natural world—like heart shapes in leaves and flower petals, and branching in trees, our veins and lightening. We explored the woods, along streams, and often landed on the beach.

There we looked for sand trees etched by the receding water, snail tracks, sand dollars and seaweed. We watched cloud formations flow by as we lay on our backs in the sand, listening to the rhythm of the waves. The energy of Mother Earth seeped into to my body and enlivened my soul. The children loved our outings, and I cherished those forays into the sacred, enhanced by their innocent and awe-struck presence. I felt connected to the energy of the earth and all existence.

Long before I read Gabrielle Roth's words above, a song came to me one night as I jogged around the neighborhood. It included the words:

The Universe is energy
From which existence springs.
Vibrations dance and laugh and sing
And permeate all things.

~

At home, Stan's rages never stopped. He could be set off by the most innocuous thing. When Rachel was about ten, she became her father's favorite because she excelled at basketball to the degree that she was competitive with the boys her age. But, as she developed into a shapely adolescent, Stan turned on her. He was vicious and punitive toward her. He called her vile names, grounded her for every minor infraction, accused her of doing things he had done as a teenager. Rachel became defiant and angry. David also acted out, but was more subtle in his rebellion. He did not openly defy his father, but quietly did as he pleased.

I had claimed one room in our big old home as my own—a small narrow room in the back of the 1690 part of the house, the birthing room. I painted the trim a deep red and covered the walls with old fashioned white wall paper featuring delicate sketches in red ink of scenes from the 1800's. Bookshelves lined two walls, and a small yellow rocking chair sat beside the fireplace. My desk was tucked into one corner. Around nine o'clock every night, after the dishes were done and the kids were settled in their bedrooms, I would retire to what I called the "library" to study. I would turn on Vivaldi's *Four Seasons* and become engrossed in my homework.

Years later, David and Rachel confessed that they would climb out their respective second floor bedroom windows on opposite sides of the house and come around to the library window to check on me and see if I was studying. Then they took off on their bikes to Windsor five miles away to meet up with their friends. I studied into the early morning hours unaware that my two oldest children were not in their beds.

During this time, we tried family counseling. It failed. What I later learned, as I continued to study and work in the field of domestic violence, was that any attempt at counseling a couple where one spouse/partner is abusing the other is unproductive and dangerous. If the children or I said something "wrong" in a session, Stan would harangue us with a tirade of anger all the way home.

The counselors would often say, "The parents should present a united front when dealing with the children."

I wanted to scream, "You want me to present a united front with a *madman?*" Instead I silently nodded in agreement.

I tried to comply with this dictate, but I never ceased defending my children behind closed doors, although I'm sure they felt deserted by me in the face of the abuse they received from their father. I wrote:

> *I swallow my anger*
> *in small sips,*
> *daily drunk on it*
> *mind unfocused*
> *I go careening*
> *through my life*
> *stopping not*
> *to taste the venom*
> *I imbibe*
> *knowing someday*
> *I shall indulge*
> *beyond tolerance*
> *vomit, choke,*
> *and die.*

> *– Kathleen, 1984*

And, I, too, could be harsh and demanding with the children. I'd become impatient, lose my temper with them, and say things I wish I could take back. The difference between Stan and me was that I was more likely to apologize for my behavior and allowed the children to have their say. My connection with them remained strong or at least so I thought. I later learned my bouts of depression were interpreted by my children as indifference or lack of caring.

~

I graduated in December 1982 with a B.A. in Psychology and a minor in Women's Studies. On my diploma were written the words *summa cum laude*. My children and husband attended the graduation and let out yelps of joy as I crossed the stage. I was elated with my accomplishment. Stan's family took me out to a fancy French restaurant the next day and gave me a leather notebook. It was clear they were proud of me.

My friend, Ann, invited me to spend the following weekend with her to celebrate while Jason and her kids went to be with Stan and my kids. She took me out to dinner and to a show and gave me a warm flannel nightgown I have to this day—now threadbare. Ann was my most enthusiastic champion as I worked toward my degree. She sent me books on how to study and one on how to write a good research paper. She was delighted I had reached my goal. I think we both saw it as my ticket out of the marriage.

Stan had his own reasons to celebrate my degree—he was counting on my getting a job and making a substantial sum to contribute to the household. His business had lost almost $20,000 in the past year. I wrongly assumed that securing a position in my field with a B.A. and my shelter experience would be easy. Everywhere I applied, I was told I needed a Master's Degree.

I had been in overdrive for so long my body demanded I rest before I did anything else. My heart rate had increased. I woke up in pain each morning, barely able to put my feet on the floor, and I was beyond exhausted. I thought it might be another bout of depression, but the doctor said there were signs of liver abnormalities in my blood work. I was told to rest—unlikely given the circumstances of my life.

Eventually, I began the downward spiral into depression. My hopes dimmed of ever getting out of the marriage. How could I support myself and my children if my body and mind kept betraying me? I forced myself to continue the job search even as depression enveloped me. After a couple months, I went back to working as a secretary for a small firm that paid a little more than the university.

I started to research graduate schools programs for a Doctor of Psychology degree (PsyD) which was a new doctoral program in Clinical Psychology. I did not know how I would pay for another degree but I was determined to get enough education to support myself and my children. I applied to the Massachusetts School of Professional Psychology, which had just opened a few years before. I was accepted for a delayed admission. I would be required to spend a year working in the psychology field before I was admitted. I was crest-fallen. A year seemed like forever. I began to look for other options.

Walking the beach and watching my children play in the waves grounded me in the reality that although things looked bleak, there was beauty and peace in small moments. Consciously embracing those moments each day became the stepping stones to the far distant shores of a new life.

~

We put a swimming pool in the back yard when we restored the house, which made us a Mecca for all the relatives in the Boston area. Just after Stan's sister, her husband and three kids, arrived to celebrate Father's Day with us, I received a call from Ann. She asked if she and Jason, and the kids could come for the day. I assured her we'd love to have them. I was surprised by the request. It was so unlike Ann, with her Yankee reserve, to reach out like that. I expanded our menu and welcomed Ann and her family into the maelstrom of seven—children running around and jumping into the water. Her two joined the fray.

Ann was unusually quiet that day. I was overwhelmed with feeding this crowd and hardly had a chance to sit down and talk with anyone. After the first group left, things quieted down.

I stood at the sink washing dishes, and Ann dried. She quietly confessed, "I'm extremely depressed again. Dr. Foss says I will continue experiencing these fluctuations in mood for the rest of my life unless I take medication. I don't want to take medication for the rest of my life!" She added plaintively, "I'm not even good for Seth anymore." Seth was Jason and Ann's six-year-old son.

"That's not true!" I exclaimed. "He adores you! I'm seeing a new psychiatrist, Dr. Ross, and he says there are new medications that can really help with depression. I can't believe I'm seeing Dr. Ross and you're seeing Dr. Foss! We must be on the right track!"

I'd had my first appointment with Dr. Ross in Boston the week before. I'd called him after I found myself standing in front of Stan's dresser holding one of the guns he kept in his top drawer "just to see how it feels." I did not mention this to Ann.

Ann's mood seemed to lighten a bit. She gave me an unusually big hug when she was leaving and said, "I love you!"—words I had never heard from her before, although I often said them to her. Normally, I would have called Jason and warned him that Ann was having a hard time, but since I had alerted him about this in the past, and Ann had denied being suicidal, I feared he wouldn't take me seriously. I trusted Dr. Foss to pick up on her state of mind.

I had been invited for a group interview being held early the next morning at Antioch/New England's Counseling Psychology Program in Keene, NH. It was on the other side of the state, almost three hours away, so I needed to leave the house early to get there on time. I was anxious about the interview and I couldn't get Ann's words about Seth out of my head.

I woke at 5:00 am the next morning with a disturbing dream. In the dream, I was supposed to meet Ann in Burlington, Massachusetts, where she and Jason lived. I was driving a sparkly silver pickup truck at high speed trying to get to her on time when I saw an outdoor camp in a field by the road. It was a camp for children with cystic fibrosis. (My friend's daughter had just died of the disease.) I could see Ann waiting for me, standing in a garden in the distance, but I felt compelled to stop and help these children even though I knew she'd be upset if I was late. I relayed the dream to Stan, something I rarely did.

I told him, "I'll call Ann as soon as I get home—it's too early now. I need to get on the road."

It was a very tense day: trying to make a good impression at the interview and worrying about Ann. I left as soon as I could and hurried home. When I walked in the door, Stan looked ashen.

He said, "Ann's missing. She went out for groceries and never returned. Jason pulled some strings and the police are already looking for her. They waived the twenty-four hour rule for missing persons."

It was a cold, rainy June night in New England. Jason kept us abreast of developments. They found her car on a back road surrounded by woods. The police and Jason searched into the night until they came to a barrier of brush and a stone wall which they assumed she wouldn't have crossed.

Jason went back at dawn the next morning and crossed over the wall and found her. She had shot herself in the left temple with the small caliber gun he had bought her to keep her safe. She was barely alive. The ambulance rushed her to Lahey Hospital & Medical Center where she went directly into surgery. When Stan and I arrived at the hospital two hours later, Ann was still in the operating room.

The neurosurgeon finally came out after the seven hour surgery and said, "I don't know about the morality of what I just did. I'm a mechanic. I did what I was trained to do. I don't know if she will live or die, and I don't know what her quality of life will be if she lives. The bullet destroyed everything that is human in her, but it missed the brain stem."

Family and friends who filled the room gasped in horror. Jason was in shock. Sobs filled the air. Ann was loved by so many; this was inconceivable. I crumpled into a heap on the floor and wept.

Why hadn't I called her when I woke up to that dream yesterday? Why hadn't I told Jason I was worried about her?

Why didn't her psychiatrist realize she was at risk? I understood her desperation and the compulsion to escape an untenable life, and I was bereft by the loss of my beautiful friend.

Seeing Ann after the surgery was heart-wrenching. There were IV lines, breathing tubes and monitors attached to every part of her body. Her hands were retracted into claws, her body twisted, her face unrecognizable. In the months to come, with the doctor's permission, I and others tried everything to bring her back—talking and singing to her, reading poetry, massaging and moving her limbs—all in vain.

~

Dr. Ross was an astute and caring doctor who listened intently to what I had to say. In our first consultation two weeks before, I told him, "I just started a new job and I can barely function." Still exhausted from my sprint to graduation, and discouraged that all I had worked for did not lead to the desired job opportunity, I felt defeated.

He helped me tease apart the issues and also encouraged me to accept the fact that I was genetically predisposed to depression. He reassured me it was not my fault that these life events had brought me to my knees. He wanted me to take a series of tests and, if they showed markers for depression, he strongly recommended I take medication. I was riding the new wave of Holistic Medicine and didn't want to take anything that wasn't natural, but I agreed to take the tests.

Then, he told me this story. "Thirty depressed yogis took part in a study," he said. "They were accomplished in all kinds of physical feats of body control, but they could not alleviate their own depression. They responded well to anti-depressant medication." He told me that controlling clinical depression is not a matter of will power or inner strength or deficient faith. I was still skeptical.

"It's a physiological disease comparable to diabetes," he said. "When a diabetic's blood sugar is low they might experience anxiety, irritability and dizziness, even coma." I remembered witnessing my diabetic friend's reaction when his blood sugar dropped—he was flailing, swearing, angry and extraordinarily strong, like my father was when he was manic. I could relate to this explanation.

Dr. Ross continued, "For someone with a genetic propensity for depression, loss and/or stress can trigger an episode."

I reluctantly said "I'll consider medication if the tests prove there is a chemical imbalance that is causing the depression."

A few days later, I dropped Dr. Ross a note. I reiterated my misgivings about taking medication. The note said: ...*I still fear I am looking for an easy way out, an excuse. Some part of me believes I can will myself into being a happy, well-functioning woman. Perhaps the depression serves a purpose in my life—gets me attention, hides a basic laziness or self-centeredness. I don't like who I am and I don't think that is going to change with any medication. I feel like a cosmic criminal doing my prison time on earth.*

Five days after Ann's attempted suicide, I had a follow up appointment with Dr. Ross to get the results of the blood and urine tests. I was shaken by the week's events and could barely talk when I arrived at his office. I told him what had happened. He was kind and tried to comfort me. "Mrs. Cohen, I am so sorry. I hope you know there was nothing you could have done to stop her; it was in no way your fault."

He speculated that she probably had the same hereditary disposition for depression as I did and would have benefited from the antidepressants her doctor had offered. Then he informed me that my test results clearly showed an imbalance in my brain chemistry. He insisted, "You need to start taking an antidepressant medication immediately." I didn't argue with him. I had taken a medication for depression before and remembered the relief I'd gotten.

I started on a low dose of Elavil, which increased over the next weeks. Elavil is called a "dirty drug" because it affects many bodily functions: my heart rate escalated, I began sweating with mild exertion. My anxiety level increased, and I could not contain my tears. Luckily, I had landed in another job where I was surrounded by supportive people.

I confided in my office manager, Marilyn, about my dear friend's suicide and my own struggle with depression. I explained that I was taking a new medication, and it would take some time to adjust to it. She said the company would accommodate my needs and stick by me. I was the secretary to the president of the company who also gave me his full support.

One day I was washing the glass coffee pot in the sink when he came up behind me and quietly said, "Kath…"

I shrieked and threw the coffee pot in the air. Obviously, my nervous system was on high alert. By some miracle the coffee pot did not break. (Another coffeepot crisis in a new job!)

"I'm so sorry I startled you! I didn't mean to upset you!"

"No, No, Mr. Carlton, it wasn't your fault!" I assured him. "It's this medication I'm on—the doctor promises my nervous system will calm down after I adjust to it."

At any other time, I would have stopped taking a medication that had so many side effects. But, several times a week through the summer, Stan and I made the trip to Burlington to offer Jason our support and to stand watch over Ann. I was reminded each time why I was taking the medication. It is likely Ann saved my life.

One day you finally knew
what you had to do, and began,
though the voices around you
kept shouting
their bad advice—

— Excerpt from "The Journey" by Mary Oliver in *Dream Work*

CHAPTER TWENTY-EIGHT
Take Back the Night

I'D BEEN ACCEPTED into the Counseling-Psychology Program at Antioch/New England Graduate School, but since the acceptance letter came in the midst of tragedy, I'd put it aside without much thought. Now the time was drawing near for me to start classes. I was still depressed and suffering with side effects from the Elavil. I couldn't imagine walking into a new situation feeling as I did.

Dr. Ross encouraged me to go forward with my plans to pursue a Master's degree. He felt I had not yet reached a therapeutic dose of the medication so he upped the dosage one more time. My heart was longing to come alive again.

A few days before I was to start school, I woke up one morning awestruck. I exclaimed, "Is this how normal people feel when they wake up every morning?" My mornings were usually abysmal—I was tired, in pain, groggy, depressed. On this particular morning I woke up feeling hopeful about the day. I felt like something had gone "click" in the middle of the night and I was truly myself. I was happy to be alive! I likened it to how I felt when I put on my first pair of glasses at twelve-years-old and could see the world as everyone with normal vision saw it every day.

~

We lived ten miles from the University of New Hampshire, which had a reputable Master's level counseling program, but I chose to travel two and a half hours across the state. The Antioch program was appealing because it was innovative, geared to older students, and had an outstanding faculty. We went to classes all day Tuesday and spent twenty hours a week interning at a counseling facility close to home. A group of students from the Seacoast area where I lived car-pooled to school each week.

The program was everything I had hoped for—in-depth training with real world experience. I interned at the local county mental health facility. Our clients were from diverse backgrounds, social-economic groups, and differing levels of psychological functioning. After six weeks of classes and orientation as interns, we were assigned our first clients. Role playing couldn't prepare us for the experience of sitting alone with a client for the first time.

I felt comfortable with the counseling skills I had acquired in the peer counseling program I had been involved with for five years, but my teachers at Antioch and supervisors at my internship were bent on dissuading me from using what I had learned. So, while I was in training, I practiced their preferred psycho-dynamic techniques, and also offered the warmth and encouragement of the humanistic psychologist, Carl Rogers. (He believed that for people to heal and grow they needed to be in a therapeutic relationship that is genuine, where they feel cared for and accepted.)

One of the cardinal sins as a therapist during that era was to talk about *spirituality or religion* with clients. Evelyn was the first client assigned to me. She was in her mid-twenties and extremely depressed. She had spent the past five years in a convent, about to make her final vows, when she was told she needed to leave. Her superiors felt she was not suited for the religious life. She was inconsolable. And I was not supposed to talk about religion or spirituality with her.

We sat together for two years and explored her childhood, family dynamics, and many psychological issues. We talked in depth about her recent experience of being asked to leave the convent and the sisters she had worked with and loved for the past five years. We explored faith issues: What was her image of God? Where was God in all that had transpired in her life? This was her exploration, not mine. I simply listened and held space for her to look into her heart for these answers. It was gratifying work.

One day a like-minded intern showed me a thick book. She whispered to me, "Look! It's on spirituality *and* psychology!" We huddled, perusing the book that put forth the theory that spirituality and psychology are entwined. Somehow seeing these words gave my work with Evelyn legitimacy. I began to gingerly explore this connection with other clients when appropriate.

Much of our education at Antioch involved group experiences. The *Tavistock* theory of group therapy, as it was practiced in the 1960s, was used exclusively in the group to which I was assigned. It was a confrontational model, exploring conflict rather than commonality, and was facilitated by leaders whose role was to remain emotionally uninvolved and aloof from group members. They offered impersonal and sometimes harsh interpretations of the group process and individual members. I felt myself disassociating during the class and remained silent through most of the sessions. I used to count the bricks on the wall to keep from crying. It did not feel like a safe space. I felt alone in the midst of twenty people.

Later, I found a quote by the esteemed author of the text, *The Theory and Practice of Group Psychotherapy*, which we used in another class. Irvin D. Yalom, M.D. wrote: *It was always my belief that…the Tavistock group approach was not only ineffective but often counter therapeutic.* I felt vindicated, but the experience highlighted for me the fragility of my ego, my lack of confidence in my own inner knowing, and my need to fit in and be accepted.

~

While I was still in my first year at Antioch, Stan announced he wanted to sell the home that I had lovingly restored. We had lived there only seven years—the longest we had lived anywhere. I said, "Absolutely not!" This time I had leverage. He needed my signature for a sale. He said that he had been offered $250,000 for the house—we had paid $80,000 and put another $20,000 into it. "We could use the money for the kids' education, if we bought something smaller in Windsor," was his sales pitch. "Besides, it would be easier for the kids to get around—they could bike to school." The two older children were going to high school in Windsor.

I held firm for a while but reluctantly consented to the sale when his badgering wore me down. This time, as we looked for a house to buy, I was determined to choose a house I did not *love*. I would choose something that was adequate for our family's needs, functional and nondescript. I found it. And, it had a book lined room called The Library that I claimed as my own.

Still, moving was painful, especially since I didn't like the buyer of our home. He was a developer. I knew he would turn the home I cherished into some kind of business because the property was zoned for commercial use. I had wanted to put the house on the registry of antique homes to protect it, but Stan had refused. I mourned that house like an old friend.

As I anticipated, the new owner destroyed the integrity of the house, stripped the ancient paneling from the walls and sold them. I'm sure he did the same with the old oak floorboards. He filled in the swimming pool and made it into a parking lot, and my beautiful home was made into a ski shop. My heart ached for my loss and for the loss of a historic landmark. From then on, I would go miles out of my way to avoid going past the house. Stan also sold the store across the street that still held a semblance of old-world elegance. It was torn down and replaced with a plain white box-like building.

Stan bought a convenience store in Windsor around the corner from our new house. The kids continued to work for him as they did in the Sheffield store, but I refused to be part of his business ventures any longer. I couldn't stand working with him. The customers grew to love our children and one said, "If I see your husband's car in the parking lot of the store, I won't stop in. You have good kids—I can't stand the way he treats them." He treated his employees the same way, although some became loyal to him because he'd help them out financially from time to time. There was always a jar on his counter for some charity, and he was the first to contribute to it—glimpses that he might have some compassion in his heart.

I was still making trips back and forth to Burlington to visit Ann. She was in a nursing home. The place was dark and depressing, but Ann was well cared for. I went unannounced and every time found her clean, her hair combed with barrettes and ribbons adorning it. The only light came from the TV. She would look at me blankly when I walked in, and I would talk to her just like we used to talk. Her eyes would begin to focus on me and follow me as I moved.

If I mentioned Seth, her son, she'd start to writhe and make moaning sounds. The nurses assured me it was just an automatic response and that she didn't understand anything I said. But, I stopped talking about Seth. Then she started to do the same thing when I would say good-bye and start to leave. I would cry all the way home to Windsor. My visits became less frequent.

~

In my second year at Antioch/New England, I was required to be in another group. This time I was fortunate to be assigned to a group facilitated by Paula Green, a wise, kindhearted woman. This group was smaller than the *Tavistock* one and much more genuine and intimate. It was held in a small, narrow, light-filled room unlike the large, dark brick-walled room in which we met for the *Tavistock* group. Paula guided us to hear and hold each other with respect and empathy. As the semester went on, we delved deeper into our core issues. I spoke about my abusive marriage, my desire to leave, and my inability to make that decision. One day, Paula drew an imaginary line on the floor.

She said, "Making the decision to leave is as easy as stepping over this line. Go ahead, step over it."

I froze. I started to shake. I was astonished by the level of fear that rose within me. Then, Paula said, "Mike, come here to the other side and hold out your hand."

Mike was probably in his late twenties, but he and I had a strong connection as a result of a few soulful conversations we had outside the group. Paula, in her wisdom, knew that if anyone could coax me to step over that line and face my fear, it would be Mike. Tears blurred my vision. The room full of friends was completely silent.

Mike gently urged me, "Come on, Kath, you can do it. You deserve better."

Those words touched the core of my heart, and I started to sob softly. My hand slowly reached out to Mike's, and he enveloped it in his own. Looking down, I took baby steps toward the line.

Paula said, "Look at Mike."

I looked straight into Mike's blue-grey eyes and stepped across the line. The room erupted in cheers as if I had just crossed the finish line at the Boston Marathon. I will always hold that day in loving memory—it was the first time I believed that I could get out of my marriage and be free.

When I was still in my undergraduate program, just beginning to explore feminism in my Women's Studies courses, I wanted to attend a *Take Back the Night* rally at UNH. It would be unthinkable to go without asking Stan's permission and, of course, he said, "No!"

Dejected and angry I went for a walk overlooking a hilly green pasture at sunset. It was fall. The air was cool with the spicy scent of dying leaves. As darkness veiled the light and the moon appeared on the horizon, a song came from the sky:

> *All women take back the night*
> *All women reclaim your days*
> *But be prepared to fight*
> *In many different ways*

Fight with all of your strength
Fight with your words
Know that you're powerful.
Tonight solemnly vow
Never to be a victim again
Chorus

Fight with all of your dreams
Fight for yourselves
And for your children
To live and grow in a world
Full of peace and equality
Chorus

Fight with all of your pride
Sisters unite, claim your identity,
A wise, loving and strong
Beautiful part
of humanity
Chorus

Fight with all of your love
All people are One
Men are not the enemy.
And fight with undaunted hope
Together we shall live joyously.

– Kathleen, 1981

This song was used the following year at the *Take Back the Night* rally. As I stepped over that invisible line, I knew, for the first time, the wisdom of the words of the song that dropped from the sky on that moonlit night.

~

Often my songs come while I'm driving—a melody begins to insinuate itself into my consciousness and then words tumble out inserting themselves into the melody—often I scribble them down as I drive. Fearing for my life, my friends bought me a voice activated tape recorder! These songs bring a surge of energy, of hope, a sense that anything is possible. Many times they speak a truth of which I am not consciously aware.

One day, I was walking around a reservoir as I often did. This day my mood was dark. I was ruminating about all my failings and mistakes. The tentacles of depression were beginning to ensnare me once again.

Then, I felt a tall full-canopied tree diagonally across the water calling to me. Almost in trance, I walked half way around the reservoir and sat beneath the tree's wide branches, my back against the trunk, nestled in its hearty roots. As improbable as this may seem, a song began streaming from the tree into me. The words were antithetical to what I was feeling that day. I knew they were coming from a sacred source.

> *I am a Light Blossom*
> *I am a Light Blossom*
> *I am a Light Blossom*
> *I am a Bloom of Light*
>
> *Light of Love shines on me*
> *Light of Love shines through me*
> *Light of Love shines in me*
> *I am a Bloom of Light*
>
> *I am a Light Tree*
> *I am a Light Tree*
> *I am a Light Tree*
> *I am a Tree of Light*
>
> *Branches reaching high*
> *Calling on the Sun*
> *Bringing from the Sky*
> *Light for everyone*

Deep within me I knew these words were true. This song quietly emerges from the depths of my soul when I most need to be reminded of who I am.

From the stones come my songs
Flow the melodies loud and strong
I hear words in my ears
Of a wisdom passed through the years.

– Excerpt of a song by Kathleen

CHAPTER TWENTY-NINE
My Path to Freedom

I GRADUATED with a Master of Arts Degree in Counseling Psychology from Antioch/New England Graduate School, in June, 1985, with the hope this degree would insure a rewarding position in the field with decent pay. My body betrayed me once more—the same thing that happened after graduating with my bachelor's degree: increased heart rate, generalize pain throughout my body, brain fog and extreme fatigue.

I was barely functioning. I dragged myself to multiple interviews for jobs in my field without success until I applied to the Family Counseling Center. A friend from my internship was director of the program. She immediately hired me. I prayed I wouldn't disappoint her as the fatigue continued to plague me. My caffeine intake greatly increased.

The position entailed working with court-referred families in their homes and meeting with the teenagers assigned to me wherever they felt most comfortable. Families were referred to the program because of child abuse and/or because adolescents or teenagers were acting out with truancy or other delinquent behaviors. We worked in pairs. My partner was a young man in his mid-twenties.

Sam and I worked well together. We were on-call twenty-four hours a day, seven days a week. We took turns covering the beeper. One of our first assignments was a fifteen-year-old girl who was truant from school and experimenting with drugs and alcohol. I was called away from the dinner table or in the middle of the night several times to look for her or pick her up at the police station. My own teenagers were acting out at the same time—the two oldest were on the verge of graduating high school and testing the limits.

In the second case we were assigned, both parents had been found guilty of child abuse. The target of the harsh physical aggression was a scrawny little six year old boy, Ray, with unkempt dark blond hair and faded blue eyes. His father, Walt, was a giant of a man, about 6'4" and over 300lbs. The mother, Terry, was obese and profoundly depressed. The house was cluttered and filthy. It smelled of rotting garbage and urine. There were two younger children, both of whom looked neglected and lethargic.

Sam and I tried to align with the parents and teach them parenting skills while encouraging and supporting the children. One of us would do an activity with the children, while the other worked with the parents. We facilitated family interactions and group activities. It was discouraging work. The parents were resistant to our interventions, and sometimes belligerent and angry. We couldn't affect change in the environment. The children were apathetic unless we brought them treats or small presents. Even then we had their attention only briefly.

One day, Sam and I walked into their home and found Ray sitting by his father's side on the couch. Ray was pale and obviously upset. He stuttered when he was anxious. "M-m-my Daddy didn't hit me! M-m-m-my Daddy didn't hit me," he asserted shaking his head from side to side. "M-m-my Daddy hit m-m-me because I was BAD!"

My partner and I simultaneously took a breath. Sam took the kids outside, and I stayed to talk with the parents. Terry told me that Walt flew into a rage because Ray didn't immediately obey his command. She said, "Walt hit him hard with his open hand and then kicked him when he fell in a heap on the floor." I knew she had risked Walt's wrath by telling me the truth. According to their religion, the man of the house was lord and master. Walt dominated everyone in the home, including his wife.

Sam and I stepped outside to regroup and call our supervisor. She told us that the provision of the court order stated that if the violence occurred again, the child was to be removed and brought to the orphanage run by Catholic nuns in the next town. We braced ourselves.

We went back inside and sent the children upstairs to play while we talked to the parents. We explained the situation to Terry and Walt. Walt got angry and aggressive. Terry started to cry—the only emotion I had seen on her face since we started working with them six weeks before. Sam had built a connection with Walt and tried to calm him down. I went upstairs to find Ray. The other children said he was hiding in the eaves of the house which had been walled off to make a storage area. I called for Sam to help.

He crawled into the tiny space and pulled Ray out, kicking, screaming and biting. Ray sobbed—crying so hard he couldn't catch his breath. He had heard us talking and begged us not to take him away. Terry packed a small bag, and Sam carried Ray out to my car, still struggling, crying and pleading. Sam got into the back seat holding onto Ray who was trying to kick out the window. I got into the driver's seat.

When we got to the toll booth Ray screamed, "Take me home! I want my mommy and daddy!"

The toll booth attendant looked at us with suspicion!

I said to Sam, "We're going to get arrested for kidnapping!" But, in truth, my heart was breaking for this little boy who was so terrified of the unknown, he wanted to go back to his abuser. I knew how he felt.

The Children's Home was a huge white farmhouse on a small knoll which had been converted into a rambling home for children. There was a large well-equipped playground on the side of the building surrounded by a high wooden fence painted stark white. Wide stone steps led to a small covered porch. I knocked on the door, Sam still holding Ray. As the door of the orphanage opened, there stood a diminutive nun in a habit similar to the one worn by the Sisters with whom I had lived when I was sixteen.

Ray had calmed down—exhausted from crying. Sam carried him inside as the nun stepped aside and pointed to the bench in the hallway. Inside, the rooms were large and painted white with colorful decorations everywhere. A young nun coaxed Ray into the playroom and offered him cookies and milk.

The nun who greeted us and who was obviously in charge looked at me intently and said, "You look like someone who has walked through my life before."

I asked, "What is the name of your order, Sister?"

"I'm *Mother* Marie Teresa," she said proudly. "The order is Sisters of Charity of Our Lady, Mother of Wisdom."

I already knew to whom I was talking, but I continued the charade. I said, "That's interesting. I was in an order called Sisters of Charity of Our Lady, Mother of Love, in Westfield, Connecticut. Would you have been known as Lucia? I'm Kathy Marino!"

Lucia was the aloof aspirant who made a display of her devotion to win the nuns favor. There was always an unspoken competition between us in our convent days together.

"Kathy, how wonderful to see you! Please tell me about our new resident and about yourself."

She had been briefed on Ray by our supervisor. Sam and I filled her in on our experience with him and his family. She seemed caring and concerned for the young boy's welfare. Sam went to help Ray acclimate to his new surroundings, and I sat and talked with Mother.

I questioned Mother about the name change of the order and she said the order had split. They were no longer affiliated with the Sisters in Connecticut.

I told her I was married and had four children and had just received my master's degree in Counseling Psychology. She congratulated me.

I said without thinking, "I'd love for you to meet my children. Perhaps you could come visit us some day and have dinner."

She responded, "Oh that would be lovely."

Then I added, "I converted to Judaism when I got married. My children are Jewish."

"Oh?" She looked stunned.

As I left, I reminded her of my invitation and said, "I'll call you to set up a time."

She replied, "You know, dear, I'll have to get Mother Provincial's permission." I knew right then she would never come. They would all be praying for my immortal soul so I wouldn't be damned to Hell for leaving the Church.

I gave my notice at Family Counseling. I couldn't bear to go through another ordeal like removing Ray from his family home even though I knew it was in his best interest. He thrived at the orphanage. His school work improved, and when I visited him he was anxious to show me his artwork. But his parents petitioned the court, and he was returned to them. I lost contact with him after that.

~

That fall, in spite of continued struggles with my body, I taught *Introduction to Psychology* and *Child Development* to underprivileged community college students in Haverhill, Massachusetts. I was shocked to find that some of these students were barely able to read or write. It was part-time work and entailed a two-hour commute twice a week. The pay was meager.

Stan ranted about my not bringing in a steady paycheck, but in spite of this, I opened a private practice in January 1986 in a small red building on a back street in the historic Windsor downtown. Stan was furious. I didn't care. This decision allowed me to pace myself and rebuild my health.

I put an ad in the paper to announce a women's support group I was forming and deposited flyers around town advertising *The Center for Life Enhancement*. Clients began to find me. As my practice grew, I became the therapist for many Baha'is, Quakers and people from the Gay and Lesbian communities. I also had referrals from the local domestic violence shelter at which I had interned. Word of mouth became my best source for new clients. I loved the work.

This was an enormous triumph for me. I envisioned a time when my psychotherapy practice could financially sustain my children and me. I longed for that day. I was driven not only to serve people in need of psychological help, but also to live free of the interminable harassment my children and I endured.

~

In November of that year, Stan tells me he closed one of our bank accounts—I find the bank book, and he had deposited $17,000 the month before. It is still open. I have no idea where he has gotten this money. I confront him about the account and tell him I want a divorce. I say, "I can't trust you—you're playing games with me." I feel empowered by the experience of crossing the imaginary line in Paula's class with Mike holding out his hand.

He says, "I have everything figured out." He agrees to the divorce, but wants me to wait three to six months so he can get another business to support the house and his own place. He becomes antagonistic when I don't agree. He badgers me and says, "You were incapacitated for three months this summer— you're not competent to have the kids. It could happen again!"

I say, "That's enough, Stan! I'm not discussing this with you."

He becomes irate. "I'm going to tear apart every paper in your library!" he screams. He goes into the library and pulls out two boxes of papers and starts ripping through them. I call the police dispatch to document his actions. He stops.

The next day I contact another lawyer, my fifth, Stewart Mills. I tell him what has happened. He says, "I'm concerned for your financial assets if we wait. Come into my office and I'll have you sign a libel." I go directly to his office and sign the paper that will lead to a divorce. I feel it is only fair to tell Stan what I have done.

That evening when I get home, Stan is furious. He starts yelling. "I spoke to your doctors today and they say you're on too high a dose of Aventle and that one of the side effects is hostility." He hounds me until I agree to put the petition on hold. Believing him, I feel I have no choice. I refuse to go to bed with him, and sleep on the couch.

I call our family therapist the next morning and she assures me none of what Stan has said is true. "Don't buy into what Stan is saying—it his distortion. You are *not* crazy and you're a good mother." She firmly states that I should proceed with filing for a divorce. "You need *space* from Stan in order to reclaim your power."

Then I call Dr. Ross, my psychiatrist, and he concurs that I'm emotionally and mentally stable and my medication dose is fine. His says in a firm voice, "It sounds like you're doing what you need to do."

That night, Stan speaks to each child and claims I'm emotionally unstable. He talks at great length to his brother in front of Jake about my irrational, unstable behavior. He threatens to have me institutionalized—*committed* is the word he uses. Pounding on the table, he shouts, "I will DESTROY you if you proceed with this divorce!" Then he tells me he's going to sell my car to David for a dollar. I almost laugh—but I'm shaken.

I never learn the source of the $17,000 deposit and all signs of it disappear.

~

As all this was unfolding, we were informed that Rachel was at risk of not graduating with her class because she had too many absences. Rachel had always been the easy one—bright, creative, funny—everything I could have hoped for in a daughter. As far as I knew, she hadn't been absent at all. When I went to the school to see what was going on, the Vice-Principal handed me a folder of notes with "my signature" requesting that Rachel be excused from school for one reason or another. No one ever called me to check if these notes were valid. When Stan and I questioned Rachel about it she was defiant and said she didn't care if she graduated or not. With this new development, I realized I couldn't make the break from Stan now. We needed to collaborate as parents.

We made a deal with Rachel. We asked her, "What do you want most of all?"

She said, "To live on my own!"

We promised that if she graduated high school with her class, we'd set her up in an apartment. She was seventeen. She graduated and was thrilled to have her own place. She was happier than I'd seen her in years.

My son, David, graduated at the same time as Rachel and had been accepted at Keene State College. Because of his premature birth, I always felt protective of him. We had our clashes, but were close. He was a kind-hearted soul and was especially devoted to his younger sister, Debbie. Along with his interest in body-building, nutrition and psychology, he was artistic and loved music.

Once, he brought home the song, *Ships Passing in the Night*, which he said was about him and his Dad. I remember watching him walking down the road with his father when he was about three, mimicking his father's swagger, but he was nothing like his father. Bringing him to Keene State and leaving him there for the first time was as excruciating for me as the day after he was born watching him being carried in a tiny incubator to the waiting police car. Both times, I could not contain my tears.

~

I was more determined than ever to make a success of my private practice after coming so close to breaking free from Stan. I engaged a supervisor, Hubert Hardy, PhD, who guided me in my first years as a practitioner. Bert was a renegade. I had great respect for him, for his courage to forge his own way as a clinician, mental health administrator and college professor. I would bring my most difficult cases to him for guidance on how I should proceed. He soon recognized I was in deep waters with some of my clients.

I'd present a case to him: "Bert, I just can't connect with this client…she cries and I can't feel for her."

Bert would say, "Use yourself as a diagnostic tool, Kath! You connect with lampposts! If you can't connect with someone—it's not YOU!"

Or, I'd say, "This client is just too intelligent—I can't keep up with her. She calls threatening suicide. I run to meet her at my office and she comes in perfectly dressed, calm, and says, "Oh, I'm fine now!" I feel completely out of control and confused when I'm with her!"

Bert would repeat his mantra, "Use yourself as a diagnostic tool! The woman is a flaming borderline!"

Bert's advice probably saved my sanity as I began to accept only those clients I could effectively serve. When I sat with someone and my inner dialogue turned to "Why can't I connect with this person—what's wrong with me?" Or, "Why can't I follow this person's line of reasoning? She must be smarter than me." And, "Why am I feeling so confused and out of control?" I honored them. They became signposts for me, leading to better assessments of my client's needs.

Clients came to me with a wide array of issues. I dealt with adults who had experienced child abuse, incest, sexual assault, alcoholic or mentally ill parents, and clients who were looking to find meaning and purpose in life. The most difficult cases for me were those adults who had been sexually assaulted as children. There were more of them than I could have ever imagined before I began this work.

One man in his thirties came to me for counseling because his supervisor advised him to "get help or look for another job." Denny was a robust man of average height with straight black hair. During our sessions, he was almost non-verbal—which is problematic when doing talk-therapy. The one thing I had ascertained was that, although he was raised as a devout Catholic, he had a great love for Native American culture and traditions. Other than that he was a mystery to me.

After a few sessions without a breakthrough, I tried a new tactic. On a hot summer day, before he came for his appointment, I put pillows on the floor. When he walked into my office, I suggested, "Why don't we sit on the floor for a change? It's so warm today I think we'll be cooler there."

As we settled on the floor, he looked around and said, "What's with all the stones?" I had baskets of stones everywhere as a result of my many hours walking the beach.

Without a thought, I said, "My songs come from the stones."

Denny's eyes opened wide. He said, "I've never heard anyone who wasn't Native American say that!"

That was the breakthrough. Denny opened up and began releasing the pain he held from being sexually violated by a Catholic priest at a very young age. It was a beginning.

The song, *From the Stones*, had dropped from the sky several years before on a rare drive alone to my Master's program on the other side of the state. The country road I took followed along a rock-filled stream. As was often the case, my mind released its death grip on my heart as I glimpsed the rocks and flowing water. I drove in a state of reverie and the song slipped through.

When my children heard another song had been bestowed upon me while driving, they'd admonish me, "Mom, pay attention to the road!"

And, I'd reply, "Don't worry. The Angels are driving when a song is coming through." Somehow that did not comfort them.

~

About two months after I advertised the women's support group, I received a call from a young woman who had clipped my ad out of the paper and stuck it on her refrigerator. She said she and two friends were interested in the women's group. All three of these women were bright, caring and full of life. It was a delight to work with them. I was still active in the peer-counseling community, so after some months, I offered to take them to a PCU workshop that was being held in Vermont. They enthusiastically joined me, and on the ride home begged me to teach peer-counseling classes.

Since this was a support group, not a therapy group, I decided to disclose my situation. "I would love to, but I'm trying to get a divorce. I'm afraid the stress would detract from my ability to be an effective teacher," I said.

They all chimed in, "We'll support you! We can help you! Please think about it."

And, thus began the Southern New Hampshire Peer Counselors United Community. It grew from these three women to over a hundred participants. As the classes filled up with friends of the original three, I realized I was doing what I loved most: teaching and counseling. And yet, because I worked on a sliding scale in my practice, I made little money.

I introduced *Creativity Days* to my community. We would gather for a picnic or indoor potluck and bring instruments, our voices, art work, and poetry to share. Groups of us would go to PCU weekend workshops in Vermont and upstate New Hampshire and continue honing our peer counseling skills. There I met other peer-counselors, one of whom became a friend. Elle was an invaluable support as I became an integral part of the Regional Community and took on a leadership role in the PCU organization. I reported directly to the Regional Leader, Keith Hanson. Keith coached me when difficult issues came up in my classes or in my community. We had an excellent working relationship.

~

That January, I received a call from my Experimental Psychology professor, Dr. Earnest Fredricks. He was now the Interim Chair of the Psychology Department at University of New Hampshire. He asked if I would be available to teach during the spring semester as several Adjunct Faculty members had given their notice at the last minute. He needed someone to teach *Test and Measurements* and *Introduction to Sociology*. I did not feel qualified to teach either, but he assured me I would do fine. I summoned the courage to step into the unknown once again.

Every semester from then on for the next two years, I taught two or three classes at UNH on a wide range of topics, including Introduction to Psychology, Abnormal Psychology, Child Development and Gender Studies. When a new department Chairman, Edward Morrell, PhD, took over, I was afraid he might not approve of my teaching methods.

In the late 1980's instructors in traditional academic settings were still expected to lecture and give tests. Instead, I put my students in a circle, talked for a while, and then encouraged discussion. I devised experiential exercises and gave weekly writing assignments. I always made sure the door to the classroom was closed and the chairs were returned to how I'd found them.

After six months of this clandestine teaching under Prof. Morrell, I was called to his office. I braced myself. He was sitting erect in his chair, hands folded on the desk, looking stern. He said in a serious tone, "I want to know *exactly* what you are doing in your classes." He paused and shifted into a more relaxed position. "From the students' evaluations it's evident you're a gifted teacher. I want to know what you are doing so I can give concrete suggestions to some of the professors in this department who would rather work with their research mice than their students." I slowly let out the breath I was holding.

I know how cold and paralyzing fear can be. I know how much strength, courage, and hard work are needed to conquer it. Most of all, I know that there are few victories in life more liberating than the victory over the low, dark clouds of fear that block our spirits from their rightful place in the sun.

– Excerpt from *The Other Side and Back* by Sylvia Browne

CHAPTER THIRTY
Now is the Time

I TAUGHT GENDER STUDIES, a Women's Studies' course in the fall semester of 1986. I had forty students, one of whom was a co-counseling friend, Greg. About mid-semester I invited a rape counselor to come and speak to my class. I introduced her and then sat beside her as she spoke. She talked about stranger rape and victim blaming, and then she introduced the topic of date rape and, finally, marital rape. These last two definitions were new to the lexicon of feminist thinking.

I sat stunned in the realization that I was a victim of both. Even after all the years of working with battered women, taking Women's Studies courses, and reading everything I could about feminism, this reality had escaped me. I struggled to keep my composure until I could thank the speaker and dismiss my class. I gathered my things and ran to my office; Greg instinctively knew something was wrong and followed behind me. As I closed the door behind us, Greg just nodded and said, "Go!"

I grabbed a pillow off the chair and began screaming into it! Fury and rage came pouring out of every cell in my body! Then I collapsed into deep sobs—*twenty years of my life, twenty years of my life*—the only words I could say. I had been doing penance for twenty years for a crime I did not commit. I wasn't culpable for *sinning against God!* Stan had sinned against me.

The next day, I made an appointment with lawyer number six, Henry Lauter, a respected attorney recommended by friends. He was a partner in a prestigious law firm. We spent an hour together. I was calm and composed telling him about Stan's abusive behavior and why I was seeking a divorce. I may have teared up talking about the children, but that was brief and my only display of emotion. Lauter drew up the divorce papers. I signed them. He said Stan would be served the next day.

I left a note for Stan, telling him what I had done, and took the two younger children to stay the night with some friends who were aware of the risk they were taking by giving me and my children refuge. I will always be grateful to them for their support. I waited all day for the call that Stan had been served. Nothing happened. By late afternoon, I could wait no longer. I called Lauter.

"What happened, Henry? You were supposed to serve Stan papers today."

He drew a deep breath and said, "I got a call from your husband's lawyer last night, and he said you are too emotionally unstable to make such a decision at this time."

I was furious! I said, "Henry, did I look unstable to YOU yesterday!"

"No, but his lawyer said you are under psychiatric care and taking medication for depression."

"Henry, half the world is under psychiatric care and taking medication!" I slammed the phone down.

I returned to the house and moved out of the master bedroom, claiming the dining room, which was off the kitchen, as my own. It was temporarily empty, so I put a mattress on the floor and a pile of books and a radio beside it. When Stan walked into the house, I ignored him.

He began to rage at me, yelling, "I will DEMOLISH you— you fucking bitch." He banged on the kitchen table and spewed venomous words at me for an hour. Then he started begging me to try to make the marriage work. His brother called and told me I should stay for "the sake of the kids." I felt trapped and defeated. I reluctantly moved back into the bedroom about a week later.

That glimpse of hope I had three years before in Paula Green's group—when I crossed that line to freedom—was shattered.

~

Things quieted down in the next few months with the two oldest out of the house, but Stan's denigration of Debbie escalated. His obsession with her weight from when she was a little girl never diminished, and my prophecy about his creating an eating disorder came true. I was also complicit in creating her weight issues because I tried to compensate when he deprived her—sneaking her food. By the time she hit puberty, she was significantly overweight. Stan continued harassing her about every morsel she put in her mouth.

When Debbie was seven, I engaged a child psychiatrist to help her. He informed me he could do nothing for her unless Stan and I were part of the therapy. Stan reluctantly agreed. After a few months of meeting regularly, the doctor told me, "No one can help Debbie until the family situation changes." He said he was terminating the therapy. "I have no hope for family therapy working with your family. Stan is intransigent, and he has serious problems. He has to stop *owning* Debbie's mouth and stomach. I'll be happy to work with you and Debbie if you become a single mother. If you ever decide to divorce him, I'll speak on your behalf in court."

I did not heed his warning and took her to several more therapists over the course of the next five years, all of whom eventually concurred with his assessment.

Debbie was now twelve-years-old. One day I came home from work and the neighbor across the street beckoned me to come over. I approached her not sure what to expect because she rarely talked to anyone. She was not smiling and her demeanor was cold. "I need to talk to you—come in."

As we stepped into the foyer, I wondered what one of my kids had done to upset her.

Her voice shook with anger when she said, "I think you should know Stan is making Debbie run around the loop while he drives behind her beeping the horn to make her go faster. It's horrible!" My heart sank.

I thanked her for telling me and stormed across the road. I slammed the door as I entered the house. Stan was, as usual, sprawled out on the couch in the family room watching television. "What's *your* problem?" he said without taking his eyes off the TV set.

"My problem is what you're doing to Debbie! I can't believe you have her running around the loop while you drive behind her beeping the horn. Are you crazy?"

"Well, it's more than you're doing for her!" he shouted. "She sits in here all day on her fat ass while you run around doing your own thing. What are you doing to help her lose weight? Nothing!"

"What you are doing is child-abuse, and if you keep it up, the neighbors are going to call social services!" In the next few days I heard from two more neighbors who wanted me to know what was going on.

Rachel, in the meantime, continued to work at Dunkin' Donuts and other jobs and maintained her apartment with a little help from us. By the next spring she decided to go to Keene State College in the fall. Before she left in August, she came over to the house and said she wanted to talk to me.

"Sure, honey. Let's sit in the living room."

We sat on our floral cream-colored couch together.

Rachel said tersely, "Mom, he's doing to Debbie what he did to me," referring to her father's cruel treatment when she was younger. "Are you going to let it happen again?"

I fell back against the couch in shock. Her words felt like a physical blow.

I knew what I had to do. During one of our attempts at couple's therapy, the psychiatrist, Dr. Dixon, who had just terminated her work with us in exasperation, whispered to me as we walked out, "Come to see me when you're ready to leave." It was time to take her up on this offer. There was no house to hold me, no hope to hold me, no dream of making it work to tether me to this man. When the two oldest were settled at Keene State, I called Dr. Dixon and made an appointment with her. We began to map out my course to freedom.

It wasn't until thirty years after my divorce that I learned the extent of Stan's abuse of my children. I saw his harshness with them. I heard his denigrating tirades. I was aware of his demanding, controlling behavior with them. I fought with him about all this behind closed doors, and tried to offer comfort to whomever was being targeted.

What I did not know was that he tormented them in ways that went beyond anything I could have imagined. I was shocked, horrified and deeply saddened when I found out he tortured them in devious, brutal ways, out of my sight and without leaving tell-tale signs. As a therapist, I always wondered how a mother could not know that a child was being abused under her roof. Now, I am that mother.

I can only assume my children did not tell me what was going on because they were threatened by their father; they did not feel safe with me; or they felt I was too impotent to help them. Were they trying to protect me, I who should have been their protector? Did they think I was too fragile to handle the truth or that I didn't care enough about them to stand up to their father in their behalf?

I cannot reconcile my failure to protect them or even give them comfort when they needed it most. That will always haunt me. I can only ask their forgiveness and continue to offer my love as they offer me theirs in spite of my failings. Forgiving myself and their father is beyond the capacity of my heart right now. It may be the work of an eternity.

~

It was the fall of 1987 and I was ready to fight! Dr. Dixon said it would be far more effective if we used Stan's belittling and bullying of Debbie as the reason for getting a restraining order. His relentless destructive and demoralizing behavior toward me would be harder to prove. I was reluctant to put Debbie in that position with her father, so I decided I would take my chances on stating my own case for emotional, mental, and what I now knew was sexual abuse.

My trust in lawyers had plummeted by the time I made my decision to leave, but one day I was walking on a side street in Danforth and came across an office with the word *PAX* in large blue letters. It was a law office. The word, which means "peace," drew me inside.

I spoke to the receptionist and told her I was looking for a divorce lawyer. She said one of the lawyers might have time to talk with me. I was led into the office of John Wholey, a giant of a man, in a tired looking suit. He was close to seventy with sparse white hair and a huge warm smile. He invited me to sit down.

I began to tell him about my marriage and why I wanted a divorce. He listened intently, and I could feel his outrage as I described Stan's treatment of me and my children.

He said, "Let me at this guy. You're a nice lady! You don't deserve to be treated like that—no one does!"

John was a bit unpolished, but he was one of the best women's advocates I've ever met. And, he could be reassuring when my strength faltered. He explained I had to file for the restraining order myself, but once that was done he would take over.

One of the judges in the court before which I was to appear for the restraining order was a family friend. When I walked into the courthouse to fill out the necessary papers, his daughter was behind the counter. I was shaken. I asked her not to say anything to her parents, and she assured me she would not.

After getting the restraining order, which would be served to Stan the next day, I took Debbie and Jake, now thirteen and fourteen, out for supper at the Pizza House and told them what was happening. They both seemed to understand my decision and let me know they were ok with it.

The children and I left the house early the next morning and I waited in my office to hear from the Sheriff. I was well aware of the possibility that Stan might come after me with a gun, but at this point it was an acceptable alternative to living with him for the rest of my life. The Sheriff called about 2:00pm and said Stan was out of the house. It was safe for us to go home. He had waited for Stan to gather some things and go to a hotel.

John Wholey, my rumpled lawyer, swung into action and had the divorce papers served a few days later. I was almost giddy with excitement. I thoroughly cleaned the house—to remove any vestiges of Stan. I began to sort his belongings from mine making a pile in the garage so he could remove them without coming into the house. I put on Cat Stevens music and danced. The symphonies and operas I loved, and Stan hated, returned to my life.

Wholey made sure I got the house in the temporary orders, and he pressed me to go after Stan financially. He said, "Let me nail this guy to the cross. I know he has money stashed that you don't even know about."

Jason, Stan's cousin whom I had treated like a brother, was one of Stan's lawyers. He was ruthless in defense of his cousin.

"No, just get me out of this marriage as soon as possible. If we go after him, he'll crucify ME."

John reluctantly proceeded as I asked. I filed for the divorce in October 1987. The divorce was finalized in March 1988, record time according to my divorced friends. I wanted to change my name back to Marino, but my children didn't want me to have a different last name from theirs. I started to call myself *Kathleen* to somehow claim my new identity as a free woman. Stan rarely called me by my name. He would bark out orders or call me by a denigrating moniker. But when he did call me *Kathy*, I felt like my name had been defiled in his mouth. There was no love or kindness in his tone.

It became clear I wasn't able to enforce the restraining order. Stan would come storming into the house and say, "It's MY house—I'm paying the bills!"

I couldn't bring myself to call the police and have him charged for breaking the restraining order. I didn't want to incite him to take more drastic measures against me, and I couldn't bear to humiliate him with his buddies on the police force. His store was one mile from the house and his new apartment a mile from the house in the other direction. I couldn't go anywhere without bumping into him—at first he was always belligerent and angry with me, but as time went on he began pleading with me to give our marriage one more try. I stood firm.

My PCU friends rallied around me and offered emotional and hands-on support. Even so, my nerves became frayed living in the same small town as Stan. Finally, as the school year drew to a close, I was frantic to get away from him. "You want the house, you can have it," I said.

He paid me half the market value at a time when the market was soft. I began my search for an apartment in Brookline, an expensive part of the Greater Boston area with an excellent school system. Debbie was entering eighth grade, and I wanted her to have all the advantages Brookline offered, even though it would stretch my budget.

The first apartment I looked at was on a narrow winding street named White Place—one of the oldest streets in town. It was on the third floor with trolley tracks thirty feet behind it. I was dubious. When the owner opened the door, I gasped. Looking straight into the kitchen, I saw *red* counters. I knew I was home.

Moving down to Brookline meant leaving my peer-counseling community, my friends, and everything that was familiar to me. And, my fifteen year old son, Jake. I'd allowed Jake to choose where he wanted to live, and he chose to stay with his father because he didn't want to leave his friends, some of whom he had known since grammar school.

I had the physical sensation of my heart being ripped open when he told me, but I was relieved by his decision because I feared the temptation for drug use would be far greater in the Boston area. I would miss him terribly.

After paying $1,200 in rent to live in Brookline, I had little money left for extras. The court hadn't given me any alimony because I had more education than Stan, although I had thousands of dollars in student loans. I received nominal child support for Debbie and had to pay half of the children's college tuition.

My lawyer, Wholey, sputtered about all this, but I was ecstatic to be free! I was immensely grateful to this bear of a man for allowing me to do the divorce *my way*—a privilege I had rarely been accorded in my twenty-two years of marriage to Stanley Cohen. My anthem became *The Journey* by Mary Oliver.

> *One day you finally knew*
> *what you had to do, and began,*
> *though the voices around you*
> *kept shouting*
> *their bad advice—*
> *though the whole house*
> *began to tremble*
> *and you felt the old tug*
> *at your ankles.*
> *"Mend my life!"*
> *each voice cried.*
> *But you didn't stop.*
> *You knew what you had to do*
> *though the wind pried*
> *with its stiff fingers*
> *at the very foundations—*
> *though their melancholy*
> *was terrible.*
> *It was already late*
> *enough, and a wild night,*
> *and the road full of fallen*
> *branches and stones.*
> *But little by little*
> *as you left their voices behind,*
> *and stars began to burn*
> *through the sheets of clouds,*
> *and there was a new voice,*
> *which you slowly*
> *recognized as your own,*
> *that kept you company*
> *as you strode deeper and deeper*
> *into the world,*
> *determined to do*
> *the only thing you could do—*
> *determined to save*
> *the only life you could save.*

– "The Journey" from *Dream Work* by Mary Oliver

All women take back the night
All women reclaim your days
But be prepared to fight
In many different ways

– Chorus of *All Women Take Back the Night* by Kathleen

CHAPTER THIRTY-ONE
Betrayal

WHILE I WAS STILL IN WINDSOR, dealing with the logistics of moving, the demands of the Peer Counselors United community escalated. The community had served as my surrogate family and substituted for a religious community. It was dedicated to individual healing, the ending of all oppression, and the ideal of working toward world peace. My peer-counseling friends were ever present as I faced the difficult decisions and the upheaval of my life. I was, at the same time, betraying their trust.

During this time, an old rumor resurfaced about the organization to which I had dedicated ten years of my life. Neil Olson, who was the founder and leader of PCU, had always denied the rumor that he was sexually abusing women in the peer-counseling community. He claimed it was a tactic often used to discredit leaders.

I had a good working relationship with the regional leader, Keith, who assured me the rumor wasn't true. I questioned no further. Keith was my mentor, friend, and the person directly over me in the hierarchy of the organization. Young and idealistic, he cared deeply about people and the state of the world. I trusted him.

Neil Olson was the ultimate decision-maker for the whole organization. A few years after its inception, PCU had thousands of members throughout the world.

In the midst of the divorce and move, two PCU counselors, Lena and Troy, whom I respected, contacted me and asked if they could address my community. They wanted to share information they had gathered concerning alleged sexually inappropriate behavior with female clients by Neil Olson and other leaders. I felt it was a reasonable request and was willing to comply, until I called Keith to clear it with him. He hadn't allowed these people to speak in his community and was furious that I'd even consider allowing them to speak in mine.

He said, "Kath, this information is inflammatory, divisive and unfounded [even though he had refused to review the findings]. If you go ahead and allow this information to be disseminated, you could be decertified as a teacher!"

I felt loyal to Keith, but I knew it was wrong to keep this information from members of our communities and not give them the opportunity to evaluate it for themselves. The week that followed was an agonizing one. I was harassed, pressured (really bullied), and denigrated by several PCU leaders who called to convince me not to allow the information against Neil to surface. I was accused of having "leadership distress," "unresolved early sexual memories," and of "acting out of a victim pattern." This was PCU jargon that meant I was not thinking rationally.

In one letter, Keith told me to *get off my high horse* and accused me of being disloyal to the organization and to him. In the course of this week of phone calls, Keith *admitted* that Neil was having sex with women he counseled. His position of power gave him leverage to coerce these victims. It was against PCU policy and the universal ethics of leadership.

Keith's excuse for remaining silent was, "I and other leaders are counseling him on the *pattern*," which really meant that Neil had unresolved issues around sex and wasn't thinking rationally. The point of peer-counseling in PCU theory was to help people undo detrimental patterns of thought and behavior held in place by past trauma and distress. When in the role of counselor, we helped each other break free of these patterns by listening with benign attention and support as the "client" expressed long held emotions. Neil's patterns appeared to include taking advantage of women who were going to him for help. This meant that while peer-counselors were working with him to undo this pattern, he remained free to sexually violate these women.

A few days later, a leader in charge of women's issues, who I held in high esteem, called me and *denied* that Neil was having sex with women in counseling sessions. She then told me, "What you need to do is to get to know Neil and counsel with him, and where he gets *funny* [sexual] hold out against the pattern and counsel him." She was thereby warning me to protect myself from him if he tried to get sexual with me. I noted that other women didn't have the luxury of a warning.

The secrecy, denial, and power-wielding became more evident over time, and I began to see the organization in a different light. I made the decision to allow Lena and Troy to present the information to anyone in my community who wanted to hear it, and I intended to invite Keith to present his side. I called Troy first and made arrangements, but before I could call Keith, he called to tell me my decision was unacceptable.

The most effective argument he used against me was that my community (and perhaps the whole Vermont/New Hampshire Region) would be disbanded if I persisted without the organization's consent. Neil Olson had already thrown out the PCU Community in another country because they had crossed him on this issue, so I knew this threat was real. Many members of my community credited peer-counseling with changing their lives. I believed it would be unfair for me to act in a way that might result in the destruction of the whole community. I rescinded my decision and resigned my leadership role.

I gave the leaders who were replacing me the information I had and left it up to them to decide what to do. It was one of the most cowardly things I've ever done. Many people were hurt and disappointed that I didn't tell them the truth myself, although I indicated I was resigning in protest over the abuse of power in the organization and possible sexual violations. I did not have the courage to defy Neil Olson.

That summer, my friend, Elle, and I attended a workshop in Virginia facilitated by peer-counselors who had left PCU. The workshop was led by Marian Kent, a former leader in the PCU organization. She confessed to being part of what she called, "Neil Olson's harem." She was not the only woman in leadership who had been lured into a sexual relationship with him, but she was the only one to stand up to him and expose the truth.

I had been in awe of the women leaders in PCU and respected their strength, intelligence and dedication. I couldn't imagine they had succumbed to Olson's sexual advances. I was shocked by this information. There was a power differential between Olson and these women leaders as well. He hired and could fire them. It's a travesty that they, too, did not have the courage to speak up to protect other women.

Elle and I weren't the only ones reeling with shock with this disclosure. The participants in the workshop bonded and supported each other through our time together. Anger, disillusionment, grief, outrage, all surfaced, as well as, tremendous appreciation for Marian's courage to share her story.

I realized that when I backed down from confronting the issue of Neil's behavior, I gave up my power and betrayed myself, my community, and all victims of abuse. I felt that same sense of failure for my cowardice in not exposing my brother's pedophilia.

~

I met many extraordinary people at that workshop. Some became life-long friends. Jeremy Sanders and I introduced ourselves and started talking while standing in the lunch line. It was the beginning of a lasting friendship. We immediately had a spiritual connection when he mentioned he was Jewish. I responded, "I'm Jewish, too, but I'm a convert."

He said, "Never refer to yourself as a convert and no one else should call you that. You are Jewish. There is no difference between those who are born Jewish and converts."

The shoulders of my heart soften with his words. I had felt like an imposter, as "other" among many of the Jewish people I knew. Now my cells filled with a deep sense of belonging. I will always be grateful to Jeremy for that.

And, we also shared a love for nature, art, music and so much more. Neither wanted strict boundaries, although we often shared counseling time. I would often join his family for their Passover Seder; he came and jumped the rocks of my river with me; I attended his graduation from rabbinic school and his wedding. Knowing my love for rocks, he once mailed me stacking stones when he was in Israel many years ago. They stand on my altar to this day.

I also met a young man named Craig Benson who had been part of an alternative peer-counseling movement in California about five years earlier. He was black-balled from the PCU community because he challenged the leaders who were using their power to sexually exploit women. He had tried to counter this form of violation from within the PCU organization and came to the conclusion that it couldn't be done. The secrecy and abuse were systemic. He was dedicated to the philosophy and practices of the peer counseling movement, and envisioned creating a new community that would ensure safety and respect for all.

As it turned out, Craig had recently moved to Boston and lived only a few miles from my new apartment. He was a Ph.D. candidate in Clinical Psychology at a near-by University. His thesis was on Domestic Violence and he interviewed hundreds of batterers and their victims and facilitated groups as part of his research. He was an extremely intelligent, insightful, compassionate young man. Tall, slim and athletic with light brown hair, he had a smile that opened my heart. We began exchanging counseling time on a regular basis.

Although he had left the PCU counseling community, he believed in strictly adhering to the ethics stated in the community's manual that delineated the non-socialization rules outside of the counseling relationships. I, on the other hand, had fostered a loose social structure as leader of my group in New Hampshire because most of the members of my community knew each other before joining PCU. I agreed to keep the boundaries as Craig requested.

During our first session together, I made Craig, whom I had just met the week before, stand diagonally across the room from me when it was my turn to be counseled. The fear of being alone in a room with a "strange" man roared through me. It would take weeks before I slowly let Craig work his way to sit beside me. He was patient and understood my request.

Craig was an expert on batterers' patterns and the effect the abuse had on their victims. He was not at all surprised by my reaction and assured me that I could heal from my abusive relationship with Stan.

When I would shake my head and cry, "Why did I stay so long? Why didn't I leave when I saw what he was doing to the kids?" Craig would quietly and firmly say, "Because the abuse is designed to keep you in your place. The abuser tears you down until you have no confidence in your ability to survive on your own or take care of your children."

Other times he would say, in response to the ever present question, "The abuser threatens, cajoles and manipulates to keep his victim confused and groundless," which was exactly how I felt most of the time with Stan, even as I began to have success in the outside world.

I had always said, "I don't understand. Stan has no empathy, but he knows exactly where to put the knife." Craig explained that this was typical of men who dominate and control their partners. He said they have an uncanny ability to see another's vulnerabilities but are incapable of empathy—this insight helped demystify Stan's power over me.

I couldn't believe my good fortune to have met an expert on domestic violence only months after my divorce. Had Craig not been an *expert*, I'd have been less likely to find him credible. His words wouldn't have had the impact to facilitate my healing from years of Stan's assaults. But, his impact on my life went beyond that. Within the boundaries of the ethics we agreed to uphold, Craig and I became close. PCU counselors are often affectionate in innocuous ways—we hugged when we greeted each other and when we parted; we held each other gently when tears began to flow, as you would hold a crying child.

Touch meant *sex* in Stan's vocabulary. He never touched me with affection—only when he wanted sex. Craig's affection was safe, conscious and tender. My body and psyche ached for that kind of touch—and I had stumbled into a fountain of it. As we knew each other better, Craig would light up when he saw me. I have so many memories of his throwing his arms around me in an all encompassing hug that made me feel seen and appreciated for who I was.

I remember, after one of our sessions in his second floor room, we hugged at the top of stairs saying our farewells. As I got to the bottom of the stairs and was about to open the door, I heard Craig bounding down the stairs saying, "One more hug!" with a big smile on his face and his arms outstretched.

One day Craig and I were walking through a park in Boston when he reached for my hand. I was fifteen years older, and I couldn't believe he wasn't embarrassed to be seen holding this older woman's hand. My heart melted.

The most profound healing came at those times when I was sobbing during a session and he held me gently in his arms until the storm passed. All my life I'd been shunned for my tears until I joined the peer-counseling group. Now, in Craig's arms, I knew in the deepest recesses of my soul, I was not alone. And, he often sang to comfort me. He had a wonderful musical ear and a soothing, mellow voice. He sang songs I had never heard from the Grateful Dead and Bob Dylan.

The contrast between Craig and Stan was so great it helped me see the deprivation I had lived with. His validation and caring gave me the strength to hold out against Stan's constant, intrusive manipulations to have contact with me. When I went to Stan's family gatherings for Passover and the High Holidays, he would corner me and try to kiss me, or insist on sitting next to me. I finally stopped going, although I missed the family and the rituals.

Layer by layer, the debris of the past was washed away through peer-counseling with Craig and others, and I began to gain a sense of myself as a competent, strong and capable woman. And, Craig reflected and encouraged that sense of myself, urging me to claim my power.

My connection with nature, with *The Holy*, with the people I loved, all strengthened as did my connection to myself. I was deeply grateful for the *Grace* that was unfolding in my life and felt the redemption I'd sought by reclaiming my own Sacred Self.

This meant I opened my heart to the unbidden mystical encounters that connected me to *The Divine*. My heart had been a tight fist in the years I spent with Stan. Now the fist began to loosen and slowly opened, ready to *receive* again. These encounters took many forms.

On one occasion, driving from Boston to my daughter's home in New Hampshire after a snow storm, I stopped for a cup of coffee to revive myself. I got my coffee and took a seat by a wall of windows, overlooking a hill covered in newly born snow shimmering in the sunlight. I sat there watching tiny rainbows appear and disappear in the snow crystals until *I* disappeared—melted into the *Oneness of All That Is*. A man sweeping the floor asked me a question and I snapped back into by body with a jolt. Disoriented for a moment, I finally mustered an answer to his question. The memory of my momentary disappearance into the *Ultimate Reality* remains embedded in my soul.

On a walk one day, fretting about money and finding a cheaper place to live, I looked over my shoulder and saw a vivid rainbow hanging in the sky. It was draped over a part of Brookline I had never explored. I found my way to this quiet corner with its narrow streets and quaint brick buildings that had been turned into apartments. There my new home awaited me.

Another time on my way to an appointment, feeling lonely and bereft, I stepped off a curb in Brookline Village and there was a tiny, pale green, heart-shaped piece of glass, roughly hewn from being battered on the city streets. I knew it was a *Love Note from God* as I called these gifts from the Universe. And, I *knew* I was not alone.

~

My private practice was still going well. I shared an office with a friend in Danforth, NH and went back and forth from Boston one day a week. I also worked as a secretary at Mass General Hospital. Between the two jobs, I was away from home over fifty hours a week. Debbie became a latchkey child. She and her friends thrived on the freedom to explore.

In the midst of this hectic schedule, Craig and I started the *International Counseling Network (ICN)* together. It was a program based on PCU principles but without the hierarchical structure that had led to such egregious abuses in that organization. We began to co-teach classes and co-lead workshops. We complimented each other. He was more cerebral than I, and I was more emotionally connected and nurturing. Our following grew.

Craig and I enjoyed working, thinking and planning together. The only place of disagreement between us was around the non-socializing rule which he insisted we adopt in our organization. I felt we needed to loosen those restrictions and allow more natural interactions, but I conceded that those who need stricter boundaries must be respected otherwise there was the potential for abuse.

I wanted Craig to be part of my life beyond our counseling connection. I wanted him to know my kids, visit my river in Connecticut with me, maybe occasionally join in a family gathering, but I respected his need to keep our relationship strictly within the bounds we had agreed upon.

Except for that one disagreement, Craig and I became closer. We continued to counsel almost exclusively with each other. There were counselors with whom I felt the same safety and support, but most lived hours away, including Jeremy, who lived in Connecticut. He and I counseled together when he visited Boston and by phone wherever he happened to be in the world. He and a core of other peer-counselors joined ICN.

On one occasion a group of ICN peer-counselors were meeting in my apartment, sitting around the kitchen table. The four men at the table were among the most enlightened, feminist men I'd ever met. The other two women were among the strongest, most articulate and powerful women I knew. As we sat there on that cold rainy day in my kitchen with its red counters and black and white tile floor, the women put forth an idea about how to make ICN more diverse, and the men at the table began debating how to go about it.

My friend, Elle, who was usually assertive and articulate, became silent. The other woman, Melissa, fidgeted and got up to make a cup of tea. I began to choke up. I jumped up from the table and went to stare out the hallway window at the rain, tears covering my face. I didn't know why I was crying, but I was embarrassed that I was. Instantly, Craig was by my side. He did not touch me or try to comfort me. He just stood silently beside me.

After a few minutes, he quietly asked, "What's going on, Kath?"

"I don't know."

"Tell me when you started to have these feelings."

"I don't know—I just started to feel like I was being choked—silenced."

"What did you notice happening?"

"Well, Elle, Melissa and I were talking about diversity, and all of a sudden only the men were talking at the table."

"That's exactly what happened," Craig affirmed. "We took over and excluded you women from the conversation. Come back to the table and tell us all what you experienced."

"I can't. I'll just cry."

"That's ok. You can just sit there and cry, but we need you to stay connected. And when you're ready, you can talk even through your tears."

I reluctantly went back to the table and sat down. I silently wept for a few minutes before I was able to explain what had happened within me. When the men began to dominate the discussion, I'd felt like a little girl again, sitting on the periphery of the huge round oak table in our dining room back home while my brothers had a vigorous exchange of ideas from which I was excluded. The other two women also talked about their reactions. They both had withdrawn in their own way, taken by surprise when the men usurped the conversation.

Elle, who worked in a male dominated environment, was shocked and disappointed to find the same gender dynamics she dealt with every day playing out in this collegial setting. Melissa had just shut down completely, going numb—not really knowing why. The men listened to us in aware silence. They acknowledged their culpability in hijacking our ideas. We began to discuss the covert sexism that even the most enlightened, egalitarian men could succumb to, and how even the strongest women lose their grounding when that happens.

I faced a similar situation when Craig and I were attending a workshop, put on by another group of renegade peer-counselors in New York City. A man stood up and started defending Neil Olson. The anger rose in my throat and as always turned into profuse tears. I ran outside into the chilly night so as not to make a spectacle of myself. Craig ran after me.

"Kath, that was outrageous! You have a right to be angry! Let's go back in. Give your anger a voice, Kathleen. You can do it! You have something important to say."

"I can't talk like this—I can't even think!"

"You are most articulate when you are being true to yourself. You can speak and feel at the same time!"

I finally mustered the strength to go back inside. Craig stood beside me as I gave voice to my outrage and anger about this man's defense of Neil. I spoke about the power dynamics and the secrets that allowed Neil to perpetrate against the women he sexually abused. I felt I was speaking for every woman, including myself.

After that, my confidence and sense of self strengthened. I felt like I was living in my own skin. I began to feel the possibility that I could make a good life for myself, that I could reclaim my lost identity. I felt like an essentially good person, not someone who needed to be *redeemed* because I had sinned in the eyes of the Church. I saw the innocent young woman I had been and embraced her. In Millay's words, *"I breathed my soul back into me."* She describes it here:

The grass, a-tiptoe at my ear,
Whispering to me I could hear;
I felt the rain's cool finger-tips
Brushed tenderly across my lips,
Laid gently on my sealed sight,

And all at once the heavy night
Fell from my eyes and I could see! –
A drenched and dripping apple tree,
A last long line of silver rain,
A sky grown clear and blue again.

And as I looked a quickening gust
Of wind blew up to me and thrust
Into my face a miracle
Of orchard-breath, and with the smell, —
I know not how such things can be! —
I breathed my soul back into me.

Bring yourself
uniquely and fully
into bloom....
After waiting
all these years,
it's time to
hope and dream
again!

– Stephen C. Paul from *Illuminations*

CHAPTER THIRTY-TWO
The Field of All Possibilities

BY SPRING OF 1989—a single mother now—disillusionment began to set in once again. The summer before, when I moved to the Boston area, I applied to multiple colleges and universities for a position as an adjunct instructor. Half-way through the spring semester, I was hired by Emerson College to replace a teacher who had become ill. I was ecstatic to have a chance to teach in Boston and was sure it would launch my teaching career there.

The class went well, but the professor I'd replaced returned in the fall. I also taught a class at Northeastern for two semesters in a huge lecture hall with over a hundred students. I wasn't comfortable with that format and the pay was dismal. I applied for counseling jobs, but was told an M.A. in Counseling Psychology was not adequate to get third party payments—I needed an MSW, PhD or a PsyD, so I continued to do secretarial work at Massachusetts General Hospital.

I moved my private therapy practice closer to Boston in Newburyport one day a week, seeing clients in an office I rented on Saturdays. Those days were always intense as I saw clients back to back without a break. I would drive home to Brookline exhausted and had one day to recuperate before I showed up for my stultifying job as a secretary. I sprained my ankle badly on the ice that winter and nursed the tender, swollen ankle as I hobbled around the office on crutches. Money was still tight, which entailed a move into a less expensive apartment, still in Brookline.

Debbie had acclimated to our new surroundings with ease and was enjoying her year in eighth grade. Her friends seemed to adore her and came running to hug her when I dropped her off at school. She was astonished to find that she had the Jewish Holidays off, and I was surprised how much that meant to her. And, she was enjoying the racial, cultural and ethnic diversity in Brookline of which we had little in New Hampshire.

Her weight was still an issue, but she was accepted by her peers, which was all that mattered to me. She even joined a dance group in high school, and we were able to see some of the finest dance companies at a discounted rate. Although she was becoming more independent, she continued to demand considerable attention from me, and she resented my relationship with Craig.

One time, when she was very young, she kept saying our black cat, Spunky, was just hers. I said, "No, honey, Spunky belongs to our whole family." This brought a flood of tears. I let her cry it out giving her calm attention as we were taught to do in peer-counseling.

After a while, she was wailing, "I want Spunky to be MY cat!" And then it became, "I want you to be just MY Mommy! I don't want you to be their Mommy, too!" (Referring to her siblings.)

Now it was Craig who was her rival for my undivided attention. I often tried to arrange my time with him when Debbie was visiting her father on weekends, but that was not always possible. Meanwhile, Craig encouraged me to set boundaries with Debbie, as he watched me struggle with her when she was being demanding. She would whine or start yelling and I would give in. Her room was a mess, with dishes and half-eaten food that she refused to clean up. I realized how much I'd depended on Stan to maintain order with the children, including Debbie, and how I didn't have the ability to stand up for myself with my teenage daughter. I saw more clearly the part my passivity had played in the marriage.

The stress of single parenting, the pain from my sprained ankle, and my work schedule, set off some of the physical symptoms I'd had in the past when I finished my degree programs. I'd push myself throughout the year to achieve my goal and then end up with generalized pain, extreme fatigue, poor sleep, brain fog and digestive problems. (I was later diagnosed with fibromyalgia, and these episodes were called *fibro flares*.) In spite of all the good counseling I was getting, I felt my mood darkening—the edges of depression closing in on me. I had convinced Dr. Ross, my psychiatrist, to lower the dose of Elavil I was taking because I hated the side effects.

At the same time, Boston was coming alive as spring weather began to break. Cherry, apple, and magnolia trees all burst into blossom overnight. Color popped up in gardens everywhere.

Crying, I said to Craig, "I can see all the beauty but I can't *feel it!*"

"The beauty will still be with you when you're ready to feel it," he said, trying to console me.

I was desolate—I thought that when I left Stan, I'd no longer have a reason to be depressed. That was not true. As Dr. Ross had pointed out before, my depressive episodes preceded my marriage and were genetically and biologically based. I didn't want to hear this. To me it meant I was defective and beyond healing. My hope for a normal life was washed away with his words. I knew how Ann felt when her doctor said the same thing to her. Now she lay comatose six years after her suicide attempt.

One night when Debbie was away, while I was lying in bed trying to sleep, I had an overwhelming urge to end this recurring cycle of depression. I had a bottle of pain pills from when I sprained my ankle. Ignoring my first psychiatrist's warning about the possibility of not taking enough pills and ending up in a vegetative state, I assured myself I had enough to do the job.

I got up to go get the pills and, instead, moving in slow motion, I watched my hand pick up the phone and dial Craig's number. It was late. Had I been in any other state, I never would have called him. He sleepily answered the phone. I didn't even apologize for waking him. I could hardly speak. I said, "I'm not safe. I don't want to be here."

Without hesitation he said, "Hold on! I'll be there in a few minutes."

Soon, he was at my door and enveloped me in a hug. I was beyond tears.

I could only say, "I am so tired. I can't sleep. I don't want to live like this anymore."

"I'll sit with you until you fall asleep and I'll sleep on the couch. We'll talk about it in the morning."

Craig pulled a chair up beside the bed. He sang quietly until I fell into a sound sleep. The next morning we agreed it was time for me to see Dr. Ross again. The lower dose of Elavil was not holding me and I needed something to help me sleep. My gratitude for Craig's presence on that night lives in my heart to this day.

~

Dr. Ross wasn't surprised to see me back. He explained that my brain chemistry made me vulnerable to the experience of loss. Although the divorce and move were what I wanted, they still entailed loss. He was right. I missed my son, Jake, whom I had left behind in Windsor, and David and Rachel were away at school. I also missed my friends and the beautiful seacoast of New Hampshire. Thus, my doctor began months of experimentation with different combinations of medication, until I finally stabilized. It wasn't the euphoria I felt on my first large dose of Elavil, but I was no longer suicidal, and I started to reintegrate into my normal life.

I started to research PhD and PsyD programs all over the country. The ones that appealed to me were all in California. I could not picture dragging Debbie across country and being so far from the other kids. I didn't have the money to go into another graduate program since I was still paying on student loans from my first two degrees. And, I had no desire to take more courses in statistics and experimental psych which would be required in a PhD or PsyD program. I feared I would end up a secretary for the rest of my life barely making enough to subsist, if I didn't pursue another degree.

My friend, Jeremy, who would later become a Rabbi, frequently came into Boston from Connecticut to visit me, and we maintained weekly phone contact. He and Craig supported me through the changes in medication, reassuring me my chemistry would come back into balance. Whenever Jeremy came to visit, we'd have a peer counseling session and then go on an adventure.

One time he took me to his favorite ice cream parlor in Cambridge—Toscanini's. I loved the name, and the ice cream proved to be the *Toscanini* of all ice cream. Another time we tracked down an obscure little chocolate shop where homemade gourmet chocolates were made fresh daily. Or, we'd go to little out-of-the-way ethnic restaurants and small art galleries.

On one of his visits, Jeremy told me he'd discovered an interfaith retreat house in Hamilton, New York, on the campus of Colgate University. He suggested I go there to get some time away to think about what I truly wanted and how I could achieve it. Chapel House was endowed by an anonymous donor, which made it affordable. I made plans to spend five days of my birthday week there in March of 1990.

When the time came, I was slipping emotionally again. I drove six hours west on the Massachusetts and New York Turnpikes in the rain. It was dusk and, as the sky darkened, I drove up and down the mountains of upper New York State. At the summit of one, I glimpsed a rainbow in my rear-view mirror. I pulled over and jumped out of the car to get a better view. Rainbows usually remind me that I am in the Presence of the Holy. But, feeling as I did, I was not moved.

I stood in the pouring rain, Bach blasting from my car radio, and said, "Thanks, God, but I can't feel it." Then, I turned the other direction to get back in the car. The dark clouds split at the horizon to reveal a sliver of radiant liquid gold as the sun slipped behind a mountain that rose from the valley below me.

I heard God say, "Here, maybe this will help!" I felt deeply touched and surrounded by Love.

I drove on with tears streaming down my face and my heart expanding. I finally reached the Colgate campus after dark and climbed the narrow road up to the retreat house which sat half way up a giant hill behind the campus. The building was a simple cream-colored, flat-roofed, cement block structure with trees around it. Further up the hill was a tree-canopied cemetery.

I was greeted at the door by a gracious elderly woman, Eva, whispering a welcome. Engulfed by a deep sense of silence and peace, I stepped into the foyer. Before me, hanging over the stairwell, was a huge Tibetan Gong whose beckoning sound would become familiar as it called retreatants to meals. There were ancient artifacts from many different traditions and cultures throughout the retreat house.

The dining room was long and narrow. A light wood Danish-style dining room set and sideboard were the only furnishings. In a carpeted music room, with a high end sound system and plush chairs, I found the huge collection of records that Jeremy had described to me. And, best of all, there was a mammoth library, with bookshelves filling three walls. On the fourth wall a massive fireplace stood flanked by bronze panels with images of Dante's *Inferno* sculpted in detailed relief. Library tables and comfortable chairs were scattered throughout the room.

A simple chapel, attached to the main building by an enclosed breezeway, could accommodate services of various traditions by sliding a panel in front of the cross at the altar.

Eva showed me to one of the seven bedrooms downstairs. It was as sparsely furnished, and almost as small and stark, as my cell in the convent, but it had a big window that looked into the woods and filled with light in the morning, unlike the dark morbid attic in which I'd slept in my convent days. The next morning I woke rested as specks of sun peeked through the curtains. When I opened them a small herd of deer came out of the woods to stop and gaze at me. We stood there enthralled with each other. Then the deer wandered off.

The gong called me to breakfast, ringing throughout the retreat house—a deeply resonant sound. We were to keep silence except for dinner in the evening. I enjoyed eating in silence as we frequently did in the convent, but some of the six other retreatants looked uncomfortable. I noted my tendency to want to put them at ease by engaging non-verbally, but I did not act on it. This time was for me.

I meditated in the chapel after breakfast and signed up for the music room for later in the day. Then I went to explore the library. Most the books were religious or spiritual in nature, although there were sections on ethics, conservation, nature, and justice. As always, I found myself drawn to the poetry section. A salmon-colored book fell into my hands. It was a slim volume of poems by the mystic, Kabir, who "…passionately sought to show the way out of delusion, including the delusion of religious identity." (A quote from Daniel Ladinsky's *Love Poems from God* I found years after my first encounter with Kabir.) I was enraptured by Kabir's words:

> *Are you looking for me? I am in the next seat.*
> *My shoulder is against yours.*
> *You will not find me in the stupas,*
> *not in Indian shrine rooms,*
> *nor in synagogues, nor in cathedrals:*
> *not in Masses, nor Kirtans,*
> *not in legs winding around your own neck,*
> *nor in eating nothing but vegetables.*
>
> *When you really look for me,*
> *you will see me instantly —*
> *you will find me in the tiniest house of time.*
>
> *Kabir says: Student, tell me, what is God?*
>
> *He is the breath inside the breath.*
>
> *– Kabir*

Something shifted in my consciousness that brought me beyond my everyday struggles and emotional lability. It was like rising above the clouds and seeing the expanse of blue sky and sunlight— the eternal and true reality. Then, the gong brought me back to the earth for lunch. Hours had gone by, and I hadn't noticed.

The music room served up another feast for my senses. First I went straight to the familiar Gregorian chants I loved. And then I began to explore the Hindu Kirtans, Native American flutes, and Tibetan Buddhist chants. Time was devoured in this room as well, and I was reluctant to leave when my time was up. It was definitely time for a nap.

As I snuggled under the covers, I could feel my whole body unwinding. I felt safe, surrounded by the Holy. After my nap, I bundled up and took a walk—up the hill, wandering through the cemetery and then up and across the field to the tree line. The view from that perch was stunning. The trees were still bare. The late afternoon sun touched them with gold and etched them onto the darkening sky. Gratitude for *Being* filled me. How could I ever contemplate leaving this beautiful earth?

I meditated in the Chapel again until I heard the sacred Tibetan Gong. As we quietly talked around the dinner table that evening, doubts about my future once again demanded my attention. A woman from Boston sat next to me. She had made the same six-hour trek I made the night before. She'd been at the retreat center for three days and was returning to Boston the next day. She started the conversation by asking, "What do you do?"

I told her it was my forty-sixth birthday, and I was trying to figure out what I was going to do with the rest of my life. I explained that my two degrees weren't enough for me to qualify to do the work I love.

She said, "Have you ever thought about Harvard Divinity School? I went there, and I loved it. I'm now in a good position within a church, running a youth program."

I shook my head. "I'd never be able to get into Harvard, and I don't belong to a faith community so I'm not sure what I could do with the degree, but thanks for the suggestion."

As the week unfolded, I was consumed by the ecstasy of each day's discoveries as I continued perusing the library and mining the gold of the music room. My walks got longer as the weather warmed, and I found myself exploring the woods at the top of the hill.

Often I thought, "I'm not doing what I came here to do—I am supposed to be figuring things out." Then I'd succumb to the next piece of music I found, or the next book that fell into my hands, or the next sunset.

As my last full day at the retreat house was ending, I once again went to the dinner table with thoughts concerning my future. Maybe I would end up a bag-lady as Stan had always predicted. I was leaving to go home the next morning. Then a new guest sat down beside me. We started talking. She, too, was from Boston.

When I told her my dilemma, I was stunned when she said, "Have you ever thought about Harvard Divinity School? I'm a graduate of HDS and have an M.Div. It's considered a terminal degree [meaning under some circumstances it has the same professional status as a doctorate]."

Shocked to hear Harvard Divinity School mentioned for the second time, I questioned if she knew the other woman who had asked me the same question. She said she had never heard the name.

I couldn't believe the coincidence (or was it synchronicity?). I questioned this woman about the program and the requirements to get into HDS. She assured me I didn't have to be interested in ministry. There were various options for studying Comparative Religions, Pastoral Care and Counseling, Feminist Theology and more. I could design the program to fit my goals for future employment, and I could take courses from any of the seminaries in Boston.

"But," she said, "if you want to get in this fall, the deadline for applications is April 1st."

I thanked her for the information and said it would be impossible for me to get the application in by that time. It was already March 11th (my mother's birthday), and I was moving to a less expensive apartment on April 1st.

I hardly slept that night. *Harvard Divinity School!* I was amazed that two women from Boston, six hours away, had crossed my path in the short five days I was at the retreat center. Their visits overlapped with mine only briefly. Both were graduates of HDS and recommended I look into the M.Div. program! It was too much to be coincidental. I felt the hand of the Holy in these encounters or, perhaps, it was my mother's hand offering me a gift on *her* birthday.

I drove home in reverie, thinking of the possibility that I could go to Harvard Divinity School. I would shake myself out of it, looking at the pragmatics of the situation—how would I complete the application in time, how would I pay for it, what makes me think I would get in? I returned home late Friday. I would have to wait until Monday to make an inquiry. The weekend seemed endless even though I was busy packing.

On Monday morning, I made the call and was transferred to Admissions. I spoke to an enthusiastic young woman who encouraged me to apply. She said it would speed up the process if I came for an interview, and she could give me the application packet.

That afternoon I met Kirsten Bijak. We talked for about an hour, more of a conversation than an interview. She encouraged me to apply and told me I had the background the admission committee looked for in applicants. She urged me to try to make the deadline or else I would have to wait until next year. I wanted this. The pressure was on.

Gathering transcripts, writing the essay, filling in my work history and answering a myriad of questions, it was late March 31st when I finished the application. I was about to seal the envelope when for some reason I felt compelled to include a tape of my songs.

I thought, "If they're going to take me, they're going to take the *real* me!" I dropped the tape into the envelope and sealed it. The tape included a song that came to me while jogging under the stars one evening. It summed up my spiritual beliefs better than the essay I had written. The words are:

My Love, my Life and everything
Are gifts direct from God
The healing touch, the songs I sing,
The visions seen afar.

I am a wave upon the sea
Of God's exquisite Love
I rise and grow as I am free
And with all life am One.

The Universe is Energy
From which existence springs.
Vibrations dance and laugh and sing
And permeate all things.

A pebble dropped upon Life's Sea
Sends ripples to the Sun.
It links the fates of you and me
And makes the world as One.

A starving child across the world
Is starving at my door
As hate and greed about us swirl
The specters rise of war.

But love enough will feed the child
And hate and greed dispel.
Believe we must in Love's great Power
And then all will be well…
And then all will be well…

– Kathleen, 1985

The next morning I was at Kirsten's office at 8:00am to hand over my application. Then I returned home to start a long day of moving. I put the application out of my mind and concentrated on the move. Exhausted, that night I fell asleep on an unmade bed with the house in disarray. The next weeks were spent settling Debbie and me into our new home.

My altar was always the first thing I'd set up when I moved. I had my mother's cedar Hope Chest, which was covered with hammer marks from children using it as a work table and stains from wet cups. It was one of my most cherished possessions. I covered it with a hand-woven red cloth, and on it I placed my rocks, shells, a clay Menorah, a picture of the Blessed Mother, little treasures given to me by my children, my Mom and my sister. I felt a *click* of recognition when it was complete, and my home was transformed into sacred space. In the midst of all this, I maintained my therapy practice and continued to work at the hospital and teach peer-counseling.

When my acceptance letter from HDS came in the mail, I was shocked and overjoyed. Then reality dawned. "That's great, God! Now how am I going to pay for it?" I hadn't even completed the financial aid application when I received a letter from HDS stating that I had a full tuition scholarship for all three years of the program. This was an *offer I could not refuse.* I deemed it a direct mandate from the Universe to follow the flow of grace that was opening before me.

Craig was thrilled for me. While I was waiting for classes to begin at Harvard Divinity School, I threw myself into teaching peer-counseling and doing workshops with Craig as the International Counseling Network (ICN) grew. I knew the demands of going back to school would strain our relationship. It occurred to me that my life revolved around Stan because I was terrified of him, and now it revolved around Craig because he was so good to me. The results were the same. I diminished myself to accommodate them.

There was a subtle power dynamic between us. I often deferred to Craig because he was so intelligent. I trusted his judgment more than my own. And I'd become too dependent on him. I wrote: "I'm not sure I can continue to work with you, Craig—you mean too much to me—I am bending my life around you. I am making painful compromises. I give you too much power."

We met to discuss my note. I told Craig I needed to take a break from our peer-counseling relationship. He was stunned. He tried to dissuade me from my decision, but said he would respect whatever I decided. I held firm.

My heart hurt. I felt like I was rending my flesh by sending him away. I had entwined my life around him, and the thought of our separation was excruciating, but it was time for me to call upon my own inner resources to survive in this world. We agreed to meet in six months with another peer-counselor to discuss our situation.

Sitting in the sun in my apartment shortly after we parted, bereft without Craig, a song came streaming through:

Having lost again all hope
of ever being held
here on earth
God, I rage against you
For not having any arms
To hold me.

Thinking it has been
So long since I've seen
A rainbow
Symbol of Your Love for me
Surely, you, too, must be
A creation of my longing
A fantasy.

Then I find myself
Engulfed in golden rays
Of morning sun
And in the light
Encircling me
I feel your heart.

Breaking open with your touch
My heart responds to yours
Sobbing in your loving arms
I look out
Through crying eyes and see
Rainbows in my tears
I see rainbows in my tears

– Kathleen, 1990

'O God! Make me a hollow reed,
from which the pith of self hath been blown –
that I may become a pure channel through which
Thy love may flow unto others.'

– Baha'i Prayer

CHAPTER THIRTY-THREE
To Be a Hospital Chaplain…

MY DAUGHTER, Rachel, had announced she was pregnant
at Christmastime. She had been going with her high school
sweetheart, Brent, on and off, since she was fifteen, but she wasn't
ready to make a commitment. She was determined to raise the
baby on her own.

The greatest gift of that summer was the birth of Amelia Rose,
my first grandchild. I was not prepared for the overwhelming
rush of love I felt for this little being. I became *Nonni*—the name
I love most to hear. I'd felt the same rush of love for each of my
children when they came into the world but then it was mixed
with anxiety and the reality of what lay before me—sleepless
nights, constant vigilance to keep them fed, clothed and alive!
This little angel was pure joy. I spent as much time as I could
with her, although we lived over an hour apart. Rachel was a
natural mother—relaxed, loving, and thrilled with this new little
person in her life.

My second grandchild came into the world four years later.
Amelia's little sister, beautiful Isabella (Bella) graced my life with
her exuberant joy and light, and her mystical spirit.

After my break-up with Craig, Amelia's presence was elixir to my soul. By then, I had developed a private practice in Brookline as well as Newburyport, although I was still working at the hospital as a secretary to make ends meet. My life was full.

In late August 1990, I went to orientation at Harvard Divinity School. I missed Craig terribly, but threw myself into this new experience. At the beginning of each semester there is a period at the Divinity School when students can sit in on as many different classes as they like before choosing what courses to take. I found this to be an exciting process and explored many different subjects. To my surprise I was accepted into all my first choice classes. I thrived on meeting new friends, connecting with faculty, and becoming part of a community.

The glass enclosed refectory was our gathering place at lunchtime. Large round tables with minimal space between them filled the room. My friends and I commandeered a table in the middle of the room each afternoon. We were a diverse group in every possible way: age, color, culture, geographical origins, ethnicity, religious traditions, spiritual beliefs, economic status and reasons for coming to Divinity School. We became a community within the larger community.

This micro-community allowed me to be who I truly am more openly than anywhere else I'd been. Spiritual discourse came naturally to me, but after leaving the convent, I ceased using that language. It did not fit in the secular world. With these friends, I could speak in my mother tongue and be heard, respected and understood.

One of my lunchtime companions, Ruth Martin, and I became friends almost instantly. She, too, was Jewish, and we were in the minority. Women had been accepted at the Harvard Divinity School only forty years earlier. Now we were the majority of the student population, but there were few Jewish students. Buddhist Monks in their saffron robes dotted the campus landscape. Students from every corner of the world inhabited the dorms. The diversity was exhilarating after living in New Hampshire for so many years. I learned as much, if not more, from my fellow students, as from academic courses.

It was autumn in New England, and the beauty was heightened by the excitement I felt on this new adventure. My love of being a student, especially with such inspiring teachers, grew as I dived into my classes. Professor Diana Eck is a renowned scholar in Comparative Religions with expertise in Buddhism and Hinduism. Ruth and I arrived early to her class every day and sat in front row seats almost directly in front of Diana. She commanded the attention of two- hundred students in the huge lecture hall, standing with impeccable posture. Her voice was mellow, steady and strong. It was a spiritual experience to sit at the feet of this extraordinary woman. Her love and deep respect for the traditions of the East was evident in the reverence of her voice and the depth of her knowledge.

The other teacher who inspired both Ruth and me was Professor William Graham who taught Islamic studies. Again, we didn't want his lectures to end. The beauty of the Koran was revealed in this man's teachings. Many times, we students walked out of class in awed silence. Prof. Graham, too, was gracious. He always made time for his students outside of class. Years later he became Dean of the Divinity School.

The class I had looked forward to the most was *Psychology and Spirituality*. Ruth and I were astounded to realize the course was being taught by a visiting professor, Dr. Mason, who encouraged competitive, adversarial discussions. I said to Ruth, "This is Divinity School, for God's sake, why can't we dialogue in a civil manner?" Something felt terribly wrong to us. We devised a plan.

Before class began, Ruth raised her hand to speak. She said, "Kathleen and I would like to propose we start class with a moment of silence." We hoped that would change the energy of the exchange.

"Absolutely, not!" was Dr. Mason's response, and most of our fellow students concurred. While Diana Eck's and William Graham's classes always seemed too short, Dr. Mason's seemed interminable.

In a course called *Power, Conflict and Community*, I began to unravel the underlying dynamics that allowed Neil Olson to gain and retain such power over the people in the PCU community. Through the lens of this course I could see PCU as an addictive and cult-like organization. Craig and I had consciously worked to form an egalitarian organization, but I still took an unequal role in the power dynamic between us. I needed to learn not to give up my power to men even if they were kind and gentle.

My weekly seminar happened to be with Harvey Cox, PhD, a world renowned theologian. We would be discussing our thesis papers with him over the next three years. It was a privilege I did not take for granted. Harvey (as we were told to address him) was interested in each student. But it was his assistant facilitator, Rev. Dudley Rose, who accompanied me on my journey through my writing project. He spent hours with me helping me mine my own experiences for the subject that would give my project meaning and purpose.

With his help, I found the subject title: *The Impact of Religion and Theology on Battered Women.* Later it would take the shape of a seminar for hospital chaplains. Dudley's kindness and soft-spoken guidance gave me the confidence to speak my truth and create a program that could help guide others who care for those traumatized by abuse.

In order to graduate from Harvard Divinity School with a Master of Divinity degree, I was required to do a fifteen hour per week internship for two years. While my children and I celebrated the Jewish holidays together and the Christian holidays with my family, I had no intention of pursuing a ministerial position of any sort. I looked for another opportunity.

At the start of the semester, the first year students were invited to a tea to meet professionals from prospective internship sites. It was there I met Rev. Katherine James—a formidable and forthright woman who was the Director of Chaplaincy at Brigham and Women's Hospital (BWH) in Boston. Rev. James became my supervisor as I joined the ranks of other seminary students who interned at BWH. I had one advantage over the other interns: I'd worked in a hospital for more than four years as a nurse's aide; I was not shocked by what I saw. We'd have two weeks of orientation and then we'd be thrown onto the floors to visit real live patients as chaplains! Like my peers, my anxiety grew as we approached the day.

~

The hospital's Pastoral Care Department had a staff of chaplains including priests, nuns, ministers of different denominations, a Rabbi, and an Imam. There was also a cadre of lay volunteers who came from diverse backgrounds and about twenty of us interns. Rev. James, who we called Kate, oversaw all the staff and volunteers, and also had to deal with the politics of the hospital, budgetary issues and numerous committees, including chairing the Ethics Committee. As a result, she did not have time to hold the hand of each new intern nor was that her style. She had chosen us carefully and expected us to quickly become working members of the team.

The first two weeks were spent on practicalities—how to enter notes into the patient's chart, learning to triage calls, working the beeper, and shadowing experienced chaplains. We met regularly to discuss our experiences as we began to integrate into the system. It was clear from the beginning that we were *Interfaith Chaplains* and there was no place for injecting our own beliefs into our visits with patients. We were to hone our listening skills, not follow our own agenda.

After that introductory period, we were assigned our Pods (patient units of different disciplines like Cardiology, Cancer, Burn Unit, etc.). In the course of our two-year internship, we rotated through a wide range of specialties caring for our diverse patient population, some with catastrophic illnesses, some newborn infants, and many who were terminally ill, supporting them and their loved ones.

The training to become a hospital chaplain is challenging, especially in a hospital as big and prestigious as this one. People come from all over the world to seek the expertise and excellent care for which the hospital is known. What started out as a modest brick building in the 1800's is now a multistoried, glass and steel, sprawling city onto itself. Just finding my way around took weeks, and the configuration of buildings was always changing with new additions to the footprint.

~

The first solo patient visit reminded me of my first session with a client as a psychotherapy intern. What would I say? What if the patient wanted me to pray with them? What if the person wouldn't talk to me? What if I said something to anger a patient? How would I handle patients with a fundamentalist religious perspective?

One of the first calls I made as a chaplain was to a treatment room where an elderly male patient was having difficulty breathing. He was surrounded by doctors and nurses trying to ease his distress, so I turned to his wife who was anxiously waiting outside his room.

I introduced myself and tried to engage her in small talk to take her mind off the tense situation. "Where are you and your husband from?"

"Lebanon."

"Oh, I was in Lebanon a few years ago. That part of New Hampshire is beautiful!" I said, trying to make a connection with this distraught woman.

She gave me a stony look, "LEBANON, the country!" I apologized for my mistake. First lesson: make no assumptions, check the chart!

Right from the beginning I learned that my patients would give me far more than I could offer them. One of my first was an elderly Jewish man named Eli, with a wrinkled wise face and sparkling eyes. He was a Holocaust survivor. He showed me the number tattooed on his arm. He clearly remembered the day he was liberated from a concentration camp by American troops in 1945. We talked for a while, and his positive attitude amazed me.

"How have you kept such a good attitude about life in spite of all you have endured? How did you keep from being bitter?" I asked.

"Some people do good things and some people do bad things," he replied in a Yiddish accent. He went on to say, "I remember a song my mother sang when I was a child about seeing the goodness in people's eyes."

I walked away in awe.

After about three weeks of doing patient visits, I visited a Catholic patient on my Pod. (Patients' religious preferences were indicated on a printout sheet and in their charts.) This man was sitting in a chair, but he was ambulatory. I introduced myself as one of the Interfaith Chaplains on the floor.

He stood up, over six feet tall, his arm raised pointing at the door and shouted, "Get OUT! GET OUT! You're a WOMAN, you're NOT a PRIEST, and you'll NEVER BE A PRIEST! I WANT A PRIEST! I'M NOT TALKING TO ANY WOMAN!"

I politely apologized for disturbing him and assured him I would get the priest to make a visit. I was trembling as I left the floor and went to the Chaplains' lunchroom. As a group of us sat around the table, I relayed the story of this encounter. We had a good laugh.

I also met one of my most endearing patients in those early days of my training. Nat and his wife, Hilda, were a devoted Jewish couple in their sixties. I had a long talk with them about being Jewish in the world today, and how some of our values and traditions were being lost. As I was about to leave, I encouraged Nat to make more noise because the nurses were concerned that he rarely talked.

Nat replied, "I talk when I have something to say."

Hilda said, "I've never heard this man yell."

Nat chuckled. "I've never had anything to yell about!"

How rare! I will never forget those two and their love for each other—a gift to know such relationships exist.

~

Another patient, Abel, and I connected deeply. He was a tall, thin, African American man, almost seventy years old, with shaggy grey hair. He was extremely ill, suffering with pain and a relentless cough. Still, every time I went into his room he greeted me warmly with smiling eyes. He always had something kind and wise to say.

He spoke simply in short sentences, but his depth and devotion to God were evident. I'd take his latest words of wisdom to the lunch table to share with the other interns. We were all touched by him.

On one visit, Abel spoke of his paper route to all the widows in the neighborhood. He said they doted on him, gave him homemade goodies, cards and money at Christmas. Then he started talking about his dog, Chips. He said, "I taught Chips to answer only to *Mr. Chips*." Chips was his faithful companion for seventeen years. He referred to Chips as "my son." Shortly before Abel entered the hospital, Chips died from an unknown cause. He believed someone had poisoned his beloved pet. Abel was still grieving the loss. He said the widows had offered to buy him another dog. "I told them Chips could not be replaced anymore than you could replace one child with another."

I offered him my condolences on his loss and validated his need to grieve.

That day he also talked of his large, devoted extended family, including nieces and nephews and their children. He spoke of his deep faith in God, although he did not consider himself religious. He shared his belief that living a good life and treating others well is all that God requires of us.

I became concerned because I didn't see Abel progressing—he was getting weaker and a little more confused. One day I went to his bedside and asked, "Abel, what can I do to help you."

"Just keep visiting me. You give me hope every time you come in."

"I hope you know I really care about you and enjoy our visits," I said.

He replied smiling, "I can feel it!"

His words offered me a sense of myself as a *real* chaplain for the first time. I realized I was making a difference in the lives of the patients I served. Chaplaincy had an immediacy that rarely happens in the long-term therapy work I did with my clients. Every day at the hospital, when I left the floors and sat down to do my notes, I felt grateful and fulfilled. I knew this was the work I was meant to do.

~

About three months into my internship, the staff chaplains had left for the day. I was on the beeper. The Burn Unit called the Chaplain's Office to have a chaplain attend to the wife and family of a man being helicoptered into the hospital with severe burns.

The person who called had no details about the case, so I proceeded to the seventh floor and checked in with the nurse on the Unit. She said that the patient's name was Timothy McShane, and he and his family were Catholic. He had been severely burned and would not survive. The family knew nothing at this point, and the nurse asked if I'd stay with them until the doctor could talk to them.

Mrs. McShane and her son, Paul, and his wife, Edna, came onto the floor, and I was instructed to take them into the family lounge to wait to speak to the doctor. They were distraught. All they knew was that Shane (which his wife said he preferred to be called) was home alone and had put the tea kettle on and forgotten it. When he went back into the kitchen the kettle had melted. She conjectured that he must have reached across the burner to turn it off and his bathrobe caught fire. She had been told that the fire damage had been contained in a small area of the kitchen. She lamented the fact that she had to work and was not there to help him.

At one point Mrs. McShane said, "I don't think it's a good sign that they took him to the hospital by helicopter."

"That probably is true," I said quietly, knowing the reality of the situation and not wanting to offer her false hope.

While we waited for the doctor, Mrs. McShane talked about her fears and her anguish at having to leave her seventy-six-year-old husband alone when he was ill and sometimes forgetful. She spoke lovingly of him and said they had many good years together. Their son, Paul, was quiet and tense, but his wife was crying, visibly upset. After about fifteen minutes the nurse came to get the family to talk to Dr. Driscoll. The doctor signaled me to join them in a long narrow conference room painted a stark white. The wooden table almost filled the room. All five of us sat together at one end, with Dr. Driscoll at the head.

The doctor told the family that Shane had been deeply burned on 99% of his body, the only part untouched by the fire were the soles of his feet. He told them that in order for him to be burned this severely, he had to have been in the fire for a long time. (All three of them gasped.) The doctor said there was no chance of survival and that the only thing the medical staff could do was keep him comfortable. He said Shane was still conscious on sedatives and pain medication, and his burns were completely covered with bandages. He had been given the Anointing of the Sick by the priest. It would be a while before the nurses would have him ready for the family to visit.

It was heart-wrenching to watch this family try to grasp the reality of what was happening. I found a private space so we could talk. I attempted to give comfort and said, "I've been told that burn victims go into shock immediately and feel nothing and do not remember what happened," anything to spare them that horrendous image of their husband and father suffering in the flames.

Paul was afraid of "making a fool of himself" by crying. I assured him that there was nothing wrong with crying—that it was exactly what he needed to do. Mrs. McShane wept openly and vacillated between being torn apart by the image of Shane alone in the fire and her own fear of being alone after he died.

Her daughter-in-law, Edna, tried to comfort her saying, "We won't leave you alone, Mother."

Mrs. McShane said, "I still can't bear the thought of going to bed at night without a good-night kiss from him." She indicated again that she blamed herself for not being there when he caught on fire.

"Don't feel guilty, Mrs. McShane, you were doing what you needed to do to support the family," I said.

She quietly responded, "I would tell someone the same thing, but the guilt is there just the same." Her eyes filled with tears.

I learned to never respond like that again. From my own life experience, I knew that guilt cannot be willed or wished away—Mrs. McShane reminded me of that.

Paul spoke of his father's kind ways and dedication to his family as he wept softly. He could not understand why God would take him in this horrific way when he had lived a good, decent life. (I had no answers for him.) I asked if he wanted me to pray with him for his father, and he nodded. Together we prayed the familiar Catholic prayers of my childhood.

I encouraged the family to express what they most wanted to say to Shane, stepping back when the nurse announced the family could see him, not wanting to intrude. Mrs. McShane asked me to come with them.

The room we entered was dark except for one light on the wall behind the bed. Shane was lying with his head raised, totally covered in bandages except his eyes and mouth. Thin plastic tubes ran oxygen into his nostrils. His eyes lit up as his family walked in.

Watching the scene unfold, I wanted the family to express their love for Shane and their gratitude for having him in their lives, and for him to do the same. I envisioned them saying their good-byes. Instead, they talked about the weather and other mundane things. I realized I needed to let go of all expectations of *how* they should say good-bye; however they did it would be perfect.

The male nurse, who was attending Shane, repeatedly addressed him as Tim. I quietly said to the nurse, "He likes to be called Shane." The nurse nodded. As soon as the nurse started to call him "Shane" he seemed to relax a little.

Shane kept asking for his bed to be adjusted, and I inquired if Paul, the patient's son, could adjust the bed for his father. The nurse agreed that would be fine and showed Paul how to do it. Paul then took charge of raising and lowering the bed. Weeping, he said, "Finally, after all these years I get to do something for him after all he's done for me."

I was present. I witnessed their agony, and I witnessed their love. That, I learned, was enough. Although classes at Harvard and the study of pastoral counseling theory gave me some insights, there was no theoretical construct that could encompass the McShane family's reality.

~

My competence and confidence as a chaplain grew. I felt fulfilled by my role at the hospital. It was a privilege to walk with patients through difficult times and make some small difference in their lives. I especially valued time spent with the terminally ill and their families. Those liminal moments, between life and death, were precious—sometimes agonizing, but more often filled with awe and peace. I was amazed at the depth of experience I could have with people I had just met. I learned to deeply witness, comfort and companion those in spiritual and emotional need as a chaplain in a way that wasn't possible in a psychotherapy session.

This new perspective allowed me to be more comfortable in my own skin; my fear of doing something wrong diminished. I was less self-conscious and more willing to take up *space*. Previously, when doing my rounds at the hospital, I tried to stay out of the way of the nursing staff unless they approached me. Now I made an effort to connect with the staff on each floor. Many nurses began to greet me warmly when I came onto their Pod. They directed me to patients who might need spiritual care, and sometimes confided their own concerns to me. I didn't feel invisible anymore.

This new collaboration between the nursing staff and me resulted in a memorable patient visit. I was called to a Medical/Surgical floor by one of my favorite nurses, Annie. She requested I visit a male patient who was within hours of dying. He had no one—no family or friends. She said she was too busy to sit with him.

Entering the patient's room, I encountered a small, frail man named Victor, leaning back against a pillow with the bed slightly raised. He almost blended in with the white sheets his skin was so pale, his hair soft white, and what must have been blue eyes now faded to gray.

I introduced myself and asked, "Annie thought you might like a visit? I'm one of the chaplains. What can I do to help you? Do you have a religious affiliation that comforts you?" He was too weak to even answer. When I saw what an effort it was for him to even lift his eyes to meet mine, I asked, "Would it be ok if I just sat beside you and prayed silently?" He nodded his consent and seemed relieved.

Praying at his bedside, I felt peaceful in the presence of this surrendering soul. Then, as inevitably happens in chaplaincy, I was paged and needed to move on to fill another patient's needs. Bending over Victor I said, "I am so sorry, Victor, I've been called away. I need to go, but you will be in my thoughts and prayers."

As I stood, I said, "May God bless you, Victor." He mumbled something in return that I did not understand. I decided not to question what he said, afraid he would strain himself if he tried to repeat it. I started for the door.

All of a sudden this wisp of a man sat bolt upright in the bed! "Stop! Wait!" he shouted in a commanding voice, his eyes blazing blue, "I want you to hear this! I said, God Bless…YOU!" And he fell back in the bed, exhausted.

I was stunned. "Victor, thank you! I will never forget you!" That was a promise I knew I could keep. I walked out of his room in tears having received the most profound blessing of my life.

As Annie, the nurse, looked up and saw my tears, she said, "That's why I sent you in—I come out of there crying every time I talk to him! He is such a beautiful man!" That was my signal to minister to her as she was dealing with feelings about losing this special patient.

That day I learned that patients have a need to give as much as receive. The rewards are great for both the giver and the recipient. I continue to carry the memory of Victor's blessing and the lesson of his soulful caring in my heart.

~

Another patient blessed my life in the short time we spent together. Helen Franken, an elderly Jewish woman, looked well groomed and elegant in her silky nightgown. As I got to know her, I found out she loved classical music. She and her brother had attended the Boston Symphony every Saturday night of the concert season in the same opera box seat for the past forty years. All that was available in her room was the TV which she abhorred. I went in search of a tape recorder and brought in my classical tapes to put by her bedside. She was ecstatic. I urged the nurses to make sure the recorder and tapes were kept where she could reach them.

Our conversations were lively whenever I visited Helen. She brightened when I walked into her room, especially if I was wearing her favorite outfit—a white flowered dress with a full skirt and scoop neck. She said, "Looking at it makes me happy!" Helen accepted her deteriorating condition and never complained.

She and I had conversations about Jewish traditions and values, her life as a child and later as a teacher. We talked about her relationship with her brother and how devoted they were to each other. She seemed to be relishing the memories. She expressed her gratitude many times for my visits, for the tapes and recorder, and for taking her to the hospital Chanukah party in December. I always walked away from her room feeling uplifted.

As days went by, Helen became weak, restless and in increasing pain. I assured her she didn't need to talk, I would just sit with her. Telling her about a book I'd been reading on Jewish Meditation, I said, "Helen, meditation was part of mainstream Judaism until 150 years ago. Maybe it would help you to repeat a Hebrew phrase in your mind. Please excuse my poor pronunciation, but one phrase the book recommends is *Ribbono shel Olam*." Helen mustered a little smile and repeated the phrase with the correct pronunciation. She must have been a wonderful teacher.

After a weekend off duty, I went to visit Helen. She wasn't in her room; someone else had replaced her. Questioning a nurse as to her whereabouts, I found she'd been moved to ICU. Shocked because she seemed to have been doing better when I left her on Friday, I ran to the ICU and found her comatose in a cubical with the pale green curtains—that were suppose to insure her privacy—wide open. Her hair was a mess, her hospital gown askew exposing her breast, a bright light glaring in her eyes and the TV speaker blaring in her ear!

My anger shot right through me! I tried to contain it as I spoke to her nurse, but it was seeping through every pore of my body. I said, "No one deserves to be left like this, but least of all this woman! She is lovely, kind, dignified and she HATES TV and would be appalled if she knew she was lying exposed and unkempt in public view. Please rectify this while I go hunt down the tapes she loves. I'll be back shortly." I forgot in that moment I was there to minister to the nursing staff as well as the patients.

Still, I feel that same fury as I write this now. I was outraged, and still am, that a patient could be dehumanized in this way. I found the music and the tape recorder and set it up at her bedside. I spoke to her nurse about keeping her music playing. I wrote a note in her chart requesting that she not be subjected to the TV and that her music be kept playing softly whenever possible. Unfortunately, no one paid heed to my note. I returned often in those final days of Helen's life to find the TV speaker once again blaring. I put a note on the TV to keep it off, to no avail. On these visits, I spoke to her softly and sometimes sang to her. One morning I came back on duty and she was gone.

~

Abel, whose words of wisdom I continued to take to the chaplains' lunch table after each visit, often had a twinkle in his eye. One day when I walked into his room he was in good humor and joking with the nurses. When they left, he said, "A sick person can be a tedious thing. Sometimes they're like this [meaning congenial] and sometimes they're like a copperhead waiting in the grass." He went on to explain. "I had to apologize to the nurses today for the way I was acting the other day—I got off on the wrong foot in the morning and nothing went right all day."

Later in the conversation he said, "I try to turn this sickness over to God, but after a while it nibbles at your faith. I've tried to carry a smile for the world—most of the time I do—but sometimes it gets hard." He used language in such a picturesque way, it often made me look at things through a new lens.

Another time I went to visit, he was with the nurses so I waited outside his room with two men who were there before me. One asked if I was waiting to see Abel. I said I was and introduced myself. They introduced themselves as Abel's older brothers, Gene and Kent, who had been visiting with Abel when the nurse needed to change the bed. Kent said, "Abel is expecting you." In spite of what Abel had told me about his large close-knit family, I knew he had been estranged from them, so I was glad to see they had apparently reconciled. When the nurse came out of the room and gave us the ok to go in, Abel was obviously delighted to see me. The four of us talked and laughed. I promised Abel I would spend more time with him on Monday and left.

On my next visit, Abel had a room full of visitors when I walked in. I shook hands with the two brothers I had met and introduced myself to the others. Abel and I had a brief talk while the others talked among themselves. Then, not wanting to intrude on the family's visit, I said, "Well, I won't keep you people from visiting," and started for the door.

"What do you mean by *you people*?" Abel said loudly. "We are all one people."

I was stunned! "Abel, I didn't mean to say we're not. You know I feel like we are kindred souls. Of course, we are one people! I wouldn't hurt you for the world!" He seemed to accept that, but I walked away feeling terrible. Although I knew in my heart it was a phrase I also used with white families, it was one I would never use again.

I trusted my bond with Abel was strong enough to weather this, but I was upset that he could believe I saw him and his family as *other*. When I got back to the Chaplain's office, I processed the visit with the only black chaplain on our team. She explained to me that the expression, *you people*, is seen and used as a derogatory term for people of color.

On my next visit with Abel, he was looking out the window. He said, "Look how beautiful the sky is. I'm so grateful God has given me the eyes to see it." He said some poignant and wise things, but his thoughts were loosely connected, and he was hard to follow. Our relationship was still warm even after the "you people" incident.

Both Abel and I were aware that this was our last visit. I was going on vacation, and he was being released to go to rehab. I said, "Abel, I hope you know I love you and will always be with you."

"I know you do and that you'll be with me. I feel you with me."

When I returned from vacation, I found that Abel was still on the census. My fellow chaplains warned me that he'd been steadily declining. He was now in the ICU. I checked with his nurse before I went in to see him. I asked her to give me an update on his condition. She asked me what I knew, and I told her all I knew was that he had emphysema and heart problems. She said rather curtly, "He abused alcohol all his life. His brain scan shows that his brain has deteriorated to the extent that there is virtually no brain left." She slapped the scan on the lighted viewer box. I gasped! I couldn't believe my eyes or ears. Who had I been talking to?

This sweet, warm, wise man with whom I had been so deeply connected, did not have a functioning brain! When I entered his room, the curtains were drawn and I could barely make out his skeletal form in the bed. He was comatose. I held his hand and spoke softly to him thanking him for all he had given me over the months and encouraging him to let go when he was ready, reminding him that God and the angels would be there to meet him. I whispered my good-bye in his ear. I knew in my heart that when I returned in the morning he would be gone—and I was right.

As I wept the next day, the other chaplains offered their support. But, Kate, my supervisor, took me aside and said, "If you continue to get emotionally attached to your patients, you WILL burn out." I knew she was right, but I could not stop myself from falling in love with those I served and grieving their loss.

When God is everything you see,
then everywhere you will see God.
Life and death—strong and weak,
It's just the One who plays hide'n seek

– From "Hide n' Seek" by Ofer Golany (2002)
from *Healing the Holy Land:*
A Musical Journey of Faith (CD): Dean & Dudley Evenson

CHAPTER THIRTY-FOUR
Not What It Seems

IT'S JUST A FEW WEEKS before Christmas 1990. Debbie and I are living in a first floor apartment with a large cream-colored living room opening into the dining room, which I've painted mauve. The windows are wide and the space is cheery during the day. There are two bedrooms and a huge closet off the living room, which becomes my study. I make this place a home, setting up my altar, hanging curtains, pictures and family photos.

The kitchen is tiny, but I love it because the landlord allowed me to paint the cabinets red. This is the sixth kitchen in which I've had either red counters or red cabinets. Having red in my kitchen has become a prerequisite for my sense of *home*. Bright colors have lifted my spirits since I was a child and requested my bedroom be painted orange. Red in my kitchen goes beyond that—it fills me with a sense of abundance, ripeness; and feeling at home in the world. This kitchen will do just fine, I think, as I put the final touches on the cabinets.

Several papers are due for my classes on which I've been working all semester. There's a paper due on the Kabbalah, one on the power dynamics in cult-like organizations, and another on Buddhism. Over the course of the semester I've accumulated hundreds of 3X5 cards color-coded with bits of information gleaned from my research. I'm overwhelmed.

As I sit in the middle of the living room sorting the cards into piles for each paper, tears trickle from my eyes. I've no idea where to begin. Debbie snaps a picture of me in this state before she goes off to her father's for the weekend. I'm thankful I don't have to tend to her needs for a few days, but I'll spend the weekend worrying that Stan might harass her about her weight and school work. She sometimes comes home after a weekend with him demoralized by his abusiveness, but she's a pragmatist and appreciates the money he has to get her name-brand sneakers or take her out to a nice restaurant.

I enter my closet study where my computer, an Apple 2E, sits. I start to type. By some Divine grace, words start to pour onto the screen. I am floating in a space where there is no time, no hunger, no need to pee. I spend hours without looking up to notice the changing light. It is almost dawn by the time I realize my body is stiff. I'm starving and exhausted and my bladder is full. I have finished one paper. This ritual is repeated two more times, resulting in three A's and a migraine that fells me for a week, although I continue to go to classes and my internship.

I've pushed myself beyond my limits as I have done so many times before. Striving for perfection is costly, and I need to re-evaluate my priorities. I'm still dealing with reverberations from my tortuous life with Stan as I revisit the experience and do the necessary research on domestic violence for my Master's project.

My days are filled with classes, the internship and keeping my practice going. And, I'm responsible for keeping the apartment, paying the bills and seeing to Debbie's needs. I try to stay in close contact with my son, Jake, who is still living with Stan, and frequently have phone conversations with my two older children.

My friend, Ruth, and I have come to know each other well and are growing closer as the semester progresses. With finals looming after the winter break, my migraines are unrelenting, even when I take medication that usually gives me relief. I am exhausted. Ruth is concerned and begs me to let her husband,

Robert, work on me. He's a massage therapist. The thought of letting a strange man touch me raises my already high anxiety level. I decline several times.

~

I have a Chanukah party in mid-December and invite Ruth and Robert. They arrive early to help me set up, so we can visit before the crowd descends on my small apartment. Robert is a tall, angular, thin man with sandy blond hair. His blue eyes are piercing, almost cold, but with the hint of something deeper, softer. He endears himself to me that night by his wholehearted participation in the party, reading part of the Chanukah service and helping me serve and clean up. He is great fun, with a witty sense of humor.

After the other guests leave, Ruth and Robert linger. Robert offers to give me a massage to relieve my head and back pain. Not knowing him well, I decline but thank him for his offer. The next day, and for several days following, Ruth says, "Robert adores you and he wants to help. Let him give you a massage, he's really good." Toward the end of the week, I'm desperate for relief. Ruth invites me over to dinner and encourages me to let Robert work on me.

The date is etched in my memory because the encounter turned out to be life-altering. It is December 22, 1990. The pain in my head, neck, shoulders and back is unbearable. After dinner I consent to let Robert give me a massage, if Ruth stays in the room. Robert says I need to strip to the waist and put on one of his shirts. I go into the bathroom and change. I'm extremely uncomfortable with this, but comply nonetheless because Ruth is there.

All three of us sit on the floor. My legs are outstretched and Ruth is holding my feet. Robert sits behind me, his long legs on either side of me holding me secure. He insists I lean back against him. An incredible piece of music, which I later learn is *Transfigured Night* by Arnold Schoenberg, is playing on his stereo.

Robert starts to talk softly in my ear, urging me to relax and totally surrender myself into his care. He is gentle in his approach, but he is doing a form of deep muscle massage that is painful. I cry, both in pain and in release as he works on me. Robert's hands are full of energy, and even behind my closed lids I sense that the room, too, is full of energy and flashing lights. The music is powerful and moving.

Robert says in a melodious, almost seductive, voice, "Relax, let go, melt into me, just surrender…" Whenever I express my concern for him or Ruth, he redirects my attention back to me, back to receiving. Meanwhile, Ruth looks vacant. I can see her, but I can't feel her presence in the room. After Robert is done, he instructs me to lie still and listen to a piece of Rachmaninov that sends me into a mystical reverie.

When I stand up, I am pain free and energized, feeling open, looser. I can touch my head without pain. Robert says, "I felt a tremendous amount of lapis energy coming through my left side. It is still running." I have no idea what this means. He goes on to tell me he has worked with some men, over a ten year period, who are spiritual teachers and masters. From them he has learned to work with the energies of precious and semi-precious stones and crystals. "My spiritual guides asked me to help you, and I always do what they ask," he says. "Your life lesson is to learn to receive. And, I'm being told that I am to become your teacher."

I am hesitant to believe all this and decline his offer. Still, I'm intrigued by his assertion that the guides have asked him to help me. That's an alluring thought.

~

I invited Robert and Ruth to join my sister, Jules, my brother, Mark, and me for Christmas dinner. On Christmas day, Debbie left for her father's in the morning, and Jules and Mark sat at the dining room table while I finished preparations for dinner. When Ruth and Robert arrived, I was still pain free and energized, happy to see my two new friends. Mark and Robert began to talk. My brother was doing most of the talking while Robert, who was sitting across the table from him, listened attentively.

After everyone was settled at the dinner table, Mark began talking about my brother, Matt, who had died in the Pacific during World War II. He told Robert that this young man, our brother, barely twenty years old, had already made an enormous difference in the lives of so many people. Mark burst into tears. I was stunned! I'd never seen Mark cry. He quickly regained control and tried to analyze why it happened. Robert quietly said, "It's not something you can figure out with your head, Mark." I looked at Robert. His thin angular face was soft and glowing. He looked transformed.

After Jules and Mark left, I asked Robert what had happened. Robert said, "When I came into the house I felt a tremendous surge of energy and thought that you must be in trouble and needed some help." (I was touched by his concern for me.) "Then," he said, "I quickly realized the energy wasn't for you, but for Mark, so I just turned my attention on him for the rest of the day." Robert and I sat and talked for a long time. Once again, Ruth seemed to have left the room although she was physically present.

Robert told me a little about his spiritual practice which can only be passed down from a teacher to an apprentice. The teachings were called *The Work* based on the practice of Alchemy. He was vague about what it actually was but described some of the practices that strengthen a seeker's connection to the *higher realms*. He had me try one of these by having me keep talking to him while I measured the distances from myself to the surrounding walls and changing the word "I" to "Kathleen" as I spoke. I couldn't do it. He said I needed to be able to function on these three different levels at once, if I was to have access to the higher realms.

Robert continued, "The guides are telling me to tell you to meditate by measuring the distances between yourself and the surrounding walls and a place about eighteen inches above the head—which is the location of communication with the higher self. And, you need to be continually measuring the distances, not just during meditation, but throughout the day." He went on to say that the Hindu meditation I had done faithfully for seventeen years was an illusion, not real meditation. He said everything I believed was an illusion. He asked me again to become his student. I'd seen the miracle Robert worked with Mark and the transformation in his face, but I was still apprehensive.

I felt uncomfortable about Ruth's lack of involvement in our discussion. She grew more distant and isolated as Robert and I talked. Reluctantly, I agreed to be Robert's student but told him I'd stop working with him if it got in the way of my friendship with Ruth. He told me, "You have this impulse to do something to fix things rather than sit with your feelings and think. Your need to take care of others is devaluing to them and is killing you."

I was surprised at his perceptive insight, since Robert had known me for such a short time. He went on, "Your behavior comes from a need to feel important."

I agreed. "That's partially true, but I also feel like my right to live is dependent on taking care of others."

At that moment, I saw an image of my mother lying on a cot across from my crib waiting to find out if her son was alive or dead. I started to cry. I believed this experience was at the root of my need to take care of others and make everything right for them. I told this to Robert. He didn't respond to my tears or my insight. It was a breakthrough moment for me, but I didn't feel met by him. I felt abandoned, a six month old infant lying unattended in the crib.

When Ruth and Robert left I had a spurt of energy and danced for about an hour. I continued to feel energy buzzing through my body well into the next day. I felt hopeful that this was the path out of my depression, pain and chronic fatigue.

The next day, I received a note from Robert. He wrote: "Pride is a pendulum which swings from I am better than others to I'm not good enough for others and, therefore, I must validate my existence to others." Again, his words resonated with me—I saw that dynamic in myself.

When I began seeing Robert for instructions, he became more authoritative, although he said to use the "stick of discrimination" and not take any of his teachings on faith. When he said, "All faith is imagination and your feeling of being connected to Spirit is an illusion," I said nothing although I was disturbed by his assertion. He told me to get a red and blue light and turn both on. Then, I was to concentrate on bringing the blue light into the left eye and the red light out from the right eye. He said this would help my chronic depression.

That stirred my hope for relief from my depressive episodes. When he told me to get a piece of lapis and remove all my other crystals and gemstones, I complied without question, although my altar looked barren and forlorn in their absence. And, he also instructed me to read *The Fourth Way* by P.D. Ouspensky.

I bought the lights, the lapis and the book, even though I was feeling resistance, anger and doubt. A few days later I went to call him to ask him about the lights. It took me twenty minutes to dial the phone, and when I got the recording, I hung up. The image I had was pounding on Robert's chest saying, "Don't make me do this!"

I liked the Robert who came to the Chanukah party and sat listening to my brother, more than this Robert who listened to entities he referred to as "they." This new Robert seemed arrogant, cold, and condescending. He had warned me not to become infatuated with him, and I imagined myself telling him there certainly was no risk of that happening.

I wrote a note to him in my own defense: "I have been "working" spiritually all my life. I have born four children, miscarried a fifth child. I have lived through incredible loss and sorrow. I have survived the ravages of depression and twenty-three years in an abusive relationship. And I have helped people and grown spiritually throughout my lifetime."

He replied, "All the more reason to spend time with you," but he continued to treat me like a novice regarding spiritual concerns and talked as if I lived in a world of fantasy. My intuitive voice kept warning me, but Robert always attributed my doubts to the ego's resistance to being challenged, so I disregarded my own instinct to run from these teachings and Robert.

Whenever my doubts surfaced I reminded myself why I had said "yes" to Robert's offer to become my teacher. I remembered the Robert who worked on my back, who was present and gentle, and how his face looked when he was listening to my brother. I felt God had put him in my path. He had come into my life when I was in need of healing.

The effect of Robert's touch was undeniable. But even more compelling was the idea that the guides had "told" him to help me and that he seemed genuinely concerned for my well-being even though I worried that what he and his guides were asking me to do would take me further from the true simplicity and connection with Spirit. I prayed that it was holy voices calling me to work with this man.

I had never before experienced the energy that I felt when working with Robert. It felt tactile and incredibly powerful. And, of course, what happened with Mark's tears convinced me that Robert had spiritual power. Mark had seemed transformed after that experience at Christmas. He regained his sense of hope for the world, something he had not expressed in many years. In the Ouspensky book, the author talked about how rare it is to find a teacher and how it's only through a teacher that this spiritual practice can be passed down.

Still, I was terrified. I did what I was told, but putting away my gemstones was painful, for they had graced my altar for years. I stopped my Hindu meditation and began meditating the way Robert taught me. I measured distances as I went through my day. But every time I thought about being dependent on Robert for instructions and information, I became furious! When I told him this in a note, he wrote back, "What character is this that takes the food out of your mouth?" Just as he dismissed my doubt, he dismissed my anger. I did not know then that a true teacher would have encouraged me to explore those emotions and allow me to come to my own conclusions about them.

Over time, the doubt and darkness increased. I cared too much about what Robert thought of me, trying to do the practice right and looking for his approval. I expended enormous amounts of time and energy in pursuing this path at a time when my emotional, mental and physical resources were low. Robert, too, was expending a lot of time instructing me. I voiced my concern to him that he was doing this without any monetary compensation. He informed me that his fee was $60 an hour, and he indicated that he expected payment for the previous hours we had spent together.

I was shocked that he had apparently intended to charge me all along, when I thought he was doing this as a form of service to humanity under the instructions of his guides. My financial resources were nonexistent—my meager income barely covered the bills. Robert was well aware of my dire financial straits when we started working together. Still, I felt obligated to start paying on my debt not wanting to owe him anything.

Although this development was upsetting and stressful, the imbalance in the relationship was more disturbing. I wrote to Robert: "You make me feel like I have nothing to give you, and that you have nothing to learn from me. I feel like I have nothing to offer you. Maybe that is part of the lesson—to receive when I feel like I have nothing to give in return. But I don't like it! It feels invalidating and humiliating."

He replied, "That nasty thing called pride can only diminish your beauty." I also protested that he seemed to know a lot about me, but I knew very little about him. There was no mutuality in this exchange. I came to understand I allowed this imbalance, just as I had in my relationships with Stan and Craig.

As the weeks went by, I felt I was regressing to an early age. I felt confused and overwhelmed and realized it was similar to how I felt as a child around all my big brothers who used words that I didn't understand. It felt like these brothers belonged to a secret world to which I did not have access. When I questioned them they gave me explanations I could not grasp, but I pretended to understand so they wouldn't think I was stupid.

Robert was engaged in the secret practice of Alchemy, which in its earliest definition is the process of taking something ordinary and turning it into something extraordinary by a seemingly magical process of transformation. I did not understand much of what Robert said, and I even had trouble reading the book that he had recommended. It contained esoteric and archaic teachings. I decided that perhaps this was a healing crisis for me and I just needed to ride it out.

My doubts resurfaced. I had learned the spiritual practice of holding God in my consciousness as I went about my day from a little book called *Practice the Presence of God* by Brother Lawrence. Now, Robert was saying that I should self-remember, stay aware of my surroundings, and measure distances around me.

Where did God fit into this? I rationalized that since we are an expression of God, self-remembering is a consciousness of that aspect of God which is most accessible to us. But Robert did not talk of God—he talked of guides, voices, and even angels.

Each time I raised my concerns, Robert would pull me back in with a demonstration of his magic, his energy. Or, I would be crying and say, "I can't do this anymore," and he'd talk sweetly and softly, encouraging me to continue. After I confronted him about his initial harshness, he became very tender and gentle. His tenderness brought up how deprived of tenderness I'd felt, until I met Craig who I'd recently banished from my life. I wanted to kick and scream at Robert, "Get away from me! You are picking at an old scabbed-over wound—leave it alone!"

In one note I wrote to him I said, *"Don't be kind to me! You're ripping me to shreds. Don't notice me, don't see me, don't care about me!"* Any kindness or evidence of someone really seeing me outside my circle of peer-counselors and friends made me feel vulnerable and unprotected; it was both what I wanted in my life and what terrified me most. I feared I would lose myself. This was the dynamic at play with Robert. I relinquished my power to him.

All this occurred in a period of less than six weeks. I felt flung like the tides from one side of the emotional spectrum to the other, mentally exhausted and confused. Bereft spiritually, I missed the comfort of my Hindu meditation. I became physically ill with a cold and sore throat (maybe from not speaking my truth!). I lost my center, which Robert said was only an illusion anyway. According to him, everything was illusion except his reality. I struggled to make a decision whether to continue *The Work* or not.

I was feeling suicidal. But my anger rose to save me. I wrote to Robert: "I want to kill you for this, Robert! In less than six weeks you have stripped me bare. I have come to doubt everything I believe and be suspicious of everything that gives me comfort. I miss my usual meditation. I miss picking up the book, *My Little Flowers* and have it speak to me. I miss seeing God everywhere I look and hearing the voice of Spirit whisper in my ear. I miss knowing my love is good and healing and an expression of Divine

Love. I shifted my awareness away from these "illusions" and found emptiness and no one to hold me there. I have nothing of value. I don't believe this is what God wants!"

This was not the end. I went to see Robert to tell him I had decided to stop working with him and he talked to me for three hours, convincing me that everything I was feeling was part of the process, the breaking down of the ego so I could experience reality. He did a ritual, this time making the *Sign of the Cross,* touching his heart with fingertips of his left hand, then his forehead, his right shoulder and his left shoulder, opposite from the *Sign of the Cross* Catholics make when they enter a Catholic Church or begin to pray. It raised a huge wave of energy in me that left me feeling "high." I agreed to continue with him.

Ruth and I prepared for finals in Comparative Religions with a study group at my house several days later. Robert came to pick Ruth up and stayed listening to the group discuss the spiritual teachers we had been studying throughout the semester including Krishna, Lao Tzu, Buddha, Christ, and Mohammed.

As the group continued preparing for the test, I turned to Robert and quietly asked, "Do you mean to tell me that all of these great teachers, masters and gurus were in a state of illusion?" He said, "Yes!" Suddenly I found clarity. I had spent months learning about these holy manifestations of God on earth and their beautiful teachings. Perhaps I could not value myself enough to honor my own beliefs, but I certainly valued these Ancient Masters enough to know they were not living in illusion. The wisdom they offered was grounded in Love, Service and Compassion. What could be more real!

"Robert, we're done! I am no longer your student," I said softly but emphatically. After the others left, I told him how destructive and manipulative I felt he had been and that he had abused both his power as a man and the power of his mystical gifts. I was very angry, and he was very quiet. Afterward I felt washed over with a feeling of relief. The next night, driving home in a winter ice storm, a song came through me summing up the past six weeks:

Who will come on a night like this?
Barren trees touched by icy kiss.
Darkness folding around my home
Finds me lonely and alone,
Lonely and alone.

Who will come on a night like this?
Bitter winds blowing from the west.
All I know has been lost to me,
As I flounder on black seas,
Flounder on black seas.

Who will come on a night like this
When the road is engulfed in mist?
Broken hearted, bereft of soul,
Wander I weeping as I go,
Weeping as I go.

Who will come on a night like this?
Evening star comes to grant my wish
Breaking through the cloud filled night
Bringing with it Holy Light,
Bringing Holy Light.

Who will come on a night like this?
Angels singing of heavenly bliss
Knock upon my heart's own door
Bringing Love forevermore,
Love forevermore,
Love forevermore.

– Kathleen, 1991

~

Studying the Kabbalah during the semester, I was awed by its
wisdom and mysticism. Our text on the subject spoke of the
mystic rabbis working themselves into a frenzy of weeping so the
feminine aspect of God on earth, the Shekinah, would appear to
them in the form of exquisite light which would send them into
ecstasy. I did not make the connection as this song was coming

through, but it had a melody that sounded like many of the songs we sang during the Jewish holidays. I realized the song was a gift of the Kabbalah.

I had a long way to go before I would be able to reconnect with my own inner knowing again. I was shattered. Meditation, which had been my grounding for years, eluded me. Sick and out of balance, I had a car accident and suffered whiplash. My head raged. I questioned everything I formerly believed. My trust in myself and others eroded.

Miraculously, I maintained my friendship with Ruth who was beginning to open up about her unhappiness with Robert who, she said, was an alcoholic. She had dabbled in *The Work* when she met Robert, but quickly extricated herself from it and delved deeper into her Jewish heritage—though she recognized Robert's healing power. That's all she had wanted for me, to experience relief from my pain, but I allowed myself to be caught in his snare, and she felt it was not her place to interfere. Robert and Ruth separated that spring and eventually divorced.

Migraines became my daily reality once again. I sought the help of a chiropractor, Martin McKenzie, who had a spiritual perspective and was a practicing Hindu. He began each session with a Hindu chant and meditation, and I was able to meditate again for the first time. I started coming back to wholeness, but the process continued for another two years.

Through that time, I could not find my gemstones. I looked everywhere. It was as if they had disappeared. I felt like a part of me was still in hiding. Finally, they appeared one day in a place I had looked a hundred times. Even now, twenty-five years later, I feel the reverberations of those six weeks with Robert—questioning my intuition, my sensibilities, my own deep knowing.

Embarrassed and ashamed for allowing myself to succumb so completely (albeit, briefly) to Robert's mesmerizing hold on me, I didn't talk about the experience. Was I so needy of male attention that I was willing to give up my soul? Although there were no sexual overtures, Robert's attention was seductive. He seemed to grasp my issues quickly and knew how to manipulate me. As I became more emotionally upset he remained calm, logical and objective—something Stan did. He seemed to get a perverse pleasure out of seeing me fall apart, as did Stan.

The annihilation of the ego was Robert's excuse for his harshness. Having spent twenty-three years with Stan, whatever ego I had was demolished by his relentless criticism, humiliation, subjugation and cruelty. I had just begun to feel myself come back to life as I entered Divinity School, and now I had allowed that fragile self to be crushed again.

~

What lessons did I learn from this experience? The main lessons were to listen to the still small voice within—even when it's an angry, resistant voice—and to remember my answers to life's questions are within me. Never again did I want to be in a one-down position and settle for less than mutually respectful, empowering relationships.

The hardest lesson of all was that I must learn to love myself, to forgive myself for being vulnerable, needy, trusting, weak, and naïve with someone who is incapable of honoring who I am. I also came to realize that I am a survivor: strong and resilient. So, I am grateful to Robert for these lessons and to the Holy Wisdom that gave me a song to heal my heart on a cold icy winter night.

~

I've been surprised by my body's visceral response to these memories in the past weeks as I wrote and rewrote this passage about my experience with Robert. It has felt like I've been detoxing from ingesting poison: stomach aches, shaking, nausea, headaches, feeling confused as if in an altered state. At times, I've felt rattled to my core. Two nights ago, unsettled and bordering on tears, I pulled myself together to attend a meditation group I belong to. As we chanted, the knot in my throat was undone and tears began to stream down my face, unbidden and without restraint. I left feeling enormously better than when I arrived.

But it wasn't until today, while sitting in a bath trying to subdue the all-consuming pain in my body, did I realize Robert's words—discrediting my life of service, disavowing my spiritual connection and beliefs—could only have affected me as they did because they resonated with something deep within me: they went to the core of what I'd experienced in the Catholic Church at a young age. He jabbed his finger deep into the wound of feeling sinful, wrong, never good enough, humiliated, invalidated, unheard.

I felt those ancient messages and Robert's messages being purged from my body as I soaked in the bathtub. I blessed them as they disappeared down the drain, doing my own kind of Alchemy as the water flowed back into Mother Earth.

I realized that as a child, my mother and older siblings told me over and over again that I had a vivid imagination, and all the things I feared were not real—they were *figments of my imagination*. I wasn't sure what *figments* meant but I assumed they were *fairy tales*. Robert had tapped into the long held belief that what I saw, heard, felt, feared and believed were merely *figments of my imagination*. A sense of compassion poured from my heart for that child who was taught not to trust her own knowing, her own intuitions, her own senses and a tender peace settled over me.

Recently, I picked up a book by Peter A. Levine titled: Waking the Tiger: Healing Trauma. *I had read it before. He describes the mechanism of fight, flight and freeze in face of a threat. It is an evolutionary defense system used by animals as well as humans. The freeze state happens when death seems imminent. If the threat disappears, the trauma victim begins to shake to release the energy that has been trapped in the body when it froze. Animals do this instinctively.*

Humans have been cultured out of this automatic response with messages like: get a hold of yourself; you need a good stiff drink; or you're being hysterical or a wimp. Sometimes people in this state are given medication to "calm them down."

I never seem to remember that this is a natural process when I start to shake during a scary event or memory, and usually try to "get control." The healthiest thing is to ride the shakes out or the tears or any other physical manifestation that arises to release energy stored in the body from a traumatic experience. It's helpful to have a caring witness with you as you process these feelings.

We must embrace struggle.
Every living thing conforms to it.
Everything in nature grows and struggles
in its own way, establishing its own identity,
insisting on it at all cost, against all resistance.

– Rainer Maria Rilke from *Letters to a Young Poet*

CHAPTER THIRTY-FIVE
In Solidarity

BY THE SPRING SEMESTER at HDS, I missed Craig more than ever. I knew that if I hadn't banished him from my life, I'd never have given myself over to Robert. Craig and I arranged to meet with another co-counselor to sort things out. After three hours of intense co-counseling, we agreed on the parameters of our renewed relationship.

It was my responsibility to claim my full power. I couldn't be dependent upon Craig as I'd been before. He could be part of my life, not the whole of it. Somehow I needed to find my own sense of worth and believe in myself as much as he believed in me. On his part, he would be more aware of the power dynamic between us.

We resumed teaching together and co-counseling on a weekly basis, but now it was I who kept the boundaries between us more defined. I went to friends and other peer-counselors more frequently instead of turning to Craig when I was slipping emotionally. I wouldn't allow myself to defer to Craig as a leader of our group, but began to take my place as a co-leader.

Still, things became complicated. As I started working on my senior project on domestic violence, I connected with the same organizations and people as Craig, who was working on his thesis in the field. I joined the organization, *Women Together Against Domestic Violence*, which put on a yearly walk to raise awareness of domestic violence and formed panels of domestic violence survivors to talk to the public. I was invited to join their Board. I also joined the *Domestic Violence Task Force* at the hospital as part of my internship.

The *Task Force* was working on a proposal to add questions about domestic violence on the hospital's intake form. If women (and men) were asked the right questions, by an empathetic and non-judgmental medical professional, during Emergency Room visits or hospitalization, they might be more likely to disclose abuse that was occurring in their life. Then, if they indicate there is some form of violence, the hospital staff could be ready to offer information on resources to help them reevaluate the abusive relationship and stay safe.

As I worked on my project and participated in activities to raise awareness of domestic violence, I had to confront my own history in an abusive marriage. Craig was the expert in helping me to find my way back from those dark memories. Despite my good intentions, I found myself turning to him for support and validation. I started having nightmares in which Stan was stalking me. I'd wake up in a cold sweat, shaking. Vivid memories of the verbal, emotional and sexual abuse started to surface even during the day, and my startle response was set off by innocuous daily events.

My psychiatrist reinforced his previous diagnosis of PTSD and recommended I go back into therapy with someone who did EMDR (Eye Movement Desensitization and Reprocessing), which was used effectively with returning veterans with PTSD. I also had migraines and constant pain, but the end of the semester was looming, so I postponed starting therapy. I continued to depend almost exclusively on Craig.

Through *Women Together*, I served on panels with other women who had also been victims of domestic violence—doctors, lawyers, stay at home mothers, minimum wage workers, women from all walks of life. We'd stand up and tell our stories at conferences, colleges and hospitals. We'd all left our perpetrators and *lived*.

That was our first message, since the headlines only herald those who are killed while attempting to escape their abusers.

We took turns speaking. The surgeon said, "I make *life and death* decisions every day in the operating room, but when I got home I wasn't allowed to make the smallest decision without consulting my husband. I never knew what would set him off and bring on a beating."

There was the lawyer who helped other women escape their violent partners but couldn't extricate herself from an abusive relationship because she was afraid of losing custody of her daughter. Her husband was a well known judge with powerful connections. She had lived in terror of his next weekend binge when he would go on a rampage, destroy the house and come after her in a rage. She finally broke free.

The woman who killed her batterer as he tried to kill her was convicted of manslaughter and spent time in prison. She stood up proudly and proclaimed her innocence. She knew she'd acted in self-defence no matter what the court said. Since her release, she had worked in prisons to help other women who were incarcerated under similar circumstances.

I began to talk about the verbal, emotional and sexual abuse I had experienced through my twenty-three year relationship with Stan. I described what his excoriating invectives and dominating behavior had done to me and my children. I talked about the role religious beliefs played in keeping me in my marriage.

Some of the other women on the panel described being stalked, vicious physical attacks, surviving gunshot wounds, gathering their children and running, leaving everything behind. Most often their abusers were not incarcerated or forced to make reparations. Often these men were repeat offenders who did the same thing to another woman, if the partner he was battering escaped.

After we finished talking, women would surround us, trying to tell us their stories, asking questions, looking for some validation and support. When I spoke at my own hospital, one of the women who came to talk to me, after everyone had left, was a head nurse on one of my PODS. I admired Kelly. She was a true leader: in control, decisive, smart and kind-hearted. Kelly confided in me that her husband had been sexually abusing her for years. She was a devout Catholic and felt she couldn't get out of her marriage and still remain in the Church. I offered to do some research for her on the Church's stance on marital rape.

I talked to several priests and learned that there is a little known precept in the Catholic Church that if a man abuses his wife *he* has broken the wedding vows and the wife can file for an annulment, which would allow her to marry again. Kelly was amazed to hear of this and promptly told her husband that that was exactly what she was going to do if he didn't stop abusing her. They ended up in couple's therapy and were still together when I left the hospital ten years later.

In spite of the physical and emotional toll it took to delve into the subject of domestic violence, I knew I could make a difference in the lives of the women struggling with these issues. I was credible because I'd lived their story, and I was proof that a woman could survive and even flourish after leaving her abuser. I felt I was making a difference every time I spoke my truth whether it was to a group of doctors and medical personnel, to clergy and chaplains, at conferences, or to an individual woman. All those years of torture could be transformed into something of value if I could help others through sharing my experience. Now that was true Alchemy.

~

While serving as a chaplain and working with *Women Together* on domestic violence issues, I was immersed in classes, writing papers, seeing therapy clients and tending to the house and Debbie, teaching and counseling with Craig—and staying connected with my other three offspring by phone and short visits. I vowed to live a more balanced life.

Martin McKenzie, my chanting chiropractor, became part of my weekly routine to improve my health and emotional balance. He also acted as a spiritual mentor as I became more enamored with the Hindu chants and meditation he introduced. Immersing myself in the reading of Hindu scriptures and texts, I felt a pull toward this spiritual perspective but wouldn't commit to it. I was still raw from my experience with Robert.

When the new semester began, I took advantage of the Boston Theological Institute which allowed Harvard Divinity School students to take courses at nine other seminaries in the area. I signed up for a course at the Episcopal Divinity School (EDS) with Demaris Wehr, PhD, called *Emerging Women's Spiritualities*.

I went into Demaris' class feeling less sure of myself than when I entered Divinity School. After taking *Power, Conflict and Community* in the first semester, I confronted my underlying prejudices and was fearful of inadvertently offending someone as I had done with Abel, when I used the phrase *you people*. EDS was especially politically correct, raising awareness of inequities and distorted perceptions, but, Demaris reminded me that spirituality includes connecting through the hard places, making sacred even our imperfections, our conflicts, our despair. I began to see that our struggles were a sacred birthing ground. This was *embodied* spirituality.

As a Catholic in my childhood, I was taught there were clear separations between body and soul, heaven and earth. Someone once said to me "You are not of this world!" meaning it as a compliment. My Catholic self wanted to be cloistered away in a convent to hone myself to perfection with prayer and sacrifice. In Demaris' class, I came to realize spirituality is about walking deeply on this earth, living in the body, reaching out, taking risks, making mistakes, feeling regretful, asking forgiveness, changing what is hurtful—learning the lessons and letting go. I saw that life itself is a prayer, and imperfection is the nature of things.

~

Little Amelia Rose, my darling granddaughter, was now almost eight months old and was the sweetness in my life. I found time to see her as often as possible. After each excursion up to New Hampshire to be with Amelia, I returned to the refectory table at the Divinity School and announced to my friends, "Amelia is my teacher! You wouldn't believe what she did this weekend."

Hearing this several times in the course of a few months, one friend said laughingly, "We know! We know! The Gospel according to Amelia!" I promptly sequestered myself in my closet where my computer resided and took dictation from the angels which resulted in a poem called, *The Gospel According to Amelia*. I have included it at the end of the book.

My days as an interning chaplain in a huge hospital exposed me to every possible human tragedy: babies born with birth defects; people dying of all forms of cancer, heart disease, AIDS, drug over-doses, traumatic injuries, assaults, suicide, burns. Working in the field of domestic violence in preparation for my project entailed witnessing many tragic situations. Amelia was the source of my balance during the three years of Divinity School. I should share my Divinity degree with her. She was my beacon of light through all the challenges I faced during those years.

CHAPTER THIRTY-SIX
Alchemy of Living

AFTER MY EXPERIENCE with Robert, questions about the role I played in being sexually assaulted by Stan resurfaced. What if I had refused to go to his apartment? What if I had refused to go into his bedroom when I was uncomfortable with the situation? What if I had fought him off? What if I hadn't worn that red dress? And, what if I had told someone? If I couldn't figure out the "what ifs" and what I'd do differently about Stan or Robert, how could I ever protect myself from the same things happening again?

There was another question. Had I been molested as a child? Could that be the explanation for my adamant refusal to learn anything about sex? In a co-counseling session a year before, I began to counsel on an abdominal pain that I had since childhood. During one session an image came to me of a lone pine grove on a hill some distance from the road, with an open area surrounded by pine trees and covered in a thick bed of pine needles. It was about a mile from my immediate neighborhood.

I recognized it as a place I played with the neighborhood kids. I'd pushed that sliver of memory aside at that time not wanting to bring it into focus.

Through the Boston Theological Institute, I took a course called *The Theology of Sexuality* with Professor Carter Heyward, PhD at the *Episcopal Divinity School* (EDS). Carter is a radical feminist. I had never heard feminist rhetoric like I heard in that class, although I had taken many women's studies courses as an undergraduate and studied Feminist Psychotherapy in graduate school.

The instructors and students in this class were ANGRY! At first I was uncomfortable with that, but as the semester went on I began to appreciate their vehemence against the systemic misogyny that exists even after the work of feminists in the 1970's, twenty years earlier. I learned the new lexicon: radical relationships, radical justice, and equal pay for equal work. And, Carter talked about the taboo subject of sexual abuse, with compassion for the victims. It was what I needed to hear.

I decided to take the risk of being in the small group on sexual abuse and violence that was part of the class. When the group identified itself as a group of childhood sexual abuse survivors, I wanted to leave because I felt I didn't belong. The other members assured me that I did. When we talked about making our identity public, I was overwhelmed with shame and voted against it.

I was astonished to find that almost everyone else in the group experienced a similar pain as I did, and that at least four of us spent time in our closets as children, feeling safe in the darkness, contained and soothed. I discovered I'd prefer to see myself as crazy for imagining the horror of being sexually abused as a child, than to believe it truly happened. I was deeply touched by the other group members' stories of childhood sexual abuse. I knew their stories might be my own—yet I didn't want to know.

Here I was at forty-seven years old, an experienced psychotherapist having worked effectively with all kinds of sexual abuse victims, including some men, still lecturing on the domestic violence circuit, and I still could not face the possibility that I might have been molested as a child. I wanted some way out of this without having to go through it.

When the class ended, Carter encouraged me to continue to pursue the memory. She said, "Find a group of women *survivors*. This group needs to be committed to moving beyond experience and feelings of *victimization* and move to empowering one another."

Craig was the only one I trusted to work on these issues. After several sessions with him, I was able to put a few pieces together: The house across the street from this pine grove was owned by a wealthy family. They had an expansive yard, perfectly maintained with lush green grass and flower gardens. A group of three or four neighborhood kids would walk to the pine grove together in the summer, jumping from one spot of shade to another to avoid burning our feet on the black tar road.

One summer, a disheveled, unkempt man appeared as the caretaker of this beautiful yard. He lived on the property in a ramshackle shed and was given three meals a day by the owners. His name was Art.

Art became one of us. He'd bring his lunch over to sit with us and play games, tell us stories and jokes. He wore the same ragged clothes every day and a dirty tan cap. That didn't bother us, but, my mother wasn't happy that he was hanging around with us. She called him a "ne'er do well."

Counseling with Craig, I described all this to him. An image slowly formed. I was about six years old, lying on my back on the bed of pine needles surrounded by tall purring pines, looking up at the sky. At least two of my playmates were lying to my right, and Art was standing in front of us. The child-me was feeling confused, but not fearful. The pine needles were prickling my back. I was afraid to move. That's all I remember.

Art disappeared one day without explanation. Our little band of neighborhood kids was upset by Art's abrupt disappearance.

I've always wondered about the root of my obsession to be pure. I carefully cultivated my ignorance during a time when other teenagers are curious and obsessed with exploring their sexuality. Was the Catholic Church's influence so deeply imbedded in my psyche that I felt impelled to deny my own sexuality? Or had some adverse experience curtailed a natural exploration of my sexual self?

~

That same semester, I was studying *Lamentations* from the Hebrew Bible with an ancient, soft-spoken scholar, Prof. Andrew Stanton, also at the *Episcopal Divinity School*. The class was held in the St. Thomas Memorial Chapel on the EDS campus, a spiraled light-colored stone edifice with magnificent stained glass windows built in 1868. The architecture was that of an English parish church: dark wood pews and soaring wood arches, stone floors and unadorned stone walls. I felt I was walking into another world every time I crossed the threshold. The prayer-soaked walls surrounded me with the sacred, and I instantly went into a state of meditation as I sat on a cold pew before class.

Carter Heyward's *Theology of Sexuality* class was loud, sometimes contentious and often disturbing. In Prof. Stanton's class, by contrast, we spoke one decibel above a whisper as we discussed the anguished cries heard in the psalms of *Lamentations*. How could two such diverse courses overlap?

For me, these psalms were entwined with the cries of all women who had been physically, sexually, emotionally, mentally and spiritually abused. The psalms of *Lamentations* began to inform the first draft of my senior project: *The Impact of Religion and Theology on Battered Women*. The psalms we were studying were usually accepted as the voices of men, but I began to hear different voices—the voices of countless women through centuries from all over the globe. I allowed them to speak through these psalms.

Hearing the Cry

It is not an enemy who taunts me—
I could bear that;
It is not an adversary who deals insolently with me—
I could hide from him.
But, it is you, my equal,
My companion, my familiar friend,
With whom I kept pleasant company;
We walk in the house of God
Together as one.

– (Ps 55:12-14 paraphrased by Kathleen)

The betrayal of a husband's friendship with the onset of abuse proved to be one of the most painful aspects of the abusive relationship for some battered women. At first they were unbelieving—"Oh, he must just be tired or stressed." "He had too much to drink tonight." Or the classic, "I should have gotten dinner on the table on time." Sometimes after the abuse appeared to stop, there was a honeymoon period in which it seemed the *friend* had returned, often with the promise that the abuse would never happen again—only it did.

The effect of this honeymoon period was to lull the female partner into relaxing her guard, and she, wanting so much to believe the man she loved was her friend, would succumb. I, too, had experienced these moments when I thought maybe Stan and I had turned a corner and the nightmare was over. It never was. There is no place to hide as this cycle of abuse plays out again and again, often escalating and, for some women, ending in death. The Psalms continue.

> *Have pity on me, O God, for I am in distress;*
> *With sorrow my eye is consumed;*
> *My soul also and my body.*
>
> *I am like a dish that is broken…*
> *But I put my trust in you, O God;*
> *I say, "You are my God.*
>
> *– (Ps 31:10-15 paraphrased by Kathleen)*

How many times did I cry out to God to help me through those tortuous years of my marriage? From the beginning I assumed there must have been a godly purpose to the ungodly union between Stan and me. I was supposed to love him enough to transform him into a kind-hearted husband and father, a good and decent person. I trusted that God would show me the way.

That was a common assumption for many spiritual and/or religious women I spoke with who found themselves in abusive relationships. Surely God wouldn't let this happen if it didn't serve a higher purpose in the end. Some women assumed they needed to learn to love and forgive. Others thought it was their job to *save* their husbands. And others thought God was testing their faith.

We were all shattered by the abuse *like a dish that is broken* and still we lifted our eyes to heaven and said, "You are my God" until we no longer had the strength to speak at all. I rewrote many psalms that semester, and my professor allowed me to use those sacred songs to express the pain, the outrage, the hopelessness and sorrow of women, including myself, who had said many times, *"My God, My God! Why have you forsaken me?"*

~

I took another class with Professor Demaris Wehr who had become a friend. It was called *Psychology of Healing*. Along with the academic work on the subject, we were required to participate in two forms of alternative healing modalities or traditions. I chose the timeless path of shamanic healing and the new age modality of *Holotropic Breathwork*.

Some of my classmates and I did a two-day workshop with a shamanic healer at her modern home lined with windows and sliding glass doors overlooking twenty acres of untouched land in a suburb of Boston. It was an exquisite day, and spring was manifesting everywhere we looked.

At the beginning of the first day, we formed a circle outside in a field as the Shaman performed a Native American ritual and taught us simple chants. We spent the rest of the morning learning about Native American traditions including journeying to *other worlds*. We ate our lunch outside, learned some more chants and then prepared to journey.

That afternoon we sat on the floor in the huge, uncluttered living room with heavy curtains drawn to block out all light and, again, witnessed a ritual and chanted. We were instructed to lie down and relax as the Shaman began to drum, augmented by a recording of Native American drummers which produced a loud, mesmerizing, rhythmic beat. Most of us soon entered a sonic-driven state of consciousness, while the Shaman gave us instructions to enter the earth through a rabbit hole, a cave, a well or some other point of entry.

As I let go I fell into a dream-like state where there was a rabbit hole. Without fear, I entered the earth through the hole.

Seeing a light shining through the darkness in the distance, I traversed the length of it and scrambled out of the hole and stood up. I looked down at my feet, as we had been instructed to do, and I saw my bare feet in dense grass, strewn with wildflowers—more real than anything I had ever seen.

Beside me was a small multi-colored puppy, black, white and caramel with a sweet face and floppy ears. I was standing in an open field on the side of a mountain, looking over a vast green valley with blue-green mountains surrounding it and a river running through it. The landscape was lush, moist, shimmering.

As I gazed at the vista below me, a bald eagle about three times the normal size swooped down close to me offering its talons so I could hold on and fly. I wanted to go, but I didn't want to leave the puppy behind. The eagle circled back around, and this time, it grabbed onto my outstretched hand while I had the puppy tucked under my other arm. We soared high above the valley, following the river, swinging over the mountains. I can see it now as clearly as I saw it then. It was a profound experience of freedom and beauty. Then, as I faintly heard the Shaman's call to return to normal reality, the eagle swooped over my mountain and gently placed me and the puppy in the grass.

I slipped back into the hole from which I came and slowly re-entered the living room of the Shaman's home. The experience of that journey remains one of my most vivid memories. I was told the puppy and the bald eagle were my power animals, and I feel they have been with me since that day.

As night fell, the Shaman once again led us in drumming and chanting. As we were chanting, I picked up the sound of deep, resonant male voices coming from the outside wall of glass. I couldn't remember if any men had sat on that side of the room. This went on for some time, and I stopped chanting myself so I could listen to these enigmatic voices. When our chanting and drumming came to an end, I was afraid to mention what I thought I'd heard. I looked around the room and the men were scattered through the circle nowhere near the outside wall.

The woman next to me, turned and asked, "Did you hear them?"

"I heard something—like deep male voices."

She said, "Those are the Ancestors. They always come when the Shaman leads a circle. This was once Native land and burial grounds."

Energy was coursing through my body that night and I couldn't sleep. The next morning we opened with the ritual and chanting and then settled in to make prayer pouches. We worked in silence as we took small circles of colored cloth and put a pinch of tobacco in the center and then tied it with red string to make a chain of pouches. As we made each pouch, we prayed for someone or something. These pouches were made to bring into the sweat lodge that afternoon where they'd be blessed to enhance their power.

Migraines were still plaguing my daily life and, in part, I had taken this course in hopes of stumbling upon a cure for them. I participated in the building of the sweat lodge on this unusually warm spring day and pushed aside the warning signals of an impending migraine. In the late afternoon we took our places on the ground in the pitch dark sweat lodge surrounding the hissing, steaming stones that were heated in the fire and wetted down over and over again. Prayers, songs and drumming filled the smoky air. It was unbearably hot, and my heart was racing and my head was beginning to pound. We stepped outside for a few minutes and then re-entered the lodge.

After the third mini-break, I told the Shaman, who also was a medical doctor that I was getting nauseous and thought I should stay out. She said that was a common reaction and to just throw up in the lodge if I had to. I was appalled by this thought, and I knew I was headed for trouble, but I went back in anyway.

At the next break, I could hardly stand up. I adamantly refused to go back into the lodge. A friend took one look at me and offered to take me home. I had a migraine that lasted a week and was too sick to go to work or classes. I had not listened to my own sense of what my body needed.

In spite of that inauspicious ending, I came away with a new appreciation of the multidimensional world of indigenous cultures. Soon another song tumbled out of the cosmos with a melody and rhythm reminiscent of the chants we had sung that weekend.

~

The Holotropic Breathwork workshop was held in a school gym with gleaming hardwood floors, folded dark green bleachers lining the walls, and sounds echoing in a cacophony. About thirty to forty people spread blankets on the floor. The instructors taught a breathing technique that when done properly would lead to hyperventilation.

The theory behind this practice is that through the breathing technique and the loud sonic-driven impulses of the rhythmic beat of drums, a non-ordinary state of consciousness is induced. This leads to accessing different levels of unconscious in-utero and birth-related imprints and memories. We were told it might lead to spiritually transcendent experiences and the healing of emotional, psychological and physical wounds from the past.

Instructed to pair up, my friend, Joyce, and I became partners. When it was my turn, Joyce sat beside me, and encouraged me to do the breathing and just let go. The music pounded through my body as I diligently tried to breathe correctly. Nothing happened. Then, I felt the presence of light on my right. It moved up my right hand and arm, which began to shake.

Finally, I decided nothing else was going to happen, so I just stopped trying and lay there. I noticed a small pain between my shoulder blade and my spine. I asked Joyce to put some pressure on that spot. Before she even had a chance to do that, the pain in my belly, which I had been dealing with in sessions with Craig, began to throb. I was quickly pulled into blackness, terror and confusion.

Joyce signaled one of the leaders, Sandy, and she was beside me in an instant. Joyce told her what was happening, and Sandy put some pressure on my belly, talking to me soothingly, telling me to let go and let it happen. She asked if I had experienced this before, and I said it was old, and I had been working on it in co-counseling sessions. I heard the music change to indicate it was time to end the session. I was struggling to come back into present reality when Sandy suggested Mary-Lou, the other leader join us, and the two of them would help me work through the pain.

Mary-Lou questioned me again if I really wanted to work with this. When I said I did, she pressed hard on my belly and both women jumped on top of me. Pinned to the floor, I experienced a pain and terror which was familiar. I pleaded and tried to get them off me. A part of me said, "This is therapeutically inappropriate!" Then something inside me got very quiet and I heard, "But this is exactly how it was."

At that point I became enraged and began fighting them off. I screamed for help, yelling at them to get off me. I was furious. I fought and fought. They gave me nothing. I had to win back every inch of my body. I almost gave up in exhaustion, but all three of them yelled, "Don't give up! Don't give up! You can do it!" I got another wave of strength and pushed them off me with a roar.

It was a powerful moment. My body pulsed with energy. I knew I owned every cell of my body again for the first time since I was very young. It was an unbelievable feeling which lasted for days. And, although I crashed a few days later, I realized it was like when I learned to ride a bike. I remembered there was a moment when I got my balance for the first time and rode alone for a few feet before I crashed. Even though I crashed, now I knew the feeling I was going for. I knew what it felt like to be in balance, and I knew I could do it again.

Although I still did not know what had happened to me as a child, I knew this experience was connected to Stan's raping me. I felt empowered to deal with any intrusion on my boundaries in the future. The belly pain disappeared and has never returned.

~

I've often said to my therapy clients that life proceeds in an upward spiral. We keep going around the same issues, but never from exactly the same place. I hoped that after this empowering experience, I'd never again betray my own intuitive knowing. This was an unrealistic expectation. About six months later, in the fall of 1992, relentless migraines drained me of strength. I dragged myself through the day. I wanted to sprint toward graduation, not haul myself inch by inch to the finish line.

I had spent the last year writing my senior project that had eventually turned into a training program for chaplains and health care workers on how to help battered/abused women. I was presenting this training all over Boston and was scheduled to present a day-long workshop to the *New England Clinical Pastoral Education Board*. Somehow I'd muster the internal resources to stand before a group and present an impassioned program about addressing the needs of this population who were just beginning to be visible. The toll each presentation took on my body would leave me wrung out and in pain for days.

After one such presentation, I made an appointment with a healer who came highly recommended by a friend. He was about an hour outside of Boston. My head was pounding with a migraine when I started out to see him that morning. Bradley Ray, the healer, owned a small rustic health food store lined with hanging herbs and shelves of apothecary jars. The store was dark, crowded, with a low unfinished wood ceiling, exposed beams and dirty small-paned windows.

I walked in and Brad greeted me exuberantly. After I told him about my deteriorating health, he said, "I know I can help you, but you'll have to follow my instructions exactly." Red flags went up immediately!

Several of Brad's regular customers came in while he and I were talking, and he introduced us. One said, "Listen to Brad! He knows his stuff. He's a real healer." Brad began telling story after story of the people he had helped.

I stood there wanting to lie down, my head pounding, the nausea getting worse with each passing minute. Smiling wanly, I thanked the customer for his advice, wishing he would leave. Finally, Brad and I are alone again, and he lays out his plan for my healing regime. I have to get off all my medications even the antidepressants that have been keeping me stable. I have to eat nothing but leafy greens, lima beans and peas. And, I have to take the herbs he prescribes.

"This is not going to work for me," I think. I thank him for the information and tell him I'll get back to him with my decision. By now, I can barely stand upright, and I have an hour drive to get home. About ten miles down the road, I can barely see. I notice an Urgent Care facility on my right. Turning into what I think is its parking lot I land in the next driveway.

There is a stretch of grass between me and my destination. When I get out of the car, I cannot stand up, so I crawl across the grass to the entrance of the Urgent Care. I pull myself up on the stair rail and enter the office on my feet. The nurse at the front desk takes one look at me and says, "Migraine?" I nod my head slightly fearing if I open my mouth I will vomit.

This petite gray-haired woman, Maggie, gently ushers me into a dark examining room and settles me on the examining table. She asks a few questions and says, "The doctor will be right in to see you." Expecting a long wait, the doctor surprises me when he walks in a few minutes later.

He speaks to me softly. His words are kind and soothing. "I have migraines myself," he says. "We're going to take care of you. I'm going to give you a shot and then you can lie here as long as you need to."

Three hours later I wake up pain free. The nurse peeks in and goes to get the doctor. I don't even know this man's name, but he talks to me for twenty minutes about migraines. "We still have a long way to go in knowing how to treat migraines," he says, "but there is hope on the horizon. The shot I gave you is effective, and eventually people will be able to self-administer it, but it does nothing to interrupt the migraine cycle."

I thank the doctor for his help and say, "I'll never forget your kindness!"

When I get to the front desk to pay for my visit, Maggie looks up smiling and says, "There'll be no charge for today." I burst into tears with relief! Money is tight, and I was getting nauseous again at the thought of paying for a three-hour treatment. Maggie and I hugged—I will never forget her either.

The good doctor's words hadn't left me with much hope about the medical profession's efficacy in treating migraines. I called Brad and told him I'd try his regime, although I was apprehensive about not taking the antidepressants. I talked to my psychiatrist, and he wasn't happy about my decision but he told me how to go off the medication safely. I began eating a diet of greens, lima beans (which I hate) and peas, and took the herbs Brad prescribed.

This regime didn't eradicate the migraines, but it lessened their length and severity. The tradeoff was an escalation of depressive symptoms: feelings of hopelessness, worthlessness, dark imaginings, lack of vitality or interest in things I usually enjoyed, welling up with unbidden tears in inappropriate settings, and, eventually, suicidal ideation. Four months of following Brad's supposedly curative regime, I was almost incapacitated by depression once again.

This time Craig was not there for me. He had gone to live with his sister in California for nine months to finish his thesis. He had promised to keep in close contact while he was gone. Soon his calls were infrequent. I told myself he was just immersed in writing.

I returned to my psychiatrist and began to rebuild my brain chemistry with medications. It was a slow process, and I was struggling through my last semester at HDS. In March, a new friend, Victoria, came from Vermont to visit me for my birthday. Vicky had graduated from HDS a few years before and was the pastor of a small Church. Just before she was about to leave, she pulled out a *Quest* magazine and showed me the back cover. She said, "Look at this!" The back cover announced:

1993 The Parliament of the World's Religions,
August 28-September 5, 1993
Chicago, Illinois, USA

Then it listed some of the attending dignitaries:

Mother Teresa—Catholic
H.H. The Dalai Lama—Buddhist
H.H. Swami Chidananda Sarawati—Hindu
Rabbi Heman Schaalman—Reform Judaism
Cardinal Bernadin—Catholic
Shaikh Kamel al-Sharif—Sunni Muslim

Mata Amritanandamayi—Hindu

Brahma Kumari Dadi Prakashmani—Brahma Kumaris

The Rev. Dr. James A. Forbes, Jr.—Christian (Protestant)

Dr. Wilma Ellis—Baha'i

Thich Nhat Hanh—Buddhist

Mr. Alfred Yazzie—Native American (Navajo)

H.E. Dr. L.M. Singhvi—Jain

As I read the list, the hair on my arms stood straight up. Almost in a whisper, I said to my friend, "I have to be there!" It was an absurd assertion. I had no money. Graduation was less than ten weeks away. I was looking for a job. Vicky prayed over me in a soothing voice that somehow this desire would be fulfilled. After she left, I dove back into my research for the papers that were due before graduation.

When my tax return of $300.00 came in April—the exact amount I needed to cover registration and airfare—I immediately called Vicky for registration information for the Parliament. The registration fee was $90 for nine days with the most eminent religious leaders in the world. I took what was left of the refund and found a discounted flight to O'Hare and booked it. I could not think beyond that. I had too much to do to finish the semester and prepare for graduation. But, I knew in my heart I would attend the *Second Parliament of the World's Religions*.

Love is quiet and gentle.
Love is fierce and strong.
Love is Spirit Eternal
Blessing you all life-long

– Excerpt of a song by Kathleen

CHAPTER THIRTY-SEVEN
Good-bye Sweet Friend

CRAIG RETURNED from California while I was finishing up the semester. It took several days after his return for him to contact me. He didn't sound like himself on the phone, and he said, "We need to talk."

"Of course! I can't wait to see you!"

"Perhaps we should talk right now," he said, his voice more somber than I'd ever heard it.

"Sure. What's going on?"

"While I was away, Angela and I began to correspond and talk on the phone." Angela was one of the students in our co-counseling class before Craig left.

"Oh?"

"We've fallen in love."

After a long pause, "I see."

My heart stopped. Everything stopped. *My breath came short and scarce at all*—a line from Millay's poem.

Silence.

"Kath, I want to see you and talk with you. I knew this would be hard for you. When can we meet?"

After six years of faithfully keeping the no socializing rule which forbids peer-counselors to have personal relationships—which Craig insisted we adhere to—he had been socializing with one of our students for the last nine months. I began to shake uncontrollably. Anger. Betrayal. Disbelief. Heart break. I was about to lose control, and I didn't want to do it with Craig on the other end of the line.

"Craig, I have to go. I'll call you later, and we'll set up a time."

Home by myself, I let the dam break, sobbing, screaming, retching, drenched in sweat. Finally exhausted, I looked up and realized the apartment was totally dark except for the street lights shining through the window. I fell asleep on the couch and woke at dawn, feeling hollowed out.

Craig and I met the next day at my place. We hugged. I could not contain my tears. My words came slowly. "Craig, I'm happy for you and Angela. I've wanted this for you for a long time. But, I've honored your need for strict adherence to the no socializing rule for all these years, then you blatantly break them with her. And, you were her teacher—we've stood up against this in Peer Counseling United for years."

He was silent.

"I can't do this anymore, Craig. This is it. I need to break off all connection with you. But, I hope you know I will love you forever."

"Kath, let's have a session with another counselor and work this out. We've been here before, and we came through it. Don't give up on us, our teaching, the years we've put into this relationship."

"My mind is made up. No calls, no letters, no contact. I'm sorry it has to be like this."

"You know I'll respect your wishes. But I don't want this. Just know you can contact me at anytime. I'll always be here for you." He looked ashen, anguished; tears streamed down his face.

Our good-bye was wrenching. We held onto each other for a long time, then we slowly and reluctantly let go. Both crying, I shut the door behind him. Grief poured out of me.

When we parted, I agreed that Craig should take over as leader of the International Counseling Network and teach the classes himself. This meant I not only lost him but the community of counselors with whom we'd been working for several years. I knew I wasn't in an emotional state to lead or teach a vibrant, growing community. I was exhausted, physically and emotionally, and there were challenges ahead in the next stretch of my life.

The adjustment was difficult. A huge chunk of my life had fallen away. There was no time for mourning. Papers due, finals looming, I threw myself into academics and into preparing for two graduations—mine and Debbie's.

~

A word about my propensity to become enamored and, sometimes, fall in love with unattainable men who treated me kindly and with respect: my hunger for connection and positive regard from men ran deep. Being deprived of affection and tenderness in my marriage made me more susceptible to men who treated me well.

But, even deeper, was my experience of men as a child. My father was indifferent to my existence, and I was surrounded by these handsome, brilliant brothers—who were the equivalent of movie stars to me. I was always disdainful of my friends swooning over the latest male celebrity, but I was no different—my brothers, who loved me dearly, were larger than life. They were young adults when I was born, launching themselves into the world. I wanted to be noticed by them, paid attention to and valued for who I was, but their visits were brief and full of adult activities. My bond with each of them grew with the years and, I know now, how much they loved, respected and appreciated me.

~

My Master's Project, *The Impact of Religion and Theology on Battered Women: A Seminar for Hospital Chaplains Ministering to Women*, was a work fueled by my passion to make a difference in the lives of women, to redeem the lost years of my relationship with Stan, to perform alchemy that would transform years of abuse into wisdom, compassion and understanding. Rev. Katherine James, Rev. Dudley Rose, Prof. Harvey Cox, and Prof. Demaris Wehr guided, cajoled and encouraged me as I struggled to complete this project. Many others gave tangible hands-on help editing the manuscript. My friend, Ruth typed it for me—all sixty pages.

My supervisor, Kate, stood by my side as I presented the full day seminar to the *Board of the New England Association for Clinical Pastoral Education*. Clinical Pastoral Education (CPE) is the official training program for chaplains. The people I spoke to that day were the ones who trained the trainers of chaplains in New England.

I told my own story and the stories of other women whom I'd worked with over the years, disguising their names and details. I addressed many issues including the most asked question: Why do women stay?

I spoke about the theological and spiritual issues such as: Does a woman's faith inform her understanding of her wifely role? And, how? And, to those who minister to women: How can we identify victims of abuse and minister to them effectively?

What strategies can we offer to keep these women safe including connecting them to resources that can help them? How do we address issues of faith when often a woman's religious/spiritual beliefs have given her strength to survive in an abusive relationship and also dictate that she stays in the marriage? And, what about the children?

I questioned: Why do we ask the question "why do women stay?" and not the question "why do men batter?" My audience was rapt. Quiet. Reflective. Respectful.

Although it was difficult for me to stand up before thirty chaplains and clergy, mostly male, to speak on the subject of domestic violence and about my own personal experience of abuse, I knew the information I was sharing with them that day would have an impact that would reverberate through generations of chaplains, making a difference in the lives of women they served. I never again thought of myself as a victim of abuse but as one who took that experience and transformed it. I had completed and presented my Project and felt honored that it could better the lives of women and men who are or have been victims of domestic violence.

~

Leaving Harvard Divinity School was another loss. HDS had become my community, a container for my passions, curiosity, creativity and sense of self. Who was I if I wasn't a student at one of the most prestigious divinity schools in the nation? I was about to become a part-time staff chaplain at Brigham and Women's Hospital, but it was not full-time employment; I planned to start my search for a permanent position after graduation. Putting that concern aside for now, my computer beckoned me to finish my papers. Again, they fell onto the page and were well received by my professors.

Finals were held in the cavernous high-ceilinged *Great Hall* of the Victorian Gothic *Memorial Hall* in Harvard Yard that echoed with clamoring chairs and the nervous voices of hundreds of students taking a multitude of different tests at the same time. The first time I took finals in this room, my shaky handwriting in the blue test booklets betrayed my anxiety. Overcome by the noise and the vastness of this imposing setting that dated back to the Civil War, I felt dwarfed by the revered company of those who came before me at Harvard and inadequate to the task of living up to their legacy.

Now, I strode into the room with a sense of place and belonging no matter what the outcome of the exams. I was two weeks away from being a Harvard Divinity School Graduate. Nothing could erase the fact that I had spent three years of my life walking this campus, attending classes and lectures in these esteemed halls, praying in the Chapel, eating with friends in the Refectory, spending hours in the library and bookstore.

I had rarely felt as proud as I did in those weeks before graduation. The program had been challenging and my life had been equally so, but I had persevered. I was certain that a Masters of Divinity from Harvard Divinity School would open doors to a rewarding, secure position as a Chaplain.

Invitations went out to family and friends for a graduation celebration for Debbie and me. Because of our small numbers, Harvard Divinity School graduates of 1993 were allotted a generous number of tickets for the graduation, so a contingency of fifteen of my family and friends arrived on campus to witness the ceremony on a sun-drenched day under a cerulean blue sky.

It was one of the happiest days of my life. My sister, Jules, and several of her children were present, and my brother, Pete, drove from Long Island to Boston to be there. Dee, my PCU friend from Sheffield, and two of her children, came. All my children and my granddaughter, Amelia, arrived from New Hampshire. I knew my sweet friend, Ann, was there in spirit—immensely proud of me—even as she lay bound to her bed beyond reach.

The Divinity School campus was tucked away from the main campus. A buffet luncheon awaited us inside *Andover Hall*, and then we prepared to line up for the procession to the tent under which our family and friends were already seated.

We solemnly and slowly marched to the beat of *Pomp and Circumstance* and were enthusiastically greeted by those loved ones who had cheered us on for the past three years. I could not contain my tears of joy and was grateful I hadn't put on any mascara! It was a simple, touching ceremony. As I walked across the platform to receive my diploma from the Dean, cheers erupted loudly from the corner of the tent where my family and friends were on their feet acknowledging my achievement. The moment was everything I hoped it would be and much more.

After the ceremony, we all went back to my apartment for the party. Debbie's friends joined us—they'd graduated a few nights before. We celebrated our two graduations well into the night: an Italian feast, home-baked goodies, music, and memories. None of my past graduations had this sense of triumph for me, perhaps because this time I had returned to school for my own love of learning—not as a route of escape.

~

The distractions of school and preparations for graduation filled my days following Craig's departure. Now, without those pressures, my grief broke open. Never before had I felt as seen and cared for by a man, as valued and esteemed. Craig believed in me: my intelligence, my leadership, my ability to make a difference in the world. And, he articulated how he saw me in a way that I could see myself, and I began to believe in what he saw. He expressed his affection openly with his huge smile and warm hugs each time we greeted each other or said good-bye.

I ached for his touch. I longed to hear the sound of his voice, to see him walking towards me, to sob in his arms with the grief of losing him. I knew I could pick up the phone and call him at any time to end this moratorium on our relationship, and he would be back by my side in an instant. But, I also knew this would not end my pain. A song poured out of me.

Good-bye, Sweet Friend

My thoughts are filled with all I know of you
Your smile, your voice, all that is good and true
The songs you sing, the words I'd never heard
The hope you bring for a better world.

The memories of all the joys we shared
And of hard times when you were always there
I cherish these sweet loving memories
And so I hold you very close to me.

I look within, my heart is filled with you.
I look without, there is no sign of you.
I know that now it must be time to part,
Although I know it will break my heart.

Our souls entwined will dance the skies at night
And by the day embrace in Holy Light
But on this earth we will not meet again
And so I say good-bye to you, Sweet Friend

But on this earth we will not meet again
And so I say good-bye to you, Sweet Friend.

– Song by Kathleen

~

After writing this piece about Craig, twenty-three years after our parting, a pall fell over me. The old deep longing returned. I took it into a recent therapy session. Always asserting my relationship with Craig was purely platonic, I finally admitted I had been and will always be in love with him. My therapist encouraged me to look at what Craig had offered me—a safe place to explore and heal the abuse I had endured. His words sank deeper than knowing—into the deepest recesses of my heart. I knew they were true. And, I knew Craig had given me the greatest gift of all—myself.

May all Beings be well
May all Beings be happy
Peace, Peace, Peace

– Buddhist Falling in love with-Kindness Blessing

CHAPTER THIRTY-EIGHT
May All Beings Be Happy

IT BECAME EVIDENT that I needed to move once more. The apartment I had shared with Debbie was too big and expensive for me to maintain. Debbie had been accepted at University of Massachusetts in Amherst, thanks to her hard work and her school counselor's heroic efforts. She would be leaving in August. It was time to go apartment hunting again.

I found a tiny apartment on the third floor of a brick building closer to the center of Brookline. I liked the location and the huge windows in the living room that opened my world to the tree tops and the sky. The day I moved in, my daughter, Rachel, helped me. My three year old granddaughter, Amelia, came, too. As night began to fall, I looked up through the un-curtained window and called to her, "Come see my moon, sweetheart." She came to the window, looked up, hands on hips, and said, "No, Nonni! That's MY moon!" I wanted to be like my granddaughter—so certain of her place in the universe, self-assured, full of spirit!

Facing the reality of my financial situation after graduation, I went back to doing secretarial work at Mass General Hospital while working part-time as a chaplain, and I began to focus on the upcoming Parliament of the World's Religions in Chicago at the end of the summer. My spirits lifted as I shifted my gaze from my loss of Craig to the exciting adventure on which I was about to embark.

A series of small miracles unfolded as the time drew nearer for my departure. I needed to find a place to stay. Hotels were out of the question—too expensive. Thanks to a friend's suggestion, I secured a room in a suite with a kitchen at the University of Chicago for $90.00 for all nine days. I asked about transportation to the Palmer House and was told, "There's a train that goes from the University into downtown Chicago. You just have to walk a short way to catch it." Everything was falling into place.

My friend, Vicky, who had alerted me to this event, was also making plans to attend. She coordinated her flight from Vermont to arrive at O'Hare Airport shortly after I arrived from Boston. I wasn't sure how we were going to find each other in the humongous airport, but I left that in the hands of the angels. As my departure date grew closer, I once again looked at my finances. I had put aside the $70.00 I owed for my room after sending a deposit of $20. I had $30.00 for buses or trains and tips, but I had not budgeted for food. I knew I would have to eat out at least once a day. Too embarrassed to mention this to anyone, I planned to buy a few groceries when I arrived there, including food to pack my lunch.

One afternoon, two weeks before the Parliament, I went to my mailbox and found a white envelop without a return address. Curious, I opened it. As I lifted the flap, the green pattern showing in the V of the envelope was unmistakably U.S. currency. As I slipped the bill out, I gasped! It was a hundred dollar bill. I looked for an accompanying note. There was none.

I tried to decipher the handwriting on the front of the envelope—I didn't recognize it. I smiled and said, "Thank you, Angel, whoever you are!" To this day, I do not know who sent that money.

~

In the early morning on August 28, 1993, I boarded the plane to Chicago at Logan Airport in Boston with one carry-on suitcase. I enjoyed flying, so the anxiety I felt had nothing to do with being in the air. There were just too many unknowns. I had no idea what awaited me on the ground at this event. The thought of taking the train back and forth to the Palmer House hotel, where the event was being held, made me nervous. Would I be able to find my way around Chicago? Who would my suite-mates be? Would I be safe?

Reminding myself that I'd jumped into unknown territory before, I settled in my seat to enjoy the takeoff. I relished the feeling of the plane lifting off the ground into the air—it always feels like a miracle that this huge chunk of metal could climb into the sky above the clouds.

When I disembarked at O'Hare, I found my way to the Gate where Vicky was arriving. I had to wait one level below and sat on a bench in a huge rotunda. The floor above formed a balcony circling it, and soon I looked up and saw my friend waving at me.

Vicky had made arrangements to stay with a friend not far from the event. She was being picked up. I had to find my way to the right train to get to my accommodations and settle in before I had to go back for the opening ceremonies that afternoon. When I inquired at the information desk as to which train I should take to get to the University of Chicago, the woman just shook her head. "Do you know how far that is?" she asked.

"Not really," I said tentatively. "How far is it?"

"It's almost an hour ride."

My heart sank. "Ok," I said to myself, "let's just do it." The woman at the desk gave me detailed directions and wished me well. I found my train, boarded and sat in a window seat. I watched the stunning city fly by as we skimmed alongside Lake Michigan into the less glamorous and poorer parts of the city. When my stop appeared, I realized it was in a desolate run-down area. I had to walk under a railroad bridge with trash and broken glass everywhere. Terrified, I walked quickly as if I knew exactly where I was going. I found my way to a more populated area, although still very shabby, and asked directions to the University.

My heart was still pounding when I finally reached my destination. I stopped at the housing office and paid what was due and got the keys. The building that housed the suite was a three-story, turn-of-the century, maroon shingled edifice. It looked decrepit on the outside but, as I opened the door, I was relieved to find it was clean, although sparsely furnished. Several people in the kitchen welcomed me and introduced themselves. They were students and hadn't even heard of the Parliament of the World's Religions taking place in their city.

I excused myself and opened the door to my room, narrow and small with a high ceiling and two large windows that looked out onto the street. It was painted chalk white, trimmed in dark green. The worn wood floor creaked. A single bed stacked with clean sheets and a green plaid wool blanket was on the far wall between the two windows. A small chest of drawers and a chair stood to the right of the door. Reminiscent of my cell in the convent, the room was perfect.

I put my things away and sat on the bed. How was I going to do this? I couldn't walk to and from the train in the dark—too dangerous. I wanted to cry. Instead, I decided I had to turn around and go back into the city. Then, on my return, I could get off a few stations before my stop and get a taxi the rest of the way even if I had to use my food money. Some of my enthusiasm had faded, but I showered, changed, ate some crackers and peanut butter I had stashed in my suitcase and started out the door.

Walking back under the trestle bridge, I could see a couple of people waiting for the train. I wavered between feeling relieved and being nervous. They were both men. One nodded to me slightly as I approached the platform and turned his eyes back to the track. I felt it was a signal that everything was ok, and I let out a deep sigh.

It was a ten-minute walk from the train to the Palmer House. My eyes widened in amazement as I walked into the lobby of the hotel. I'd never seen a more ornate, opulent, luxurious hotel. It dated back to Victorian times with elaborately carved furnishings, lush brocade upholstery and curtains, elegant paneling, and magnificent chandeliers hanging from brightly painted ceilings. The hotel was buzzing with excitement.

Everywhere I looked a diversity of people, colors, clothing, languages and smells spun around me. There were Jains in their white robes, turbans and mouth-coverings which they wore to prevent even the tiniest creatures from flying into their mouths risking death. The Jains, like the Hindus and Buddhists, practice the philosophy of *ahisma,* the sacredness of and non-violence toward all living beings—which extends to the avoidance of harm and violence to even miniscule forms of life.

Eastern Orthodox Bishops, in their elegant embroidered garments, and Orthodox Jewish Rabbis, in black suits and hats, prayer shawls, with beards and side locks, mingled with Catholic monks with shaved heads, in leather sandals and coarse brown cassocks. Long rosary beads beat a rhythm as they moved. Representatives of the Wiccan tradition, some in elaborate costumes, wandered through the halls. Native Americans in full regalia gathered in small circles talking, drumming and chanting. There was only one elevator in the main hallway of the hotel and, as I stepped in, this crush of sacred diversity engulfed me.

Since I was about two hours early for the opening program, I decided to find out where I was supposed to be. Most of the over 8,000 participants were staying at the Palmer House or other hotels in the vicinity, so many seemed already familiar with their surroundings. Signs led me to a huge room on the second floor set up with long tables for registration and information about the Parliament.

At the registration table, I was given a sturdy blue envelope with a famous Norman Rockwell print on the front cover—an iconic image of diversity in America. The envelope contained all I needed to know about the schedule, the keynote speakers, the break-out sessions, restaurants, bathrooms and, most importantly, the location of the meditation room.

I went to check it out. It was a large, high ceilinged, square room, with dark paneling and a massive fireplace with an elaborately carved white mantel. The lights were dimmed, and it was difficult to make out who was in the already crowded room. I saw white turbans of Jains and Sikhs, women in saris, and the saffron monastic robes of Buddhist monks dotting the area. Muslims had laid out their tightly woven prayer rugs in the middle of the floor and were prostrating themselves in the direction of Mecca. Catholic priests and other clergy dressed in black, disappeared against the dark paneling except for the white collar at their throats.

There were cushions, blankets, and pillows strewn across the dark wood floor. The silence was vibrating with energy. I grabbed a round cushion and a little piece of wall and sat in the vibrant energetic soup all around me.

The Opening Ceremony would start in an hour. I decided to find the best seat in the mammoth hall where it was to be held—a huge ornate, gold-gilded auditorium with multiple entrances of cream-colored double doors. Pockets of people were scattered about in small groups. Many seats had already been saved. I wandered around and tried one seat, then another, and another—not knowing why I kept moving. Finally, I sat on an aisle seat about twenty rows back from the right side of the stage. Again the feeling: This is perfect!

I turned to the man sitting next to me on the left and noticed his name tag, which said, "Winn McIntosh" and identified him as belonging to the "Federation" of something I can't remember. I introduced myself and asked about the Federation. He was very congenial and said, "Oh, don't bother about that. My wife and I are Baha'is." He introduced himself and his wife, Nancy.

I exclaimed, "Baha'is! Oh, how wonderful!"

Winn smiled, slightly amused by my reactions. "You know about Baha'is?"

"Oh, yes!" I replied. "I'm a friend of the Baha'is, and back home I am the counselor for many in the Baha'i Community on the seacoast of New Hampshire. I participate in their devotions, Firesides, Race Unity Day. Now I know why I chose this seat!!"

Both Nancy and Winn were in their sixties, from the Midwest. We continued our conversation, sharing how we came to be at the Parliament. I recounted all the small miracles that had to happen to get me there, "But," I said, "The only thing that hasn't worked out that well is my getting to and from the Palmer House. I'm all the way out at the University of Chicago and taking the train is pretty scary, especially at night."

They laughed in unison. "We're staying out there, too," Winn chuckled, "and we have a car! We'll see to it that you get back and forth every day!" I was awe-struck by the synchronicity of my choosing that seat after trying so many others. And, as unlikely as it may seem, I spotted my friend, Vicky, in a room that held 5,000 people. We waved to each other as the music began for the Opening Ceremonies.

~

Solemn, majestic baroque music performed by *Music of the Baroque Chorale and Orchestra,* filled the vast space of what was called *The Great Ballroom.* Following that performance, the *Drepung Loseling Tibetan Monks,* in their saffron robes and elaborate gold-feathered headpieces, began to chant in their deep resonant voices, accompanied by twelve-foot-long Himalayan horns with an ear-shatteringly low timbre, high trumpets, bells, chimes and drums. Vibrations reverberated in my body as I was transported into an exotic, mysterious world.

When the lights dimmed and the music faded, the Native American Singers began to process into the Great Hall, chanting and drumming their way to the stage. They took their places and continued to provide the music for the solemn procession down the three middle aisles of the ballroom: 600 dignitaries and individuals representing over 250 traditions. I was filled with a sense of awe as I witnessed this moment in history.

Jewish and Islamic leaders walked side by side. Native Americans, who had been banned from the first Parliament in 1893 because they were considered *heathens,* took a prominent role at this Parliament in 1993. Islam, which had been represented by one American convert in the previous Parliament, had a contingency of representatives from all over the Islamic world. Baha'is and Buddhists, introduced to Americans for the first time a century ago at the First Parliament, were now organizers and major contributors to this event.

About thirty seats on stage began to fill with dignitaries dressed in the ceremonial attire of the major religions of the world. I was suspended, barely breathing, afraid I would wake up from this dream. Eight thousand participants in two huge rooms spontaneously held a collective sacred silence as the procession continued.

It seemed everyone was held in suspended animation, absorbing the sights and sounds, the excitement, the energy of this magnificent gathering. This display of unity among such diversity of traditions and cultures was heady stuff. If we could come together in this place and time, united in purpose to bring peace and love to this planet, surely *anything* was possible.

As the last of the processing dignitaries took their seats almost two hours later, the invocations and blessings from eighteen religious leaders of the world's faiths began. Blessings were offered by five Native American elders from the Onondaga, Navajo, Hopi, Crow and Patowatomi tribes, representing the four directions and the center. Cardinal Bernadin, of the Catholic Archdiocese of Chicago; Swami Chidananda Saraswati, a Hindu leader from India; representatives of different Christian denominations; Unitarian Universalists; Jewish Rabbis and Scholars; Zoroastrians, Baha'is, Buddhist, Muslims, Jains, Wiccan and others offered invocations or blessings in the voice and language of their faith traditions. Although these prayers were raised in different tongues, they expressed common hopes and ideals: peace, justice, and compassion.

After a welcome address and introduction by my esteemed teacher, Professor Diana Eck, Sri Chinmoy, a world famous Indian spiritual leader and peace activist, walked to the middle of the stage in a light blue silk Chinese style tunic and pants to lead us in a meditation. His hands in prayer position, standing perfectly still he lowered his eyes and bowed his head. I waited for this great spiritual leader to utter the words that would take us all into a deep meditative state.

Then it dawned—THIS IS the meditation. Stillness and silence deepened with each passing second—soon 8,000 of us were breathing one breath, hearts beating in unison. I believe that initial meditation profoundly bonded the diverse community of the Parliament for the next nine days.

Awestruck by Robert Muller's insightful and visionary keynote address, *Interfaith Harmony and Understanding*, describing his dream of a World Spiritual Center, I succumbed to travel fatigue. After the third respondent, Winn suggested we should leave to get a good night's sleep. Filled with gratitude for both the ride and the suggestion, I fell asleep in the back seat as Winn found the way through the streets of Chicago. Winn and Nancy assured me they'd pick me up at 8:00am so we could get some breakfast and explore the city before the morning program started. It appeared they had adopted me!

The 150 page catalogue we were given at registration listed an overwhelming array of programs. The Program Director described the book as containing an "embarrassment of riches." He said, "The catalogue you hold in your hands is simply an extraordinary sampling of human religious and spiritual reflection at the close of the twentieth century."

Our time was filled with choices over the course of the eight remaining days: two dozen major addresses, seminars, classes, musical presentations. These were led by outstanding theologians, religious/spiritual leaders, university professors, researchers, and CEO's of business organizations. It was a daunting exercise to figure out what I was going to do on any given day.

I committed myself to attending the afternoon and evening Plenary Sessions which were rich sources of information, inspiration, music, and performances, ending in the communal prayer of 8,000 people.

One of the first workshops I attended was that of Yogi Bhajan who taught Kundalini Yoga. He was a tall, imposing man dressed all in white with a white turban in the Sikh tradition.

At first I was intimidated by his looks and booming voice, but his smile and warmth won me over. He spoke about the Oneness of all things and urged us to "see God in all." This resonated with my own beliefs. We chanted and learned several mudras, hand positions that enhance concentration and the movement of energy. Yogi Bhajan died the following year. I am grateful I had the chance to experience his teachings.

I arrived early for Thich Nhat Hanh's afternoon talk. I chose a seat in the second row about four seats in from the center aisle. I sat quietly in meditation. When I opened my eyes, I was shocked to find my professor, Diana Eck, sitting beside me! We nodded our greetings honoring the silence. Her eyes shined with excitement.

As Thich Nhat Hanh, the renowned Vietnamese Zen Monk, called Thay (Teacher) by his followers, took his place in front of the audience, three feet from us, she reverently whispered, "This is my guru!" I smiled. I was sitting next to mine.

Thay sat in a state of deep serenity. He spoke slowly with simple eloquence on how to live life mindfully with compassion. The slow pace allowed each word to drop on my consciousness like a flower petal on a pond. Listening to him was a meditation, leaving me in a state of profound peace. His wide smile was a silent blessing, and the kindness in his eyes will always be with me. I felt palpable grace in his presence.

Jean Houston was to present *Ecological Postmodernism: A New Appreciation of the Great Spiritual Traditions,* and the actress, Ellen Burstyn introduced her. Ellen stunned me with her authenticity, insight and depth. She spoke about living from the heart, living in harmony with the earth, living from the center of our being—the All Abiding silence within—the birthplace of compassion and peace. I learned many years later that she had been initiated in the heart-centered tradition of Sufism. Jean Houston's talk, on the other hand, was intellectually stimulating and visionary, but lacked the warmth, simplicity and sincerity of Ellen's.

Riane Eisler, Ph.D. became one of my heroes when I read her book *The Chalice and the Blade* a year earlier. The book explains how we ended up with the patriarchal structure that has perpetuated war throughout millenniums, created the dichotomy of extreme wealth and abject poverty, and brought us to the point of destroying the earth. It describes how we can return to the ways of the peaceful, egalitarian, cooperative societies which once existed around the equator.

Her topic at the Parliament was: *The Return of the Goddess: Ecology, Spirituality and Partnership.* She reawakened the passion of my youth to work for change and sparked my hope for a new world that I had once envisioned before it had been suffocated in disillusionment. I felt invigorated and ready to begin anew to help this change happen.

In talking with some women who identified as Wiccan, I found our beliefs were not radically different. They said my long-held devotion to the Blessed Mother was equivalent to their devotion to the Divine Feminine in whatever form it appears. And, my sense of the Holy in nature and in all I see is aligned with their connection to the natural world. Many were environmentalists, working to restore that which has been destroyed and to stop further destruction of the earth. These women were my sisters.

The program each night had a theme. The theme of one of the most difficult and moving nights was: *The Voices of the Dispossessed*. The participants in this program were to speak about their personal experiences of dislocation against their will within their homeland. These were supposed to be personal stories without reference to the perpetrators or the politics behind the oppression.

The first person to take the stage was a Kashmiri refugee. He stepped up to the microphone and began recounting the Indian government's brutal repression of his people in Kashmir.

We heard a roar as some fundamentalist Hindus rose in unison to protest. Their fury was frightening. Someone said, "I think I see a gun!" Police and Security flooded the room, removed the speaker from the stage and herded the protesting Hindus out of the ballroom.

I ran to the restroom in tears, traumatized by the angry voices. I felt a loss of hope that we'd ever find peace in the world if we couldn't find peace here. I returned to the hall to find a woman had started singing *We shall Overcome* and everyone joined in. Things calmed down.

The announcer returned to the stage and assured us that the next presenter had agreed to adhere to the rules and not politicize his story. The protesting Hindus promised to remain calm. The next speaker, a tall Sikh man from Punjab, made taller by his white turban, stepped onto the podium. The Hindus quietly filed back into their seats. The Sikh began to speak in the same manner as the Kashmiri—telling of the atrocities committed against the Sikhs by the Hindu government of India. The Hindus erupted again more ferociously than before.

This time, as the police were hauling the offending persons out of the ballroom, a tiny Native American woman went to the microphone and, on tiptoes, began to tell her story of being dispossessed in her own land—what was now called "The United States." Her name was Jennie Jim, a Navajo holy woman from New Mexico. She spoke about the tragedy of her peoples' history.

As she spoke with dignity and strength, Native Americans in the audience began drumming and softly chanting. They emerged from every corner of the Great Hall. Some moved onto the stage and others formed a circle around this enormous room, inviting us all to join them. Soon a huge circle of people from all traditions were dancing and chanting. Burton Pretty On Top, a Crow spiritual leader, explained that "the earth itself is a sacred spirit and the circle symbolizes world unity." As peace was restored, he said, "The gift of the circle can unite everyone in the world." Hope tentatively rose up again.

Another night, Louis Farrakhan of the Nation of Islam, commandeered the stage with his armed bodyguards around him. The group of Baha'i youths, who were in charge of planning the evening, naively allowed him to speak when he approached them, saying he just wanted to say a few words. He spewed anti-Semitic rhetoric as Jewish religious leaders angrily filed out of the room. Some refused to return. After speaking for over twenty minutes, Farrakhan finally relinquished the stage.

One of the central goals of *The Second Parliament of the World's Religious* was to create a document called *The Global Ethic*. Each afternoon a group of religious and secular leaders gathered to hammer out an agreement on moral values and ethics shared by all in attendance. The most divisive aspect of their dialogue related to some traditions wanting to eliminate the word *God* from official prayer and communication at the Parliament, and from the *The Global Ethic*. After much discussion, the word *God* was removed to accommodate those traditions that do not believe in a supreme being.

As a result, some Christian Orthodox religions and other groups withdrew. Despite these examples of disharmony I was impressed with the valiant attempt at unity. The Parliament still engendered connection through Interfaith Dialogue and the building of an Interfaith Community of 8,000 people for nine days, even if it sometimes frayed at the edges.

During the nine days of the Parliament, the Dalai Lama seemed to be everywhere. I would catch a glimpse of his saffron robes in a hallway and hear his hearty laugh or see him getting into an elevator surrounded by a group of young monks—shaved heads, flowing robes and broad smiles on their faces. The vibration around him and his entourage was one of joy, good humor and loving kindness—he lived and breathed his message. I felt loved and accepted in his presence even though we never spoke a word or ever got closer than twenty feet from each other.

This was a huge contrast to my experience in the Catholic Church where I'd been taught that my sinfulness was the reason Jesus had died on the Cross.

Yet, here was this saffron robed man beaming love at me, enveloping me in a sense of worthiness and peace. I've had many occasions to be in the presence of the Dalai Lama since then, and each time I am embraced by the palpable stream of love I feel coming from him. I know I will continue to feel that even when he leaves this earth.

~

At the age of three, I sat on the floor crying as I listened to my brother sing *I'll Take You Home Again, Kathleen*. That became my theme song throughout my life! One foot was always ready to step from the earth to a place of peace, my true home. Here, at *The Second Parliament of the World's Religions*, I was walking among spiritual giants, great thinkers, illuminated souls, and everyday people like myself, who were formulating plans for peace and unity.

I sat among peoples of ancient traditions bringing their wisdom and celebration of life into our circle, and 8,000 hopeful hearts prayed together as One. I absorbed this energy that was all around me and felt at home on the planet for the first time in my life. I did not want this to end—ever!

As the event came to a close, a joyous outdoor celebration was held at Grant Park. The Dalai Lama took the stage. As always, a smile on his face and his eyes dancing with humor and joy captivated our attention. His self-deprecating humor about his "broken-English" elicited laughter. He spoke of and exuded Love! I thought, "This is my native tongue—it is the music of my heart!" I was home. I began to call myself a *Jewish Hindu Witch of Italian Catholic descent with Baha'i, Quaker and Sufi leanings and deep respect for indigenous peoples' traditions*. Everywhere was home!

> *Ah, up then from the ground sprang I*
> *And hailed the earth with such a cry*
> *That is not heard save from a man*
> *Who has been dead, and lives again.*
> *About the trees my arms I wound;*
> *Like one gone mad I hugged the ground;*
> *I raised my quivering arms on high;*
> *I laughed and laughed into the sky;*
> *Till at my throat a strangling sob*
> *Caught fiercely, and a great heart-throb*
> *Sent instant tears into my eyes:*
>
> *O God, I cried, no dark disguise*
> *Can e'er hereafter hide from me*
> *Thy radiant identity!*
> *Thou canst not move across the grass*
> *But my quick eyes will see Thee pass,*
> *Nor speak, however silently,*
> *But my hushed voice will answer Thee.*
> *I know the path that tells Thy way*
> *Through the cool eve of every day;*
> *God, I can push the grass apart*
> *And lay my finger on Thy heart!...*

We are One

Epilogue

Dear Readers,

Thank you for journeying with me through the first fifty years of my life. To bring some closure to this book let me give you a glimpse of what has transpired in the past twenty-five years.

As you have read in the last chapter, the 1993 Parliament of World Religions was life-changing for me. After returning home, I boldly claimed my new inclusive identity. I became an Interfaith Minister and officiated at weddings, funerals and other rituals. I maintained my psychotherapy practice and chaplaincy work. I retired at sixty-three, but continued to teach courses on psychology, comparative religions, spirituality and health, and death, dying and grief at local community colleges. Ten years after my divorce, I met a man with whom I had a two year relationship which ended abruptly—a story for another day.

In January 2001, I was hired by a small-town hospital to create a Spiritual Care program and serve as their full time chaplain. This was a dream come true. I became an integral part of the hospital and served on the Domestic Violence Task Force, the Palliative Care Committee and the Ethics Board. I also worked with local faith communities and the Interfaith Council in our area. My love for ministering to terminally ill patients and their families deepened into a passion.

Next, I went to Texas where I was Director of Pastoral Care for five hospitals. That was a challenging position—only seven miles from the border. I was in culture shock. Gunshot wounds, overdoses, victims of violence, and babies with severe birth defects filled my days. It was beyond anything I had seen in the big city hospitals in Boston.

I was diagnosed with bladder cancer in 2003, and was in treatment until 2009. In January of 2010, I was pronounced cancer free. I made the decision to do something I had wanted to do since I was six years old. I had dreamed of making a bus into a home-on-wheels and having someone drive me around the country to find my younger sister Rosie who had died that year. I decided now was the time to take that road trip.

At the age of sixty-six, I packed up my little blue 2001 Ford Focus and began my pilgrimage around the United States. My first stop was Camden, Maine, where I did a silent retreat for five days. Edna St. Vincent Millay had lived there as a young woman when she wrote "Renascence" at the age of nineteen. I climbed Mount Battie, the mountain she had climbed many times, and I saw what she had seen:

> *All I could see from where I stood*
> *Was three long mountains and a wood;*
> *I turned and looked the other way,*
> *And saw three islands in a bay.*

Centered and calm, I was ready for my journey.

During the first few weeks, I traversed through New England and upper New York State. Then I drove north through Pennsylvania and picked up the northern route across the country. I let my heart guide me. Some of my stops were planned, but most were made on a whim as I slowly wended my way to the West coast. I visited my niece and her family in Campbell River, BC, then traveled down the Pacific Coast highway hanging over the ocean. Throughout my travels I stayed at retreat houses of different spiritual traditions, spent time at National Parks I had always wanted to see, and visited family and friends.

On October 15, 2010, I stopped to rest in the little town of Prescott, Arizona. I planned on being back east for Christmas. After two days of exploring the beauty of this mile high town, and encountering its warm and welcoming inhabitants, I knew I *was* home. I called my daughter and told her my plans had changed. I've lived here ever since.

~

Stan, my ex-husband, died in 2012 at the age of seventy-two. He was not a happy man. He continued to sexually harass women until the very end. But, in the years after the divorce, his focus turned to our children and grandchildren, and he made his peace with them. I now refer to him as "the pebble in my oyster shell around which I built a pearl."

If he had been a kind, gentle man like the men with whom I was prone to fall in love, I might have been content to stay at home. However, his abuse sent me into the world to pursue an education that would enable me to leave him. In doing so, my life took on a meaning and purpose beyond anything I could have imagined.

My children have floundered at times, and ultimately, flourished. They are compassionate, wise, loving people, and my two sons-in-law and my daughter-in-law are equally so. Amelia and Bella, my first two grandchildren, are now young women, fulfilling their dreams and beaming their Light into the world. I savor every moment of our time together. And, my oldest son, David, and his wife, Linda, have gifted me with five amazing grandchildren ranging in ages from ten to two-years-old. These darlings bring tremendous joy and love into my life.

Our family has lost three brothers, Jim, Tom, Pete, and his wife, Lisa, who was a sister to me; three nieces and two nephews have died of cancer and my nephew, Stevie, committed suicide—all since 2003. All three of my remaining siblings, Jules, Joseph and Mark, died this year. I am the only one left, out of ten.

Still, every two years, over seventy of us gather for our Marino-Rossi family reunion to continue the family tradition, enjoying good Italian food, music jams, story-telling, memories, and love.

~

One of my clients, who came to me long ago, was the victim of father-daughter incest at a very young age. She told me, "I would stand at the window and look out, repeating over and over again: *There is always hope. There is always hope.*"

May that be the message of this book. We can heal from the abuse and trauma we have experienced. We will be changed. Our healing may lead us down a different path than we had intended to travel, but it will be *our own* path nonetheless.

And, I keep on singing. One of my favorite quotes is by Carl Perkins:

If it weren't for the rocks in its bed, the stream would have no song.

The Japanese tradition of Wabi Sabi celebrates imperfection. When something breaks, instead of discarding it, a repair is made that celebrates the article's singular history by filling the fractures with gold. This often makes the repaired piece more beautiful and valuable than before, giving it new life and purpose.

And so too, we are made stronger, more beautiful and more precious as our cracked places are restored with the support and love of others, with self-compassion and respect for who we are. This is the alchemy of taking our pain and suffering and transforming it into Healing Light for ourselves and for the world.

May it be so.

Kathleen Rossi Marino
Prescott, AZ 2020

Parting Words

Dear Ones,

I am filled with gratitude for you, dear readers. You have lived in my heart for a long time, and I am forever grateful for the inspiration you have given me. It is for you I have spent the past ten years pushing through my resistance to telling the truth. And, it is because of you that this book has manifested and taken on a life of its own. I am thankful for each one of you.

If you have been wounded by life, traumatized, or feel unloved or disassociated from the world (most of us have experienced these things and more), I urge you to take time to heal. This calls for radical self-compassion and self-love. Learn to put yourself first. We betray ourselves if we say "yes" when we want to say "no;" when we defer to others' needs rather than our own; when we constantly put ourselves down or criticize everything we do; when we push ourselves beyond our limits because we don't feel good enough or feel like we have to *earn* the right to live. Discard the old stories and begin to live in the awareness of your own worth.

We expand ourselves when we willingly and lovingly reach out to help others. When we give from a full coffer, and refrain from giving when we ourselves are depleted. We enrich ourselves when we recognize and celebrate others for being who they are and do that for ourselves as well.

Reclaim your childhood wonder, your connection to the earth, your sense of oneness with All That Is. We come into the world as liminal beings—floating between heaven and earth, undifferentiated, feeling no separation between ourselves and those who care for us. We do not individuate until much later. Experiencing even a momentary state of Oneness is our birthright. It is sometimes called bliss or ecstasy or enlightenment.

Lie on the grass and watch the clouds. Allow yourself to drift into reverie and peace. Walk barefoot on the earth. We are energetic beings and the energy of the earth feeds our energy field enhancing our health and sense of well-being. Stop by a stream, the ocean or a placid lake and take in the smells, sounds and beauty of that place. Hug a tree or a child or your beloved pet. Make music or listen to it. Let it seep into your cells. Honor your body with good food, exercise, restful sleep and a playful heart.

Create! Let go of the negative self-talk, the need for perfection. Rejoice in the act of creating. Celebrate your creation. Celebrate the Life you have created! You have woven an exquisite tapestry with your days—the dark strands give depth to this piece of art, the muted colors create the background on which the shining and brilliant colored threads shimmer in the Light, reminding you of the joy you have lived.

Meditate. Pray. Sing. Do what brings you joy and comfort. Walk, run, kayak, do yoga or martial arts or any bodywork—physical activities strengthen you physically, empower you, open your heart, and help to make you flexible and conscious when facing any challenge.

Loss and grief enter every life—if your heart is as heavy as dark clouds full of raindrops, let the tears fall. Talk about the loss of your loved ones, your pets, your dreams. Bring to mind sweet memories and gratitude for your loved one's presence in your life, for the blessings you have received. Never forget the love you shared. And, keep your heart open to love, even at the risk of losing again.

Lastly, nurture your connection with The Holy whatever that may be to you. Beware of cultish and dogmatic teachings, or spiritual leaders that demand complete allegiance to *them* not to a higher good or principle. As my granddaughter Bella wrote when she was twelve years old:

"Find that small river of love, and follow the flow of your own ways."

One friend was a professed atheist. His sustenance came from his connection with nature. My brother's religion was science. He was an avowed atheist, but he came to believe in angels when there was no explanation for why his car stopped abruptly avoiding a catastrophic accident. The Dalai Lama says, "My religion is simple. My religion is kindness." Some have a connection with Jesus, Buddha, Krishna; the Jewish, Christian, Islamic or other religious traditions. Some follow Taoism, Sufism, the Baha'i faith, Quaker or Indigenous Spiritual practices to name but a few. There are a myriad of ways to connect to that which is Holy or Precious to you. As Rumi says:

"Let the beauty we love be what we do.
There are hundreds of ways to kneel and kiss the ground."

Gratitude is a potent spiritual practice. We can find the vein of gratitude in all that we experience: in moments of beauty, discovery and joy; in times of discouragement and despair or when looking at a child's face. Mine the gold of gratitude every day, wherever you are, however you feel.

And, one last note: Nothing you have experienced defines you. From *The Gospel According to Amelia*, I leave you with these words:

You are unique in all the Universe.
You are Love.
You are Joy.
You are Holy and Divine.
I come to remind you.

Blessings and love to all,
Kathleen Rossi Marino

RENASCENCE
Edna St. Vincent Millay, 1892 – 1950

*All I could see from where I stood
Was three long mountains and a wood;
I turned and looked another way,
And saw three islands in a bay.
So with my eyes I traced the line
Of the horizon, thin and fine,
Straight around till I was come
Back to where I'd started from;
And all I saw from where I stood
Was three long mountains and a wood.*

*Over these things I could not see;
These were the things that bounded me;
And I could touch them with my hand,
Almost, I thought, from where I stand.
And all at once things seemed so small
My breath came short, and scarce at all.*

*But, sure, the sky is big, I said;
Miles and miles above my head;
So here upon my back I'll lie
And look my fill into the sky.
And so I looked, and, after all,*

The sky was not so very tall.
The sky, I said, must somewhere stop,
And — sure enough! — I see the top!
The sky, I thought, is not so grand;
I 'most could touch it with my hand!
And reaching up my hand to try,
I screamed to feel it touch the sky.

I screamed, and — lo! — Infinity
Came down and settled over me;
Forced back my scream into my chest,
bent back my arm upon my breast,
And, pressing of the Undefined
The definition on my mind,
Held up before my eyes a glass
Through which my shrinking sight did pass
Until it seemed I must behold
Immensity made manifold;
Whispered to me a word whose sound
Deafened the air for worlds around,
And brought unmuffled to my ears
The gossiping of friendly spheres,
The creaking of the tented sky,
The ticking of Eternity.

I saw and heard, and knew at last
The How and Why of all things, past,
And present, and forevermore.
The Universe, cleft to the core,
Lay open to my probing sense
That, sick'ning, I would fain pluck thence
But could not, — nay! But needs must suck
At the great wound, and could not pluck
My lips away till I had drawn
All venom out. — Ah, fearful pawn!
For my omniscience paid I toll
In infinite remorse of soul.
All sin was of my sinning, all
Atoning mine, and mine the gall
Of all regret. Mine was the weight
Of every brooded wrong, the hate
That stood behind each envious thrust,
Mine every greed, mine every lust.

And all the while for every grief,
Each suffering, I craved relief
With individual desire, —
Craved all in vain! And felt fierce fire
About a thousand people crawl;
Perished with each, — then mourned for all!

A man was starving in Capri;
He moved his eyes and looked at me;
I felt his gaze, I heard his moan,
And knew his hunger as my own.

I saw at sea a great fog bank
Between two ships that struck and sank;
A thousand screams the heavens smote;
And every scream tore through my throat.

No hurt I did not feel, no death
That was not mine; mine each last breath
That, crying, met an answering cry
From the compassion that was I.
All suffering mine, and mine its rod;
Mine, pity like the pity of God.

Ah, awful weight! Infinity
Pressed down upon the finite Me!
My anguished spirit, like a bird,
Beating against my lips I heard;
Yet lay the weight so close about
There was no room for it without.
And so beneath the weight lay I
And suffered death, but could not die.
Long had I lain thus, craving death,
When quietly the earth beneath
Gave way, and inch by inch, so great
At last had grown the crushing weight,
Into the earth I sank till I
Full six feet underground did lie,
And sank no more, — there is no weight
Can follow here, however great.
From off my breast I felt it roll,
And as it went my tortured soul
Burst forth and fled in such a gust
That all about me swirled the dust.

Deep in the earth I rested now;
Cool is its hand upon the brow
And soft its breast beneath the head
Of one who is so gladly dead.
And all at once, and over all

The pitying rain began to fall;
I lay and heard each pattering hoof
Upon my lowly, thatched roof,
And seemed to love the sound far more
Than ever I had done before.
For rain it hath a friendly sound
To one who's six feet underground;
And scarce the friendly voice or face:
A grave is such a quiet place.

The rain, I said, is kind to come
And speak to me in my new home.
I would I were alive again
To kiss the fingers of the rain,
To drink into my eyes the shine
Of every slanting silver line,
To catch the freshened, fragrant breeze
From drenched and dripping apple-trees.
For soon the shower will be done,
And then the broad face of the sun
Will laugh above the rain-soaked earth
Until the world with answering mirth
Shakes joyously, and each round drop
Rolls, twinkling, from its grass-blade top.

How can I bear it; buried here,
While overhead the sky grows clear
And blue again after the storm?
O, multi-colored, multiform,
Beloved beauty over me,
That I shall never, never see
Again! Spring-silver, autumn-gold,
That I shall never more behold!
Sleeping your myriad magics through,
Close-sepulchred away from you!

Oh God, I cried, give me new birth
And put me back upon the earth!
Upset each cloud's gigantic gourd
And let the heavy rain, down-poured
In one big torrent, set me free,
Washing my grave away from me!

I ceased; and through the breathless hush
That answered me, the far-off rush
Of herald wings came whispering
Like music down the vibrant string
Of my ascending prayer, and—crash!
Before the wild wind's whistling lash
The startled storm-clouds reared on high
And plunged in terror down the sky!
And the big rain in one black wave
Fell from the sky and struck my grave.

I know not how such things can be;
I only know there came to me
A fragrance such as never clings
To aught save happy living things;
A sound as of some joyous elf
Singing sweet songs to please himself,
And, through and over everything,
A sense of glad awakening.
The grass, a-tiptoe at my ear,
Whispering to me I could hear;
I felt the rain's cool finger-tips
Brushed tenderly across my lips,
Laid gently on my sealed sight,
And all at once the heavy night
Fell from my eyes and I could see! –
A drenched and dripping apple tree,
A last long line of silver rain,
A sky grown clear and blue again.
And as I looked a quickening gust
Of wind blew up to me and thrust
Into my face a miracle
Of orchard-breath, and with the smell,
I know not how such things can be!
I breathed my soul back into me.

Ah! Up then from the ground sprang I
And hailed the earth with such a cry
As is not heard save from a man
Who has been dead, and lives again.
About the trees my arms I wound;
Like one gone mad I hugged the ground;
I raised my quivering arms on high;
I laughed and laughed into the sky,
Till at my throat a strangling sob
Caught fiercely, and a great heart-throb
Sent instant tears into my eyes;
O God, I cried, no dark disguise
Can e'er hereafter hide from me
Thy radiant identity!
Thou canst not move across the grass
But my quick eyes will see Thee pass,
Nor speak, however silently,
But my hushed voice will answer Thee.
I know the path that tells Thy way
Through the cool eve of every day;
God, I can push the grass apart
And lay my finger on Thy heart!

The world stands out on either side
No wider than the heart is wide;
Above the world is stretched the sky, —
No higher than the soul is high.
The heart can push the sea and land
Farther away on either hand;
The soul can split the sky in two,
And let the face of God shine through.
But East and West will pinch the heart
That can not keep them pushed apart;
And he whose soul is flat — the sky
Will cave in on him by and by.

Lessons I Learned

For those among you, dear readers, who find yourself on the pages of this book, I offer you some of the lessons I have learned and my loving support.

The following is in no way prescriptive. I am a psychotherapist, an educator and a retired chaplain. I am not a physician or psychiatrist or an expert in the fields I address here. I am speaking from my own experience. Always listen to your own heart to determine what is best for you and your loved ones.

This is my message to all who remain encased in abusive relationships of any kind or have experienced partner abuse in the past. (There are Crisis Line numbers at the end of the book.) You are a victim—the abuse is not your fault or your shame—it is your abuser's. And, being a victim is not a life sentence. It can be transmuted into triumph.

A new life awaits you—you deserve to be safe and free! You are stronger and more capable than you know. Remember that partner abuse is designed to keep you in the relationship by destroying your self-esteem. Trust in your ability to survive without your perpetrator. Reach out for help—you don't have to do this alone.

If you are in immediate danger, call 911. Without putting yourself in danger, seek the help of Domestic Violence or Sexual Abuse services; speak the truth to medical and mental health professionals—they can document evidence of the abuse and lead you to local organizations and resources, including safe houses. I and millions of others stand in solidarity with you.

Healing is, in part, an inside job, but there are many guides along the way. Seek them out. Find a mental health provider who has experience dealing with domestic violence. Couples counseling is contraindicated when there is partner abuse and can be dangerous. In most circumstances, counseling from clergy is, too—most members of the clergy have not been trained to deal with these issues, and often have a religious bias against dissolution of a marriage no matter what the reason.

Self care and patience are required. Tell your story to empathic listeners who will allow you to feel and express your emotions. Talk about your strengths and triumphs, and things for which you are grateful. Allow yourself to emerge from the darkness of shame, victimhood, and despair, and revel in the Light of your own Being. You are whole, not broken. You are good, beautiful, and lovable. Remind yourself daily.

This quote helped me live a new reality. "But whether you stay or go, the critical decision you can make is to stop letting your partner distort the lens of your life, always forcing his way into the center of the picture. You deserve to have your life be about you; you are worth it." (From Why Does He Do That? *by Lundy Bancroft)*

Relationships are complicated and hard and rich and rewarding. No relationship comes without struggle even your relationship with yourself and with that which you deem Holy in your life. Take care of yourself and keep healthy boundaries to insure you will not lose yourself in a relationship or allow yourself to be mistreated. Remember, you and your loved one are separate people—honor and celebrate your differences as well as your commonalities. Love is not just a word. It must be lived and expressed in the small moments of everyday life.

For victims of sexual assault or any kind of trauma as a child or adult, you, too, can heal and transform the pain and terror of your experience. There are therapists who are trained to help with these issues, and centers for sexual abuse survivors which offer counseling support and group therapy. Often, resulting PTSD can be addressed with modalities like Eye Movement Desensitization and Reprocessing Therapy (EMDR), neuro-feedback, mindfulness training, and Somatic Experiencing® originated by Peter A. Levine. (Waking the Tiger: Healing Trauma) or similar body oriented therapies that address the healing of trauma.

If you grew up without the love and nurturance you needed, with family dysfunction in the form of domestic violence, addiction, mental illness, secret keeping and/or physical, emotional, sexual or spiritual abuse, you have been exposed to what is now being called Adverse Childhood Experiences (ACE). Through scientific research, we now understand the profound and long lasting psychological and physiological damage these traumas do. They alter the child's quality of life and health into adulthood.

Seek the help of professionals who are aware of this research and the protocols which have been developed to work with trauma and Complex PTSD. Talk softly to that confused, wounded, frightened, and often angry child-within. Slowly form a healing relationship with your child-self. Listen to his or her needs, be patient. Trust comes hard to these little ones. Often, this lack of trust spills over into the child's adult life and makes forming healthy relationships difficult.

And, if you're facing the challenges of physical or mental illness contact a physician, psychiatrist, psychotherapist or others. Choose professionals who are caring, compassionate, good listeners and respectful.

Be honest about your struggles and invite trusted family and friends to support you through difficult times. Hold your head high— you are not "less than" anyone who walks this earth. You are whole and beautiful even though you may not believe that in your darkest days. When you glimpse the Light, walk into it even if it's only for a moment—allow it to expand within you and illuminate the truth of who you are.

If you are dealing with addictions now or in the past, reach out to organizations like AA, Al-Anon or Alateen, or other support groups; or turn to professionals who are trained to treat them. Remember you are not defective; you do not lack moral principles or willpower. Addictions to any substance are complex diseases. They change the brain in ways that make quitting hard.

Researchers are discovering the genetic, biological, neural and sociological vectors that lead one to become addicted. With these new insights, better recovery treatments and therapy modalities are available to help people recover and lead productive lives. Do not give up hope. Seek treatment. Seek support. You are worth fighting for. You deserve to be free.

I realize these suggestions may not be available to many of you. An advocate can help you find the resources you need. There are government agencies that have social services, religious communities that offer help, local hospitals, your physician, and even your child's teacher may be able to help you. I've often found it hard to ask for help, but when I do, I'm filled with gratitude for the support I receive.

I believe we are created as "perfectly imperfect" human manifestations of The Holy in whatever form that takes for us. Our imperfections are the pathways to growth, deeper understanding of life, and connection to the Divine. Let us embrace them and remember we are loved and held in the arms of the Pure Love that sustains us all. And, remember you are that Love.

May you be blessed… always, Kathleen

REFERENCES

Partner Abuse

Bancroft, Lundy. *Why Does He Do That?* Inside the Minds of Angry and Controlling Men. Berkley Books, 2002.

Bancroft, Lundy; Patrissi, JAC. *Should I Stay or Should I Go? A Guide to Knowing if Your Relationship Can—and Should—be Saved.* Berkley Books, 2011.

Bancroft, Lundy. *When Dad Hurts Mom: Helping Your Children Heal the Wounds of Witnessing Abuse.* Berkley Books, 2005.

Evans, Patricia. *The Verbally Abusive Relationship: How to Recognize It and How to Respond.* Bob Adams, 1996.

Fortune, Marie M. *Keeping the Faith: Questions and Answers for the Abused Woman.* HarperSanFrancisco, 1987.

Hoff, Lee Ann. *Battered Women as Survivors.* Routledge, 1990.

Jones, Ann, Schechter, Susan. *Where Love Goes Wrong: What to Do When You Can't Do Anything Right.* HarperPerennial, 1993.

Suicide

Jamison, Kay Redfield. *Night Falls Fast: Understanding Suicide*. Alfred A. Knopf, NY 1999.

Lukas, Christopher (Editor). *Silent Grief: Living in the Wake of Suicide Revised Edition*. Jessica Kingsley Publishers, 2007.

Ramsay, Richard F., Tanney, Brian A., Lang, William A., Kinzel, Tarie. *Suicide Intervention Handbook*. Livingworks, 2004.

Smolin, Ann; Gulnan, John. *Healing After the Suicide of a Loved One*. Touchstone Books, 1993.

Sexual Abuse/Healing Trauma

Bass, Ellen; Davis, Laura. *The Courage to Heal: A Guide for Women Survivors of Child Sexual Abuse, 20th Anniversary Edition*. William Morrow Paperbacks, 2008.

Finkelhor, David; Kersti Yllo. *License To Rape: Sexual Abuse of Wives*. Free Press, 1987.

Fortune, Marie M. *Is Nothing Sacred? When Sex Invades the Pastoral Relationship*. Harper & Row, SF, 1989.

Herman, Judith L. *Trauma and Recovery: The Aftermath of Violence—From Domestic Abuse to Political Terror*. Basic Books, 2015.

Levine, Peter A.; Frederick, Ann. *Waking the Tiger: Healing Trauma*. North Atlantic Books, 1997.

Lew, Mike. *Victims No Longer: The Classic Guide for Men Recovering from Sexual Child Abuse*. HarperCollins Publisher, 2004

Maltz, Wendy. *The Sexual Healing Journey: A Guide for Survivors of Sexual Abuse, 3rd Edition*. William Morrow Paperbacks, 2012.

Naparstek, Belleruth. *Invisible Heroes: Survivors of Trauma and How They Heal*. Bantam Dell, 2005.

Rutter MD, Peter. *Sex in the Forbidden Zones: When Men in Power—Therapist, Doctors, Clergy, Teachers and Others—Betray Women's Trust*. Jeremy P. Tarcher Inc, 1989.

Salter PhD, Anna. *Predators: Pedophiles, Rapists, And Other Sex Offenders.* Basic Books, 2003.

van der Kolk MD, Bessel. *The Body Keeps the Score: Brain, Mind, and Body in the Healing of Trauma.* Penguin Books, 2015.

Religion/Spirituality

His Holiness The Dalai Lama. *Toward a True Kinship of Faiths: How the World's Religions Can Come Together.* Double Day, 2010.

Kuchler, Bonnie Louise (Editor). *One Heart: Wisdom from the World's Scriptures.* One Spirit, 2003

Moses, Jeffry. *Oneness: Great Principles Shared by All Religions.* Fawcett Columbine, 1989.

Teasdale, Brother Wayne & Howard MD, Martha (Editors). *Awakening the Spirit: Inspiring the Soul.* Skylight Paths Publishing, 2004

Tobias, Michael; Morrison, Jane; Gray, Bettina. (Editors). *The Parliament of Souls: In Search of Global Spirituality.* KQED Books, 1995.

Death, Dying & Grief

Byock, MD, Ira. *Four Things That Matter Most: A Book About Living.* Free Press, 2004.

Callanan, Maggie & Kelley, Patricia. *Final Gifts: Understand the Special Awareness, Needs, and Communications of the Dying.* Bantam Books, 1997.

Prend, ACSW, Ashley Davis. *Transcending Loss: Understanding the Lifelong Impact of Grief and How to Make It Meaningful.* The Berkley Publishing Group, 1997.

Smith, Rodney. *Lessons from the Dying.* Wisdom Publication, 1998.

Quotes

Bancroft, Lundy. *Why Does He Do That?* Inside the Minds of Angry and Controlling Men. Berkley Books, 2002.

Bancroft, Lundy; Patrissi, JAC. *Should I Stay or Should I Go? A Guide to Knowing if Your Relationship Can—and Should—be Saved.* Berkley Books, 2011.

Browne, Sylvia. *The Other Side and Back.* Penguin Random House, 2002.

Berry, Wendell. *Collected Poems 1957-1982.* North Point Press, 1985.

Gibran, Kahlil. *The Prophet.* Alfred A Knopf, 1968

Ladinsky, Daniel translator. *Love Poems from God.* Penquin Books, 2006.

Ladinsky, Daniel translator. *The Gift: Poems by Hafiz.* Penquin Books, 2002.

Oliver, Mary. *Dream Works.* The Atlantic Monthly Press, 1986.

Oliver, Mary. *Thirst.* Beacon Press, 2006.

Paul, Stephen C.; Collins, Gary Max. *Illuminations.* Harper San Francisco, 1991.

Paul, Stephen C.; Collins, Gary Max. *Inneractions.* Harper San Francisco, 1992.

Rilke, Rainer Maria. *Letters to a Young Poet.* MJF Books, 2000.

Foster, Jeff. "First you Must Ride." "The Extraordinary Painting of You." www.lifewithoutacentre.com. Accessed June 2018.

Louden, Jennifer. *Celebration of Being Ordinary.* https://jenniferlouden.com/in-celebration-of-being-ordinary/. Accessed November 2018.

Roth, Gabrielle. "Energy Move in Waves." *5RHYTHMS.* www.5rhythms.com. Accessed November 2019.

RESOURCES: CRISIS LINES

Domestic Violence

Note from the author: I have chosen to focus on women in this *Resource* section because I am speaking of my experiences as a woman in this memoir, and my work in the field of Domestic Violence was with women. Men in heterosexual relationships, men and women in same sex relationships, and people of all gender identities are also affected by domestic violence. Most of the Crisis Numbers given here will help anyone affected by Domestic Violence.

In an emergency, call 911.

The National Domestic Violence HOTLINE: available 24/7 at 1-800-799-SAFE (7233) in more than 200 languages. All calls are free and confidential.

The National Domestic Violence (TTY for Deaf/Hard of Hearing) HOTLINE: 24/7/365 1-800-787-3224

Mental Health

In An Emergency:

If you or a loved one is in immediate danger **calling 911 and talking with police** may be necessary. It is important to notify the operator that it is a psychiatric emergency and ask for an officer trained in crisis intervention or trained to assist people experiencing a psychiatric emergency.

NAMI HelpLine: 1-800-950-NAMI (6264)

The NAMI HelpLine can be reached Monday through Friday, 10 am–6 pm, ET.)

Suicide

National Suicide Prevention Lifeline: 1-800-273-8255

Trained crisis workers are available to talk 24 hours a day, 7 days a week. Your confidential and toll-free call goes to the nearest crisis center in the Lifeline national network. These centers provide crisis counseling and mental health referrals.

In An Emergency:

Call 911 or the National Suicide Prevention Lifeline at 800-273-8255

Stay with the person, or if you must leave, ask someone you trust to stay with the suicidal person; do not leave them alone.

Remove all lethal weapons, medications, and other means of potential harm from the premises.

Accompany the person to an emergency room or psychiatric clinic with walk-in services.

Avoid putting yourself in a dangerous situation; call 911 for your own safety, if necessary.

Sexual Assault

National Sexual Assault Hotline: Call 800-656-HOPE (4673)

Connect with a trained staff member from a sexual assault service provider in your area that offers access to a range of free services.

How does it work? When you call 800-656-HOPE (4673), you'll be routed to a local **RAINN affiliate organization** based on the first six digits of your phone number. Cell phone callers have the option to enter the ZIP code of their current location to more accurately locate the nearest sexual assault service provider.

Child Abuse/Sexual Abuse:

Call 911 in case of emergency.

National Child Abuse Hotline: Hotline: 800-4.A.CHILD (422-2253)

Provides local referrals for services. A centralized call center provides the caller with the option of talking to a counselor. Connects to a language line that can provide service in over 140 languages.

Military Resources: Safe Helpline: Hotline: 877-995-5247.

Department of Defense (DoD) Safe Helpline is a crisis support service for members of the DoD community affected by sexual assault. Provides live, one-on-one support and information to the worldwide DoD community. Confidential, anonymous, secure, and available worldwide, 24/7 by call or text.

My Gift to You
The Gospel According to Amelia

Beloved Ones,
I have come to walk among you
to remind you who you are.
You are Holy.
You are Divine.
You are One with All That Is,
you are unique in all the Universe.
You are Love.
You are Joy.
I come to remind you.

I come to remind you of your brilliance.
You marvel at what I have learned
in eight short months upon this earth.

You, too, learned with grace
when you were young,
before the clouds set in.
You loved to learn as I do,
you were wonderfully curious
as I am,
before you became afraid.
I come to remind you.

I come to remind you of your goodness.
You look at me and all you see
is sweetness, purity and innocence.
Why do you believe in your guilt
when you and I are one?

I know how intrinsically good I am.
I celebrate myself.
I deeply believe I deserve to be
cherished and cared for,
just as you once knew these things
about yourself,
before you heard their angry voices.
I come to remind you.

I come to remind you of your joy.
Sitting here in the middle of the floor
the joy of my existence
bubbles up from within
and I begin to giggle
for no apparent reason.
I delight in the sensations of my body.
I live totally in the present moment
for I know no other.

Do you remember what it was like
to live like this?
Do you remember?
I come to remind you.

I come to remind you of your
innate capacity to heal.
Yes, you have been hurt
and will be again.
But watch me.

I cry when I am in need or in pain
or when I'm lonely.
I rage viscerally when I'm angry.
And, I laugh and laugh…
Healing is very simple.
I come to remind you.

*I come to remind you of your ability
to dream, to hope, to believe
that anything is possible,
just as I do.*

*Already I dream of walking,
I who have barely learned to crawl.
I know I will fall many times
before I master even one step,
but I am ready for the challenge
because I hold the vision in my heart.*

*Remember the dreams of your childhood
within them is your passion
and your power.
I come to remind you.*

*I come to remind you of your lovingness.
I search out your eyes.
I blossom with your touch.
I put my trust in you.
I know how deeply and lovingly
we are connected.*

*Within you is the memory
of our Ultimate Oneness.
I can feel it in your response to me.
You are Love. I feel it. I know it.
You are Holy.
You are Divine.*

I come to remind you.

— As recorded by Amelia's adoring grandmother

Made in the USA
Middletown, DE
27 April 2021